Missions
1924–1997

(numbers correspond to the legend on pages 319–20)

Newfoundland

Quebec

Prince Edward Island

Ontario

New Brunswick

Nova Scotia

TO DO AND TO ENDURE

The Life of Catherine Donnelly, Sister of Service

BY

JEANNE R. BECK

Catherine Donnelly, Founder of the Sisters of Service

TO DO AND TO ENDURE

The Life of Catherine Donnelly, Sister of Service

BY

JEANNE R. BECK

Dundurn Press
Toronto • Oxford

Copyright © Sisters of Service of Canada Inc., 1997

All rights reserved. No part of this publication may be reproduced, stored in a retrieval system, or transmitted in any form or by any means, electronic, mechanical, photocopying, recording, or otherwise (except for brief passages for purposes of review) without the prior permission of Dundurn Press Limited. Permission to photocopy should be requested from the Canadian Reprography Collective.

Editing: Diane Mew
Manuscript Preparation: Heather Duncan
Design (Text): Barry Jowett
Design (Cover): Sebastian Vasile
Design (Photo sections): Scott Reid
Printer: Best Book Manufacturers
Index: Claudia Willetts

Canadian Cataloguing in Publication Data

Beck, Jeanne Ruth Merifield.
    To do and to endure

Includes bibliographical references and index.
ISBN 1-55002-289-X

1. Donnelly, Catherine, 1884-1983. 2. Sisters of Service - Biography. 3. Nuns - Canada - Biography. I. Title

BX4237.B42 1997   271'.97   C97-930771-6

1 2 3 4 5 BJ 01 00 99 98 97

We acknowledge the support of the **Canada Council for the Arts** for our publishing program. We also acknowledge the support of the **Ontario Arts Council** and the **Book Publishing Industry Development Program** of the **Department of Canadian Heritage**.

Care has been taken to trace the ownership of copyright material used in this book. The author and the publisher welcome any information enabling them to rectify any references or credit in subsequent editions.

Printed and bound in Canada.

Printed on recycled paper.

Dundurn Press
8 Market Street
Second Floor
Toronto, Ontario, Canada
M5E 1M6

Dundurn Press
73 Lime Walk
Headington, Oxford
England
OX3 7AD

Dundurn Press
250 Sonwil Drive
Buffalo, NY
U.S.A. 14225

TABLE OF CONTENTS

Preface... 7

Acknowledgements.................................. 11

Foreword... 15

I   THE LAND OF HER YOUTH :
      THE ADJALA COMMUNITY......................... 17

II   LIFE AS A TEACHER IN ONTARIO, 1904-1918 29

III ADVENTURES IN ALBERTA:
      AM I CALLED TO BE A RELIGIOUS?................. 43

IV CATHERINE PURSUES HER VISION:
      THE FOUNDING OF THE SISTERS OF SERVICE 65

V   THE NOVITIATE YEARS............................ 91

VI THE FIRST MISSION AT CAMP MORTON 121

VII RETURN TO ALBERTA: PIONEERING IN VILNA...... 141

VIII SERVING IN A DEPRESSION-WRACKED
      COMMUNITY..................................... 161

IX CREATING A NEW RULE FOR A NEW ORDER........ 185

X   PIONEERING IN THE CARIBOO 197

XI KEEPING THE ORDER ON COURSE................ 223

XII THE HARDEST YEARS 239

XIII BACK IN HARNESS:
      THE LAST YEARS OF TEACHING 255

XIV I DON'T WANT TO GROW OLD
       GRACEFULLY — USEFULLY — YES 275

NOTES 295

SISTERS OF SERVICE MISSIONS, 1924-1997 319

INDEX 321

PREFACE

IN THE AUTUMN OF 1992 I WAS ASKED BY THE SISTER General of the Sisters of Service, Frances Coffey, if I would consider writing the biography of Sister Catherine Donnelly, the founder of their order, the first English-speaking Canadian women's Roman Catholic religious order.

I was not completely unfamiliar with the Sisters of Service, as I had come across tantalizing references to their work during my research on my Ph.D. dissertation on Catholic Social Thought in the Archdiocese of Toronto. Henry Somerville was editor of the diocesan newspaper, the *Catholic Register*, from 1931 to 1954, and in that period wrote articles and editorials promoting this new group of women religious who had been freed from the confining traditions of the cloister in order to undertake the traditional good works of charity, nursing and education for the immigrants and Canadian citizens, particularly those living in the West in isolated settlements. The majority of the recent immigrants who were staking out prairie homesteads lived too far from the cities where these services were being given by the traditional Roman Catholic religious orders.

I was attracted to this project because I had long believed that the role played by the Roman Catholic women's religious orders in the educational, social and religious history of Canada has been largely neglected by the historians. As well, the glimpses I had gained of Catherine Donnelly from my reading indicated that she was a fascinating person; someone who was unafraid to question traditional attitudes and customs in order to accomplish a greater good. Her recognition that new methods must be used by her Church to minister to human needs in the twentieth century seemed to exemplify in a practical way the theology underpinning the Papal Social Encyclicals.

Sister Coffey invited me to come to the motherhouse in Toronto to meet their archivist, Sister Catherine Schmeltzer, and to see if their archives contained sufficient material on which to base a biography. At our meeting, Sister Schmeltzer explained that while many of the papers

Preface

pertaining to Catherine Donnelly's life had not survived her many transfers from place to place, some valuable letters were still turning up. A search was being conducted in all of their mission houses, and requests for relevant information had been made to the various dioceses where Catherine had worked. As Sister Schmeltzer had joined the Sisters of Service in 1938, I concluded that she herself would also be an invaluable source of information.

When I indicated that I would be interested in undertaking the biography, Sister Coffey said that the order's only stipulations were that the book was to be centred on the life and work of Catherine Donnelly, rather than the order itself, and that the book was not to be written as a memorial but as an examination of a life in which the techniques and standards of a historian would be applied. She hoped that sufficient information could be located to reveal the complete story of Catherine's long life of ninety-nine years, and assured me that all the order's records would be made available, including those which dealt with its finances and personnel. I was also given permission to interview members of the order privately, particularly those who had worked directly with Catherine Donnelly.

I have found this to be a stimulating professional assignment, made all the more challenging because complete freedom of access to the records allowed me to tell the story as I saw it emerging. At no time did I encounter any attempt to influence my conclusions. When I required additional information on events or people that was not in the written records, it was willingly given to me by the many sisters I questioned, and with complete candour. The only direct comment on the text which I received was when I requested Sister General Frances Coffey, her successor Sister General Anna McNally, and the Council of the Sisters of Service, to peruse it for clarity and accuracy of fact or definition.

Chief among the members on whose expertise and memory I had to rely was the late Sister Catherine Schmeltzer, who died suddenly only two months before the last chapter was completed. Her devotion to her work as an archivist, her sparkling sense of humour, her thoughtful answers to my innumerable questions, and her unfailing kindness made writing this story a joyful personal and professional experience.

Sister Catherine Donnelly's story has been written for the general

Preface

reader, of any or of no religious persuasion, who is interested in the history of Canada, and in the struggles of the peoples from every country who settled this land and battled its harsh climate to make homes in a new environment. To succeed against poverty, adversity and loneliness they needed help in a multitude of ways. This book is about them and about one woman's attempt to break the bonds of tradition so that she and the order she founded could provide for their educational and spiritual needs. In so doing she became a pioneer in extending the role of women in Roman Catholic religious orders.

The title of this biography, *To Do and To Endure*, is taken from the second verse of the hymn, "Breathe On Me Breath of God," which is common to both Roman Catholic and Protestant hymnaries.

Jeanne R. Beck
St. Patrick's Day, 1997

ACKNOWLEDGEMENTS

Telling the story of a person who lived as long and productive a life as did Sister Catherine Donnelly, was a great challenge, for the archival sources had some gaps which had to be filled in before I could understand her motivation and her problems. When I first dipped into the Archives of the Sisters of Service at their Motherhouse in Toronto, two facts about her collected papers were soon apparent. The good news was that Catherine obviously enjoyed writing letters and brief memoirs, for they were forthright, interesting in style and content, and meticulously punctuated. The bad news was that some of the most important documents from her early career had not survived her many changes of location; I would have to use as clues the brief references in letters written long after some of the most important events had taken place. The best news was that her various versions of these incidents, even those written at an advanced age, were consistent with earlier versions.

I knew that I would need help in locating much of this information scattered in letters and memoirs on other topics. I am very grateful to three members of the Order who spent many hours aiding me in the search for biographical details. First, I owe a great debt to the Archivist, Sister Catherine Schmeltzer, who provided constant personal assistance during my search for missing links, and supplemented the Order's archival holdings with extra details from her amazingly clear recollections of events and of people with whom Catherine Donnelly was involved. Her work was supplemented by that of Sister Leona Trautman, who had undertaken to organize the Archive's photographic records. She also wrote invaluable notes on her own experiences in the order, particularly the period when she was a student of Sister Catherine. I thank her also for her help in the selection and identification of the photographs which add so much to the biography. I owe a great debt to Sister Mary Phillips, who organized the collection of documents and letters from the Archdiocese of Edmonton as well as interviewing and collecting the memoirs of many sisters who were not

Acknowledgements

able to come to Toronto for interviews. When her packages of documents arrived, the contents were like a Christmas box of goodies!

I am deeply indebted to those Sisters of Service who in interviews provided anecdotes about their encounters with Catherine, as well as personal experiences which led to their becoming Sisters of Service. Each detail they recounted gave me valuable insights into the great variety of women who were attracted to the order, of the use that was made of their talents and the additional qualifications they acquired which enabled them to broaden the scope of their service.

I am also very grateful for the words and notes of encouragement that I received from those Sisters who were not acquainted with Catherine Donnelly, but who were pleased and excited at the prospect of learning more about her. Their assurance of support for this work was much appreciated.

To former Sister General Frances Coffey, Sister General Anna McNally, and Assistant General Patricia Burke, I owe special thanks for unfailing support which was given in so many personal and practical ways. The gracious hospitality I received during my working days at the Motherhouse, their encouraging comments, and their helpful explanations and comments on their lives as religious, enriched my understanding of their own and Catherine's vocation.

I owe much to the archivists of other religious orders and institutions from whom I requested documents and information. In particular, I am indebted to Sister Esther Hanley, IBVM, Toronto, Sister Collette Ryan SSND, Waterdown, Sister Mary Jane Trimble CSJ, Toronto, and Sister Mary Rose Pautler CSJ, Hamilton, and Sister Mary Olga McKenna SC, Halifax. As well, Father James Mason CSsR, of the Edmonton and Toronto Province of the Redemptorists, gave me generous access to the CSsR Archives, and valuable additional information on Father George Daly's life.

I was fortunate to receive help also from Mrs. Margaret Sanche, Archivist of St. Thomas More College, Saskatoon and the Archivists of the Archdiocese of Toronto, in particular, the former Archivist, Sister Frieda Watson CSJ, the present Archivist Marc Lerman, and the Assistant Archivist, Linda Wicks.

Fellow scholars have been generous in their moral support; as well they offered practical advice on the task of writing religious history, and valuable information garnered during their own research.

Acknowledgements

Their published works, and suggestions for sources enabled me to place Catherine in the social and religious contexts of her times. I am particularly grateful to Dr. Mark McGowan, Dr. Brian Clarke, Dr. Elizabeth Smyth, Dr. Ruth Compton Brouwer, Dr. Gerald Killan, Dr. Paul Laverdure, Dr. Robert Bérard and Mrs. Sheila Ross.

Information and letters from Catherine's Alliston connexions and information on her early family life were provided by Mrs. Mary Munnoch, Mrs Margaret Donnelly, Mrs. Theresa Quayle Reich, Mrs. Shirley Gibson and Catherine's nephew Robert Gifford. Catherine's cousin, Mrs. Betty Ogle of Calgary, provided gracious hospitality, a splendid interview and a treasure trove of Catherine's letters.

I received helpful information and advice, along with large doses of encouragement from Dr. Terence Fay S.J., Father Joseph O'Neill, Dr. Margaret Denis, Father Kenneth Bernard, Sister Veronica O'Reilly CSJ, Father Ronald Synnott, Maurice Villeneuve, Lorene Hanley Duquin, and Sister Barbara Frank, SSND.

As the written manuscript evolved I was given the priceless gift of having it read by Dr. Goldwin S. French and Dr. Maurice Careless. Their suggestions and advice were invaluable, and I do thank them for bringing their wisdom, their vast knowledge and experience, and their acute sensitivity to the art of writing history to their critiques of this work.

The final preparations for publication were done by Diane Mew, whose copy-editing skills and dedication to the correction of the text, brought order to my frequently chaotic footnotes and inconsistent form. She and Heather Duncan, who prepared the computer disk, formed a team which, with unfailing good humour and skill worked late on many nights to meet the publisher's deadline.

Finally, very special thanks are due my husband Robin, whose constant enthusiasm for the project, and astute observations on the text, were of value equal to his skills at keeping the home fires burning while I was utterly absorbed by the epic story of this woman who accomplished so much and endured to the end.

FOREWORD

In her portrayal of the life of Sister Catherine Donnelly, founder of the Sisters of Service, author Jeanne Beck has succeeded in weaving a tapestry rich in texture, broad in scope and deeply revealing of the character of a memorable Canadian woman. To a remarkable degree the thematic details of Sr. Catherine's life and times, 1884-1983, reflect those of her country and church. These details cluster around a unifying triad consisting of her sense of space, mission and self.

In the late nineteenth and early twentieth centuries Canadian energies focused on twin developments: the movement from dominantly rural to urban populations and pursuits, and the exploitation of the vast expanses of the West. The tasks associated with incorporating millions of immigrants included assisting with the multiple adaptations to foreign cultural, linguistic, educational, technological and political expressions. All of this in a time before social workers, or the array of government-assisted social programmes, which would develop later in the century.

Catherine was born shortly after the First Council of the Vatican (1870) and lived well beyond the Second (1962-1965). Until the Second Vatican Council the dominant model of religious life experienced and expressed by Roman Catholic communities of women in Canada was the monastic model. It is important to recognize the normative dominance of this model of religious life in order to appreciate the myriad of difficulties she experienced in proposing to pioneer the implementation of a novel and opposing approach to service which her missionary vision entailed.

In the preceding century the Catholic Church had responded to the increasing challenges of the secularized and materialist world view promoted by Enlightenment philosophies and hostile political agendas. The highly centralized and rationalized re-structuring of the Church which resulted, succeeded in providing clear identity and focused direction. But this was at the expense of developing a non-traditional character which tended to be defensive, reactive and hostile in turn

Foreword

towards innovation in general. This was particularly so with regard to alterations in the form and function of women's communities.

This ecclesial conservatism was reinforced by cultural expectations resistant to the emergence of women from private sphere to public space, at least through the first half of the century. In fact, taking into account both ecclesial experience and cultural expectation, hindsight suggests that Catherine's success in winning acceptance, or at least toleration, of adaptations with regard to such things as habit, residence and form of ministry, are really remarkable. Such contextualization should not underrate the immediacy and depth of successive painful passages and personal humiliations. It should, however, validate the clarity of her vision with regard to the needs of the mission, and highlight the resilient sense of self which sustained that vision in the face of challenges from landscape, religious institution and social convention.

The biography is refreshingly candid with regard to conflicts and tensions internal to character, institution and her own religious community. The treatment is both sensitive and critical throughout and the result is a three-dimensional life, personal in detail and instructive with regard to the true measure of its subject: a woman sacramentally rooted in time and place and deeply moved by a vision of service and human care founded on the love of her God.

Brian F. Hogan, C.S.B.
Dean, Faculty of Theology
University of St. Michael's College
Toronto, Ontario

CHAPTER 1
THE LAND OF HER YOUTH: THE ADJALA COMMUNITY

IN MANY OF THE BRIEF BIOGRAPHICAL SKETCHES which Catherine Donnelly wrote throughout her long life, she frequently referred to her belief that the land and the attitudes of the people who tilled it were vital determinants in both an individual's and a nation's character and destiny. Thus it seems suitable to begin her story with a description of her own family heritage, of the land and the people of her community.

The area of Ontario where she was born in 1884, and considered her home territory for her first thirty-four years, was Simcoe County. It extended from Newmarket to its southwest boundary at Mono Mills, north to Nottawasaga Bay, east to Lakes Simcoe and Couchiching, and north to the Severn River. In 1794 Lieutenant-Governor John Graves Simcoe had discussed purchase of some of that land with the Lake Simcoe Chippewa Indians, and negotiations and treaties were completed by the British government by 1818. The county had been surveyed and was made available for settlement by the time the first immigrants arrived from Northern Ireland in the 1820s. They were mainly farmers, and although they were not destitute, they possessed more optimism and determination than money and worldly goods. In religious allegiance, they were a mixed lot; but Roman Catholics, Anglicans, Presbyterians, Quakers and other Protestant groups lived in the new settlements in relative harmony. One contributing factor may have been that the immigrants could acquire more acreage of freehold land than was ever dreamed possible in Ireland. There the tenant farmer had to support his family on five or ten acres of leased land, which he would never be able to purchase. His life was an unending struggle with little prospect of advancement. For these tenant farmers their real security came from their strong kinship ties and a devotion to the religious traditions in which they were raised. This was the glue which held their society together and enabled them to endure, whether their religious allegiance was Roman Catholic or Protestant. However, one legacy from the stormy history of Ireland was that, living as they had in close proximity to their neighbours for many generations, the Northern Irish were very conscious of their own religious and class differences. In some of the early settlements in various parts of Ontario, around Peterborough for example, the old-country tensions and prejudices were carried into the new lands, where they lasted for long years.

When more immigrants arrived during the 1840s at Mono Township, adjacent to Adjala Township where the Donnellys settled, their futures seemed much more hopeful. Uncleared land could be bought from 5 to 15 shillings an acre.[1] The settlers' social and religious energies would be directed to creating wider kinship groups and building many churches, where they could continue to worship in their own way, and establishing schools to see that their children got an education.

Although Simcoe County was forbidding in its isolation from the bustling city of Toronto, the settlers found it an attractive area for homesteading. As they had travelled north from the city, the ground had risen steadily to the dividing height of land in the area of Newmarket, from where all streams flowed northwest into Georgian Bay. Within three generations this terrain to the north would become one of the most beautiful agricultural areas of Ontario. Its many creeks and rivers wended their way through pretty valleys flanked by rolling hills. Moraines and drumlins caused by ancient glacial action made picturesque eruptions in the landscape. But not all this land was good for tilling. Glacial debris of sand and stone made the moraines unsuitable for grain crops, and these areas would eventually be used for pasture. But before the crops could be sown, the land had to be cleared of a heavy forest cover, and the debris burned. Cedar and tamarack swamps that dotted the area had to be drained. Although money, tools and labourers were scarce, the settlers had to erect barns, sheds and fences to shelter valuable animals, and build houses for their families. These were not tasks for which the Irish immigrants had been trained. "Forests in nineteenth century Ulster were protected on estates; most immigrants had never used an axe and knew nothing of land clearing."[2] Only by co-operation and sharing could they survive the loneliness, the exhausting physical labour, and the climatic extremes of Ontario's summers and winters.

During the early 1840s the Irish immigrants continued to arrive in a steady stream, but not in such overwhelming numbers that they could not be absorbed economically into Ontario's towns and countryside.[3] It was in 1846, according to one of Sister Catherine Donnelly's memoirs, that her grandfather Hugh Donnelly, with her grandmother Mary Ann and their children, emigrated from Armagh to Simcoe County. Little Hugh, Catherine's father, was still an infant. They had left one of the most thickly populated areas of pre-famine Northern Ireland, and were able to secure land on Lot 1, Concession 5, facing the town line between Tossorontio and Adjala townships. Their farm was located on what is now Highway 89, about four miles west of Alliston. The nearest settlement was the small village of Arlington, a mile south. Most of the Roman Catholic immigrants who had arrived earlier lived in this section of the township, for their church had encouraged them to settle in kinship and religious groups.

The closest Catholic church for the area was St. James at Colgan, eight miles south of Alliston. A swamp separated the North Adjala settlement from Colgan, and so the settlers attended Mass at the home of Hugh Ferguson, one of the more prosperous Catholics in Arlington. A priest from Colgan made regular visits for that purpose. When an additional group of Catholic immigrants came into the area following the Irish famine of the late 1840s, the "house church" was no longer adequate. In 1854 Hugh Ferguson donated two acres of land for the erection of the Church of the Immaculate Conception. The Colgan clergy oversaw the construction of the simple frame building at Arlington, and the church was blessed on 19 July 1857. As the Arlington Catholic population had increased by 1866, the North Adjala parish was separated from Colgan and a new rectory built for the priest next to the church. By 1871 51 per cent of the population of Adjala Township was Irish Catholic. This became a religious and ethnic base on which Catholic culture could thrive and yet not threaten their Protestant neighbours.[4]

In nineteenth-century Irish farming communities in Ontario it was the custom for the youngest son to take over his parents' farm, with the understanding that they could live with him for the rest of their lives.[5] According to Sister Catherine's family memoir of 1975, such an arrangement was made by her grandparents with her father Hugh when he was twenty-five years old. In 1876 Hugh married Catherine Donnelly, aged twenty-three, the daughter of Patrick Donnelly of nearby Essa Township. They were not related, and Sister Catherine noted that she was never sure of her maternal grandmother's maiden name because "she must have died when the children were young. My mother seldom talked about her childhood days, but she seemed to be familiar with facts about people of the Scotch line of Essa township, especially the Haydens and the Ellards."[6]

Patrick Donnelly was married for the second time to a young Protestant woman from the nearby village of Everett. As in his first marriage, he again had three sons and a daughter, and they lived on a farm northeast of Alliston, near Everett. It is perhaps for this reason that Sister Catherine's mother was living with the Ellard family at the time of her marriage.

In a remarkable document, written when Sister Catherine was ninety-one, she listed the names and locations of her three maternal uncles (Patrick, Thomas, Christopher), the names of their wives, the ten children they had produced, and the names and fate of those children's children! This is followed by a similar listing of the children and their descendants from her grandfather's second marriage — a total of over sixty people she could proudly claim as relatives on her mother's side of the family.

Hugh and Catherine Donnelly had seven children: Mary Gertrude, born in 1880, died when she was eleven; Bridget Ellen, born in 1881, died when she was sixteen; Joseph, born around 1882, died in infancy; Catherine Donnelly born on 26 February 1884, lived until she was ninety-nine; Thomas Ambrose, born in 1888, died in 1892 from sunstroke. (He was the only sibling for whom Catherine listed a cause of death.) Elizabeth Theresa (Tess) was born in 1890 and died at the age of seventy-four; Mary Loretto (Sister Justina CSJ), the youngest child, born in 1894, was eighty-seven when she died in 1981. Sister Catherine's grandparents, her parents, and five of her brothers and sisters are all buried on a knoll marked by a fine tombstone in the little cemetery adjacent to the Church of the Immaculate Conception, within sight of the old farm property.

In addition to raising their three surviving daughters and caring for Hugh's mother, Catherine's parents also took Hugh's nephew and niece into their family. These were little Hugh Donnelly Jr. and Annie,

The Land of Her Youth: The Adjala Community

the children of Matthew Donnelly, Hugh's eldest brother. Matthew's wife had died when little Hugh was two years of age and his sister Annie was four. "Matthew was an alcoholic ... lost his farm and lived alone in Alliston before he died."[7] Such an arrangement was not unusual at that time in the Irish community, for it was the custom to look after their kinfolk if at all possible. This family situation was described in her typical cryptic fashion by Sister Catherine when she was in her ninety-sixth year, in a letter to her nephew:

> Little Hugh, my cousin, was a worker — was needed on the farm. His great joy was *horses* and a *dog*. He only got an elementary schooling at the local school. My generous mother was good to him and to our grandmother — Mary Ann (Johnson) Donnelly a convert, who never spoke about her life as a young girl ...
>
> Little Hugh left when quite young to seek his fortune in North Dakota. After some years of dray work and jobs he handled well, he married a good woman ... There was one little child died very young ... I went to see Hugh once at Superior, on my way to Fargo N.D. Tess came ... It was in the late 40's or early 50's.
>
> Hugh was a very lovely man and had worked hard to save and own some property. He made a will and left most to his wife's close relatives, some of whom had been really good to him.[8]

Catherine Donnelly's memoirs, and my own interviews with present residents of the area, emphasize two noteworthy characteristics of the North Simcoe County Irish community. First, although it was a composed of disparate groups of closeknit Protestant and Catholic families which were separated from each other by religion, they lived in relative harmony and goodwill in Adjala Township.[9] True, there were annual, isolated raucous incidents. These usually took place on 17 March when the Catholics observed the feast day of their beloved St. Patrick, and also on 12 July when the local Loyal Orange lodges celebrated the 1690 Anglo Protestant victory over the Catholic King James II at the Battle of the Boyne with parades and fiery speeches. (Some cynical Scots viewed these festivities as religiously permissible party times for the Irish Catholics, giving everyone a break in the long forty-day Lenten fast demanded by the Church at that time; similarly, for the Protestants 12 July was an occasion to take a holiday from their farm labours by holding big neighbourhood, midsummer picnics after the parade.) In sum, it was a community in which there was mutual

To Do and to Endure

respect with no serious and permanent rancour between the Catholics and Protestants. This was in happy contrast to some parts of Ontario where the two religious groups were so mutually antagonistic that walls of suspicion and hostility kept them apart for many years. Both Catholics and Protestants felt secure in the acceptance and practice of their own faith, to the extent that regardless of their religious differences, they co-operated in community enterprises, aided each other in times of disaster, and formed warm friendships with people outside their own religious and social circles.

Second, in an era when few families were able or willing to educate their children, particularly their daughters, beyond the bare minimum demanded by law, an unusually high percentage of Catholic parents in Adjala struggled to keep their children in school so that they would be eligible for higher education. This was true not only of Hugh and Catherine Donnelly's daughters, but also of several other families whose children would later become prominent in the secular and religious worlds beyond Alliston.[10] Many of these local children went into the Church's teaching orders. For example, in this period, Adjala Township produced a higher number of vocations to the Community of St. Joseph than any other area in Ontario.[11]

The Donnelly family were faithful Catholics and well respected in the Adjala community. Catherine was baptized in St. Paul's Church, Alliston, and attended Mass every Sunday with her parents at the little mission Church of the Immaculate Conception, only a mile from the farm. However, in the absence of a separate school, she was sent to the local public or 'common' school. These schools did not ignore religion, for in the nineteenth century there was a profound Christian moral and religious component in the public school curriculum. Appropriate Bible readings and prayers, carefully selected so that particular Christian doctrinal differences would be avoided, began each school day. The School Readers, at all grades, contained passages from the Bible suitable for memorization, and many of the poems, fables and stories were selected to teach Christian ethics.

This continuous exposure to a mixed religious environment as a child would prove invaluable throughout Catherine's teaching career — one which she often declared far outweighed any religious advantage she might have gained from attending a separate school. She felt that it helped her to understand, appreciate and feel comfortable with people of other religious denominations. Indeed, one of her dearest school friends, Nettie Wright, was the daughter of the local Anglican rector. In return, her beliefs were respected and this "positive approach to society" resulted in "a big share of kindness from such God-fearing, lovable Characters provided by my Creator. In my childhood, neighbours who were Methodists or Orangemen, had been the best mutual co-workers for good."[12]

Catherine credited her mother, whom she frequently described as "generous, wonderful and good," with nurturing in her and her sisters a profound love and understanding of their Catholic heritage. She recalled that in her childhood the little church was not open during the week for any religious classes for children (nor was there any local religious order to teach them). They learned their religion at home, from their mother. The services on Sundays lacked the musical splendour of the large town churches, as they had no choir, but the family attended faithfully. In their community, there was no church hall where the little congregation could have choir practice, or organize church groups for the adults.

From her mother Catherine learned the skills of keeping a farm home, but it was her father who trained her in the Donnelly tradition of expertise in the care and training of horses. She recalled fondly, "My hard-working father was a sort of perfectionist in his farming and care of animals — not a money-maker. I loved to work outside with him handling horses and he taught me very strictly ... I owe a great deal to my Father though I did not fully realize it till comparatively recently."[13]

Like most of the rural farm children of that era, Catherine Donnelly received her elementary education at a one-room public school, No. 5 Tossorontio Township, later known as Meadowbrook School. Although these schools are now scorned as inadequate, there was very little else the taxpayers in the rural areas could afford, since the community did not have the resources to build elaborate structures for a scanty, scattered school population. The towns built larger elementary schools, and a high school was built as soon as the taxpayers decided it was a necessity. But only a small percentage of the farms were within walking distance of these centres. When a farm child was ready for high school, the family had to be able to afford some school fees, entail the expense of boarding their child in town, and do without their labour on the farm as well. Although some children might try go to high school on horseback, it was an unreliable form of transportation during the long winter months; snowstorms could block the country roads of Simcoe County for days.

Catherine's parents were able to send her to Alliston High School, where she went on to obtain her junior leaving certificate (Grade 11) in 1901. She loved school and wanted ardently to become a teacher. Her school principal in Alliston gave a glimpse of her character at that time when he wrote a recommendation for her as she was seeking her first teaching position:

> Miss Katie Donnelly attended Alliston Public School ... and she showed herself possessed of energy and ability, pluck and determination which carried her successfully through all her examinations in less than the average time ... she has been a most fruitful, persevering and clever student ... I can with pleasure recommend her to any Board of Trustees in need of a teacher who will fully justify any confidence which may be placed in her.[14]

Before Catherine could begin her career as a teacher she had to qualify for a certificate of training from one of the province's Model Schools. These were special county schools set up after new teaching regulations had been mandated by the province in 1877, to ensure that prospective teachers hired by local school boards had received a minimum of training. Model School courses were a popular substitute for the more lengthy and expensive course offered at the provincial Normal School in Toronto. The entrance requirements were low, as were the fees, and the course only lasted fourteen weeks. It was also usually situated close to the candidate's home town, which kept residence and travelling costs to a minimum.

Between 1877 and 1907, over 36,000 elementary teachers qualified for a third-class teaching certificate by attending the fourteen-week course. The apprentice teachers received highly practical training in classroom management and teaching methods given by fully licensed and experienced teachers. The certificates, issued by the County Board which ran the Model School, were valid only for three years. Teachers who wished to become fully qualified had to upgrade their certificate to either second or first class by enrolling in the Toronto or Ottawa Normal Schools for advanced professional training.

The most valid public criticism of the system was that only one-quarter of their graduates upgraded their qualifications. As a consequence, fully qualified rural teachers often found they had priced themselves out of a job, as many school boards would hire a less-qualified candidate for a smaller salary. Boards could do this with impunity since teachers' contracts were only for a year. Teachers' salaries, particularly those for women, were very low, so the teaching force became a very transient one, as women sought positions with better wages and working conditions. School inspectors complained about the harm caused by the "Arabs of Ontario ... They have no fixed abode, and are here this year, there the next and nowhere the third." Indeed, fifteen schools in Oro Township, south of Adjala, averaged eleven teachers each in the 1874-1900 period.[15]

In the summer of 1901, at the age of seventeen, Catherine Donnelly enrolled in the Model School at Bradford. Even then, she seemed to have the intellectual curiosity and natural ability to communicate ideas with which a good teacher must be blessed. When she graduated in October of that year, her principal gave her an enthusiastic recommendation:

> The bearer Miss Donnelly has been known to me since the beginning of the present Model term as a teacher-in-training. Seldom have I met a student as diligent and attentive as Miss Donnelly. Her work in every respect is eminently satisfactory. In teaching she is diligent, pains-taking intelligent and thorough. She will doubtless put into actual practice in her own school those qualities she exhibits as a student teacher.
>
> It is with the greatest pleasure and confidence I recommend her to the favorable consideration of School Trustees.[16]

Catherine was eager to start her teaching career. Her prospects were good; she and her family were well known and esteemed in the township. She had a strong body and a firm will. These were both necessary attributes for a teacher who was going to cope with fifty or sixty children distributed among Grades 1 to 8, in a one-room school which would lack electricity and running water. Catherine was not daunted by the prospect of being on her own in an isolated rural setting; indeed, she was happy at the prospect of living in the country among farmers and tradesmen. Like her, they understood man's utter dependence on the earth for life, and on the God whom they believed had created it. Throughout her life, her own religious faith would be grounded in her gratitude for the earth and the people who tilled it, and fuelled by the natural beauty which she always found in the Canadian countryside. Many years later this was perceptively observed by one of the Sisters of Service with whom she lived for many years:

> Sister Donnelly expressed much of her spirituality in the great love she had for nature. She saw the hand of the Creator in the beauty and songs of the birds, the trees, the animals and all of nature ...
>
> She loved going for walks in the bush behind our place with our faithful dogs and appreciated their company both inside and outside the house. She said that they were good therapy and made her think how faithful and wonderful the Creator is.[17]

One of Catherine Donnelly's traits, already evident in her youth, which would endear her to many in the future was her generous and forthright nature. Although she did intimidate some with her dominant personality, she could be a good companion and an excellent raconteur, and was never hesitant about seeking and developing long and lasting friendships with a great variety of people. She made new friends during her summer term at the Model School. Several of her letters many years later recalled young men and women with whom she was still in contact. But her term at Model School was particularly enjoyable because one person taking the course with her was her dearest friend, Nettie Wright, also from Alliston. Seventy-seven years later she described their relationship:

> ... lovely good and constantly my faithful friend for the rest of her life. She lived to be a little over 90 and her Anglican father and home-training made her strong in morals and ethics. I hear regularly from her niece, Marion Harper — Mrs. J.F. MacKinnon of Toronto, a widow now. Her Mother was Frances Wright, wife of Dr. Harper. Only Marion is left of that bright good family.[18]

By January 1902 Catherine had obtained her first position as the teacher, responsible for grades 1 to 8, in the one-room Bandon School No. 10 at Adjala, near Colgan, at the south end of the township. She boarded with the Gunning family and with them attended the splendid Colgan church on Sundays, getting there by horse and buggy. She remained there until January 1903, when she transferred to her old No. 5 School, which she had attended just a few years before. It was a mile from her parents' home, and she was able to save more of her scanty salary to pay for her forthcoming study year at the Normal School in

Toronto to upgrade her teaching certificate.

Reflecting on her first teaching experience among her own people, Catherine remembered that "the people of that Adjala area were very kind to me — to any teacher. The pupils were very obedient and respected and loved the teacher. The families were good. They were good to me and God was good to me and to them."[19]

CHAPTER 2

LIFE AS A TEACHER IN ONTARIO, 1904-1918

When Catherine Donnelly left Alliston to attend the Toronto Normal School in September 1904, she left behind the quiet routine of her parent's farm home, her younger sisters, Teresa (Tess) age fourteen, and Mary Loretto (Mamie) age ten. Her grandmother, Mary Ann Donnelly, had lived with them until her death the previous year, shortly after passing her hundredth birthday. Her mother had cared for her mother-in-law all her married life. Now she herself was not well and needed help to care for their home.

The decision to stop teaching and take the year of study in Toronto to fulfil the required Normal School year had not been an easy one for Catherine. Tess was boarding in Alliston while attending high school, and had a very good teacher. If Catherine left, she would have to stay home, as she would be the only person available to look after their mother. Was it right to interrupt her sister's schooling and leave her with such a heavy responsibility at that time? In one way, the circumstances were right for her to go to Toronto because she had been asked to share lodging with her friend Nettie, who would also be fulfilling the mandatory year's attendance at the Toronto Normal School for the Ontario permanent teaching certificate.

When Catherine sought her mother's advice, the sick woman had replied, "No, you go, you know what you can do." They agreed that it was important that she obtain professional qualifications because she could command a higher salary and be eligible for advancement.[1] Moreover, Catherine's mother had always approved of her friendship with the Wrights, and felt that she would benefit from living with such a congenial room-mate. Sharing a room also meant that Catherine's meagre funds would go further.

To Do and to Endure

Many years later Catherine recalled the importance of this decision to seize the opportunity to deepen her relationship with the daughters of the Anglican rector:

> Nettie Wright was just 2 days younger than me and was a great Christian — one of great physical beauty too — as well as spiritual strength. Nettie Wright and her sister Amy too, were at Alliston School with me and were my best friends — continuing through my life. Nettie Wright and Amy were faithful admirers of the S.O.S. work and often said so. Nettie died May 28, 1974, 90 years old. They were truly Christians of a very noble type.[2]

Catherine worked hard in Toronto, and was enjoying her year when, shortly before she was to write her final examinations in May, she was unexpectedly called home. Her mother's illness had been diagnosed as tuberculosis. The doctor said he could do nothing to save her and she required more care. Catherine was devastated; now she would not be able to complete her school year. Nevertheless, she prepared to leave Toronto immediately. Her problem was solved by the compassion of the Normal School principal, William Scott, who was sympathetic when she told him her plight. Her marks to date were excellent, and so he granted her full credit for the year's practical work, waived her final examinations, and certified that she would receive the Ontario permanent teaching certificate in June. To the end of her days, Catherine Donnelly always recalled his kindness with gratitude.

Catherine returned to Alliston to a deeply disturbed household. Apparently she had not comprehended the hopelessness of the situation when the doctor had discovered the then fatal disease a few months earlier. As her father reeled from the shock, friends and relatives persuaded him that he would not be able to carry on the farm without his wife, or make the arrangements for his two younger daughters to attend high school in Alliston. Their mother had always attended to such things. He had decided to sell the farm and move into Alliston.[3]

The major factor in making this decision was probably his concern that his fifty-acre farm was heavily mortgaged,[4] and it was unlikely that, at the age of fifty-nine, he would ever be able to pay his debts. In her memoirs, Catherine never mentioned the crushing mortgage, but she did refer many times to the shortage of money when she was growing up, and attributed it to her father's "bad business ventures," and the periodic economic depressions which afflicted the

Life as a Teacher in Ontario, 1904-1918

Ontario farm economy in the late nineteenth century. According to the old provincial directories, Hugh Donnelly was a woollen factor as well as a farmer — that is, a person who dealt in wool futures by buying up the fleeces from the farmers before the mills had established the yearly buying price. If the woollen factor received less money when he sold the wool to the mill than he had already paid the farmers, he could be in serious financial trouble.[5] Land records in the Ontario Archives show a continuing series of smaller loans against the Donnelly property for many years, and even though they were paid off, they indicate a chronic cash shortage.

Even in her old age Catherine still recalled the sale of the farm with sadness. She felt that if she and her sisters had been given the chance, they could have managed to run the farm and thus keep the land and the old homestead she had loved. As she ruefully remarked to her nephew, "I thought I could teach near home and come home on weekends. The neighbours didn't think it would do for us girls to be out harvesting and ploughing — everyone thought so."[6] Yet in the circumstances of farm work and teachers' incomes in 1905, the local Alliston neighbours were probably right.

The terms of sale had permitted the Donnellys to remain on the farm for a time. During the summer and autumn of 1905 Catherine struggled to look after her dying mother and keep the farm household going. During this period Catherine expressed to her mother her gratitude for urging her to attend school in Toronto. The suffering woman knew that she was going to die soon and had accepted it, but she was very distressed about leaving her two younger daughters before they had completed their education. Catherine allayed her mother's fears about their futures by promising that she would provide for her sisters and see that they completed their education. Although Catherine wrote of her father's grief and loneliness with pity, and described him as "dear" and "hard-working," she never referred to him as being helpful or supportive during the long ordeal of waiting for her mother to die from "the wasting disease." She described her mother as "wonderful, deeply religious, actively Christian, self-sacrificing, a loving mother, loved by our neighbours."[7]

A small news item in the *Alliston Herald* announced that on 20 November 1905,

> A sad affliction visited the home of Mr. Hugh Donnelly,

To Do and to Endure

Tossorontio, on Monday at noon, when Mrs. Donnelly passed away after a lengthy illness. The deceased was a woman who was held in very high esteem by all who knew her and will be mourned by a large circle of friends. She is survived by her husband, and three daughters, who have the sympathy of the community in their sad loss.[8]

While still mourning the sad loss, Catherine had to start preparing immediately to resume her teaching career, as her family needed her income. Only two weeks after the funeral, she obtained a character reference from her parish priest, Father I.F. Gibney:

I have much pleasure in testifying to the good moral character of the bearer, Miss Catherine Donnelly, whom I have known for years.

She has good credentials as a Teacher, and I feel convinced that she will give good satisfaction in that capacity.[9]

In April 1906 Hugh Donnelly and his three daughters moved to Alliston, and James Quayle, to whom the farm had been sold, took over the property. (The Quayle family still owns the land; the old farmhouse was destroyed by fire in 1918.) Catherine did not move in with her family because she was successful in finding a position for the final two months of the year (May and June) at Central Public School in Galt, as the teacher of the boys in the "slow learner class." This brief teaching assignment she always regarded as one of the most fortuitous of her life, because it was in Galt that she met and arranged to board with the MacDonnell family. Robert MacDonnell was an accountant, and a successful businessman. His wife Irene was a warm-hearted motherly person, and they both took to Catherine immediately. Their two daughters, Achsah and Ruth, were of an age with Catherine, and in her two months' stay in their home an enduring friendship was created which was a great support and joy to Catherine all her life.

The MacDonnells were all deeply devout Baptists, and Catherine was helped by their sympathy and understanding at such a difficult time in her life. Even more meaningful for her was their sincere acceptance and appreciation of her religious allegiance as an equally devout Roman Catholic. Like her Alliston friends, the Wrights, she found that the faith and moral outlook which they all held in common bonded them together as Christians in a mutual love and respect for each other which transcended their denominational differences. These and other friendships which she had made outside the Catholic community became the source of Catherine's fervent belief in the value and necessity of ecumenism, which she later declared should be the true destiny of the Christian church. However, ecumenism as she defined it was of the spirit, and not in the outward forms of service or governmental structures of the various Christian denominations. It should be demonstrated by love and co-operation between Christians regardless of whether any institutional unions ever took place. In practical terms, ecumenism meant that neither she nor the Wrights nor the MacDonnells, nor any other of her non-Catholic friends, ever sought each others' conversion. Rather, they supported each other in the carrying out of their own denomination's religious obligations as expressions of a mutual faith. These ideas took shape and became part of her own religious philosophy during that spring, in the quiet and peace of the MacDonnell home. But they were rooted in the Alliston community in which she was raised, particularly as exemplified by her parents and her childhood friends.

At the end of June, Catherine moved into the new family home in Alliston. The difficult events of the past year had taken their toll on her. Nursing her dying mother while keeping the farm going, moving the family to Alliston and then leaving immediately for a strenuous teaching position in Galt, and worry about her family's future and the heavy financial responsibilities which had now fallen on her twenty-one-year-old shoulders had by July caused her to break down "with almost fatal results."[10] "I was worn out mentally and physically for a few months quite convinced that I could never be capable of teaching school. It was almost a complete and incurable breakdown."[11] Catherine never disclosed any of the medical details on how she managed to overcome her illness. She only stated that "God provided and I went through the experience of using my *faith* and the opportunities God had provided and still provides if we humbly ask Him."[12]

By January 1907 Catherine had recovered sufficiently to take a teaching position at the Apto School, a hamlet north of Barrie, not far from Alliston. On 5 January she enrolled Tess in a boarding school in Toronto, the prestigious St. Joseph's Academy for Young Women, founded by the Sisters of St. Joseph. Catherine paid the fees, although her father was listed in the academy register as guardian.[13] Not quite seventeen years old, Tess was like her elder sister in temperament,

To Do and to Endure

strong-minded and energetic. Catherine described her at this time as "very clever and lively and attractive."[14]

Catherine took young Mamie with her to Apto and arranged to have her enrolled in the school where she was now teaching. Lodging was found with the Loftus family "who kindly took us both to board at their fine home." There was an elementary school in Allison which Mamie could have attended, but Catherine apparently wished to oversee Mamie's studies for her Grade 8 elementary school certificate. Mamie had no objections to this arrangement, as she was a quiet, dutiful child whom Catherine always described as gentle, serious and co-operative, but who "perhaps gave in to worry too much at times."[15]

The adolescent Tess was harder for her to handle, and Catherine admitted that it was often gentle Mamie who helped advise her. Tess became the centre of the next family crisis when, according to the St. Joseph's Academy records, after only two weeks in the school, she left. The register stated that she "Took French leave, Saturday Jan. 19, 1907." She never returned to the school; the next entry in her school record noted that Catherine Donnelly was sent a refund of $61.25 out of a total of $65.50 which she had paid for board and tuition for "Teresa Donnelly" for the term ending June 1907.[16] These sums were a substantial portion of Catherine's income, since her salary at Apto School was probably less than $500.[17]

Why did Tess leave and how did she manage to do it? Her son narrated her story many years later, beginning with Tess's impression that

> she was in the pipeline to becoming a nun in a Toronto Convent school, something that she did not want to do. One day the Convent school-children were on a field trip on a Toronto trolley, and got off. My mother stayed on until the trolley got to the Toronto train station, where my mother took a train to New York, enrolled in the Mount Sinai nurses school, became a registered nurse and rose to become chief scrub nurse in the Mt. Sinai operating rooms. Probably in 1916, she volunteered to go to France as a Red Cross nurse, and spent no more than a year in hospitals in Nantes and Brest, where she met my father.
>
> Why my mother came to New York is a matter of speculation. I suspect that she thought she would have to distance herself from Aunt Catherine, who I know to be an exceedingly strong-willed person, in order not to be convinced to re-enter the convent school and then the convent. My mother's relationship with Aunt

Catherine was one of great affection and caring.[18]

This is a near tragic example of the misunderstanding between the two sisters and Tess and her teachers at school. Catherine at that time was, by her own admission, not particularly interested in or particularly approving of convent life, either for herself, or anyone in her family. Her main intent was to see that her sisters were educated to support themselves in a profession. Nor was it likely that the Sisters of St. Joseph tried to influence their graduates unduly to enter the order. Protestant and Catholic girls attended the school, for it was one of the best in Toronto. Only 2 per cent of the Catholic girls who were boarders at the school in this period entered the order.[19] Fortunately the situation worked itself out. Catherine remained on good terms with her sister and was always very proud whenever she mentioned Tess's career in nursing. But she omitted any reference to the event, and never explained how a good Catholic girl from Alliston ended up in a Jewish hospital in faraway New York City.

After completing two years' teaching at Apto School, Catherine herself resigned, as she felt it was necessary to search for a post with a higher salary to meet the anticipated cost of tuition and board for the latter part of her sister Mamie's high school education and her session at Normal School. Mamie, too, wanted to be a teacher. "Schools offering the highest salaries had to be hunted out by me and handled successfully. It was a must!"[20] Mamie returned to Alliston to begin her secondary education at the local high school. Catherine had no qualms about the rightness of this decision, for "she was where she observed good people and saw their life-style and mingled with all kinds of pupils in an ordinary High School — but knew there were dangers."[21]

Most of the school boards paying higher salaries were in districts far from the Alliston-Barrie area, or else they were facing emergency situations caused by unexpected teacher resignations in mid-year. As she began to search for her next position, Catherine carried with her good references from her last employers. The first was from the West Simcoe County inspector Thomas McKee:

> I hereby certify that Miss Katie Donnelly taught a Public School in my Inspectorate for four years and during all that time performed every duty pertaining to her Profession with zeal, ability, and complete success.
>
> I have very great pleasure in recommending her to any Board of

> Trustees desirous of securing the services of a skilful, able and Conscientious Teacher whose heart is in her work, and who knows how to bring her work to a successful issue.[22]

The Apto school board wrote:

> The trustees of any school engaging the services of Miss K. Donnelly, as teacher, May not be anyway anxious as to the moral qualifications of this good young lady in the classroom or elsewhere. [She is] scrupulously exemplary. Mr. Mills, the Inspector is my authority for saying that she is an excellent teacher and a good proof I think, of her ability as a teacher after this year's experience in the Apto School is the desire of the school section not to lose her.[23]

Mr. G.K. Mills himself wrote:

> This is to certify that Miss Catherine Donnelly has taught in my inspectorate for the past two years. She has been an earnest, hard-working, and successful teacher. Both years she had large Entrance classes and had good success. Such was the work being done in the school and the influence of the teacher that several young people who had left school returned to take up Entrance work. For the past year and a half she has had a 5th class doing good work. She has succeeded in inspiring a number with a desire to take up higher work and they are now attending High School. Her work has been very much appreciated by the people of the community.
> I can with confidence recommend her to any Board of Trustees as a capable and successful teacher.[24]

Thus well supported, Catherine Donnelly began her odyssey through the rural schools of Ontario. Her primary reason was to earn more money for her family's responsibilities and to advance her own career through appointments with more responsibility. But she also later admitted that she was something of a "scamp," in that she loved the adventure of new challenges and new places, and she adapted easily and well to new situations.

The new teaching position that Catherine found in January 1909 was, as she had anticipated, much farther afield than her previous Simcoe County posts. But it was a step up the professional ladder for her, since she was hired by the board of Forrester's Falls to be the principal of their two-room school. This was a small community west of

Ottawa in the Renfrew County North Inspectorate. There were no Catholic families in the community, and only one Catholic child attended the school; but it was the kind of assignment that Catherine was beginning to prefer. "Something in my letter of application appealed to the School Board members. They wanted a disciplinarian. I had written that I could do it — but I must have a way to get to Mass on Sundays. They were prompt to reply that they would provide a way."[25]

Sure enough, when she arrived in January there was a team of horses and a cutter ready for her use, and at no expense to her. All that winter and spring she drove her team alone twelve miles every Sunday to the nearest Catholic church, which was across the Ottawa River at Portage du Fort in Quebec. She could not recall missing a single Sunday. Catherine attended church so faithfully, not only out of her personal religious conviction, but also because she felt that teachers, by their very lifestyle, should publicly exemplify their moral priorities. "Christian principles meticulously followed while living among the families and teaching school subjects which a completely-developed child must know are what produce a fruitful harvest."[26] The lesson being taught to her students by her example on Sundays should, she believed, be one which they could apply to their own lives. This was as important as her duty to guide her students through the regulated academic drills which were such an integral part of classroom teaching at that time.

She liked the local community and they liked her; the people were kind and appreciative. "In ... Forrester's Falls I received cooperation greater than in any other in many ways. Respect for my Christian principles was tops ... Never have I enjoyed stauncher support. It was completely against their wishes when I finally accepted a school with a higher salary and resigned."[27]

The school inspector, E.B. White, summed up the local feelings toward her: "I consider that Miss Donnelly is doing excellent work in the school and I would be sorry to see her leave my Inspectorate. She has shown herself a capable teacher in organization and in governing power. She has a good grasp of the subjects to be taught and a pleasant manner in presenting them to the class."[28]

From 6 August to December 1909 Catherine next taught at the Killarney Public School, which was in an isolated community on the northwest coast of Georgian Bay. Her salary was around $500. In

January 1910 she moved south to become a principal again, for six months, at a two-room school in Heidelberg, a German settlement near Waterloo. Her salary was about $525. In August she signed a contract to teach for a year at No. 1 Public School, Culross Township, a farming area in West Bruce County, where she boarded with one of the local farmers. Twenty-five students attended her school, and her salary was now $600. Then in August 1911 she was able to get a year's contract in the same inspectorate at the Riversdale Public School near Chepstow, which paid her a salary of $650. A deciding factor in her getting this job was probably the excellent recommendation she was given by W.F. Bald, the public school inspector for West Bruce.[29]

The salary increase which she achieved with this move was especially important, as in September 1911 she enrolled Mamie in St. Joseph's Academy in Toronto for her last year of high school. Her sister's board and tuition for the year cost her $150.[30] After paying for her own clothing and room and board, Catherine did not have much money to put aside to support Mamie's tuition and board for Normal School, which they planned she would be attending the following year. Still, the elder sister felt her sacrifice was worth while, for Mamie was a good student, who would win the prize in English, donated by the Academy's most illustrious graduate, Miss Gertrude Lawler.

An opportunity to regain the rank of principal caused Catherine to leave Riversdale after one year. In his glowing testimonial, Mr. Bald wrote: "I am sorry that you are leaving West Bruce Inspectorate and particularly Riversdale School. Wishing you every success in your work."[31]

In August 1912 she accordingly moved to Manley in the East Bruce Inspectorate, not far from Seaforth, to be principal of a two-room school, again at a salary of $650. She was thus able to pay Mamie's tuition to the Normal School and her board for another year at St. Joseph's. The Academy, moreover, had an arrangement with the Normal School that their graduates could be registered as boarders at St. Joseph's and attend classes at the Normal School.

Mamie wrote three religious poems which were published in 1913 in *St. Joseph's Lilies*, the St. Joseph's alumnae magazine which had been started by Gertrude Lawler. The poems indicated a religious sensitivity and fervour which was exceptional for a young woman of nineteen. She had wanted to join the St. Joseph's Order the previous year when she had finished high school, but Catherine insisted that she was to attend Normal School and teach for two years before making her final decision to become a nun.[32]

Catherine meanwhile taught at Manley from August 1912 to December 1913. Her sister had just started teaching at S.S. No. 2 Nottawasaga, near Creemore, and was then offered the opportunity to teach at St. Peter's Separate School in Toronto, starting January 1914. But to do so she had to find a replacement teacher at Nottawasaga, so Catherine resigned from Manley at Christmas in order to complete the teaching year for her. The salary was the same, and she would be nearer home and able to keep an eye on her father, who was feeling lonely with all his daughters away. But by September 1914 she was off to northern Ontario, to Hudson Consolidated School, near New Liskeard. Her only comment about that post, which paid her a salary of $600, was that the pupils came in a horse-drawn van. To attend Mass in Cobalt, Catherine walked eight miles (and in Northern Ontario winters too) to New Liskeard, and took a train to Cobalt. Later, the secretary provided a horse and buggy to New Liskeard.

From August to December 1915 Catherine held forth in the separate school in Merriton, near St. Catharines. Her salary was only $550, which was considerably below her former levels, but by January the following year, she was back in her own home district as principal of Caledon East Village School. Yet this brief posting to St. Catharines became one which she later felt was providential for her future career, for here she met Adeline McConnell, who took the junior grades in the school. They became close friends.

That summer Catherine made a great professional breakthrough, when she was offered the principalship of the public school in Penetanguishene at a salary of $850. It was a fine brick school of nine rooms with three hundred and sixty students. Adeline McConnell was hired too, and Catherine was also able to add to her staff three other friends who were good, experienced teachers: Marion Tyrell, and Helen and Mary O'Connor. She shared many interests with Mary, including a sense of adventure. The school was controlled by a Roman Catholic board because the great majority of the town's students and the ratepayers were of that faith. Penetanguishene was one of the few instances in Ontario at that time where the "separate school" was that attended by non-Catholic children.

To Do and to Endure

The town was attractively situated on hills which bordered Georgian Bay, and had been largely settled by French and Irish Catholic immigrants. It was famous for having played a historic role as a naval station, provisioning and repairing the British ships which fought in the War of 1812. On a hill overlooking Georgian Bay was one of the town's finest buildings, St. Anne's Catholic Church. It had been built in 1902 as a memorial to the Jesuit Canadian martyrs, in Italian Romanesque style, of Credit Valley limestone and Nottawasaga sandstone. In contrast to the more modest brick or wood Catholic churches of Adjala township, it was indeed splendid, with its very large interior walls faced with pastel marble and made brilliant by striking frescoes and large stained-glass windows. In 1911 the town population was only 1,134 people, but in the next ten years it had nearly quadrupled to 4,037. The Dominion census also recorded that the Catholic population was 2,466, and the rest of the townsfolk were divided among many small Protestant groups.

Catherine was very happy teaching the highest grade here, as well as being school principal. She had a reliable staff, and by 1918 her salary had been raised to $925, which was well above the average of $580 paid to female teachers in rural Ontario at that time. However, the school was not without its problems, for it had a high truancy rate. The social unrest caused by the First World War had produced profound distresses which struck deep into Canadian society, even in the smaller more cohesive communities, and many families became what would now be termed dysfunctional. Years later Catherine mused that "it was a social worker, well-trained, whom we needed instead of a truant officer whom the boys defied. I ought to have made time to visit the families myself. The Pastor, Father Brunet came to the school now and then. His load was very heavy, so was mine."[33]

Life for the teaching staff at the school changed very suddenly when the school board investigated the possibility of bringing in a religious teaching order to take over the school. Unknown to Catherine, plans were being made in the early spring to replace the lay teachers with Sisters of the Community of St. Joseph, Toronto.

> On May 20th [1918], His Grace the Archbishop [Neil McNeil] called to make the request that four Sisters take charge of the Penetanguishene Public (Catholic) School in the coming September. Reverend Mother's consent to the opening of the

Life as a Teacher in Ontario, 1904-1918

Mission was obtained by wire from B.C. Reverend Mother raised one objection, — the School was a public School. His Grace stated that it was an objection to have the School a Public School, but that at the present such an objection had to be borne with. The Council decided on the following conditions being agreed to by the authorities in the Mission before the Community take charge of the School.

1. Each Sister to receive $500.00 per annum.
2. The Community to be provided with a furnished home free of charge.
3. That the house be put in a state of good repair, the heating made satisfactory, and two additional rooms built at the rear to do service as Kitchen and laundry. The house is to be only an arrangement for a year or so until a suitable residence can be built.[34]

It is not surprising that the local board agreed to the terms imposed by the Sisters of St. Joseph, as they were well known for their teaching vocation. Like other religious orders, they had worked in Catholic schools in the Archdiocese of Toronto for many years, and always received salaries well below the average paid by Catholic school boards for their qualified lay female teachers. In many places in Ontario their salaries were half those paid in the public system. The new principal was to receive only $500 per annum, the same as her staff. Moreover, their single status was a certain guarantee of staff stability, for lay female teachers were expected to stop teaching when they married.

On hearing this news about the impending arrival of the St. Joseph Sisters, Catherine and her four colleagues resigned. Her work in Penetanguishene was acknowledged with a cursory note from L.F. LeMay, the board secretary: "Your letter of resignation as Principal of our school was read at the regular meeting of the School Board held last evening and accepted with regret. The School Board instructed me to convey their thanks to you for the excellent manner you have conducted the school during your stay here and wishing you every success for the future."[35]

Catherine immediately thought of applying to a public school board; but her school inspector, Joseph Garvin, told her that she was not likely to get as good a school position anywhere in Ontario. This was disheartening news from a man who had certified that "I consider

41

To Do and to Endure

Miss Catherine Donnelly is one of the best teachers in North Simcoe."[36] But it was not a propitious time for a Catholic lay teacher to be seeking employment with a public school board. Protestant-Roman Catholic tensions had increased in Ontario during the war. Quarrels had erupted in the Toronto press over whether Catholics (particularly Irish immigrants) were contributing their fair share to the war effort by answering the call to arms. In spite of a proportionate enlistment in the armed forces by Catholic men, Catholic loyalty to the Allied cause was suspect in some circles.[37] It was an opportune time for suppressed anti-Catholic prejudice to surface, and it was manifested in unreasonable public utterances and actions. Public school board hiring committees were not immune to these pressures, and were beginning to be cautious about hiring a Roman Catholic. Catherine decided to investigate opportunities elsewhere.

CHAPTER 3
ADVENTURES IN ALBERTA: AM I CALLED TO BE A RELIGIOUS?

CATHERINE SAID THERE WERE SEVERAL REASONS why she decided "to try my luck in a western province," but the only one to which she usually referred was the greater possibility of getting the better position and salary that her ability and experience merited. "I realized that openings for Catholic teachers which would suit me were scarce in Ontario."[1] She was quite right. Teachers were in such short supply in the Canadian West, particularly in the rural areas of the prairie provinces, that her religion was less likely to be an impediment. After her recent experiences teaching in Catholic schools in Ontario, she felt more secure working for the public boards. She also believed that it was beneficial for children of all faiths to be educated together. A good salary was still of prime importance, for in September 1918 Catherine was still the only person in the family who could give financial support to her seventy-three-year-old father, who was living alone in Alliston. Her sister Tess had joined the American Medical Corps and was nursing wounded troops in France, while Mamie was now Sister Justina CSJ. On 5 July 1917, at the age of twenty-three, Mamie had entered the Community of St. Joseph in Toronto. On 5 January 1918, having completed her term as a postulant, she had begun her two-year novitiate.[2]

Working in western Canada also offered Catherine the prospect of new sights, new people and new adventures. She looked forward to seeing a part of the country not visited very frequently by easterners. She sent out some job applications, and while awaiting replies, received the good news from Inspector Garvin that "as she had taught successfully for two years as principal of a 9-roomed school in Penetanguishene, Ont," he was recommending that "her certificate (II Class) be endorsed for Urban and Rural Schools of 4 or more rooms."[3]

To Do and to Endure

She decided to use the holidays to upgrade her academic qualifications and enrolled in summer school at Toronto. Her friend Mary O'Connor, who had also resigned from the staff of the Penetanguishene school when she had realized she too would be displaced by the St. Joseph Sisters, joined her there. One day she announced suddenly, "Chief, I'm going with you, and if possible, I'm going to teach in the same school with you."[4] Catherine was delighted. The only one who did not feel any joy about her plan to move was her father. He pleaded with her not to go so far away, but she said she still needed as high a salary as she could possibly earn, as she had to look after him.

Preparations were made to leave in late August 1918, and the two women travelled west together. They went by boat to Fort William, and in Winnipeg they arranged at a school employment bureau for a school at Kerrobert, Saskatchewan, for Mary O'Connor's sister, Helen. She, too, had decided to join them in the western adventure, and arrived shortly to take up her duties at the Saskatchewan school. Catherine had also found positions for Mary and herself in Stettler, Alberta, a small town in the ranching country about 120 miles northeast of Calgary. But they thought they might prefer southern Alberta, so Catherine went to investigate the possibilities south of Lethbridge while Mary proceeded to Stettler to inspect the territory. As the Lethbridge lead proved false, Catherine caught the train to Stettler. There Mary and the school inspector, Mr. Thibodeau, greeted her at the station with the welcome news that everything was now arranged. Two vacancies were available in two rural one-room public schools, about five miles apart. Catherine would teach in one of them and board at the Claey ranch; Mary would teach in the second school, board at a ranch near her school, and join Catherine on the weekends.

They were soon introduced to western ranch life, as they were hospitably received by new friends who took them around the beautiful countryside and also arranged for them to go to church. They heard that although some Catholics were settled in the area, there was no Catholic parish church in the district. Their friends introduced them to a French Catholic family who lived in the area on the Genore Ranch and had built their own tiny private chapel in their house. When a priest was available, which might be about once a month, Mass was celebrated there for their family. They were told that they were welcome to attend. Catherine solved her transportation problem by breaking in a young horse which belonged to her landlady, Mrs. Charles Claey. She could now ride to visit her friends and also go to nearby Erskine, five miles away, for the mail. Classes at their schools commenced in September 1918.

The First World War ended in November, and brought the first contingents of soldiers home to families and friends. A delirium of joy swept through the nation, as Canadians anticipated happy reunions. But an epidemic of influenza had started in Europe in early 1918, and soon spread rapidly. It was brought into Canada by soldiers who had small resistance to the disease, for they had been weakened by constant fatigue, poor food, and years of living in the cold, damp trenches of the Western Front. The two women had only been teaching in Alberta for about six weeks when the dreaded Spanish flu struck their district with sudden and widespread virulence. It was a particularly dangerous strain of the disease, as it struck down young and healthy parents as well as their vulnerable babies and the elderly.

The Alberta government acted swiftly; by mid-November the schools were ordered to close indefinitely, and the teachers were requested to volunteer their services as nurses for the desperately ill families. Living in isolated farmhouses, often miles apart from their neighbours and far from the town, the poor homesteaders had no means of getting medical aid. In many cases, the whole family was struck down with the disease which could kill within a few days of contagion. In the Stettler area, the young couple whose private chapel Mary and Catherine had occasionally attended both died after only four days' illness. The two women themselves felt they had to answer the call for volunteers, and prepared to undertake home nursing duties. They had taken a St. John Ambulance course in Penetanguishene, but neither of them had ever worked under such life-threatening conditions.

They were immediately assigned to their first case out in the country by the local doctor who, with the help of his wife, was struggling to organize help for his patients. In a farm home a father, mother, their baby and a baby cousin (who had been taken from his home when his sick parents became unable to care for him), were all dangerously ill. There were no drugs and many patients were dying from secondary pneumonia infections. The only curative measures the doctor could suggest were rest, nourishing fluids like chicken soup, and the traditional home-made mustard or onion plasters (the latter were to be used on the babies) to relieve chest congestion. There was no suitable food in the house, so Catherine went out to their hen-house, killed two of the chickens and prepared chicken soup for them all. Throughout the night Catherine nursed and fed the parents while Mary cared for the little ones. By morning Mary had also caught the flu, and Catherine now had five patients. When the doctor came by, it was obvious she needed help. He arranged to get all of them driven into Erskine, where he had commandeered the local Protestant church and turned it into a makeshift hospital. The beds were all occupied. After much difficulty, Catherine managed to scrounge another bed for her friend. For the next week she herself used a bench or a mat on the floor when she could take a break from nursing her five patients. Miraculously, Catherine escaped infection although she was ready to collapse from fatigue when finally more nursing help arrived. Catherine and Mary were then able to return to Claey's ranch.

She soon took on another flu case: a farmer whose wife had recently died, and whose housekeeper had left him and his two children alone and sick. Mary O'Connor came too, although she was still too weak to do anything strenuous. It was fortunate that Catherine was a farmer's daughter, for in addition to her nursing duties, she had to look after their valuable farm animals.

> We slaved inside the house and out. The cattle had to be watered. We ran the pumping apparatus ... We got the patients on their feet again. The boy and girl raced to the telephone to listen to the neighbours' conversation. Then we knew they were O.K. We knew too, that materialism was the god of the home. The man had set his heart on securing a good wife — Miss O'C. We left as soon as we could possibly get away.[5]

By Christmas they were back home in Catherine's quarters where they discussed the harrowing experiences of the last seven weeks. The most disturbing aspect of their nursing experiences, they agreed, was the absence of any recognition by their patients that they might also need some spiritual help when they were all facing possible death. Nor was there ever any expression of gratitude to God for their survival for, "There was no sign of faith in God, or resort to prayer in the homes where we nursed; rather the atmosphere everywhere breathed materialism."[6]

They liked the people in the district, and Catherine knew that they

Adventures in Alberta: Am I Called to be a Religious?

were trusted and accepted. Working through the crisis, however, had made them realize that what was missing in the settlements was the communal bond which is created when a group recognizes that they have a mutual religious faith in a power which can lift them above their obsession with material security. Catherine and Mary were not unsympathetic to the immigrants' fierce drive to succeed. They had seen how precarious was the life of the rancher and the farmer. Illness, accidents, crop disease or bad weather could destroy their prosperity overnight. Several people in the community had died, and many more of them had come close to dying, to leaving behind all that they had striven for. Yet the survivors did not seem prepared to face the fact that even if they had escaped this time, they too would eventually die. Their lack of a spiritual preparation was of great concern to Catherine and Mary. Could any community spirit or bonding ever develop in such a religious void? They had discovered that there were quite a few Catholics in the area, but the majority no longer practised their religion.

This was particularly true of many of the immigrants from Central Europe where Catholicism had been the religion of the majority. They had come as foreigners into rural communities where, unlike Europe, there were very few Catholic churches and "no [Catholic] missionary workers anywhere near these people."[7] There were Protestant churches in the area, and although their religious services were unlike what they were used to, some Catholic settlers had been attracted. With no church leadership of their own, it was not long before many of the European Catholic arrivals had begun to disregard their own spiritual heritage, and concentrate solely on achieving security and prosperity. The two women thus concluded that the settlers could not really be blamed for their indifference to religion. It was their Church which was at fault, for most of its resources had been allocated to the prairie cities. It was true that for many years some male religious orders had been working among the Indian tribes, but the female religious orders had been establishing their hospitals and schools in the urban settlements from Winnipeg to Victoria. The needs of the Catholic country folk had been largely ignored, with the result that "the spiritual condition in the homes was like a barren place, a Godless foreign country."[8] As Catherine said, "the worldliness and lack of Faith made one homesick."[9]

Catherine and Mary also concluded that although it was their own

47

strong constitutions which had enabled them to work so hard during those weeks of crisis, it was their own deep religious faith that had enabled them to ignore their fatigue and continue to work even in the most desperate situations. They appreciated more than ever that they had been raised in God-fearing families and communities who had taught their faith to them as children. After they had left home and begun teaching in Ontario, they had always found a supportive group of people who believed as they did in the worth of religious faith and practice. Church buildings, clergy, and religious teachers had always been available. Catherine was particularly perturbed when she discovered her Church's neglect of the rural West, for she felt that this did not bode well for the future of the people, the Church or the nation.

What could be done about it? Each woman admitted that during that autumn they had, unknown to each other, "been doing some special thinking." Had they saved people's lives only "for them to go back to cold paganism?" Most of the Catholics they had met "had become quite lax ... seldom got to Mass, and didn't seem to try any too hard."[10] They had both begun to think more seriously about their futures in the light of their heightened awareness of the reality of their faith in God. Was it His will that they continue teaching as laywomen? Catherine said that because she was not satisfied to continue simply teaching school in such conditions, she had even written to her sister Tess in France, asking if she should give up teaching and undertake to train as a nurse. Tess had not been very encouraging, pointing out that she was now over thirty and the hours in training were long and arduous. Furthermore if Catherine ever married, she would have to give up working as a nurse or a teacher, even if her skills were urgently needed. Should she therefore commit her life solely to teaching and working with people? If so, did this mean that she should join a religious community dedicated to teaching in these areas where the Church's presence was so urgently required? In religious parlance, this meant accepting that her present spiritual unease was a sign that she had a vocation to be a religious — to be a sister.

It was a very serious decision, one which Catherine would find particularly difficult to think through. Since 1905 she had worked hard to fulfil her responsibility to support her father and educate her sisters. But her father still needed help, and she was the only one in the family who could give it. He had already been saddened by her departure; he was not in good health and he was lonely. Was it right that she change the course of her life at this stage? Up to this time she had never considered becoming a nun, and she was ignorant of the particulars of convent life. Nuns had never played any role in her education. As a child she had attended "a small public school two miles away — never a Catholic teacher ... never a nun anywhere near except when they came for my father to drive them around to collect for the House of Providence. Nuns were something very mysterious and austere, in my mind, but high above other women."[11] She did not even know how to get information about the work of the various religious orders.[12] Catherine had been pleased when Mamie had been accepted by the Community of St. Joseph, but she had also insisted that her sister become professionally qualified as a teacher before she applied to enter the order. Young Mamie, as Sister Justina, now lived according to a strict Holy Rule. Its details were carefully guarded as private information within the order, but the Rule was designed to keep the sisters physically and spiritually separated from the secular world. They were not allowed to eat meals away from the convent, or leave it for any reason without permission, or unaccompanied. Personal relations, even within the convent, were carefully controlled, and visits home were rare and of very short duration, except for exceptional circumstances.[13] Catherine was an extroverted, gregarious person; she prized her friends and sensed that she would not find it easy to give up the emotional obligations which deep friendships entailed. Nevertheless, she decided to investigate if she could "join some Order which could be induced to come out there."[14]

There was also a final factor about which little is known, but which might have been an additional cause of her concern. In 1916, when she was teaching in Caledon, Ontario, Catherine had written to Neil McNeil, the Archbishop of Toronto, requesting that he help a Mr. Wellington Mackenzie "with his case." She stated that she had "taken time to study well, the circumstances of his case, and even if I were not promised to him in marriage, would do all in my power to help him." She said she believed him " worthy of any assistance you may be able to give him" and that she "admired his patience and deep seriousness."[15] In the letter, the problem which concerned them was never identified, but it was clear that Archbishop McNeil was already apprised of it. To date no other record has been discovered which discusses Catherine's relationship with this man, or mentions that she once made a promise to marry. But the clarity and sincerity of her short, hand-written letter testifies to its authenticity. If she had still been engaged to him in January 1919, she was faced with a very difficult decision indeed. Even if the engagement had by then been terminated, it is proof that, up to that time, she had not ruled out the possibility of marriage.

In an effort to sort her way through her personal dilemma, Catherine decided to search for a position where she could teach and "be able to contact an experienced and wise priest. (I had the Bishop in mind) about entering a community which would work in the abandoned west."[16] Mary was quite happy to come with her. She did not wish to return alone to the Stettler district when the schools were reopened, and they both needed their salaries. By Christmas 1919 they had their next jobs in hand. Catherine chose the principalship of a Catholic school, Sacred Heart School in West Calgary, and Mary O'Connor was hired by the Innisfail Public School Board to teach in their high school.

Catherine was not long on her new job before she discovered she had fallen into a touchy situation. "A neglected school, the pastor of the parish overseas ... The teachers on the staff were bitterly dissatisfied with their salaries and general conditions. The discipline was something not to be described in a few sentences." The board did not support the staff because "it consisted of volunteer business men who were over-ruled by Bishop McNally."[17] He was a "domineering Bishop, very conservative, Dictator type — little sympathy for mere women teachers — one who wanted to get teaching nuns to take schools and be made parochial — directly under his commands."[18] In addition she herself had a "very weak grade eight class, promoted haphazardly and belonging to proud parents who must have their children pass." The physical plant was so bad and "the school furnace so inefficient that we couldn't settle to work till March."[19] Catherine supported the teachers; but as she was the principal of the school and legally responsible directly to her superintendent, she was at a loss to devise ways to change their working conditions without authorization.

While struggling with these distracting matters she met Father William Cameron, the founder and principal of St. Mary's Boys College and also a diocesan priest on the staff of the cathedral in Calgary. He was a discerning, kindly man whose academic ability and personal qualities had earned him a Rhodes scholarship. He was also highly regarded in Calgary for his support and leadership in Catholic charitable endeavours, particularly Holy Cross Hospital. Catherine found him to be an attentive and sympathetic listener, an experienced administrator and a brilliant teacher, whom she could consult with confidence about the troubles at Sacred Heart School. Her reminiscences about the situation in Calgary did not give many more details, except to state that Father Cameron gave her sage and helpful advice, and that in his professional discussions with her, he always treated her as an equal and a colleague. His reassurance about the rightness of her stand gave her the courage to insist, against the superintendent's wishes, that she would present the school's problems to the school trustees at a board meeting. The result was that "for me it was a complete triumph which boosted my desire to dare and fight for the right under all opposing forces."[20] Improvements were made and "the school settled down to business." She was particularly proud of the fact that "all my grade 8 pupils passed the dep'l exam and two of the prizes of the 3 always secured by St. Mary's pupils taught by FCJ Sisters came to my pupils."[21]

In the months following the school board incident, Catherine abandoned her idea of consulting the bishop about her concerns regarding her personal future: she found him haughty, uninterested and aloof.[22] She turned instead to Father Cameron for advice "my wisest and best friend there."[23] She confided to him her deep distress over the Church's indifference to the spiritual and educational needs of the people in the rural areas in the West. She was certain that this would result in irreparable harm to these abandoned souls, and also damage the Church's reputation and the welfare of the nation. She had developed such a longing to be a part of the solution to this situation, that she was perplexed as to whether this restless dissatisfaction with her present life was really a call from God to devote her future life to His work in a rural apostolate. Did this mean that she had a vocation to become a teaching sister in this unserved territory? Or on the other hand, was it her duty to give priority to her financial and moral obligations to her father? Could these conflicting obligations be worked out so that she could seriously consider making the necessary preparations to enter a religious community? During the many hours they spent discussing her mission to bring education and the Catholic faith to rural western Canada, her longing to serve never wavered. Her passionate eagerness to undertake what they both knew would be a difficult and arduous task convinced Father Cameron that she did indeed have a vocation. Their discussions then turned to an investigation of the steps she should take before applying to a religious order. But which order?

They both agreed that it should be a teaching order, but Father Cameron felt that none of the religious communities working in the West at that time would be suitable for her envisioned apostolate, as most of them were French in origin with motherhouses overseas. However, he had heard that Bishop McNally had invited the St. Joseph Sisters in Peterborough to come to teach in Calgary next year. He suggested she contact them as they were the community most likely to be willing to consider her plan. Catherine was not enthusiastic about the Community of St. Joseph. She thought their religious habit was severe, cumbersome and so elaborately fashioned as to be quite unsuited to the rural conditions she had recently encountered. However, she agreed that when the time was opportune, she would discuss her ideas with them.

As the school year was now over, she joined Mary O'Connor at a cottage for a six-day holiday before the two of them went to Edmonton to summer school. She was informed that in September she was to be transferred to the principalship of another Catholic school in Calgary; the Sisters of St. Joseph would be taking over Sacred Heart School in September. Father Cameron's information had been correct. Catherine was not keen at the prospect of working again for the Separate School Board in Calgary. She was torn between her duty to return east so as to be near her father, and her desire to experience more of Alberta by continuing to teach in rural schools. She decided to accept a teaching position in the town of Coleman about 175 miles southwest of Calgary, in the Crow's Nest Pass area, and arranged for Mary O'Connor to take over her new Calgary posting in September. Neither of them was ready yet to make an application to a specific religious order, but they admitted to each other that they had made a private, spiritual commitment to enter religious life when the time was right. Catherine justified her decision to stay in the West for the time being because "I knew that I still needed plenty of salary for my expenses of different kinds. And I had matters to settle, problems to solve."[24]

Adventures in Alberta: Am I Called to be a Religious?

Her father was one of the problems. Was Wellington Mackenzie another? There is no answer to that question, for Catherine never again made any direct reference to him or to any commitment to him. Mr. Mackenzie had written to Archbishop McNeil while she was at Stettler stating that, "At present I'm calling at the Monastery at 141 McCaul St. where I take instructions from Rev. Father Coughlan, once a week." In May of that year he had written again "hoping that the time will not be long now before I shall have the pleasure of being received by you into the first and only true Church." His last letter was written on 22 January 1919, in which was enclosed "a little gift to you as a token of my gratitude" for the "kind and sympathetic letter which you sent to me while at my home at Hillview, Ont, with reference to the death of my Father."[25]

In the meantime, Catherine had been writing to another old friend from her Penetanguishene staff, Adeline McConnell, urging her to join them in their western adventure. Adeline was intrigued and replied that only family duties were keeping her from accepting the enticing invitation. In late summer of 1919 she wrote saying she could come if she could get a position on staff at Coleman School. This Catherine managed to secure, and Adeline joined her in her cosy apartment in the town. Mary O'Connor came from Calgary one weekend for a joyous reunion celebration.

A week later, on a Saturday morning in early November, a telegram announcing that her father was seriously ill summoned Catherine back to Alliston. She asked the chairman of the school board to secure a substitute, and if possible, a permanent teacher, as she felt it would be impossible to give the board a definite date when she would be free to return. She caught the train that night and she arrived home three days later to find that her father was unconscious. A local practical nurse was doing her best to cope, and her aunt and cousin were also there. Sister Justina had arrived a few days earlier, having been granted special permission to leave her community for a few days. Now that Catherine had arrived, Mamie had to return to Toronto at once, as she was completing her novitiate and was preparing for her first profession on 5 January. Their sister Tess was not free to come home either, for she had been married in August, and was now living in the western United States.

As she had done so many times before, Catherine took charge in the family emergency. She hired two nurses from Toronto, and when her father had recovered sufficiently to travel, she took him to St. Michael's Hospital in Toronto, to see if he could undergo a cataract operation. It was deemed to be too risky due to his heart condition. She managed to secure work as a supply teacher in Toronto, for her father's medical expenses and the wages of the home help had depleted her savings. As Sister Justina was teaching and living at the House of Providence in Toronto, Catherine persuaded her father to go there for a while to recover further. But he became very homesick and begged to return to Alliston. On 18 December when the fall school term was completed, Catherine brought him back home. "Worry and weariness and a feeling of insecurity brought on another delirious attack that evening. Sister Justina came as quickly as she could. He died on 23 December and was buried two days after Christmas. Sister Justina left that day for Toronto and I was alone."[26] Only one line in the *Alliston Herald* reported "the death of Hugh Donnelly, aged 73 years." Dr. Harper listed the cause of death as "apoplexy."[27] In the following years Catherine regretted that she had left her father when he was so lonely, and felt guilty because his sadness had contributed to his illness. Her remorse was a gnawing grief that she carried for many years. She accepted without resentment the fact that the circumstances of her sisters' lives had exempted them from physical and financial responsibility for their father. She believed that the task had been hers alone, and in times of discouragement and depression her self-reproach would resurface and become a heavy burden.

Early in the new year she sold the Alliston house, paid up the debts and disposed of the family's belongings.[28] Now free to follow Father Cameron's advice, she went to Peterborough to discuss her vocation with the Mother General of the St. Joseph's Community. It was not a rewarding encounter for either of them. The Mother General was cool and reacted negatively to Catherine's resolve to teach in the remote areas of western Canada as a sister of St. Joseph. As Catherine admitted later, hers was not an acceptable way to request entry into a religious order. Prospective nuns were not supposed to announce the kind of work they would do, and where they would do it. Such an attitude was defined in the holy rules of all of the religious orders as a grave offence against the vow of obedience. Catherine had never read the Holy Rule of the Community of St. Joseph, which warned that the sisters must "be on their guard against the spirit of independence; they shall set aside all considerations of personal qualities and advantages which they possessed in the world, and shall make no pretention to privileges on account of education or talent."[29]

The Mother General concluded the interview with the firm declaration that "they were expecting to go to Calgary, but they might not remain there ... She did not think I should be accepted into their Community."[30] Before she left Peterborough that day, she spoke with Bishop O'Brien, but he did not offer any direction or encouragement. The Peterborough incident, she once ruefully recalled, "deflated me considerably ... tired and discouraged, I was in tears the whole way back to Toronto."[31] But she recovered enough to make the decision to seek an interview immediately with Father Arthur Coughlan, a Redemptorist priest who was the Canadian Provincial of his order and lived at their residence on McCaul Street, next to St. Patrick's Church. She sought him out because a few years before, Sister Justina had spoken so highly of him that Catherine had "once talked with [him] about some matters and remembered that he was a very understanding man. I had some confidence in him."[32]

Father Coughlan was an American who belonged to a missionary order, founded in 1732 by St. Alphonsus Liguori of Naples, whose members had become particularly dedicated to an apostolate of conducting missions in Catholic parishes. Because of a great shortage of clergy, Bishop Michael Power had invited the order to come to Toronto in 1845, and they had soon become famous for their dramatic, effective preaching. Their homilies were carefully constructed to give instruction in doctrine, and at the same time to renew the faith of all who attended their services, particularly those who were lax or lapsed Catholics.

Father Coughlan was now fifty-one years of age, and had been educated by the Redemptorists since he was eleven. He had entered the seminary when he was nineteen, was ordained in 1892 at twenty-four, and in the early part of his career he had taught English at a Catholic College in Pennsylvania, and worked in parishes in New York and Baltimore. In 1913 Archbishop McNeil had requested the English-speaking Canadian Redemptorists (whose headquarters were in Baltimore) to provide a priest to work among the Italian immigrants in Toronto. Father Coughlan, who spoke Italian, was assigned to the task

To Do and to Endure

and performed it brilliantly. In 1915 he was made rector of St. Patrick's Church and secretary councillor of the order's vice-provincial. He soon became well known for his kindly and practical advice on spiritual matters and was a popular retreat master and confessor for several religious orders. His duties were expanded when the order made Canada and Newfoundland a separate English-speaking Redemptorist Province. Soon after, he took over most of the administration when his Superior became ill. In 1920 he was officially appointed Provincial of his large Canadian Province.[33]

As his order was already working in western Canada, Father Coughlan understood Catherine's concern, and was impressed not only by her compassionate presentation of the plight of rural immigrant families, but also by her revolutionary solution to provide them with teachers and religious instruction. Like Father Cameron, he too believed she had a vocation, for the spiritual and physical dedication which such a task required could only be sustained through a vowed commitment. The key to her plan of attack was to become a teaching sister working in rural schools in the western settlements outside the orbit of existing urban Catholic schools and churches. In this way she could provide urgently needed school instruction for students of all religious persuasions during the day with her salary paid by the public school board, and on Saturdays and during the summer give classes in religion to the children of Catholic families who had hitherto never been taught the faith. She was insistent that it was folly to wait for the establishment of a separate school system because the western Catholic population was so scattered among the small prairie settlements, there would be too many instances where a separate school, funded by the provincial department of education, would not be viable.

Father Coughlan advised Catherine that the only way for her to begin this apostolate in the public schools was to join an established order and persuade them that this was a promising field for both secular and religious education. He too was unable to suggest any women's religious order, other than the St. Joseph's Community, which might give serious consideration to her plan. He urged her to present her ideas to Mother General Alberta CSJ, in Toronto, because he believed that she was planning to open a Novitiate in Vancouver. If Catherine could enter the order there, she should be more sure of working in the West. Catherine indicated that this was not an order she felt would suit her.

Adventures in Alberta: Am I Called to be a Religious?

Undoubtedly the refusal from Peterborough still rankled, and she had already experienced their strictness and rigidity in applying their Holy Rule during her recent family emergency. Nevertheless, she agreed to apply, especially since Father Coughlan could not think of any alternative.

She was gratified when Mother Alberta received her kindly; Catherine described her as "capable and friendly."[34] Mother Alberta accepted her as a prospective applicant; however, she added that she was nearing the end of her term of office and did not know what the attitude of the new Mother General would be. As the next group of postulants would not be received until July 1920, and it was now only January, she advised Catherine to make a formal application, return to the West, teach for the rest of the school year, and make plans to enter the novitiate with the next group of postulants. Catherine agreed, for she had to earn money to pay for her living expenses until June, and also for the dowry and trousseau which were required when she entered as a postulant.

Catherine returned west in February to an excited reunion with Adeline and Mary. She refused an offer to rejoin the staff in Coleman, and took a higher-paying position as the principal of a two-room school in Morrin, seventy-five miles north and east of Calgary. All went well, and as she had to leave for Toronto before the end of June, Father Cameron found a high-school student willing to take on her duties until the school year ended.

On 2 July 1920 Catherine and four other young women were received as postulants of the Community of St. Joseph, Toronto, at their novitiate at Scarborough-on-the-Lake. The donning of the postulant's simple black dress affirmed the sudden and severe transition which Catherine was about to undertake. At thirty-six, she was older by at least fifteen years than most of her classmates. For seventeen years she had been an independent career woman who had supported herself and her family. She was a successful teacher who had advanced steadily, by making her own decisions on her career direction and her employers. On occasion she had acted aggressively and confronted her employers when she felt measures should be taken to remedy untenable situations in schools where she taught. When she had left Penetanguishene, very few women teachers in Ontario at that time were principals of such a large school or were earning her salary. By nature she was a plain-spoken person who had never hesitated to take the initiative in a situation if she felt comment or action was required. Did she fully appreciate the great transformation that she was expected to undergo?

The purpose of the postulancy was twofold. First, it was a period of probation for the candidates, during which their personalities and their beliefs would be scrutinized thoroughly by the Novice Mistress and the Mother General to ascertain the validity of their vocation — that is, their willingness to offer their lives completely and unreservedly to the service of God. Second, it was designed to determine whether the temperament and the spiritual qualities of the candidate would fit well with that of the community, and were suitable to the carrying out of its designated mission. For her part, the postulant during this period was expected to examine her motives for becoming a nun and to become confirmed in the certainty that this particular order would satisfy her desire to serve God. The regulations which governed the conduct of postulants were designed to introduce the candidate to the lifestyle of those vowed to follow the Way of the Evangelical Counsels, which were the vows of poverty, chastity and obedience that they would take after they had completed a further two years of training as novices. In the next six months therefore, both the candidate and the order had to find out if the novice was called to make this commitment, and whether she was suited to become a member of that particular order.

The commitment to become a nun demanded of the postulant, first of all, the surrender of her own will to the Holy Rule by which the order was governed, and to the direction of the Mother General and the Novice Mistress who were responsible for her training. In practical terms this meant that in every aspect of each day's activities she should "faithfully and joyfully fulfil the orders of their Superior, seeing God alone in her person and His Will in her commands."[35]

Catherine found the atmosphere of the novitiate more austere and strict than she had expected. Postulants were admonished if they did not fulfil with careful attention the minutiae of the Holy Rule. She blamed the severity of the discipline on the new Mother General, Mother Victoria, who she felt was more punctilious than Mother Alberta. It was more likely the demands imposed by the ancient rules and customs of the order, rather than particular personalities, which determined the prevailing atmosphere of the novitiate. The reasons for the myriad of regulations and customs which governed every aspect of the postulants' lives were not explained, nor were queries on their origin and purpose welcomed. As the Holy Rules of all religious orders stipulated that postulants and novices be kept strictly segregated from the professed sisters, Catherine had no opportunity to contact Sister Justina (who was now teaching in St. Catharines) for advice or comfort. The candidates were expected to accept their daily routines as given, without expressing any doubt or question as to their effectiveness. At that stage of their formation as nuns, they were being tested for their physical and spiritual endurance, their patience, and their willingness to accept criticism about minute details of their behaviour. These were all qualities which they would need to cultivate if they were going to survive in the conditions they would encounter from time to time as professed sisters. They would then be full members of a working community in which perfection of their lives was their goal, and abnegation of self in the performance of their assigned tasks was the means of achieving it.

During this time Catherine did become very fond of her Novice Mistress, Sister Avila, who came from Everett, just north of Alliston. She described her as "a brilliant, sweet character, very frail — my good friend for the rest of her life."[36] She was, as their constitutions instructed, a person who possessed "great prudence and charity; she should be serious, yet affable, and firm without ceasing to be gentle."[37]

In all her descriptions of her experience as a postulant in the St. Joseph's novitiate, Catherine admitted that she was, from the beginning, very open in expressing her own vocational expectations, which she announced would be "teaching in the public schools of the rural west," and she "couldn't be satisfied with any other destination."[38] Mother General Victoria chastized her for having predetermined her future service, and stated emphatically that "You will go just where you are sent."[39] This rebuke did not stop Catherine's protests about the Church's neglect of the rural West — also a serious breach of the Rule. She did adjust, however, to the daily routine; Sister Avila did not find her lacking in humility or diligence in the performance of her spiritual or work assignments, but it was clear to her superiors that she was bored and worried. She realized there were now no plans to open a Vancouver novitiate, and that the whole mind-set of the order was against the principle of allowing their sisters to be in direct contact with

59

To Do and to Endure

the public school system.

Two months before the postulancy was completed, the candidates were scheduled to be measured for their religious habits. They would put these on at the end of the colourful ceremony which marked the postulant's official reception as a novice of the order. Each women's religious order had it own distinctive style of habit, and great care was taken to make them all identical in every detail according to the regulations set out in their constitutions. The "holy habit" of the St. Joseph's Order was of plain black material, with sleeves twelve inches wide which extended to the end of the hand; its softly pleated skirt was two yards wide and did "not quite touch the ground." The head-dress consisted of six parts: a black veil which extended six inches below the elbow; an underveil of the same material; a white cornet (bonnet) which extended under the chin; a white band across the forehead; and a white guimpe (a very deep broad linen collar) "which shall cover the breast."[40] The measuring procedure was usually a source of joyous expectancy for the postulants, for now they only awaited official approval of their acceptance as novices by the Mother General and the Council. Yet as the time approached, Catherine did not conceal her dislike of the garb; she thought that it was unsuitable for work in isolated districts where roads were often dusty tracks, and where the poor immigrants were barely eking out a living from the land.

Instead of being measured, Catherine was called before Mother Victoria and told that she would not be accepted into the order, and that she should prepare to leave immediately. No explanation was given for the decision which, as the Holy Rule stipulated, had been made by the Mother General after conferring with her councillors and the Mistress of Novices. Catherine was shocked. She had gone into the order with some misgivings, but never for a moment during the past four months had she doubted her vocation. She asked if the decision could be reconsidered but was told it was final. She then asked if she could delay leaving for a day or so until she could make plans, for now she had nowhere to go. Permission was granted, and she fled back to her room where she lay inert in bed, unable to plan her next move. "That night a dear little postulant (afterwards Sister St. Edwin) ... came to my room, lay on the floor and wept hysterically — then left and I was alone to take my few belongings and move into the great unknown."[41] Many years later Catherine rationalized her rejection by stating that

Adventures in Alberta: Am I Called to be a Religious?

from the beginning she had been uncomfortable about entering the order, and not too hopeful of persuading them to alter their centuries-old traditions. "In the Novitiate I was never happy. There seemed to me, always, something inconsistent about my being there ... Mother Victoria rejected me, Thank God."[42]

In another document, however, her real feelings at the moment of rejection were candidly revealed. "Never shall I forget the feeling of being utterly without sympathy or understanding from Catholics! I felt scorned, despised and terribly alone!"[43] Where and to whom could she turn now? If she were not acceptable to the Community of St. Joseph, which had been recommended by two priests who knew her well and whom she trusted, did that mean that she was deluding herself that she had a vocation to be a nun? It was in this mood that she phoned the one person to whom in her desolation she could feel close, her old friend Irene MacDonnell, with whom she had boarded when she was teaching in Galt in 1906, and with whom she had maintained a firm friendship ever since. The family had moved to 36 Park Road in Toronto. When Catherine phoned to say that she was leaving the convent, no questions were asked; she heard only the welcoming words, "Come right here." Her leave-taking from the convent in November 1920 remained vividly etched in her mind.

> There was a lane to the street and a regular street car would take me to Park Road — no one to come with me to the street car, no one to say Good-Bye — but at Park Road the most beautiful love and kindness awaiting. God surely provides! It strengthens my *Faith* yet, to think of it ... On that street car moving towards that loving, intelligent, family of Baptist Christians I repeated over and over —
> God around me, God above me,
> God to guide me, God to love me.
> Darling, beautifully-cultured, sweetly-Christian, Mother Irene MacDonnell was at the door. "Come and stay as long as you like." Ruth, Achsah, and Mr. and Mrs. MacDonnell had a home saturated with heavenly love and refined culture — days there for me that I can never forget.[44]

While Catherine was recovering from her shock and humiliation, she was comforted by a letter forwarded to her by Sister Justina. Sister Avila had gently informed Sister Justina immediately after Catherine

To Do and to Endure

had been rejected; for she knew that the quiet, gentle Mamie would be very upset at her sister's failure and need consoling.

> My dear Sister Justina,
> The accompanying news will grieve you, I know. Yet there is much I might tell you to lessen your grief. Your dear sister has been an exemplary postulant, and has never given me a moment's anxiety. In one accustomed to govern, I naturally expected to find much evidence of self-will. It will surely greatly comfort and edify you to know that I found none.
> Your sister won the esteem and affection of her companions, and her going is a real grief to them. I am confident that the Divine Providence of God which orders and rules all things so sweetly has designed this experience for your dear sister as a preparation for some special work He has set aside for her capable direction. Pray hard that light may abound to lead her steps aright.
> Miss D. is brave and cheerful. I feel she is realizing the truth of Father Faber's words: "There is no disappointment to him whose will is buried in the will of God." May that same precious conformity lighten your heart dear Child, and bring you comfort and consolation. God bless you.

Sister Justina's note accompanying Sister Avila's letter assured Catherine that "it is the Holy Will of God and while it is a disappointment there is consolation in the thought that 'every cross is a crown begun' and 'absence of trials is not God's usual way of rewarding faithful service.'" She invited Catherine to visit her late in December and assured her that "Sister Superior will welcome you most cordially." She closed her note with "all the love of a fond sister's heart to one who has been brave in the battle of life and who some day will hear the Master's own 'well done'."[45]

Although these letters helped dull some of her pain, Catherine always credited the MacDonnell family for her recovery of faith in her own worth and in her vocation. With loving care in the form of good meals and gentle understanding, they halted her descent into a despair from which she might not have otherwise recovered. Just before Christmas she decided that the time had come to report her recent disaster to Father Coughlan. He listened calmly to her story, and his only comment was, "I guess you talked too much about the West." Catherine had to admit that she had. There was silence, and then to her astonishment he burst into hearty laughter and said, "You had better start a community of your own."[46] For Catherine, that moment on 20 December 1920 was the instant of the birth of the Sisters of Service; this priest, whom she esteemed and trusted, still believed that she had a vocation, had understood that her ideas were so revolutionary that no established religious order in the Canadian Catholic Church would be able to bring them to fruition. Their traditions were too entrenched to enable them to make the transition into a new era of Catholic education and apostolic mission.

Father Coughlan then said he needed time to get his regular duties completed, and as it was getting close to Christmas, they should wait until after the holiday before beginning their discussions about the new religious order. Catherine returned happily to report the amazing turn of events to Irene MacDonnell, who immediately invited her to stay with them as long as she needed. Now they would all be able to enjoy Christmas together. Catherine rejoiced that at last she had found the road leading to the mission she had envisioned. She felt vindicated, and confident in her ability to present her plans for the new order in a clear, logical and persuasive way when the time was ripe.

CHAPTER 4
CATHERINE PURSUES HER VISION: THE FOUNDING OF THE SISTERS OF SERVICE

SHORTLY AFTER CHRISTMAS, FATHER COUGHLAN began a series of discussions with Catherine to put into specific and orderly form her ideas on the purpose and function of their new religious order. Whenever he could spare the time, she would be summoned to his office on McCaul Street in Toronto where they discussed her vision of service in the light of her experiences in Ontario and Alberta:

> I explained to Father Coughlan that dedicated women could use rural schools, publicly administered and organized in all settled Western Areas, for peripheral missionary work. There would be no treading on ground already accepted by older communities, no overlapping. The magnetism which would draw suitable motivated women was not to be any city, but something quite new, the untouched farming areas west of Ontario. Such untrodden or abandoned areas were vast and were slowly filling up with Ukrainians and others from Europe, people certain to be confused for years to come, about Canadian economics, politics and especially religion.[1]

Catherine's knowledge of the inner workings of religious orders was, as she admitted, very scanty. Father Coughlan gave her some instruction in the processes which, by canon law, must be followed to accomplish their mutual goal. She always recalled these discussions with pride and gratitude. Father Coughlan was not just sympathetic to her ideas, he also indicated that he thought she had been truly inspired in devising a new and creative approach to meeting the spiritual and educational needs of the neglected settlers in western Canada. Her ideas were based on principles and methods which, at that time, were not followed by any of the female religious orders working in the Canadian West. She now saw that the Community of St. Joseph could not have been expected to undertake a new apostolate at the urging of a postulant who, in effect, was trying to deflect a stately ship from its own safely predetermined course. To change so drastically would have required fundamental alterations to the Holy Rules and Constitutions of the order, which had been approved by the Vatican at their founding. To obtain Vatican consent to this would have been lengthy and difficult, even if the Mother Superior of the order had actually agreed with her.

Father Coughlan perceived that Catherine would always be on a collision course as applicant to any order which was committed by its rule to an apostolate which was intrinsically different from her own vision. She was impetuous and determined; but she was also a practical and enthusiastic person who was willing to attack a serious problem with great faith and total dedication. He recognized, too, that these were the personal traits of many of the Church's most creative visionaries, who in the past had also suffered rejection when their insights into the needs of the Church ran counter to its current practices. To those not inspired by her warm desire to introduce new methods of reaching the immigrant communities, she appeared to be wilfully disobedient. He recognized that this new order would be grounded in orthodox Catholic theology, spirituality and discipline, but through its Rule would introduce new concepts in carrying out the traditional work of the womens' religious orders. Catherine herself described her approach as adopting a spirit of ecumenism, in the method of carrying out its mission to rural settlements.

"Ecumenism" by her definition was still the same principle she had believed in and lived by as early as 1903, when she had chosen some non-Catholic Christians in the Alliston community as her closest friends, and with them had sought out teaching positions in Ontario's public schools. Her recognition of them as faithful Christians was still a rarity in Catholic circles, for many of the parish clergy and laity were still "deeply immersed in the ghetto complex"[2] which had encouraged them to avoid, and in some instances even to forbid, contacts or co-operation with non-Catholics.

In practice, her project meant that sisters of her new order were not to be separated from the secular world by regulations which restricted their social and religious contacts with any of the laity,

Catherine Pursues Her Vision

Protestant or Catholic. Given the wide gulf which then existed between the Catholic and non-Catholic world, and between the lay and clerical world within Catholic society, this in itself was a revolutionary idea which ran counter to centuries of a traditional lifestyle. Yet, as Father Coughlan and Catherine agreed, the essence of the life of a Catholic religious, which was the dedication of sisters wholly to the service of God and the Church, was retained. Indeed, she explained further:

> We could use the conditions just as they existed and develop a teaching Order for the rural West of Canada. I had already proved that the ordinary public school system would suit. Like St. Paul, we could earn our own living and have rural public schools for anchor holds. There were many teacherages attached. Thus our living quarters would be supplied.[3]

Father Coughlan said that before proceeding on this project, they must seek the approval of Archbishop McNeil, as canon law decreed that the bishop must give his approval for every new foundation in his diocese.[4] Archbishop Neil McNeil had been appointed Archbishop of Toronto in 1912, and by 1920 he was acknowledged as the most forward-looking and influential of the English-speaking hierarchy in Canada. He was a Nova Scotian of Scottish descent, a legacy which made him far less defensive in his attitude to the non-Catholic world than the Irish bishops who had been his predecessors.[5]

In his youth he had been a brilliant scholar, having received doctorates in theology and philosophy in Rome. While studying there he also became an enthusiastic supporter of Pope Leo XIII's social encyclical, *Rerum Novarum*, and was determined to see its reforming principles adopted by the Catholic Church in Canada. On his return to Canada he was made Rector of St. Francis Xavier University, where he spoke out as an ardent defender of poor fishermen against the local fish merchants who exploited them. At age forty-five, Neil McNeil became Bishop of St. George's in western Newfoundland, where he ministered to a population of seven thousand Catholics living in little Irish, French, Scottish and English settlements along the rugged coastline. For fifteen years he gave them practical as well as spiritual leadership, for money was scarce and skilled labourers a rarity. He taught his people how to build their own churches and schools from local materials and, as one of them, adopted a simple lifestyle himself.

Thereafter, Bishop McNeil was transferred to Vancouver, where he now worked as archbishop of a huge diocese which included all of British Columbia except Vancouver Island. That diocese urgently required restructuring. Founded in 1863, its first priests had been the Oblates of Mary Immaculate, a French missionary order who had worked mainly in the French and Indian rural frontier villages. The province's population mix was changing rapidly by 1900, as English-speaking immigrants settled in Vancouver and its environs. In his short tenure of two and a half years, Archbishop McNeil earned respect as a builder of hospitals and welfare projects which benefited the whole community as well as erecting schools and churches for his own Catholic flock.

Vancouver was a boom town, and the archbishop became very incensed about the plight of poorly paid workers, particularly the young women who were desperately seeking work in the new factories and businesses. He spoke openly about their difficulties in finding decent places to live at reasonable rent, and told businessmen who paid these low wages that they had a civic as well as a moral obligation to undertake projects to provide some form of low-cost, safe and respectable housing for their employees.

In his sermons and letters to his Vancouver flock, the archbishop pointed out that Catholics should not remain sequestered from the community outside their church. The most effective way, he said, for them to express their faith publicly was to participate in public affairs with goodwill and charity. Charity, as he frequently pointed out, was not mere almsgiving, but was a generosity of spirit which accepted differences without rancour or condemnation.

After he became Archbishop of Toronto, McNeil worked to promote a spirit of reconciliation between all citizens in his new archdiocese. Many of the prewar immigrants were Roman Catholics from Central Europe who had experienced difficulties in adjusting to a new language and the predominantly Anglo-Celtic cultural and religious patterns of the city. In his inaugural address to the Toronto diocese he lamented the insularity exhibited by some Catholics and declared, "We must enlarge our hearts and widen our horizons. The people of this church in Canada need to know each other better." During the First World War the archbishop was troubled by the instances of racial or religious rancour which endangered national unity. As a patriotic Canadian, he urged Catholics to support public events contributing to Canada's war effort. He warned that "if we are wanting in Catholic charity we can make it seem that we had no part in the upbuilding of this great nation, as if we were innately selfish, looking after local and small issues."[6]

Like Catherine, Archbishop McNeil was worried about the spiritual dangers and cultural isolation facing the Central European immigrants, and did his best to find priests who spoke their language so that they would become more comfortable with Canadian ways. In the days before any government aid, he urged the Catholic churches to provide them with language classes and emergency relief, lest they lose their faith because their Church seemingly had deserted them when they were lonely strangers in a strange land.

With such a broad background in the difficulties faced by the rural and urban immigrants, the archbishop was prepared to be sympathetic to Catherine's particular contention that it was a matter of great urgency that the Church begin now to broaden the scope of its mission to include the vast unserviced sections of western Canada. At their first meeting, he grasped immediately that Catherine had also hit upon a new method to carry out this difficult task. This differentiated her from the usual applicants to the religious life who accepted without question the ministry assigned to them by the Superiors.

Moreover, the archbishop was not at all alarmed at the prospect of Catholic sisters avoiding separate schools in order to teach in the rural areas which in most locations across the West had only public schools. The western rural population was so scattered, and this new order's potential mission field would be so large, they would not infringe on the useful ministries of those Catholic orders already established in larger western centres and employed there by the separate school boards. Nor was the archbishop troubled by the prospect of some of the new order's employers objecting to their school staff wearing religious habits. He agreed with Catherine's plan to avoid their displeasure at the public display of their teachers' Catholic affiliation by having the order wear a less conspicuous form of dress than the traditional religious habit. At one of their meetings, Archbishop McNeil even went so far as to suggest that they not use the word "Sister" in their official title. This idea was later discarded, in case it might not be acceptable to the Roman authorities.

Catherine stressed repeatedly at these meetings that the key to reaching the lapsed Catholic rural immigrants was through the provision of education for their children. It seemed the most immediate and practical way of approaching these people, as the lack of schooling for their children was one of their great worries. Even if the parents did not speak English, their children would be making progress in English every day in school, the sisters would be meeting their parents to discuss school affairs, and this would give them an opportunity to offer to help with many of their other needs, including religious education. Other services might come later, but she held firmly to her theory that schooling was the first and most important service they could offer.

Archbishop McNeil and Father Coughlan do not appear to have disagreed with her logic; but early during the several conferences which Catherine's memoirs indicated took place in January 1921, she noted that the archbishop asked that "health work be included to supplement and help the prestige ... A couple of small hospitals in the West could give the claim to caring for health ... other rural endeavors could be anything to help families, provide clothing, medicine, encouragement, guidance and thus come under the head of social work."[7]

Archbishop McNeil, Father Coughlan and Catherine also held many discussions on the particular aspects of the sisters' lifestyle which would have to be incorporated into their Holy Rule and Constitutions. Catherine put forward her objections to several regulations common to all female religious orders in Canada which she felt would thwart the mission to be undertaken by the new order. She rejected the excessively early rising hour, which had been the custom in the medieval enclosed monastic orders, and had been continued even by the semi-enclosed orders. It would be detrimental to the health of teachers working under the difficult physical conditions found in remote areas: "6 a.m. was as early as I could manage day after day, so it was definitely decided on."[8] Eliminated also should be the rules which restricted the sisters' freedom to eat their meals away from the convent community when necessary, forbade them to go out alone, or to stay overnight in other than their own or another religious order's accommodation. The severity and uncertainty of prairie weather, and the great distances they would travel in their work, made such restrictions impractical. A rule which severely restricted participation in secular activities would not be conducive to attracting the community's co-operation and goodwill.

In practice, Catherine's goal of promoting ecumenism required a different attitude to the secular world than that held by the traditional female orders, whose Rules regulating their clothing and behaviour restricted them from mingling freely even with fellow Catholics. The new order would permit its members to participate in local public educational and welfare projects which benefited all the people. These activities would provide opportunities for the sisters to reach out to lapsed Catholics, and even those who were indifferent to any religion might be drawn into the Church.

Father Coughlan himself was familiar with the poverty and loneliness which was the lot of most of the Ukrainian immigrants then struggling to make a living on the prairies. Priests of his order had been working with them in Yorkton, Saskatchewan, since 1904, when the first great wave of Ukrainian immigrants had arrived. Both he and Archbishop McNeil were also very aware that the Protestant denominations, particularly the Presbyterians, had been working steadily for some time among the rural immigrant communities. They were now well entrenched in some areas and well equipped to proselytize the second great wave from the Ukraine which had begun again after the war. McNeil and Coughlan agreed with Catherine that unless the Church began soon to increase its efforts to reclaim those whose birthright was the Catholic faith, it might never succeed in doing so. They also agreed, however, that before proceeding further with their plans, Catherine should work for a short time in a western rural Ukrainian settlement to investigate whether these people would be receptive to the idea of women committed to the religious life working as teachers in their communities. She agreed to return to the West and seek a teaching position in a Ukrainian immigrant settlement and assess the situation for them.

Then Father Coughlan mentioned that he had heard of an Australian religious community, the Sisters of St. Joseph of the Sacred Heart, known as the "Josephites," which had been founded to attack a problem similar to the one identified by Catherine. Its work had now extended to New Zealand. The two clerics thought that it might be worth while to investigate the Josephites' experiences as a useful preparation for the mission that Catherine was proposing to undertake in Canada. Archbishop McNeil said he intended to write the order and ask for suggestions on a training program for novices which they had found suitable for this type of enterprise.[9]

Obedient to their request, Catherine returned to Regina in early February. She replenished her dwindling savings by working as a substitute teacher for three weeks with the Regina Separate School Board. At an interview with the Saskatchewan Chief Inspector of Schools and the Inspector for the District of Macklin, she was told that no schools in Ukrainian districts were available, but they promised to keep her in mind if a need arose. In the meantime, would she accept a position as principal of a two-room school in Denzil, near Macklin, starting on 1 March at a yearly salary of $1,600? She accepted at once, for this was a splendid salary; and Denzil was not too remote — only 135 miles west of Saskatoon on the Alberta-Saskatchewan border. They also offered to hire Adeline McConnell for the school's junior section, but unfortunately she was unable to leave her Alberta post. The board instead hired a teacher from Ottawa, who arrived on 1 April, and the two women decided to share the rent of a furnished house in Denzil. Catherine remembered this posting with great pleasure, one which was both interesting and successful. She worked hard, even giving classes at night so eager were the children to catch up on their schooling. An added bonus was that her colleague, Miss Lenore Ferry, was a willing helper, a superior teacher, a cultured companion, and a Roman Catholic who was in sympathy with Catherine's future plans. Together they managed to prepare all of the Grade 8 students for the provincial departmental examinations in June.

On 12 March, Father Coughlan wrote to Catherine with the disconcerting message that Archbishop McNeil had not yet written to the sisters in New Zealand, nor had he taken any other action to establish their new order. The archbishop had said that he was considering asking the Sisters of St. Joseph of the London diocese to undertake the Ukrainian missionary work. Father Coughlan said he was able to dissuade him from that plan by pointing out that it would not work, and that "I had obligations towards yourself and perhaps others who wished to devote themselves as religious to the Ukrainian mission work and that I wished to help you attain your desires." Father Coughlan had then offered to write the New Zealand sisters himself and "propose to them to receive you and perhaps some others in their Novitiate and when the Novitiate is over, to send you back here with some other Sisters of their Order to start the great work."

Father Coughlan then broke the news that if this plan worked out,

Catherine would have to finance her own way to Australia, as neither he or the archbishop had any funds available. He said he could do no more at present as he was leaving shortly for Rome for a meeting of his order's general chapter, and would not return until mid-July. He assured Catherine that she could rely on him not to forget and that he would "do all in my power to further this great work and I shall also help you all that I can to attain the realization of your holy desires."[10]

Catherine responded immediately, hoping to reassure him before he left for Rome that she was still enthusiastic about their project. She had asked Mother St. Andrew of the Sacred Heart Academy in Regina about the Josephites. She was from New Zealand and was familiar with the order whose motherhouse was in Australia, but who had a house in Auckland. "She informed me that they have greatly modified their rule and are no longer going out into the outlying villages as they did when the Order started. That is the great necessity here — sisters who could live in places like Denzil." She went on to describe the local situation. The present principal of the school was a good teacher and a faithful Catholic, but as often happened he had made enemies in the community because of his involvement in local politics, and he had lost his job. It was but "one case in thousands in these wild western places." The girl who had taught the junior class had formerly been in a rural school, living in a teacher's residence. "Then she came here but boarding conditions even here, were very disagreeable for her so she left for her home in P.E.I. There are several schools around here which cannot get teachers and where the teachers do come, they start planning to leave just as soon as possible ... These schools are not fit for lady teachers and even men can't stand it."

> I'll be making one hundred and sixty a month with forty for board and will be able to save a few hundred between now and July.
>
> There are many Catholics all around here — Germans. The priest speaks English very poorly. He has several little churches to attend and lives four miles from Denzil at St. Henry's Church. We have Mass here twice a month and sometimes during the week. Fr. Bieler seems to be suffering greatly from nerve strain.
>
> The only solution for the teacher problem here would be sisters. Catechism is supposed to be taught in the school after hours but there has been a distressing clash caused by misunderstanding between the Priest and teachers. It has been so hot lately that I don't teach catechism yet. I am waiting for the troubled waters to

calm a little bit. I'm "lying low" ...

Yes, I certainly am ready to go to Australia, if that happens to be the best thing to do. And, I am happy to be able to say that I can finance myself in every way. With the scheme only in the head it would be difficult don't you think, to get people really interested in it? When there is something definite and sure arranged, I would not be surprised if many find it exactly what they've been looking for. The western girls want to work in the West. Would it be a good plan to advertise in the Catholic papers for applicants, and also have some good convincing writer like Rev. Father Daly compose an article on the subject for the Catholic Press? ...

I am enclosing here a letter from the Rev. Mother at Graymoor, the place you told me about. She also sent a booklet and an application form. Aspirants are received between the ages of 15 and 35. One of the printed questions in the application form is "Have you been in any other Community as Professed, Novice or Postulant? If so explain cause of leaving." I sent a reply to the Rev. Mother Superior explaining that I was waiting for counsel from my spiritual adviser.

Your letter was most comforting and encouraging. Father Coughlan, as you say, "if we fail we can feel that we have done our best." If we fail in what we are attempting to do now, something better will develop, don't you think? ...

I don't think I'm praying enough. I had hoped to be where there is a resident priest but I wasn't lucky enough for that. It seems difficult to pray enough in a place like this, but I'll find a way to do better in that line ...

You are certainly unselfish in your efforts for me, Father Coughlan and you have already given much of your time for me, with no apparent results even. May God bless all your labours.[11]

The preoccupation of her clergy advisers with contacting a religious order so far from Toronto was trying for Catherine. Privately she felt it was a fruitless quest to attempt to persuade a religious order on the other side of the world to embark on a venture in western Canada. But she did not openly object because she knew that they were trying to solve the first difficulty which must be overcome when establishing the new Canadian order. To be approved by the Vatican, a prospective order had to have arranged that its first applicants would complete their regular training through a postulancy and novitiate, for

Catherine Pursues Her Vision

Church canon law stipulated this was a requisite for all women religious. Of necessity, this training would have to be given to the first candidates in a new order by an experienced sister in an already accredited women's religious order. Any order which could be persuaded to undertake this task would have to be willing and able to make some adjustments to its own staffing arrangements, and to its interpretation of its own Holy Rule, so that the fledgling sisters would be trained in a way which was compatible with the proposed mission of their own new order. This would be especially important, since Catherine intended that their Rule would break radically with Church tradition. The Church's supervision of the female religious orders was structured so that the overtures to begin this process would have to be conducted by the bishop of the diocese or his designate.

Catherine wrote to Father Cameron about these developments and his reply indicated his own misgivings. " New Zealand Sisters! Are these Maori? Why go so far afield to find a nest ... My advice just now is pursue your pious endeavors along the lines suggested by Rev. Fr. Coughlan because it means ultimately Canadian labours."[12]

When Catherine started her summer holiday no word had been received from the Josephite Sisters. But in early July, shortly after she had arrived in Calgary to visit Helen O'Connor, a telegram from the Chief Inspector of Schools informed her that a school in a Ukrainian settlement five miles from Stornoway, near Yorkton, Saskatchewan, would be available for her on 15 August. She accepted and prepared to go to Yorkton, trusting that somehow a way would be found to establish an apostolate to the immigrants that she knew were living in many little isolated communities.

On her arrival she found that there was a teacherage on the school site, but it was in a very lonely location. She preferred to live in the village five miles away and was able to arrange her meals at the home of Mrs. Beam who, she had discovered, was a very good cook. Catherine was able to persuade her to allow her to sleep there too. A minor flaw in the arrangement was that the Beams' house was so small that she had to share the room and the bed of their young daughter. But "they were nice friendly people, and I felt safer in the village."[13] At first she walked the five miles to school, counting herself fortunate if she got a lift from someone going her way. Then she was given the loan of a horse; and shortly after, the secretary of the board, a friendly

To Do and to Endure

bachelor, loaned her his team of horses and a buggy. The horses were thin and the buggy and the harness threatened to fall apart at any moment, but it was luxury compared to trudging to and from school across the dusty prairie. Accompanying her loaned chariot was the following note:

> Just a word or two about the team. They are broke just about to suit my whims on some occasions, so you will find them tough bitted and they will not always stop just when you tell them too [*sic*], so you want to watch yourself over bad places as they might take you through at a pace that you would not care to travel. I would advise you not to put them through fast as they had two strenuous days of it rounding up horses and cattle. The one on the right is Kate and the other is Jane. You will have to keep an eye on them all the time as one cannot trust them. They do not seem to mind an auto. Always check them up when you drive and keep the buggy top up, as it has been in two runaways and somewhat sprung so that it does not fold back very easy.
> Wish you would bring me 4 cans of Pork & beans
> 4 packages Corn Flakes
>
> Frank J. Muzik[14]

There was a Ukrainian Catholic Church five miles out in the country in a different direction from the school. To the astonishment of the Beams, Catherine attended Mass there on Sundays. The congregation were farmers, and as was the custom they stood during the service. In spite of the differences in liturgy and language, Catherine felt that "it was my Church and I was glad to be there."[15]

On 24 August Catherine received a long letter from Father Coughlan updating her on his recent discussions with Archbishop McNeil. Since no response had been received from the Australian order, they had concluded that

> the only practicable plan was to establish a new Order for the work among the poorer children in the west. He [Archbishop McNeil] spoke principally of educational work but I would judge that medical work might also be added. How would you like to be the head of this new Order? I know you have a number of the qualities needed for that office, but I do not know whether you possess all.
> Our plan would be to have the Order Diocesan (Toronto) for the present, so as to be under His Grace & also not to be obliged to

Catherine Pursues Her Vision

have recourse to Rome for approval. Together with yourself as many others as could be gotten to go, would enter a Novitiate of some Existing Order and be trained there for a year, then make the vows & then start your own Community. His Grace thinks we should have at least half a dozen young ladies to make this beginning together. But where are we to get them? Do you know?[16]

There followed a summary of their discussion on which religious order should be asked to undertake the novitiate training. Archbishop McNeil felt that since Catherine had been "dropped" by the St. Joseph Sisters, it would be better if the Sisters of Loretto would set up a special novitiate for Catherine and the other applicants at their convent in Niagara Falls. Father Coughlan said he preferred that their novitiate be located in Toronto so that he and Archbishop McNeil, as their clerical advisers, could help directly and guide their formation. The archbishop had reconsidered the problem of their location, noting that probably neither of these orders would have room for the new novices in their novitiates. As well as agreeing to locate their own novitiate in Toronto, the archbishop had also promised to donate a building suitable for the purpose. This meant that either the Loretto or the St. Joseph Sisters could now be asked for the loan of a novice mistress for their initial training. After a time she could return to her own community and the new order could undertake that work themselves.

They had then discussed this with an experienced Passionist Father who approved of the whole scheme, and had given some helpful suggestions. All three had also agreed that the order should undertake medical and social welfare work as well as teaching, and that a traditional religious habit was not suitable for their particular apostolate. The style could be decided later, in consultation with Catherine and others. They were also trying to think of a suitable name for the order.

Then Father Coughlan discussed the two principal obstacles to be faced in forming the new order: lack of candidates and lack of money. Neither he nor the archbishop had any available funds, but they hoped that a circular letter to priests might net some donations for their new venture in missions. They would also try to recruit suitable young women candidates seeking entry to an innovative religious order. His concluding words, although assuring Catherine that he thought of her as "our mainstay in this bold enterprise," cautioned her:

Of course you must leave yourself in the hands of His Grace and myself to do what is best, even to make a sacrifice of your own wishes — for example if we see fit to place someone else at the head of the Order. I don't think you are ambitious for any position, rather to do whatever good you can for God's poor. We have determined not to restrict the work to the Ruthenians, though it would be principally among them, but to extend it to all poor children of Canada.

His Grace told me he spoke of the Order to Archbishop Soptensky, head of the Ruthenian Catholics, who is now in Canada and the latter said it was "A magnificent idea" ...

Though I am burdened with many cares, I would be willing to act as spiritual director of the New Order, and His Grace is very willing too that I should ...

The Archbishop and I will be glad to have any ideas or suggestions you may see fit to make, so do not hesitate to tell us your mind. I wish you were here to consult with but you better continue where you are, till we call you East. We don't wish to take a decisive step until we are sure of our ground. We do not wish to make the matter too public and then have a failure.

I have written all this hastily — I hope it is not confusing. We will inform you of what we are doing. We desire to start as soon as the thing is feasible. Will you be able to come without delay as soon as we notify you? But do not come before we call you ... His Grace and I will await your reply. Take your time to consider the matter well, but do not delay answering unnecessarily.[17]

Thus encouraged, Catherine continued to teach and observe the Ruthenian community.[18] About fifty children attended the school. They had never had a Catholic English-speaking teacher, although the Stornaway area contained several settlements composed almost entirely of Ukrainian Catholics. Catherine reported to Father Coughlan that the teachers who had been employed in their schools had obviously been enthusiastic Protestant missionaries. The previous teachers at her school had kept their pupils well supplied with Methodist magazines and Sunday School lessons. She found the children "lovable" and wonderfully obedient and anxious to learn, and they had listened closely to the religious education which was given by their teacher. Her immediate and strongest impression was that in Saskatchewan, becoming Protestant was regarded by the teachers, inspectors and school trustees in these western public school districts as the first positive step the immigrants should take on the way to their "Canadianization."

When Catholic church services were held by visiting priests, who conducted them in the Latin Rite, the parents did not attend as they did not understand it, nor wish to be identified with Latin Catholicism. Catherine did not get involved in, or comment on, the politics of the disputes going on in the Canadian Catholic Church at that time between the Latin and Ukrainian Rite Catholics. Among other differences, the Catholic Ukrainian Rite clergy were allowed to marry, and the Canadian hierarchy were trying to supplant this group with Latin Rite priests for whom marriage was forbidden. Some Redemptorist priests stationed at Yorkton learned the language and adopted the Ukrainian Rite; but many of the Ukrainians would not accept them for they still believed that ultimately they were expected to give up their language and religious customs.[19] Some were so determined to maintain their culture, that if they changed their religious allegiance, it was more likely they would become Protestant. Catherine's only comment on the situation was that "for a considerable time, at least, their Ruthenian Rite must be left to them in Canada. This means that it is absolutely necessary for the children to be taught faithfulness to their own church, and at the same time the difference between Catholic and Protestant Canadians. In the course of time conditions will change." Evidently Catherine hoped that if these Ruthenians could be kept in the Catholic faith, even though it was the Slavonic Rite, they would eventually accept the Latin Rite. She felt that the most effective way of achieving this was for the Catholic Church to send in a new order of women religious who would provide secular and religious education for their children. She expressed these ideas very forcefully in a manuscript written some time later to attract recruits and funds to the Sisters of Service.

> Who can save the situation? Not the priests, nor Catholic lay teachers, nor any Order of nuns working in Canada at present. The priests cannot be spared, for Canada was already short of priests when these people flocked in. Catholic [lay] teachers, unless they could bring companions would be compelled to live alone in the teachers' residences. This is, more than ever, an unwise thing to do. Apart from the oppressive loneliness, there is the ever increasing danger in these times of unemployment and crime.

There are no Latin Catholic churches near and there is no companionship.

Only an order of nuns whose rule would not forbid their living in these teachers' residences, whose habit would not be in the least conspicuous and who would be qualified to teach in the Prairie Provinces and capable of handling the situation tactfully, would serve the purpose.[20]

Father Coughlan and Archbishop McNeil continued to exchange ideas, and on 9 September the former, in a note to the archbishop, agreed with him that medical and social work should be included among the aims of the contemplated society, if they were to be successful in reaching the immigrant population. One title for the order which Archbishop McNeil was considering was "The Teaching Sisters," but Father Coughlan rejected it as they might have applicants who would not be able to teach but "who could render other valuable services. Moreover, there would have to be some in the community who would devote themselves to the domestic duties of the convent ... Miss Donnelly has suggested 'Sisters of Service.' That seems good too, and is broad. I could send a telegram to Miss Donnelly to come to Toronto at once and attend to the mailing of the letters and replying to them etc."[21]

Catherine replied on 3 September, and Father Coughlan responded immediately. He reported that he and Archbishop McNeil had a letter ready to send to the priests of Canada which, although not asking directly for funds, would they hoped induce a good response to a later appeal. The archbishop had decided to ask Mrs. Ambrose Small to help finance their work as she was a good friend.[22] The Catholic Women's League would also be approached. They felt that at least six novices were required before they could go to the trouble of securing a novice mistress. They could not, as Catherine had suggested, start with only one or two candidates, and this would likely cause some delay, but he "hadn't the least doubt that after the work is well started, we shall have many applicants, the only trouble is to secure enough for a start."

Another heartening piece of news was that Archbishop McNeil had spoken to Mother Victoria CSJ about their plans and "she gave His Grace a very good recommendation of you." He did not think that there would be any difficulty in getting a novice mistress from the Sisters of St. Joseph, but it was not likely that they would be able to spare their

Catherine Pursues Her Vision

own Novice Mistress, Sister Avila, as Catherine had suggested. But he would consult with Sister Avila when he was at the convent during the next week. The matter of the title, habit, rule and so on could be settled later. He thought "Service Sisters" was a good suggestion for a title, as "we have decided to include medical and social work among the doings of the Order as well as teaching. We hope some day to establish smaller hospitals in the West, as the Presbyterians and Methodists are doing." He concluded by advising her not to take a university course the coming summer, but to come to Toronto as soon as she could conveniently leave Stornoway. They would provide clerical work and a desk for her at the Archdiocesan office. He was leaving Toronto soon and would be away until early November. He concluded:

> I should like to meet you before I leave, but if that is not possible His Grace will instruct you what to do. You can send me word when you expect to reach Toronto.
>
> So again, let us pray hard especially to Our Lady of Perpetual Help and St. Joseph that God may bless this great work and bring it to a successful issue. I wish to say I was very much pleased with your willingness to serve, not to lead. That is the right spirit and God will bless you for it. Leave yourself entirely in the hands of your Superiors to make use of you for the greater glory of God, as they see fit. Praying God to make you a fit instrument for His Service I remain
>
>   Yours sincerely,
>   Arthur Coughlan, C.Ss.R.
>
> P.S. Archbishop Sinnott of Winnipeg was here for a few days. His Grace and I both spoke to him of our plans and he was very enthusiastic in his approval.[23]

Father Coughlan also wrote that month to Father George Daly CSsR, one of the priests under his jurisdiction, who had recently been transferred from his post as rector of the cathedral in Regina to Saint John, New Brunswick. One of his new duties included meeting the immigrants at the docks during the summer months when the harbour was open to transatlantic ships. It was a newsy note, typical of the kind of letters sent to keep members of religious orders in touch with the happenings at their headquarters. In it he remarked:

> You will be surprised to learn that Archbishop McNeil and I are trying to establish a religious order of women to do educational,

medical and social work among the poor in Western Canada particularly the foreign-born. The undertaking has come about naturally, though I believe providentially. Modern conditions will require a modification of the usual rules and customs of ordinary religious Orders. For example, we think the nuns should not have a special religious habit but dress ordinarily. They would have to go by twos into lonely settlements and be deprived of Mass and Holy Communion for a long period etc. What we need now to begin the foundation is money and candidates. But I think with God's help we can surmount all difficulties. I wish I could have a talk with you on this matter and learn from your experience.[24]

Catherine taught for six weeks at Stornoway before concluding that she had discovered all that she and her clerical advisers needed to know about conditions on the immigrant frontier. Anxious to return to Toronto and continue making plans with her clerical advisers, she was relieved when the former teacher said that she was willing to take over the school again. She arrived in Toronto in late September 1921, took a room at 29 Breadalbane Street, and asked her friend Brother Rogation for a teaching job.[25] She did not want the proffered clerical work at the archbishop's office, for she could earn more at her own profession and it was evident that money was urgently needed for the new order. She was pleased and grateful when he put her to work at St. Francis School teaching a class of fifty boys, and made her salary retroactive to 1 September. After Christmas he asked her to continue on staff, but as a substitute teacher as he knew she would not be teaching permanently in Toronto, and he had another experienced teacher who wanted a full-time permanent position.

Brother Rogation continued to be a sympathetic supporter and advised Catherine strongly against sending their first applicants into the novitiate of any other order for their initial training. He felt that instead of developing a spirituality suitable to their own order, they would inevitably be influenced by and eventually absorb the spirituality of their older tutors. He thought also that she should move as soon as possible into the building suitable for their own novitiate promised by the archbishop. He mentioned that Newman Hall (at one time used by the students of St. Michael's College) at 97 St. Joseph Street was partly furnished and vacant, and it was an ideal location, across the street from St. Basil's Church and next door to the House of the Christian Brothers. All the necessary permissions were obtained from Archbishop

Catherine Pursues Her Vision

McNeil for the new order to use this house, owned by the archdiocese. They were given it, rent free, and Catherine moved in some time in late autumn 1921.[26] She was heartened when the Catholic Women's League arranged to have an altar and pews placed in the large front room, making it a pretty little chapel.

Catherine had continued to teach during the autumn of 1921. She was living as frugally as possible, for she hoped that start-up funds would soon be needed. Whenever he could spare time from his onerous duties as Provincial, Father Coughlan continued to give her spiritual advice and together they consolidated their plans for the order. But she began to grow impatient, as both her teaching career and progress in starting the order seemed to be reaching a dead end. True, some decisions had been made. Archbishop McNeil and Father Coughlan accepted her choice of name for the order, Sisters of Service, and her advice on their apostolate and living style would be incorporated into their Rule when it was written. This would be the first English-speaking, Canadian-founded religious order in Canada, and its Rule would enable the sisters to bring succour and education to the rural settlers in western Canada. They would have a lifestyle which would provide them with opportunities to mingle with the secular community unencumbered by conspicuous clothing or rules which curtailed their freedom to share in the social and religious activities of the people they served.

The three of them had also agreed that an established local order would be asked to lend an experienced sister to organize and head their novitiate until one of the Sisters of Service was trained to take that position. Either a St. Joseph or a Loretto sister was deemed suitable and it was Catherine's responsibility to decide which one. She was thinking hard about that one. She liked the Loretto order, and her friend Mary O'Connor had recently entered it. On the other hand, the Community of St. Joseph was experienced in both teaching and medical work. To choose the latter would vindicate her own earlier rejection by that order, and also please Sister Justina, her beloved Mamie, who had been so dismayed by her order's refusal of her sister. She decided to request that a St. Joseph sister head the novitiate. But she knew there would be a further delay even if they accepted. The Mother General would have to decide on the person suitable for the task, make arrangements to release her from her current duties, and assign another sister to fill her place.

83

To Do and to Endure

By December 1921 Catherine was decidedly edgy about the future. She knew that Father Coughlan was very busy but she did not know the particulars of his problems. These were revealed in a letter he wrote to George Daly:

> On account of my travelling the plans for the New Order have been held up. His Grace has been quite unwell lately and can hardly be bothered with business.
>
> However, I have not been idle. I have launched in one good quarter a campaign for funds for the Novitiate. I expect soon to get the other campaign for subjects under way.
>
> Fathers DeLaere & Descamps with whom I spoke in the west, are very enthusiastic about the usefulness of the New Order, and have already offered schools at Komarno etc. They foresee difficulty with Bishop Budka, but I think Archbishop McNeil can obviate that.[27]

Shortly after Father Coughlan wrote this letter, Catherine met with him and told him they were moving so slowly that something different would have to be done. He was sympathetic, for she was approaching her thirty-ninth birthday and was anxious to return to the West as a sister committed for life to carry out the mission she believed in so passionately. He shared her concern and regretted that his duties as Provincial did not permit him to allot more time to the practical details involved in founding a new religious order. The only solution was to appoint another priest of his order to bring their plans to fruition. He suggested that Father George Daly was a person well qualified to undertake it. He spoke fluent French and was well qualified to promote the new community financially and in other ways too, for he was well connected, a good organizer and an excellent writer and speaker. Although he had not been in his present post at Saint John for very long, if Catherine approved, he would ask him to come to Toronto immediately. "Then send for him," Catherine responded.[28]

When Catherine recounted the incident many years later she said that up to that moment she had never heard of Father Daly. She might not have met him, but she must have been aware of him and his ability as a communicator for the Church's causes, for she had referred to him in her letter to Father Coughlan on 20 March 1921, as "a good convincing writer" who might be asked to produce some publicity about their new order. Her memory of the date of her first knowledge of Father Daly can probably be attributed to the deep distress and guilt she felt about her impatient pleas to Father Coughlan which precipitated his decision to assign Father Daly to the position of official clerical supervisor of the Sisters of Service.

When Father Daly arrived in Toronto on 14 January 1922, his appointment to the Toronto Provincial House of the Redemptorist community was listed as "unofficial," but it was confirmed in his order's records on 11 March.[29] There was no doubt about Father Daly's energy and purposefulness in undertaking his task. An article was immediately prepared for publication in the Toronto *Globe* on 17 January, announcing the founding of the Sisters of Service as a new Roman Catholic religious order for women. It was also arranged that he would speak on 24 January at the bridge party being given by the Catholic Women's League to raise funds for the order.

At that event he stressed that although the order's motherhouse would be in Toronto, where applicants would be received and trained, the sisters would be dispersed to other locations, particularly in western Canada where they would work with immigrants. The sisters would not be cloistered, would not wear a religious habit, nor would they live in large city convents. Rather two or three of them would live together in the small settlements, and bring religious, educational and medical help to all, but especially to the neglected and lapsed Catholics who so desperately needed these services. These were the very objectives which in 1920 Catherine had insisted were an intrinsic part of her vision, and which would remain the particular mission of the order in the future.

With great vigour, Father Daly attacked the two main problems in founding the order — vocations and financial support. He began a whirlwind speaking and writing campaign explaining the uniqueness of the order's approach and its need for applicants ready to undertake a difficult but adventurous life of service. He organized a special financial appeal which sought one thousand Catholics in Toronto each of whom would sponsor the Sisters of Service with donations of ten dollars a year for five years.

Shortly before Father Daly left for the West on 30 March, Adeline McConnell joined Catherine at 97 St. Joseph Street. Brother Rogation was able to find her a teaching position, for she was a splendid, experienced teacher. To Catherine her friend's companionship "was

85

like a heavenly gift."[30] Adeline's health was not strong, but she was optimistic that she would be fit to join the order with Catherine.

For the next three months Father Daly solicited the western bishops for their support in the form of donations and invitations to the order to come and work in their dioceses. The western dioceses did not produce many donations, for even the Catholics who lived in the cities did not have much money to spare. However, some of the hierarchy, particularly Archbishop O'Leary of Edmonton and Archbishop Sinnott of Winnipeg, were very interested in the prospect of sisters who could work in the outlying areas of their dioceses. When he reached Vancouver, Father Daly sent a warm letter to Catherine. They had been introduced shortly after he had arrived in Toronto, and she had been impressed with his sincerity and his enthusiasm. She felt that "he was a very intelligent, zealous and capable priest."[31] As they were both so busy, there was not much opportunity for many meetings before he had left Toronto, but his optimistic letter certainly indicated a tactful awareness of her concerns:

> I am sure that by this time you think I have forgotten Toronto and the S.O.S. — yet, I am always and everywhere speaking of them.
> The idea of the S.O.S. is meeting everywhere with great favour. Especially, Reverend Father Cameron of Calgary is an enthusiastic supporter of the idea. The Bishops throughout the West have already laid a claim on the first Sisters who are to go out into the field.
> I hope to be back in Toronto the first week of June. I will be glad to get back for it is tiresome knocking around from pillar to post. I am keeping well, thank God, and hope that by the time I return I will hear of many applications for the S.O.S. Let us, by a worthy life, prepare ourselves for the great work awaiting us in the West. God bless you! Best regards to your friend, Miss McConnell. Write to me at 2161 Cameron Street, Regina.[32]

Father Coughlan wrote to Father Daly and reported on their campaign's progress in Toronto. There had been some inquiries about admission to the order, but he was waiting for Father Daly to interview these candidates before he approved their applications. Unfortunately none of the serious applicants were school teachers, and so Miss Donnelly and Miss McConnell were the only prospects to date.

He reported that their financial campaign was also in the

doldrums for "the Ten Dollar Drive, I am sorry to say is not meeting with much success; confined as it is to Toronto. I believe we will have to make a Dominion-wide appeal to the wealthy Catholics to make it a success."[33] He had appealed however, to the Catholic Women's League to continue their support and a fund-raising garden party was being planned.

Father Daly returned on 1 June and began immediately to search for a more suitable house for the novitiate. It had been discovered that the basement of 97 St. Joseph Street was afflicted with incurable dampness, but the archdiocese did not have any other suitable property or funds to spare for the impending purchase. Thus on 23 June Father Daly went to Winnipeg to speak for the SOS cause at the convention of the Catholic Truth Society, and a week later he was in Ottawa for the same purpose. He was searching for benefactors who could give sizable donations.

To relieve Father Coughlan of the work of processing applications and inquiries, the Mother General of the St. Joseph's Community loaned the new order two nuns, Sister St. Charles and Sister Mactilde. They met the applicants and if they were serious about a vocation, arranged for them to be interviewed by Father Coughlan. The appointment of the Novice Mistress would be announced by the time a suitable building for the novitiate was found and made ready to open.

Father Daly was soon successful in locating a big house for $35,000 in a good location at 2 Wellesley Place, within a few hundred feet of the archbishop's residence. The lot was 91' by 136' and overlooked the grounds of the Wellesley Hospital. It was an impressive three-storey, brick and stone building, with hardwood flooring on the first two of the upper floors, and one of the rooms in the finished basement had a fireplace. The purchase was completed on 31 July, the sale being made to the Congregation of the Most Holy Redeemer (the CSsR) as the Sisters of Service were not yet an incorporated order.[34] With the novitiate location settled, Archbishop McNeil notified the Mother General that the Sisters of Service novitiate would open on 15 August.

When Catherine finished teaching in June she enrolled in summer school at the College of Education and was successful in completing her courses for her first class certificate. She was now qualified for a higher salary and more responsibility when she returned to a permanent teaching position. But her joy was blighted by a serious decline in Adeline's health; more rest during the summer vacation had not brought any improvement. When her illness was diagnosed as Bright's disease, at that time an incurable kidney ailment, Adeline's only recourse was to leave Toronto for Port McNichol where her sister could look after her. This was a serious blow to Catherine, for Adeline was not only a dear friend, she was ideally suited to the new teaching order which she had intended to join as soon as she had recovered her health.

One happy incident happened to Catherine during the spring which had the fortuitous result of attracting one of the order's most successful candidates. Mary Ann Bridget Burke was an Irish immigrant girl who had arrived in Toronto in March 1920 to work in the home of the son of a family she had worked for in Scotland. She also had introductions to good people in the Irish Catholic community who were kind to her and appreciated her gentle thoughtfulness. One Sunday morning when she was at Mass, probably in late April 1922, the priest at St. Monica's Church, Father H.J. Murray, announced that Archbishop McNeil was to speak that afternoon at the Knights of Columbus Hall on the new religious community, the Sisters of Service, which was being sponsored by the Catholic Women's League. One of the church members took Mary Ann to the meeting. The audience waited expectantly, but the archbishop did not appear. After a lengthy delay Catherine Donnelly rose and spoke to the meeting. She kept them spellbound for two hours while she told of her work in the West and the sad physical and spiritual deprivation she had encountered among the poor Catholic settlers. She pleaded especially for teachers and nurses and others who were willing to help in other ways to join her in a wonderful adventure to work among them and educate their children.

Mary Ann Burke left the meeting determined to join the community. But when she sought advice from Father Murray, he expressed scepticism about the future of the new order. It wasn't well established, and if the Catholic Women's League disbanded, what then? Why not consider the Sisters of St. Joseph, a well-respected and solidly established order? Mary Ann decided to present herself as an applicant to the Sisters of Service and find out more. Sister St. Charles looked at the tiny, five-foot woman who was now thirty-five years old and said, "You know, Miss Burke, the life of a Sister of Service will be a very hard life." The applicant replied, "Very well, Sister, but hard or soft, I am willing to try."³⁵ She was accepted by Father Coughlan, given a list of clothing she would need as a postulant, and told to plan to enter on 15 May. When no house for the novitiate was found, her entry was postponed until June. Again, she was told there would be a delay. It was with great relief Father Coughlan was able to reassure her that certainly all was now arranged for 15 August.

Two other applicants were interviewed and accepted, a Mrs. Mary Whittaker and a Miss C. Allard. Several others were refused, mainly because of poor health. Including Catherine Donnelly there were now four candidates, and it was hoped that others would arrive soon. When Catherine moved into the big house on Wellesley Place in August, the place needed cleaning and organizing. She arranged first for movers to bring the altar and furnishings from the chapel at 97 St. Joseph Street, and had them set up in the room she judged most suitable for their chapel. Her old friends from Alliston, Amy and Nettie Wright, came to visit. She was delighted, and thought it particularly fitting that "these loyal and beloved Protestant friends, refined in their education, and spiritually superb" were the first people to view the building in which the order was to be founded.³⁶

Next day as she was working, an Irish voice on the phone inquired, "Is there room for me trunk?" An amused Catherine answered the door shortly after and greeted little Mary Ann Burke for the first time. Sister Burke later remembered that after Catherine had shown her upstairs, she looked around and suddenly felt the strangeness of her surroundings. Loneliness swept over her; the big, barely furnished house seemed cold and barren and she knew no one in it. Nevertheless, she put on her new apron, came downstairs and offered to help Catherine with her tasks. The ice was broken; a sisterhood was being formed and a new friend was made. Tomorrow they would begin their great adventure together.

CHAPTER 5
THE NOVITIATE YEARS

IN THE EVENING OF 14 AUGUST 1922, A TAXI BROUGHT Sister Lidwina of the Community of St. Joseph, and the two sisters of her order who had been designated to accompany her from her own convent to 2 Wellesley Place. In the front hall she met for the first time the four postulants for whose religious formation she was now responsible. Her escorts bade her a fond goodbye and returned to St. Joseph's.

The sister selected by the Mother General to undertake the unusual and arduous task of being the first Novice Mistress of the new religious order was not, as Catherine had hoped, her former Novice Mistress, Sister Avila. Fifty years of age, Sister Lidwina was a woman of very different temperament, talents, experience and background. She had been born and raised in Toronto, the eldest of the nine children of Peter and Mary Henry, and was baptized Anne Teresa in St. Mary's Church.

Anne Henry received her entire education from the Sisters of St. Joseph. When she was quite young, they had perceived that she was a very conscientious child who had exceptional ability in music. They took particular care with her music instruction, a discipline in which the sisters were well respected in Toronto for their expertise as teachers. When Anne was in her late teens her music teacher, Sister Aloysia, asked her if she had ever considered becoming a nun. Anne replied that she had not; she intended to continue studying music, and stay home and help her mother. Sister Aloysia suggested she think and pray about her life choice. Some time later Anne told her mother that she felt she had a vocation to be a nun, and asked if she would be able to manage without her. Her mother had replied, "Annie, if God is calling you He will take care of us, but be sure He *is* calling you."[1]

On 6 January 1892 Anne Teresa Henry was one of nine postulants who entered the St. Joseph's Community in Toronto. She was given the

To Do and to Endure

name Mary Lidwina when she was received as a novice. She was a tall slight girl, whose lack of a robust constitution was emphasized by her thick-lensed glasses and pale complexion. The story is told that one day, when she was a novice, one of her classmates, Sister Majella, concerned about her frail appearance asked, "Why don't you go home and have your mother look after you, until you become stronger?" Sister Lidwina replied crisply, "Sister Majella, when the Community sends me home, I'll go, but not before."[2] She continued in the novitiate and made her first and final profession in August 1894 at the age of twenty-two.[3] She was destined to spend seventy-two years in the order, outliving all of her class, including Sister Majella.

As a fully-professed nun, Sister Lidwina's assignment for the next twenty-two years was to be a music teacher and choir leader at St. Joseph's Academy in Toronto and in other Ontario branches of the order. Then in January 1916, the Mother General received a request from Father E.M. Bunoz OMI, the Prefect Apostolic in Prince Rupert, British Columbia, asking the St. Joseph Sisters to take charge of the local Catholic school. Sixty pupils were without a teacher and he expected many more would arrive soon. The town was the terminus of the Grand Trunk Railway, and settlers were being attracted by the expectation of fortunes to be made in the area's new mining, fishing and lumbering industries. He also hoped that the sisters would be able to establish a boarding school in the town for the children of the homesteaders in the newly opened hinterland "to make a strong establishment of Catholic Education."[4]

Sister Lidwina was one of the four sisters selected to undertake the establishment of this, the most westerly mission of their order. One sister was to be the housekeeper, two were to teach school, and Sister Lidwina was to be the Mother Superior of the mission as well as the music teacher. She remained there six years, the full term of office for a Mother Superior. In that time the boarding school was successfully established in Prince Rupert. Although Sister Lidwina learned much about conditions on the Canadian frontier, neither she nor her staff went out among the people to any greater extent than the contacts allowed by their Holy Rule. As Mother Superior, she made certain that their routines and living conditions resembled as much as possible those of the regular convent life in which she had been trained.

In early August 1922 she was instructed to return to Toronto. She prepared to leave immediately and selected a sister to be her travelling companion. In this, she was obeying to the letter the Rule which decreed that the Sisters of St. Joseph carried out their Superior's decisions immediately and without question, and did not travel anywhere alone. The two nuns took the boat to Vancouver and boarded the transcontinental train which took four nights and three days to reach Toronto. On her arrival Sister Lidwina was informed that her next appointment was to be the Novice Mistress to a new religious order, the Sisters of Service, to whose motherhouse at 2 Wellesley Place she was now to move. There, on the Feast of the Assumption (two days hence) at the first Mass to be celebrated in their new chapel, Archbishop McNeil would proclaim the founding of the Order of the Sisters of Service and she would be inducted as their Novice Mistress. Sister Lidwina was startled and apprehensive; she knew what a daunting task she was undertaking, and the personal qualities that she was expected to exemplify, for the Holy Rule was very explicit on these matters. First of all, to qualify for the position one had to be at least thirty-five years of age and ten years professed, and "be distinguished for her piety and fidelity to the observance of the Constitutions." The Rule then demanded of her:

> To instruct and guide those under her charge, and to form them to the spirit of their holy vocation, the Mistress of Novices must be a person of interior and mortified life, and possess great prudence and charity; she should be serious, yet affable, and firm without ceasing to be gentle.
> She shall explain the Constitutions and the duties of the religious state, the practice of the vows, and how to make mental and vocal prayer. She shall train the novices to the practice of solid virtue, especially to self-denial, obedience, mortification, tolerance of others' defects, the spirit of prayer and recollection, and the avoidance of particular friendships.[5]

While she was still in a daze from travel fatigue and bewilderment at being assigned to a task in which she had no previous experience, with an order of which she had never heard, Sister Lidwina was summoned to an interview with Archbishop McNeil. At the conclusion he smiled and said, "I was anxious to know whether or not you would be motherly, and I feel confident that you will be."[6] The remark was a perceptive one, for the successful launching of the order would depend very much on Sister Lidwina's skills in so inspiring these first novices through her own personal warmth and zeal in teaching them an understanding and love of their vocation, that they would not falter when confronted with the physical hardships and loneliness which awaited them in their chosen apostolate.

Sister Lidwina was assured by Archbishop McNeil that she would be receiving special guidance in her task from Father George Daly CSsR, the experienced and dynamic Redemptorist priest who had been assigned by Father Coughlan to be the clerical superviser of the order. He would interview and approve the admission of all applicants and be responsible for all publicity releases informing the public about the Sisters of Service. He was already planning a campaign to secure religious and financial support from the bishops and clergy in the various dioceses where the sisters would work, and he would use his excellent contacts with many prominent members of the laity to rally their financial support for this, the Church's important new pioneering venture into home missions among the immigrants in western Canada. As well, Archbishop McNeil promised that he would be giving as much of his personal attention to the spiritual development of the novices as his timetable would allow. Father Arthur Coughlan, the Provincial of the Redemptorist Order, and Father Daly's Superior, had consented to be their official confessor and spiritual adviser.

It is unlikely that Sister Lidwina was told at this time about the important role Catherine Donnelly had played in founding the order, or given any information on Catherine's successful eighteen-year teaching career, prior to her decision to become a religious. Nor do we know whether the archbishop mentioned the specific tactics and objectives that she had persuaded him and Father Coughlan the Sisters of Service should follow in their apostolate. Conversely, Catherine was never consulted or informed about the talents and experience of the sister appointed to the vital role of Novice Mistress in the formation of this new religious order. Unfortunately, these omissions would contribute to the absence of empathy between the two women during Catherine's novitiate. The great contrasts in their temperaments, their family and educational backgrounds, and especially their career experiences, would soon become apparent, and they had the initial effect of obstructing rather than intensifying what in later years became a much warmer relationship. At times during her novitiate, Sister Lidwina would find Catherine strong-willed, and Catherine would find her Novice Mistress inflexible, even though they were both ardently committed to the same vocation and did not hesitate to work themselves to exhaustion for the success of the new order.

The rushed schedule for all the participants prior to the opening ceremonies precluded any meetings where their talents and experiences could be mutually revealed. Catherine had only two days after she had moved alone into 2 Wellesley Place to get the chapel and the big house cleaned and ready for their first Mass. The two novices who arrived on 14 August were unwell and unable to do any heavy work. Until Mary Ann Burke put on her apron and took up the floor mop that first afternoon, Catherine's only real help was one hired cleaning lady.

All their hard work seemed worth while the next day when the flowers and lights were put in place and the candles lit on the chapel altar. The Toronto branch of the Catholic Women's League had used some of the funds they had raised for the new order to provide the proper fittings for the chapel, some necessary furniture and kitchen equipment for the house, and the refreshments for a reception after the inaugural service. Archbishop McNeil celebrated Mass and in his homily explained the importance of the work the new order was destined to undertake. He and Father Coughlan, as well as Sister (now Reverend Mother) Lidwina received the four candidates: Catherine Donnelly, Mary Burke, Mary Whittaker and Miss C. Allard. The rest of the congregation consisted of several members of the Catholic Women's League, among whom was Gertrude Lawlor, a retired secondary school teacher in the Toronto public school system, who was one of the most respected and influential laywomen in the diocese. She had been the first pupil of St. Joseph's Academy to attend the University of Toronto, from which she graduated with high honours in 1890. In 1919 she had organized and was the first president of the Toronto Catholic Women's League.

Father Daly, who would play the major role in organizing and developing the Sisters of Service, was unable to be present, for he had been previously assigned by his Superior to conduct a priests' retreat in New Brunswick. However, he sent the novices a warm, personal message of blessing, congratulations and good wishes. In his letter he also introduced them to the motto which they and all subsequent members would make their watchword, and which still undergirds the order's coat of arms — "I Have Come to Serve."

> You have together to give to God, to His Church and to the most abandoned souls your best services. I mean the services of your Life. Your motto will be that of your divine Master, "I Have Come not to be served, but to Serve." And like Him you wish to be in the Great West, "As he that serveth."[7]

Father Daly also sent a personal letter to Mother Lidwina wishing her "courage and inspiration for the great work you begin tomorrow ... a work which I am sure ... after many *crosses* will grow."[8]

During the week, several members of the St. Joseph's Community as well as clergy from Toronto parishes called at the new motherhouse. The social duties of welcoming these guests did not hinder Mother Lidwina from introducing her charges to the Order of the Day which would become for many years the first year daily prayer and work schedule for novices of the Sisters of Service. As Brother Rogation had anticipated, it followed as closely as possible that of the Community of St. Joseph. This was the only way in which the canonical regulations which applied to all female religious orders could be met, for it would be a few years before the official Rule and Constitutions of the Sisters of Service would be written and approved by the Sacred Congregation for Religious in Rome.

During the first week of September, Father Coughlan introduced the four women into their canonical year by leading them in a five-day retreat. During the first novitiate year all religious orders severely restricted their novices' contacts with the outside world. They were not allowed to socialize away from the convent, visits from their families were limited, they did not read secular literature or newspapers, and only undertook studies prescribed by their Novice Mistress. They were also forbidden to do any professional work outside the convent. To make such a sudden switch from a world in which they had been free to decide personally the use of their time and their choice of work, to that of the religious who must now accept complete submission of their own will on all matters to that of their Superior, was recognized by Sister Lidwina as a difficult transition for her novices, but one which she was duty bound to help them achieve. They were preparing to pledge themselves to a lifestyle which would be marked by a constant awareness of the all-encompassing nature of their vows. This novitiate was where they would be taught the discipline this abnegation

Catherine's parents — Hugh and Catherine Donnelly.

The first Christmas after their mother died in 1905: Hugh Donnelly and his daughters, Tess, age 15, Mamie, age 11, and Catherine, age 21.

Parents and students at Meadowvale School, Tossorontio Township, which the three Donnelly sisters attended. Tess Donnelly age 8 is third from the left, front row.

Mamie, Catherine and Tess at the Alliston house.

1906 – Catherine with her Alliston friends.

Sisters Mamie and Tess at the Alliston house.

A pensive picture of Catherine – the breadwinner.

Tess Donnelly, Red Cross nurse in France, 1918.

Mamie Donnelly just before she joined the Sisters of St. Joseph in 1918.

The Claey Ranch, Stettler, Alta., August 1918. Catherine boarded at this ranch until the local school was closed by the "flu" epidemic, November — December 1918.

Mary O'Connor gets a riding lesson from rancher Jim Robinson, September 1918.

Catherine's Grade 8 class at Sacred Heart School, Calgary, Alberta. She was also the principal of the school 1919-20.

School at Stornoway, Saskatchewan where Catherine taught in an immigrant community, August 1921.

Frank Muzik loaned Catherine these horses and buggy so she would not have to walk five miles to the Stornoway school.

Local friends with Catherine, Stornoway, Saskatchewan, 1921.

Shortly after this was taken, Catherine decided to join the Sisters of St. Joseph.

The Novitiate Years

demanded, by living according to a strict schedule, regulated by the convent bell which indicated the times to be spent at prayer, study, work, meals and recreation from the first ring at their 6 a.m. rising to their final communal night prayers at 9 p.m. As one member of the order wrote, "The *sound of the bell* calling us to spiritual exercises we looked upon as God's calling us to do His Will by going to those exercises."[9]

Their day began with their short rising prayers said aloud in Latin in their rooms, followed by morning prayer said together in the chapel. A private meditation preceded the daily Mass in the chapel at 7 a.m. At breakfast and at all other meals, silence was observed while the person assigned as reader for the week read reflections on the life of one of the saints. Talking in the refectory was permitted only at dinner on Thursdays and the noon and evening meals on Sundays. The convent was a quiet place, for talking was permitted only at specified times and places, and strictly forbidden in all bedrooms, dormitories, hallways and stairways.

No outside household help was employed and the novices were assigned in rotation to do all the domestic chores as well as other duties in the big house. These began after breakfast and might also be fitted into other short periods, so that adequate time could be given to their religious exercises and classes which occupied most of their time. The bell had to be rung punctually, for it regulated the convent day. The sacristan cleaned and prepared the chapel for all services; the portress answered the door and telephone; waitress duty included waiting on table, clearing and resetting for the next meal; those assigned to the kitchen cooked and washed dishes and kept all supplies in order; others cleaned and waxed floors in the halls and common rooms, and did the laundry.

At 9 a.m they again visited the chapel for private prayer and saying the rosary. Sister Lidwina then gave a class on meditation, or on different aspects of life as a religious. Following class, a half-hour of talking was permitted until another fifteen-minute visit to the chapel for a private examination of conscience, followed by the communal prayers of the Angelus and Litany. After lunch at noon they had a short break for recreation, which was always taken together in the common room of the convent, or outside in their garden on fine days. Sometimes Mother Lidwina would recount the early days of her own community and her experiences in Prince Rupert. The novices were also read selected sections from the newspaper or church mission publications. Time was also allotted for listening to a spiritual reading by a designated sister, while they all mended or did needlework. Late afternoon was a time for completing their unfinished chores or private visits to the chapel.

Talking was permitted for a short time before dinner, and in the early evening they all relaxed for a longer recreation period. They frequently sang to Mother Lidwina's piano accompaniment. Her musical knowledge enlarged their repertoire of songs suitable for group singing, and would prove to be very useful when they were sent to the prairie schools and summer missions. They also played games in which she enthusiastically joined. After more young women joined the order they also wrote plays and skits which they performed on holidays and feast days for the amusement of their clergy visitors.

Planning programs for recreation time was a good way to discover the talents of the novices. Some revealed ability in singing and dancing, others wrote and narrated amusing poetry or patter songs, and the costumes and sets for their plays revealed other young women's talents in design, drawing and sewing. Everyone had to take part and the shy ones learned to overcome their self-consciousness when they acted or sang in front of the community. It was not long before Mother Lidwina began giving them choir training. The memoirs of the sisters and the carefully preserved scripts of some of the plays formed a useful archive of material on which some of them would draw in years to come when they were in charge of country schools and city hostels and needed material for Christmas concerts. The convent day ended at 9 p.m. when night prayers were said together in the chapel. Strict silence was then kept until after Mass the next day.

For many applicants, this was a physically and mentally strenuous routine, as few allowances were made for individual temperaments or needs. One of Mother Lidwina's principal responsibilities was to study the novices, and correct any infractions of the Rule or personal faults which might hinder their adaptation to convent life. Permission had to be sought for any impending deviation from their set tasks or the order of the day, even for necessary visits for medical or dental treatment. Negligence in applying for a permission, lateness, careless performance of a task, or inattention were faults which must be reprimanded. If a

The Novitiate Years

novice was aware of any infraction, she was duty bound to report it herself, kneeling penitently before the Novice Mistress or the Mother Superior (and Mother Lidwina fulfilled both roles), who then assigned a penance. One novice recalled that

> Mother Lidwina was very kind and "Motherly" but her kindness was never softness ... She led a disciplined, mortified life and never complained of anything ... She could never countenance anything that was not refined or in good taste ... and was a firm believer that as Religious we should bring dignity into our lives whether it be prayer, work or play.[10]

Not all of this novitiate routine came into full force immediately, for two of the four initial applicants, Miss C. Allard and Mary Whittaker, soon had to withdraw because of serious health problems. Applications did come in, however, albeit slowly. It took time for the first publicity releases sent by Father Daly to the Catholic press and the clergy to filter down to the parish level. He had to refuse many of these applicants because it was obvious their state of health was so precarious they would be unable to undertake the tasks awaiting them on a prairie posting.

When Father Daly returned from New Brunswick, he immediately established his office at 2 Wellesley Place, where he worked every day (unless other duties took him out of town), attending to all aspects of the affairs of the Sisters of Service. He lived until his death in 1956 at the Redemptorist Rectory attached to St. Patrick's Church on McCaul Street in one of the small simple, rooms occupied by the clergy staff who were affiliated with the parish, but who were available principally as missioners to parishes and religious orders. Throughout his career in Toronto, he would carry out his dual obligations as Director of the Sisters of Service, and a missioner of his own order.

Father Daly was fifty years of age when he was called to Toronto. His had been a varied career which in many ways reflected the great changes which his religious congregation underwent in the early years of the twentieth century. He was born in Montreal in 1872, one of nine children of William Daly, his Irish-Canadian father, and his French-Canadian mother, Josephine Morin. His father was a bank manager, whose position gave him a secure income and an assured social status in the community. George was a short, husky lad whose strong will, great sense of curiosity and daring, and impulsive behaviour got him

To Do and to Endure

into the usual childhood scrapes. He liked people and they liked him, for he had an engaging, outgoing personality, with a great capacity for friendship. He was always energetic, with great physical stamina. He did have a defect in one eye, the result of a childhood injury, but he was a fairly good student in spite of it.

His family's social life revolved around the community in the parish of St. Ann's Church in Montreal. Both his parents were devout Catholics, and very conscientious about ensuring that their children had good examples to follow both within and without the family. George Daly admired and respected his father, but he credited his mother with nurturing him in the faith and encouraging him to fulfil his dream, expressed when he was but a young boy, to become a priest. His models and mentors were the Belgian Redemptorist priests who staffed St. Ann's Church. As he was raised in a bilingual household, it seemed only natural that when the time came to leave the Catholic Junior College he attended in Montreal, he should continue his education under the tutelage of the Belgian Province of the order.[11]

He was only fifteen when he sailed from Montreal in June 1888, and entered their novitiate at St. Trond. The adolescent George Daly would not have an easy time of it. The Belgian branch of the Redemptorists were well known for their very strict adherence to a Holy Rule that was considered one of the most ascetic of all the male religious orders. As well as overcoming the natural pangs of homesickness, young Canadian recruits found the harsh living conditions of the Belgian novitiate wore down both their physical and mental health. The buildings were unheated and their regular diet was restricted; fast days were very strictly observed. Their Superiors could not understand why young Canadians had such difficulty adapting to life in the seminary, since they had survived years of living in the cold Canadian winters. They did not seem to understand that Canadians survived because their buildings were heated, and their winter diet was heavy with protein and fat to help them withstand the cold. Some of the young men who had the spiritual fortitude to endure loneliness, the intense religious discipline, and strict withdrawal from the world, were sent back to Canada with impaired health.

George Daly went through a difficult time adapting to a new religious and social culture, but his strong physique, his determination and his faith carried him through. As he progressed in his studies, he

100

The Novitiate Years

became recognized as a very promising student, and after he was ordained in September 1898 he undertook more academic work until his eye trouble prevented him from completing it. He was ordered to return to Canada in 1900 and took up his first post as assistant director of the new minor seminary which the order had established at Ste. Anne de Beaupré, just outside Quebec City. At this school boys who aspired to be Redemptorist priests received their first experience of Redemptorist education and spiritual discipline. After three years he took over as director, for he had gained a reputation as a man of sound judgment. He was also popular with the students because he did not believe it was necessary to replicate the spartan existence he had undergone in the Belgian minor seminary. He introduced small but important changes in matters such as heating, food and recreation. Some of his Superiors disapproved of what they felt were his concessions to the young students because they feared it would result in a weakening of the Redemptorist ascetic tradition, and wanted to accept only mature applicants willing to accept the European way. But George Daly argued that it was important that the order begin training their prospective candidates at an early age, for if they did not admit Canadian youths to their minor seminary, they would seek out other orders. He felt that he had benefited by beginning his own religious formation when he was only fifteen. True, he had to work through a difficult adjustment period, but the long years of preparation in Belgian seminaries had given him a profound understanding of Redemptorist spirituality and their mission. He did not believe, however, that the young Canadian candidates for whom he was responsible would benefit if their initial exposure to life as Redemptorists in North America was a replica of the spartan existence of his youth. It was very advantageous for candidates to spend some of their years of preparation for the priesthood in a Canadian milieu. This would enable them to discern the difference between automatic conformity to their Rule, and mature adaptation which maintained the spirit of the Rule, yet allowed them to work effectively in a rapidly changing Canadian society.

During the twelve years he was at Ste. Anne de Beaupré, Father Daly played a prominent role in the vigorous discussions among the Redemptorist Superiors on the urgently needed reorganization of their order's administrative structure in North America. Too frequently national, linguistic and cultural differences dominated their approaches

101

To Do and to Endure

to their work. Father Daly hoped some of their educational and jurisdictional problems in Canada could be resolved through the creation of a distinctly Canadian bilingual Redemptorist Province, and the order did try this solution for a short time when he was at Ste. Anne's. But money and staff were too scarce to give it a real trial and not many in the order supported the idea. A different administrative division had to be devised.

In 1912, a new English-Canadian Vice Province was created and Ste. Anne's became part of the French-Canadian Province. From his headquarters at St. Patrick's Church in Toronto, the new Vice-Provincial would oversee the English-speaking Redemptorist Houses in Saint John, New Brunswick, St. Patrick's Church in Quebec City, and St. Ann's in Montreal. Father Daly transferred to the new English-speaking section and was appointed pastor of his old Montreal parish of St. Ann. During the three years he was there, his fame grew as an extraordinarily effective conductor of retreats for the clergy. He also introduced temperance programs for the parishioners and had a kindergarten for children built at St. Ann's. With men away at the war and so many women working in the munitions factories, it was an urgently needed social service. He was highly regarded for his way with people, but his enterprises were costly and the financial burden had to be assumed by the order, as it was not a wealthy parish. In July 1915, in spite of Archbishop Bruchési's protests about the loss of such a valuable priest from his diocese, Daly's Superior demoted him to the much smaller centre of Regina as Rector of Holy Rosary Cathedral.[12]

In Regina, Father Daly immediately attacked the work which he felt needed to be done with his usual directness and vigor. He was an ardent Canadian patriot and very aware of the accusations directed at Catholics that they were shirking their wartime duties. To show his loyalty to Britain and the Empire he travelled across the prairies supporting the Canadian Army's recruiting drives and appeared on a public platform with the Prime Minister, Robert Borden, in support of the war effort. Direct participation in the war effort was a delicate issue within the order for many of the American Redemptorists were from Germany. That problem would be solved in 1917 when the United States entered the war and the American Redemptorists, as patriotic Americans, then gave the war whole-hearted support.

Father Daly pursued a wide range of interests from his Regina post. As a person familiar with both the English and French aspects of Canadian culture, he tried to act as a go-between in alleviating tensions between the French-speaking western bishops and the increasingly large numbers of English-speaking Catholics in their dioceses. He also began a popular series of Sunday night sermons in Regina for non-Catholics. As well, he promoted the founding of a Catholic College, which was to be affiliated with the University of Saskatchewan.

All these activities, which Father Daly combined with his regular parish work, he believed were useful ways to establish the Redemptorist presence in southern Saskatchewan and allay criticism of Catholics by the Protestant majority in the West. But in 1916, his Superiors found it "profoundly upsetting" that he was using a car which was given to him as a gift, as his mode of transportation in Regina. They declared this was a breach of his vow of poverty and ordered him to use the streetcar and give up the car. They had obviously not investigated the sprawling settlement pattern of a western Canadian city which even in 1916, made a car a necessity for anyone involved in ministering to the population at all hours of the day or night. He complied, but "very slowly and reluctantly."[13]

As the war dragged on and the need for army recruits became more urgent, Father Daly's public statements in the press and on the platform increased. This dismayed his Superior, Vice-Provincial Patrick Mulhall, an American, and he reminded Father Daly that a Redemptorist's mission was souls, not Canadian army recruits. When he did not stop travelling about and giving lectures, his Superior decided that Father Daly had "no idea of religious life. He wants to be in the public eye all the time. He cannot content himself at home with his community."[14] Father Mulhall consulted his Roman advisers and they confirmed that the activism of Father Daly and his use of a car, and his involvement with Canadian politics and national issues was detrimental to his religious vocation as a Redemptorist vowed to poverty, self-sacrifice and obedience. No consideration was given to the fact that Father Daly was trying to adapt the obligations of his religious life to Canadian wartime conditions. He was transferred early in 1918 to Saint John, New Brunswick, where his assignment was to do some work with immigrants, but his main task would be giving missions.

Around the same time, the Toronto Vice Province was raised to the status of a full Province, Father Mulhall was appointed Provincial, and Father Arthur Coughlan was appointed one of his assistants or advisers. When Father Mulhall resigned due to ill health and returned to the United States, Father Coughlan succeeded him in 1921 as Provincial of the Toronto Province.

Among the most vexatious of the problems confronting him at that time was that of the future of the Redemptorist missions in Saskatchewan. Their work among the Ukrainians and other settlers was beset with difficulties. More money for churches and more priests who spoke Ukrainian might have helped to stop the leakage of these people from the Church. But money and personnel were in very short supply. Catherine Donnelly's report to Father Coughlan and Archbishop McNeil in 1921 on the probable response of the Ukrainians to a Catholic teacher in their schools had pinpointed the problem. In her emphatic fashion she had stated that as an educator she had been well received, but she had noted that priests who could not or would not minister to them in their own language and ritual were not. She had observed that the Ukrainian Catholics of the Eastern Rite were strongly resisting attempts to introduce Latin Catholicism into their communities. Only a few Redemptorists were proficient enough in the language and ritual to be able to transfer to the Eastern Church.

Father Coughlan respected Catherine's acuity and zeal and realized that her plea to speed up the process of founding the new order of women to do educational and medical work in the isolated areas was one practical and immediate remedy to staunch the leakage of these Catholics from the Church. It was time to act, and his response was to advise her that the task now required the guidance of a priest who had the time, the knowledge and the skills for such a huge task.[15] In selecting Father George Daly to take control of the process of founding the new order, he was aware that Redemptorists complained of Father Daly's shortcomings. They felt he did not fit the mould of their traditional Redemptorist way of exemplifying their vow of poverty and a communal style of life; that he was too headstrong and independent by nature; and he was not prudent in handling money, especially when he thought it necessary to spend it to accomplish his goals. But Father Coughlan felt his other qualities outweighed these faults. Whenever he had consulted Father Daly about Redemptorist affairs, his advice always indicated that he had broad vision, a great personal devotion to

The Novitiate Years

Redemptorist spiritual ideals, and a kindly, personal touch in his dealings with both clergy and laity. Moreover, Father Daly's recent book, *Catholic Problems in Western Canada*, showed that he had grasped the serious problems facing the Catholic Church. In it he pointed out that Catholic missionary efforts in the West were too scattered and meagre when contrasted with the massive and co-ordinated surge of missionary work being initiated by Protestant denominations who were pouring personnel and money into their western missions.

Father Daly's assignment as director of the Sisters of Service would require many skills and much energy. His immediate tasks would be to inform the Canadian Catholic Church of this new religious order, and to search out and admit suitable candidates. At the same time he would have to launch a vigorous financial campaign to raise money through appeals to the laity and the hierarchy, for it would be at least two years before sisters could be sent out west to earn money to support the order. Not the least of his tasks would be drawing up their Holy Rule, which would define the sisters' dress, spiritual life as individuals and as a community, and the constitutions by which they would eventually govern themselves. These and other documents would then be translated into French or Latin and submitted, in accordance with canon law, to Rome for approval. As the clergy director, Daly would be in charge of the order's affairs until it was deemed that it had achieved a financial, administrative and spiritual development of sufficient strength to be able to manage its own affairs. In any case, Father Coughlan felt that George Daly was ready for such a challenge.

In meeting that challenge, Father Daly's next few months were undoubtedly a round of hectic activity. He wrote press releases for all of the Catholic diocesan newspapers as well as the secular press, he delivered speeches and preached sermons to whoever would give him a podium or a pulpit. One of his most important targets was the Catholic Women's League. He went to their second national convention in Winnipeg in late September 1922 to lobby for their support. He gave a short but spirited address explaining the Church's need for such an order, which would use new ways to carry out an apostolate among Canada's immigrants and poor rural settlers. Their work as teachers and nurses would link the important tasks of promoting good citizenship

105

and patriotism with teaching the faith to their children. It was a theme he would repeat many times in the coming years, as seen in notes he drafted for his presentation to the Catholic Women's League.

> To put ideas into execution requires money. The financial requirements to realize our objective are commensurate with the extent of the need, with the immensity of the field of operation. The need is national, the field is Dominion wide ...
>
> This brings me to you, Ladies of the C.W.L. — my proposal to you tonight, ... is to adopt the work of the S.O.S. as one — if not the principal of your national works. As the Marquis of Lorne said, "Canada is the land of magnificent distances & unlimited possibilities."
>
> You have been thinking in Canadian terms; now I wish you to act on Canadian lines. Long enough have we been bound by the fetters of parochialism & diocesism. The work we offer you to protect is national; Therefore it requires a national body to help it. By identifying your organization with the S.O.S. you will help to keep to your organization its national character ... to remain a Catholic Dominion wide organization & not degenerate or lose itself entirely in local interest —
>
> Look at big maps!
>
> I leave to you to decide the way in which you will propose to help financially the S.O.S. Only remember the small amounts make the big sums. The consistent recurrence of small offerings often proves more profitable to a cause than large but too often solitary amounts ...
>
> The figures that appear in today's paper of the sum of $1,500,000 collected by the Methodist Womens' Missionary Soc. tell us eloquently — may I add reproachfully what coordinated effort can produce.
>
> Ladies — Canada needs the S.O.S. The S.O.S. needs also the Church and Canada. The Church & Canada expect everyone to do his duty.[16]

Daly then drafted a motion, which was moved by Gertrude Lawlor, declaring that the Catholic Women's League "heartily endorses this work of the Sisters of Service and willingly adopts it as one of its national works." The convention then resolved to form a national committee to study means and ways to give it support. As well, each member of the League would be asked to make a contribution to help financially "this truly Catholic & nation-wide endeavour."

The Novitiate Years

When Father Daly returned to Toronto from his speaking trips, much of his time at the convent was spent conferring with Mother Lidwina, for she needed instruction in several of her important tasks, not the least of which was keeping an accurate account of all donations received, as well as the convent expenditures. As she was not experienced in office procedures, she found this very stressful. Fortunately her brother, who was an accountant, offered to come once a week to help. When a new novice revealed she was experienced in bookkeeping, Mother Lidwina gratefully assigned the task to her.

Looking ahead to the day when the four postulants would be ready to be clothed as religious in their order's uniform, Father Daly decided that it should be grey, and ordered a 100-yard bolt of English grey serge for the purpose. He and Father Coughlan had agreed that some form of distinctive dress was necessary, not only for economy and propriety, but also because the Canadian railways only gave fare discounts to clergy and religious workers if they wore distinctive dress which identified their occupation. Catherine Donnelly's original strategy that the sisters would not wear a traditional Catholic religious habit was followed. It was agreed that the outfit should resemble the type worn by the Victorian Order of Nurses or the Salvation Army women. Mother Lidwina, who had worn the black and white, voluminous, floor-length habit of her order for thirty-one years, admitted that she had no ideas about appropriate dress for the Sisters of Service. When she asked the postulants for suggestions, Catherine offered the novel idea that a riding skirt should be part of their attire so that they could ride horseback on the prairies! A new postulant, Katherine Schenck, suggested they consult Fairweathers, a fine ladies' department store, who in turn suggested Edgeleys, the specialists in designing and making exclusive uniforms for college students.

Taking Katherine Schenck as her adviser and companion, Mother Lidwina visited the company. She asked if they could incorporate a type of long sleeve that she had seen on a nurse's uniform. Sister Schenck suggested that these sleeves be attached to an under-bodice, so that the uniform would have two pairs of sleeves. Edgeleys then designed a uniform which incorporated these two ideas. The grey sleeveless dress had the currently fashionable lowered and belted waistline. Deep pleats extended from the left shoulder of the left front, and the right shoulder of the right back to the bottom of the hem. The full skirt, slightly gathered on the sides and back, was to be worn eight inches from the floor. As requested, each dress had two sets of sleeves attached to separate under-bodices for ease in laundering. A narrow white linen collar and large white cuffs completed the uniform. They were all pleased with the result; with only a few alterations this would be the dress worn by the Sisters of Service for forty years.[17] The novices wore them for the first time to the 8 a.m. Mass at Our Lady of Lourdes Church, Toronto, on 17 June 1923.

In the early discussions on suitable uniforms for the order, Archbishop McNeil, Father Coughlan and Catherine had also agreed to reject the traditional nun's long veil worn over shorn hair and white undercap. Archbishop McNeil suggested that headdresses were unnecessary, even in chapel. But in 1923 fashion decreed that genteel women wore hats in public. Holt Renfrew designed and made the matching grey serge hats. Mother Lidwina's friend, who was a milliner, donated fashionable black straw sailor hats for Sunday best, and the novices were delighted. These attractive hats had to be abandoned later; when they went out of style they would no longer be obtainable. They also proved impractical on a windy day in a dusty prairie town. It was also decided that they could not adopt Father Daly's suggestion that their voluminous blue capes be lined in blue, because that colour would soil too easily. They did follow his suggestion that their only visible religious symbol, a simple silver cross, be hung on a blue cord.

The only parts of the uniform to which Father Daly objected were the black silk gloves and the black Oxford shoes selected by Mother Lidwina. The former were worn by all St. Joseph sisters, but he felt that silk was too luxurious a fabric and incompatible with the vow of poverty. The shoes were a more contentious matter. Sister Katherine Schenck was called to the office one day and when he saw her new black Oxfords he declared:

> It is my wish that the Sisters of Service wear high shoes [a high laced shoe of ten or more eyelets].
>
> Mother Lidwina remonstrated, "Father, no person in this day and age wears high laced shoes, the Sisters of St. Joseph do not wear them, excepting a few of the older Sisters or those with weak ankles, perhaps."
>
> Father Daly very firmly stated, "The Sisters of Service are going out to work on the Prairies as Religious, and they should

The Novitiate Years

wear high shoes."

Mother Lidwina, in a very modified tone of voice but very earnestly warned that the Sisters of Service "will never receive subjects ... I don't think personally, I could wear high shoes during the heat of summer. The Redemptorists no longer wear them and even today, Father, I notice you have on low shoes."

Poor Father Daly seemed quite perturbed. Mother Lidwina, God bless her, had won the day.[18]

Sister Schenck had one other tale to tell about the selection of the order's clothing. One day she asked Father Daly if there was any particular reason why he had chosen grey for their uniforms. He replied he just thought it would be a nice colour for the sisters. Sister Schenck commented that only a man would chose grey for womens' uniforms, as it was too hard a colour for older women to wear when their youthful complexion had faded. Quickly Father Daly retorted, "Keep young at heart, Sister."

Catherine did not record that she had any private discussions about the order with Father Daly during her first months in the novitiate. She does state that she was able to talk with Father Coughlan, for he was her confessor and it would have been to him in private that she spoke of her impatience with the imposition of the St. Joseph's Rule. She worried that its emphasis on what she considered were the minutiae of their training was not a practical way of preparing them for the isolated conditions that awaited them in the West. There is no record of her speaking out to Mother Lidwina on this, but perhaps the admonition that she stated she received from Father Coughlan, that she should just stay back in the corner, like an old broom, was his way of cautioning her not to complain.[19]

She was startled however, when, on 23 April 1923, it was announced that Father Daly and Archbishop McNeil had agreed to purchase the house next door, 4 Wellesley Place, in the name of the Sisters of Service, to be used as a women's hostel. It was to be a home for young working women, particularly immigrant Catholic girls. They were being assisted by the Canadian government through loans for their ocean fare of $120, and they needed homelike, safe, inexpensive living quarters in Toronto where they could stay until they were secure financially and socially. Father Daly persuaded the Catholic Women's League to take charge of the hostel until the Sisters of Service would be ready to take over its supervision. As early as 1912, Archbishop McNeil had urged the Vancouver business community, which employed young immigrant women as well as untrained country girls seeking jobs in the city, to sponsor reasonably-priced housing for them; but he was not heeded. For many years it had been the Christian churches, or institutions affiliated with them such as the YWCA, which had taken the initiative and tried to provide this type of accommodation for young women.[20]

Catherine had never considered hostels for working women as part of her vision of service when she was planning the order with Father Coughlan. She thought they had agreed it would provide teachers and nurses, with social work as a service which would derive from their working contacts with rural people. This new addition to their apostolate would, she feared, divert the order from its original founding intention of a rural apostolate.

But Father Daly was facing a difficult situation. Archbishop McNeil saw a real need in his own diocese which he knew a new and modern order like the Sisters of Service would be able to fulfil admirably. Moreover, very few Catholic teachers and nurses were indicating any interest in joining the order. They were joining other orders which had established reputations as experts in education and nursing, and who had school and hospital structures already in place. Most of the young women who had made serious inquiries in the first few months did not have the educational qualifications to be trained in these professions, and sufficient money was not being donated to educate those who would desire it. Father Daly believed some of these applicants did have a genuine religious vocation, and accepted them.

Catherine was not told any details about the order's current difficulties in finances and recruiting. The situation certainly troubled Father Daly and Sister Lidwina, for her entry in the SOS *Annals* of 19 January 1923 quoted from Father Daly's latest letter: "It is hard to get money — I can assure you that begging is no joke! But let us have confidence! It is not our work, but God's work. We are but instruments in His hands! If He wants the work, it will succeed."[21]

Sister Lidwina herself wrote a plaintive note in the *Annals* on 11 April, "Father Daly returned from the west. Delighted to see our dear Father, but oh, such regrets things are not brighter. Evidently the dear Lord is trying him longer or else I am failing somewhere." She had

The Novitiate Years

such moments of self-doubt in spite of Father Daly's assurances that she was the right person for the task. Her stamina was being depleted by worry and responsibility, and some days she was confined to her bed. When these attacks were severe, another sister from the St. Joseph's Community would come and relieve her for a few days.

Catherine, too, was despondent when the spring of 1923 did not bring new postulants. "We seemed to be facing nothing but defeat. I was puzzled and confused, expected to do the work and discuss nothing and know nothing of what was going on." She became so depressed and lethargic that Mother Lidwina decided she should see a doctor, whom Catherine noted that Sister Lidwina herself selected. His only prescription was, "Get out of that place. Get a school and start teaching." When Catherine returned, she asked to be allowed to drink milk as a tonic. Permission was granted but she was depressed by a system which was quashing all her initiative so that even the addition of a medical prescription required a permission. "I was not supposed to have ideas."[22]

Then one day in June, Archbishop Sinnott of Winnipeg called on Mother Lidwina. The reason for his visit was revealed to Catherine after he had departed. She was informed that in August, on completing her first novitiate year, she was to be posted to Archbishop Sinnott's diocese. He needed a teacher for one of his Indian schools. Instead of meekly and happily accepting the assignment, Catherine was aghast. She knew that the directive had really come from Father Daly, and it was proof to her that neither he nor Mother Lidwina understood the nature of her vision, and so it was about to be further undermined. She said firmly, "No, I will not go, that is not our work."[23]

Mother Lidwina was displeased, and not at all mollified by Catherine's explanation that other Catholic women's orders were already involved in Indian work, and that the Sisters of Service was founded to bring education and spiritual help to the rural immigrant people in the areas where no Catholic sisters had ever ventured before. As Novice Mistress, Mother Lidwina could not reconcile Catherine's passionate declaration that she had "an inspired road to follow" with all that she was trying so hard to teach her in the novitiate about the meaning of obedience. Catherine had also put Mother Lidwina in a very awkward position. She could not insist that Catherine accept the posting, nor could she recommend that Catherine be refused admission

111

to this new order, which as yet had no Mother Superior of its own, or members who had taken vows. To her, the refusal was a direct subversion of her ability to so train her novices in obedience to accept her direction, especially in matters concerning their work assignments.

Catherine, for her part, felt that as a matter of conscience she could not be a party to subverting the purposes of an order which she had been told (by two priests and the archbishop) was a God-given solution to a serious problem which was rooted in the Church's conservative approach to new challenging situations. It was not that Catherine did not wish the Church to minister to the native peoples; rather, she feared that once drawn into the Indian missions, an undertaking which required so much money and personnel, the Sisters of Service would never be able to recover the momentum to carry out their original apostolate. And in this, she was undoubtedly right. That assignment could have established a precedent which would have taken her projected order in a different direction.

Catherine never recorded any repercussions from her refusal that day, other than a detectable coldness, an "arctic atmosphere" which Mother Lidwina exhibited in their encounters. Nevertheless, it must have been very embarrassing for the Mother Superior to have to report Catherine's refusal to Father Daly. There is no record that he ever discussed the incident with Catherine herself. She undoubtedly told Father Coughlan, and he was probably the person who informed Archbishop Sinnott that the order's apostolate did not include working directly in the Church's Indian schools and other institutions, and suggested that the sisters would welcome an invitation to do teaching and social service work among the European immigrants in his diocese.

Catherine was not looking forward to spending her second novitiate year in Toronto, but no other requests for a teacher had been received from other dioceses. Then her spirits were lifted by three fortuitous events. On 15 August 1923 a new postulant arrived, Catherine McNally, "a young, well-educated, talented lovable girl with great potential, who sang and played beautifully, was frank and outspoken. From the time she arrived full of laughter and kindness, I had no more black days of confusion and near despair." Catherine was also heartened when she was given permission by Mother Lidwina to study privately by correspondence, to upgrade her academic qualifications. A month later, Margaret Guest was received, "young,

The Novitiate Years

buoyant, ready for anything, a qualified teacher at last."[24]

In several memoirs, Catherine wrote that she did not like her two years in the novitiate at 2 Wellesley Place. But the contemporary records do not reveal serious discontent. A letter from Sister Avila thanking Catherine for her letter and gift on the occasion of her silver jubilee stated, "I am so glad to know that you are happy dear Sister and that the outlook for your great work in so bright and promising."[25] She was remembered as a person who could tell entertaining stories at recreation, who participated wholeheartedly in all of the activities, and who cheerfully carried out her domestic duties. If she had been told by her Superiors that they were trying to find a posting which would fulfil the purpose of the order as she understood it, and had been asked to use her excellent contacts with the western public school boards to locate teacher vacancies, she would have felt less frustrated over the delay in returning to the west. Nor did they tell her that Rome had not yet given its approval for the order, since it was not the custom to inform novices about the order's business affairs. Postulants were not to be distracted from the spiritual side of their religious formation at that stage of their training.

The machinery to obtain Vatican approval had been set in motion in March of 1923, when Father Daly prepared the documents of the *Petitio ad. S.Sedem ad canonicam erectionem faciendam*, which was the official request to the Sacred Congregation of Religious in Rome seeking their approval of the Sisters of Service whose founding Archibishop McNeil had himself approved in his archdiocese in August 1922. When no reply was received after three months, Archbishop McNeil wrote a strong letter to the Cardinal Prefect of the Congregation of Religious appealing for prompt action. The serious situation that he outlined at some length, and its solution, was exactly what Catherine had been describing for over two years as one of real crisis for the Catholic Church in the west:

> Your Eminence:
> In Canada the Catholic Church has to encounter very serious problems and difficulties. During the past twenty years the number of Catholics who have left the Church in Canada is not less than one hundred thousand, and the probabilities of the future are much more serious. The losses have occurred in the Western Provinces, Manitoba, Saskatchewan, Alberta, and British

Columbia. Catholic immigrants came from Europe, especially from Austria-Hungary, and Protestants were better organized to help them than we. Protestants helped them by supplying hospitals and schools and in other ways. The Catholics have been much divided by differences and antagonisms of race and language, as well as by the absence of co-operation between the various dioceses.

One of the means used by the Protestants is the public school in Catholic rural districts. The teachers employed are mostly Protestants. They distribute their tracts by means of the school children, and teach religion to the children on Sundays. The priest cannot prevent this. In very many cases he knows nothing about it, because he has charge of a vast area and it is only every two, three or more months that he can visit any particular place. The parents become indifferent or hostile.

Many of us have discussed this problem and tried to devise some means of protecting the faith of Catholic immigrants. One plan which Bishops in the West approve unanimously is that of forming a new religious community of teachers and social workers, and of sending them to teach in the public schools of the West. Many of those schools have dwellings attached for the use of the teacher, and Sisters could use this dwelling. Not less than two Sisters would live together. It was by a plan of this kind that the Church in Australia protected the faith of her scattered members.

We have proved that it is possible to found such a community in Ontario. The Redemptorist Fathers have undertaken to develop it and to guide it spiritually, and the Sisters of St. Joseph have loaned one of their best Sisters for the training of the first Novices of the Sisters of Service, as the new community is called.

We have all that is needed in Canada to inaugurate the new community, namely, vocations, spiritual guidance, and financial support. What we still need is to comply with Canon 492. As far as I am concerned I complied with Canon 492 in March of this year, when I gave to the officials of the S. Congregation of Religious all the necessary information and recommendation of Bishops in writing. All concerned are anxious to begin this work of zeal and piety. We need this work not only for teaching the children of immigrants but also to obtain missionary undertakings. The area of those Provinces is so great that Bishops and Priests cannot know much about the intimate lives of the people. Three of the four Provinces named above, Manitoba, Saskatchewan, and

Alberta, have a combined area that is greater than the combined area of England, Scotland, Ireland, Denmark, Holland, Belgium, Switzerland, France, Italy, and Spain, and have only ten Episcopal Sees and 621 Priests. British Columbia is much larger than any one of the other three Provinces.

Protestant activities are well organized and well supported in those Provinces. We get few of theirs and they get many of ours.

In the absence of any central executive committee through which all the Catholics of Canada could bring their forces to bear upon such problems, our Catholic hospitals are placed in cities where they can be self-supporting. The Protestant bodies have such committees and they place many small hospitals in rural districts in the midst of Catholic populations, thus gaining the good will of our people. Through the Sisters of Service we hope to compete with Protestants in hospital service.

I therefore beg your Eminence to enable us to place another organized Catholic activity in those Provinces of the West.

With profound respect I beg to remain

Your Eminence's humble servant,
Neil McNeil
Archbishop of Toronto[26]

To Archbishop McNeil's dismay, the response on 15 May 1924 to his request was a refusal to proclaim the Canonical Erection of the Sisters of Service. The Congregation of Religious gave two reasons: first, they felt the name of the order implied that their mission was personal service to people such as is given by domestics or waitresses, and second, they felt that the financial provisions for the order were inadequate.

McNeil's response in French was tart and to the point. They had misunderstood the meaning of the English word "service": "En anglais ce nom n'a pas la moindre soupçon de servitude."[27] He noted that their letter seeking approval might have translated their title as "Soeurs de Bon Secours," but the word service in this context in contemporary English is understood to mean service to God and to humanity. Contemporary dictionaries had among the several definitions of the word listed "office of devotion: official religious duty performed." The order's name, like those of other religious orders such as the Sisters of Charity and the Sisters of Hope, told the world of the special virtue which they would practise, namely service, especially to the poor.

To Do and to Endure

Finally he noted, "le titre de Filles de la Sagesse ne suggere plus de religion que celui de Soeurs de Service."

As for the order's financial situation, McNeil pointed out that in one year the Redemptorist Fathers, mainly as a result of Father Daly's efforts, had collected and spent $11,600 for the Sisters of Service. The Catholic Women's League, which had 35,000 members, had contributed $4,580, and would continue its contribution until the new order was solidly established. He noted also that "trois de ces Soeurs vont commencer l'enseignement en Manitoba. Leurs salaires montent à mille six cents dollars par an."²⁸

When no reply had been received by March 1924, Father Daly tried to hasten the laborious process by enlisting the support of Archbishop O'Leary of Edmonton, who was an enthusiastic supporter of the Sisters of Service. He asked him to lobby the Sacred Congregation on their behalf. The Apostolic Delegate had referred their request to Rome, with a strong recommendation for approval, "but I think if your Grace would drop a line [to] Msgr. Gentilli it may expedite the giving of the long awaited permission."²⁹

Father Daly's constant travelling away from the Toronto Redemptorist community, and his seeming total absorption in the affairs of the Sisters of Service, had caused to be resurrected many of the criticisms raised in former years by some members of his own order about his personality and methods. They had reached the order's high command in Rome, and Father Coughlan was notified in April 1924 to make arrangements to have Father Daly transferred to Edmonton to be Superior of their small mission there. Father Coughlan was very disturbed, for he recognized that the injunction was an attempt to thwart Father Daly's activities at a crucial time for any new order, but especially for the Sisters of Service. He wrote a long, urgent and frank letter to his superiors in Rome pleading for them to rescind their instructions. His review of the situation aptly summed up Father Daly's role in the Canadian Catholic religious community at this time:

> I shall try to explain the matter conscientiously and without bias. It is true, Father Daly spends a great deal of his time and energy in the interests of the Sisters of Service, the Catholic Truth Society, the Catholic Women's League and Catholic Immigration ... At the same time, being an indefatigable worker, he is ever ready to labor at the works of our vocation — he is just at present preaching

Retreat for the Sisters of St. Joseph at Peterborough, Ont. He is almost the only one I have who can preach a retreat for priests, & I was reserving him for this work for the summer. He has already an engagement for a double Retreat, French or English, for the Ottawa clergy in July, a very delicate task on account of the language troubles in that diocese. His travelling I may say costs him very little for the C.P.R. & the C.N.R. Railroads have given him annual passes on account of his interest in Immigration. Father Daly is a man of unbounded influence in the entire Dominion among the laity, clergy and part of the Episcopate ... There is no priest in Canada, secular or religious, who is so influential and much in demand. Because of his great usefulness, and of the immense good he does for the Church in general in Canada, I was loth [sic] to curtail his activities and his travelling, which I would certainly not allow to any other Father. But I always felt that Father Daly's was an exceptional case. He does not travel for mere pleasure, but for work in some good cause. Perhaps I made a mistake in encouraging him in all his undertaking, for I confess I have so encouraged him & he has done nothing without my approval; but I am sure he has brought more honor to our Congregation in this country than any of us or any number of us together. Outside of the undertakings & the travelling, no one can complain of Father Daly's conduct as a religious & Redemptorist for this is indeed edifying.

Of course his nomination to Edmonton will practically put an end to his share in the above mentioned undertakings & his travelling, and would put an end also to the criticisms of him ... On that account alone things would be made easier for me during the next trinium.

But there are several other matters to be considered in this connection. There is for example the foundation of the Sisters of Service. Again perhaps it was a mistake, but the fact is Father Daly and I are the founders and main support of this Institute. Their vocation is one that I feel would please St. Alphonsus, the care of the most abandoned souls, (especially among the Ruthenians and other foreigners) in the country districts of Canada. The undertaking has the approval of practically the whole hierarchy of Canada and of the Apostolic Delegate, principally because there is no other Institute for Sisters attending to this neglected field. Now while I care for the spiritual guidance of this growing community of religious, and I may say I have never neglected even the minutest Duty as Provincial for this purpose,

Father Daly bears every other care financially and otherwise, on his shoulders, and is indeed their main prop. I do not see how his services can be dispensed with by the Institute at this time ... I have no other Father to whom I could or would ever care to entrust this task of F. Daly's and if Father Daly leaves I am sure the whole burden of this Sisterhood would fall on me. Now I cannot do more for them than I am doing now, and I will not attempt to do more. So if Father Daly goes, the only thing it seems to me I can do is to turn the whole affair over to the Archbishop & let him manage as best he can ...

Mons. McNeil has the greatest confidence in Father Daly and is continually calling on him for aid for the Catholic Women's League, Immigration, Catholic Extension etc ... Now to tell the truth his Grace will be very much grieved to know that Father Daly has been moved to Edmonton, and how could I explain satisfactorily to him the reasons for this removal? ... And there will be many others who will be astonished & will not understand why Fr. Daly is exiled, as they will surely say. Of course I would do my best as a loyal son of St. Alphonsus to smooth over the misunderstanding, but I am afraid I would not succeed well.

Now as to the charge that I am too much under the influence of Father Daly, I can quite understand the usefulness of His Paternity's and your warning in this respect. I may say ... that while I have frequently sought Fr. Daly's advice, I have a very independent mind in all matters, and I have never followed any suggestions or opinions of his that did not commend itself to my good judgment ... I think there exists a feeling of jealousy of Fr. Daly in the minds of some for truth to tell he is head and shoulders over all of us in many respects. I am not however a blind admirer of Fr. Daly — he has his faults, particularly a lack of prudence at times in speech and I have called his attention to these. But I do think those who criticize him do not realize what a power for good he is and what a hold & influence he has ... especially among those outside the congregation.

Now Very Reverend Father, I have laid all this before you and I request you to lay the same before his Paternity, merely as a matter, I feel, of duty. Whatever you decide in Rome, I look on as the will of God, and you will know how to dissipate our fears and anxieties. If you still believe Fr. Daly should go to Edmonton as Superior, I shall accept it as God's will ...[30]

Fortunately, only a few weeks before Archbishop McNeil had

written his letter of explanation and protest, Archbishop Sinnott had made another visit to Toronto in June with a new and different request for the Sisters of Service. Shortly after, Catherine was overjoyed to learn that he had arranged for the order to begin their work in a suitable location in his diocese in August. She and Sister Catherine Wymbs RN would be leaving together on 9 August for Camp Morton, Manitoba, a small immigrant settlement on the shore of Lake Winnipeg, sixty miles north of Winnipeg. Catherine Wymbs would set up a small nursing station, and bring medical aid to the district. Catherine Donnelly would be the teacher of a one-room elementary school in the hamlet of Camp Morton, and her employers would be the local public school board. The board had a second school in the area which also required a teacher immediately. Archbishop Sinnott was told that the order would send another teaching sister who had been selected for this apostolate, as soon as she had completed her canonical year, and would thus be ready to leave the Toronto novitiate. As well, suitable living quarters would have to be ready for three sisters.

In late June, Catherine wrote her final examinations in Algebra and English, the two subjects that she had been studying privately from texts throughout the year. Then she began packing — clothes, books, school lessons and some school supplies in preparation for the great move. Father Daly applied for the first of the many reduced railway fares for which members of the Sisters of Service, garbed in their official uniform, would now be eligible.

Catherine Donnelly and Catherine Wymbs were the first members of the order to make their first vows, which were to observe poverty, chastity and obedience for the period of one year. The quiet, impressive ceremony took place at a Mass celebrated on 2 August in the novitiate chapel. At the reception afterwards, Archbishop McNeil announced that the *Annals* of the Sisters of Service should record the day's events:

> The first thing I want entered is the item, that the founders of the Sisters of Service are Rev. Fathers Arthur Coughlan and George Daly. I have cooperated, the St. Joseph Sisters have cooperated, but the founders are really Fathers Coughlan and Daly. I want this entered in the annals.[31]

It is not surprising that Archbishop McNeil did not credit Catherine Donnelly for her initiatives in founding the new religious order. For centuries, the hierarchy had thought only in terms of the

To Do and to Endure

regulations in canon law on the founding of religious orders, and these required the sponsorship of the hierarchy and their designated clergy. Priests were considered the most important authorities for women to consult if they felt called to undertake forming a religious order with a new apostolate, or if they wished to join an established religious order. Catherine kept silent on this occasion, for she had never emphasized her own direct role in the founding of the order except on the occasion of her disagreement with Sister Lidwina over her assignment to an Indian school. Nor does she seem to have ever mentioned publicly that she had contributed all of her savings to Father Daly, a sum of over $2,000, as seed money for him to use in starting the order.[32]

On 5 August, Catherine, now Sister Donnelly, was permitted to take a brief trip to Port McNichol for a final visit with Adeline McConnell, whose struggle with Bright's disease was now in its final stages. Catherine knew it was going to be hard to say goodbye to her old friend. But she found her cheerful and quite accepting of her impending death. Her only regret was that she would not be going west with her dear "Chiefie" to begin the apostolate they had dreamed of undertaking together.

CHAPTER 6
THE FIRST MISSION AT CAMP MORTON

CAMP MORTON, THE SITE SELECTED BY FATHER DALY and Archbishop Sinnott for the first missionary venture of the Sisters of Service was in a farming and lumbering community sixty miles north of Winnipeg. It was originally called New Iceland, for it had been first settled in the 1880s by Icelandic immigrants of the Lutheran faith. In 1897 the Canadian government opened the unclaimed land in the district to the German, Ukrainian and Polish Catholic immigrants. They were happy to leave the Austro-Hungarian Empire, where they were tenant farmers, and take up the free land available in western Canada. Some of these new people who claimed homesteads created a small settlement on Lake Winnipeg in 1904 and named it Haas, after Adam Haas, a local farmer who was also their first postmaster. In the same year the King Edward School District was established, and a small log schoolhouse was constructed two miles west of the lake. Gimli, five miles south on the lake, was a larger settlement, being a village with twenty houses and a small schoolhouse.

Within eleven years the increase in population made the Haas school inadequate, and the King Edward Public School Board decided to close it and build two new one-room schools. Thus in 1915 King Edward School No. 2 was erected, three miles west of Haas, and a year later King Edward School No. 1 was built only a mile to the west of Haas. As the Manitoba Public School Act of 1890 did not provide for the public funding of Catholic schools, and the Catholic population could not afford to build their own, children of all religious persuasions attended these public schools.

In 1920 Monsignor Thomas W. Morton, the rector of the cathedral in Winnipeg, purchased for the diocese some of the Haas lakeshore property and buildings from a settler, Mr. J. Maier. Here he

To Do and to Endure

founded a summer camp for the Catholic population of the diocese of Winnipeg. Haas was renamed Camp Morton, after the monsignor, and the camp was opened in 1923. Archbishop Sinnott built a church and rectory in the vicinity of the schools, in preparation for the establishment of a parish.

The immigrants who settled this area were very poor. It had been a difficult struggle to establish farms out of the virgin territory by the lake. At first their main source of revenue had come from felling the trees on the land assigned to them as their homesteads. Trembling aspen, black spruce and tamarack were found in the marshy areas, and elm, white spruce, maple and willow in the sections bordering Lake Winnipeg. The cordwood and lumber cut on this land had to be taken by horse and wagon or sleigh to the railway which the Canadian Pacific had begun to build north from Winnipeg. Then it was transferred to trains going west, and used to build and heat the prairie towns. With the advent of the new summer camp, the CPR completed the line right into the settlement, and built Camp Morton station.

Life on the Manitoba frontier was made exceptionally difficult by the extremes of the climate. In the summer the temperatures soared; if there was no rain, the crops burned out and the parched soil blew away. The winters were bitterly cold; blizzards swept over the landscape, creating danger of frostbite for animals and people if they were exposed unprotected for even a short time. The melting snow in the spring, and the heavy autumn rains, turned the clay soil into morasses of mud, and the settlers found that travel by horse-drawn vehicles was almost impossible until the land dried or frost hardened it.

When Archbishop Sinnott had written to Father Daly in May about the procedures necessary for the sisters to secure teaching positions in Manitoba with the public school board, he had assured him that there would be no difficulty, as the local school trustees were all Catholics. The salary in one school was to be $90 a month for ten months, and $85 for the second school. He advised that for living quarters, "there is a little house near the Church, where I am going to put a priest this summer, with eight acres of land attached, which is for sale just now and which could be purchased for $900. I think it a good buy and suitable temporarily for the Sisters."[1]

At this point, the negotiations regarding housing between Father Daly and Archbishop Sinnott became a sparring match, for in spite of

The First Mission at Camp Morton

their mutual eagerness to get the new venture started on a secure footing, both the archdiocese and the Sisters of Service were short of funds. Father Daly went out to inspect Camp Morton and wrote to the archbishop from Regina, where he was conducting a retreat:

> I looked over the ground, visited the two schools, had a conference with the trustees, and came to an arrangement subject to the approval of Your Grace. The trustees offer $80 a month to each teaching Sister, with a bonus to defray expenses of transportation of the Sisters to school during the winter season. In the Summer, I told them that we would provide the Sisters with a Ford car.
>
> The only matter which remains unsettled is that of habitation. All considered, I find that property you had in view most suitable for this purpose. Only, as I told you, we would not like to burden ourselves with real estate, so my proposal is this. Let the Episcopal Corporation buy the property, and we will cover the interest by paying it in rent. This would enable you to carry the property without any burden, and, were the Sisters to leave in any future time, you could dispose of it or keep it for parochial purposes. The reason why the location appeals to me is that the Sisters would be near the Church and also find protection. As to the matter of a third Sister as a nurse, I will give it consideration as soon as I get back East. Anyhow, a third Sister will come and she could busy herself visiting the Homes of those poor people and instructing the children in Catechism.
>
> As I have to rush home after the C.W.L. convention [in Edmonton], I allow myself a day in Winnipeg, Friday, July 11. I would like very much, if possible, to meet you in Winnipeg on that day to come to a final arrangement. In the meantime a letter would reach me addressed c/o Archbishop O'Leary.[2]

On his stopover in Winnipeg, Father Daly also had a successful interview with the Deputy Minister of Education of Manitoba. He reported to the archbishop that it was "very gratifying. He showed himself most sympathetic to our work and was willing to second our efforts."[3] Father Daly also confirmed that two sisters, Catherine Wymbs, a qualified nurse, and Catherine Donnelly, a teacher, would be leaving the first week of August, and the second teaching sister, Margaret Guest, would arrive in the first week of October for she would only finish her novitiate year on 29 September, and "we think it

123

only fair to her and to our work that she would have the full benefit of her year." The school board would have to find a substitute teacher for two months. On the problem of housing, Father Daly felt it best to have the sisters live for the time being in the small house the archbishop had offered at the Camp; a more permanent solution would be discussed later.

Archbishop Sinnott replied immediately, urging that the sisters arrive as soon as possible:

> I will not be just sure until the contract is signed ... As to the residence, I do not agree with you. They will be at liberty to stay at the Camp, when it closes after September 1st, but that will be too lonesome for them and too far from the Church. You must get busy and get the funds to build a bungalow. That will prove more satisfactory in the end.
>
> Of course we can settle this when you come here in the middle of August. But in the meantime, kindly pick up $1500 or $2000.
>
> We will find shelter for them during August, but it will lack the privacy of their own community. That they will understand.
>
> If it be not possible to get the substitute for two months, you must face the possibility of shortening the Novitiate of Sister Guest. We cannot let the opportunity pass.[4]

The school board and Archbishop Sinnott had little choice but to accept Father Daly's decision that Sister Margaret Guest must complete her first novitiate year and make her profession before she left for Camp Morton. The Ministry of Education had accepted the two teachers' Ontario professional certification as valid in Manitoba. Father Daly had attended to that important matter before making the final arrangements with the district school board. Sister Wymbs was a Manitoba-trained nurse, so there was no difficulty about her qualifications to open a nursing clinic and also act as a visiting nurse. He had also appointed Sister Wymbs as Sister Superior of the Morton mission.

Father Daly was strongly supported in his stand by Father Coughlan, who wrote, "I would not consider sending Sister Guest under any consideration, until she finished her canonical year. She has already expressed to Mother Lidwina her great joy that she has not been sent on the Missions before she shall have taken the vows." He said also that he had spoken with the first two missionaries of the order before they left, and they "were in the best of spirits ... I tried to prepare them for the worst, without discouraging their ardor."[5]

Thus it was that on 11 August 1924 only Sister Donnelly and Sister Wymbs, dressed in the grey serge uniforms of the order, got off the train at Camp Morton. From the station, the only signs of settlement were St. Anthony's, the partly built parish church, a small building used as a rectory, and a few small scattered farmhouses in an otherwise deserted landscape. A half-mile from the station down a dirt road was their temporary home, a small cabin set amid the trees. It perched on the edge of a bank sloping down to the shore of Lake Winnipeg which extended north and south for nearly three hundred miles. It was the original Maier farmhouse, a small uninsulated building of only two rooms, with no electricity or water supply except the lake. Obviously this cabin would be inadequate for living quarters for three people in the winter. A decision on winter housing for the sisters was made soon after they arrived, for Catherine noted in their Annals, "It was decided to build a cottage near the Church. The Mission to meet interest on same."[6]

The first two weeks were a whirl of activity as they prepared for school opening, and located a stove (loaned), table and beds. But the most important acquisition was their horse, Pat, for he was to take the sisters to their respective schools. He was not very strong or fast, but Catherine was pleased to have him. A second horse would have to be found soon, as Sister Wymbs would also need transportation when she made nursing calls in the scattered settlements.

Thanks to Father Daly's persuasive talks to the Catholic Women's League of Winnipeg, several of their members drove the sixty miles to the cabin bringing staple food supplies and canned goods, home-made treats of jam, cakes and pies, and books for a library. All were urgently needed, for there was no local store and the sisters always offered some form of hospitality to visitors. To give a warm welcome to all who called on them was one of the most important ways in which they tried to exemplify to the community their motto, "We have come to serve."

By 19 August the two schools were opened. Sister Catherine took King Edward School No. 1 located a mile from their cabin at the summer camp, and Esther Sullivan from Winnipeg was hired by the school board to teach at King Edward School No. 2, three miles away. The first day only four students came to school; the others were at

To Do and to Endure

home working in the fields, and bringing in the harvest. Each day their numbers increased until there were twenty-five students in Catherine's school. When Sister Guest arrived on 8 October, thirty-five students were enrolled at King Edward School No. 2. Catherine was heartened and touched by the eagerness of the children to attend school. Besides the regular academic curriculum, she and Esther Sullivan taught catechism for half an hour each day, as allowed in the Manitoba school regulations. Most of the families were nominally Roman or Ukrainian Catholic and were of Ukrainian, Polish, German, Irish and Icelandic origin.

As there was no resident priest in the district, regular church services had not been available for some time. The local residents might hear Mass once a year, and then only if a missionary priest was passing through the district. The two teachers offered to give classes in catechism on Sundays at their schools to the young people who were beyond elementary school age. Many of them now working on the farms had never received any religious instruction for their first communion or confirmation. This offer was well received, and each week the classes grew larger. By October they were able to report that the class numbered fifty-one, and "all who might be supposed to attend have now started."[7]

Sister Wymb's services were soon in demand. There were thirty-three families in the immediate vicinity of Morton, and the district had a rural population of 1,942, of whom 382 were farmers. The nearest doctor was in Gimli, six miles away, and the nearest hospital was in Winnipeg. Most of the farmers could not afford those services except in extreme emergencies and often that was too late. Disease, illness and farm accidents could become serious trouble for an isolated family unable to get any expert medical help. Sister Wymbs made visits by horse and buggy to those unable to come to her at Camp Morton, and several cases required more than one visit. She reported:

> We are most welcome among them all; mothers especially are very grateful for the nurse's advice.
>
> The people are poor. The majority of the houses have only two rooms. They have large families. I have already made twenty-three visits in the surrounding district. The field for a health worker is as immense as the prairies that surround us.[8]

The patients were supposed to pay a small sum for her services, but most of them do not seem to have been able to afford even a modest donation for a house call.[9]

On 29 August, Father Daly arrived at Camp Morton to conduct a three-day retreat for fifty men from Winnipeg. Near its conclusion, Archbishop Sinnott called a meeting of the Winnipeg Diocesan Men's Committee to discuss how they could help the new Morton mission. They offered to collect clothing, especially shoes and stockings, heavy pants, underwear and sweaters for the needy children, and deliver it before the cold weather arrived. Books for the school libraries were also promised. In return, the sisters offered two beautiful white kittens which had been left to fend for themselves at the camp. Catherine was pleased when two men took them home to Winnipeg. She was also happy to record that Father Daly and the archbishop "walked to the site of the new S.O.S. house and made plans for its erection."[10]

The next week brought two cheering events. King, a fine, spirited horse, was acquired, and Catherine received Sister Lidwina's letter congratulating her on having passed the three upper school examinations she had written in June, following her year of solitary study at the novitiate. Her Algebra mark was in the 50s, but she had achieved third-class honours in English composition and literature.

September was a busy month with every day bringing unexpected tasks. They entertained a constant steam of clerical visitors from Winnipeg and eastern Canada, as well as receiving the local folk. Archbishop Sinnott had a cottage on the camp property and came frequently, bringing guests on fine weekends to hunt and to see the mission. When he was unable to bring his housekeeper, the sisters' duties included cooking and cleaning for him and his guests as well as for other visiting priests who came by, often on very short notice. These guests usually did bring gifts of food or books, or later mailed money or thoughtful personal gifts.[11] Another day they were pleased to be visited by four Benedictine sisters, who lived in a fine convent at nearby Arborg, where they were in charge of an orphanage. Another pleasant surprise was the donation of an organ which arrived by train and was cheerfully delivered by Paul Biys, a local farm boy. A week later the lad was brought to the mission with a serious head injury which required all of Sister Wymbs's skills.

For Catherine, the month brought the distressing news of the death of her old friend, Adeline McConnell. Her sorrow was hidden in

To Do and to Endure

her entry noting the event in the Annals, "Surely her suffering here, so cheerfully and lovingly endured has secured for her a rapid passage to Heaven."[12]

The two sisters worked very hard under difficult circumstances during those first two months at Camp Morton. The lack of any conveniences made their domestic chores doubly time-consuming and tiring. Living so close together in the crowded little cabin, with no privacy, could be wearing on the nerves. Hauling all of their water by hand from the lake in all kinds of weather was exhausting. They were short of money so they made do with minimum kitchen equipment, much of it purchased secondhand. Shortly after the stove was installed, the oven door fell off and they had to prop it up. These conditions were a foretaste of similar situations they would have to cope with many times in the coming years when they were assigned to a new mission.

Many of the outbuildings at the camp had seriously deteriorated, but they had money for only the most urgent repairs. The first heavy rain revealed the poor condition of the stable, and Catherine noted with concern, "Stable roof leaking — water coming down on Pat in his stall." Catherine was responsible for the care of the horses as she had more expertise. This could cause difficulties if she was away from camp when the horses required care. Catherine was particular about keeping Pat comfortable and in good condition, for although he was a willing creature when properly handled, he tired quickly. She knew that he could not work if he was not watered and fed, or was feeling stressed. It distressed her when she found out one day that Sister Wymbs and Esther Sullivan's mother had driven in the buggy to Gimli and back and neglected to feed the tired horse on their return. As a result, Esther had to walk the three miles home from school that day, for Pat was not fit to do another six miles.[13]

Gradually they were able to establish a daily routine centred on the private and community prayers prescribed in their Rule. After teaching or attending to callers' medical needs all day, their evenings were devoted to marking and preparation of school lessons, cooking, washing and housecleaning. Sundays were busy days too, for another of their duties was to clean the little church and prepare the half-finished building for Mass on Sunday, in case a priest did come. When, as happened on many occasions, no cleric arrived, the sisters led the few people assembled for the service in saying the rosary and a litany.

The First Mission at Camp Morton

In the afternoon Catherine, aided by Esther Sullivan, drove out three miles to No. 2 School to teach catechism to the older students. She recorded:

> Miss Sullivan taught at #1, I took six of the big boys and went on walking the last mile or so to save Pat. Had about thirty at No. 2 — 11 from Berlo [a hamlet five miles away] — all respectful earnest children.
> Sr. W. and Mrs. Payne [the Matron of the Diocesan Camp] prepared dinner and took it to Archbishop's cottage while we were away. We returned very hungry as we hadn't had time to have a meal all day. Dinner was ready. We did it justice.[14]

After Catherine had walked home from school on 2 October, she made some preparations for dinner, hitched up Pat and drove to the station to meet Sister Margaret Guest, who was now a professed sister, and had come to replace Esther Sullivan. It was very dark, and the only light was from farmer Biys' wagon lantern. He and his son Paul (now recovered from his recent head injury), and his friend Metro, had driven behind her buggy to the station to help with the trunks. In the dark, Catherine could only identify her friend by her giddy laugh as she alighted from the coach and caught sight of a "weird and rustic-looking" Catherine perched on her wagon. When they arrived at the cabin, a tired Catherine was grateful for the boys' help as they cheerfully unloaded the luggage and "took Pat to the stable and fixed him up for the night."[15]

At dawn next morning the two teachers went by wagon and train to Teulon, a small town thirty-five miles southwest of Morton, to attend the teachers' convention. It was a refreshing change for Catherine to hear professional papers, meet other teachers, and hear a talk by her school inspector, Mr. Hartley, with whom she had already established a cordial relationship. She was also pleased to be appointed to the executive committee of the Teachers' Association. When the local teachers gave their visitors a tour of Teulon, the two sisters saw the mission work being done by the Presbyterian Church in Canada. They noted that they had built two separate homes for Ukrainian girls and boys, and also an area hospital in the town.

The next day, when Catherine introduced Sister Margaret to their Sunday routine, which began at St. Anthony's, the latter was surprised to enter a church building that was only a bare shell, full of lumber and

To Do and to Endure

building supplies. There was no sheeting on the interior walls so the drafts were blowing in and there was no stove. About twelve people were waiting, and in the absence of the priest, joined in the prayers led by the sisters. That afternoon they taught catechism at their schools to twenty-seven local older children.

The three sisters had no leisure time; there was always a task awaiting them. Sister Wymbs stayed at the cabin to be available at the little clinic she had set up in a nearby building, and tried to have dinner ready when the teachers arrived home late in the afternoon, tired from teaching children who were scattered across all grades of the elementary curriculum. But many times they found the house empty and the fire out, as their nursing sister colleague had answered an urgent call for help.

Mental stimulation, relaxation and entertainment had to be found in the daily round of events at the mission, for trips to Winnipeg by train were a rare treat and they had no car. The gifts of food and garden produce from the Camp Morton farm women were always a welcome supplement to their very plain diet. A link with the outside world was established when one great day a visiting Redemptorist brother brought them a radio. Another useful gift came from Archbishop Sinnott and the Winnipeg laymen's group — a buggy and a sleigh, complete with harness. Excitement of a different kind occurred the day Archbishop Sinnott arrived at their house the same time as their new dog, Rastus. In the confusion the excited dog took after their cat, who escaped just in time and cowered behind the organ. Catherine was amused to record that the cat "was saved by his Grace."[16] The next week Rastus sinned again when he tore Catherine's beaver hat into small pieces. She observed only that he was "very thorough" about what he did.

The antics, personalities and physical condition of the missions' pets and horses would always be one of Catherine's great concerns. She was passionately fond of animals, and believed that these faithful companions, guardians and means of transport, were gifts to mankind from God. They should be cared for with love and rewarded with praise, for they contributed to human welfare. Neglect and cruelty to animals roused her to indignant anger, for she believed their protection was a moral obligation.

Catherine was also very moved by the natural beauty of Camp Morton. She was thrilled one night in September when Archbishop

The First Mission at Camp Morton

Sinnott called the sisters outside to observe a spectacular display of Northern Lights. Three months later winter cold had arrived and the shortened daylight hours meant they drove home in the spectacular beauty of a prairie winter sunset:

> As Sister G. [Guest] and I drove home from school, the skies were glorious with color. All along the western horizon, long stretches of crimson cloud lay along the sky. We saw it through the trees as we came through the woods. It was there when we reached the house and made us wish to linger longer to gaze upon the loveliness. A little fall of fresh snow has kept the ground pure white. Among the shrubbery, the Jack-rabbits are dashing here and there. We saw a little group of them as we came along. Something tempts them out beyond the danger line and, sad to say Rastus gets them and we find dead rabbits often now.
>
> These evenings, when the glory of the sunset is gone, the clear crescent moon is in the west.[17]

Cold weather also made even more evident the severe poverty of the settlers. The children arrived at school ill-clad even for the first snow flurries which heralded the winter freeze-up. When they saw their pupils in thin cotton dresses and shirts and lacking warm jackets and sweaters, the sisters distributed the clothing donated by their Winnipeg supporters and requested them to send more if they could.

The onset of winter also showed up the deficiencies of their own living quarters. It was impossible to heat their two rooms, and they had to close off the smaller one which had been their kitchen. The three of them would now work, cook, eat, wash, sleep and pray in the one room until their new quarters were completed. Also in December, a newly appointed priest, Father Macieszek, took up residence in St. Anthony's rectory. His first Mass was held in a frigid church on a bitterly cold day. Everyone except the priest wore warm hats and mitts, and the men, who composed most of the congregation, only removed their toques for a few seconds, for the prayer of Consecration. At the conclusion of the church service, the priest told the men that they should donate enough money to fix their church as they were doing it for God, but they flatly refused.

At school, the sisters began rehearsals for the Christmas concert and for the special Christmas services. At first, this was disheartening work, for Christmas meant little to a poor community deprived of religious celebrations for many years, and with little cash for necessities, let alone luxuries like presents. Attendance at the Sunday catechism classes dropped because the young men worked Saturdays and Sundays hauling water to flood a little skating rink in a local farmer's field. Their industry prompted Catherine to observe, "The cold was intense — had they a similar spirit about getting their church built, they could have finished it in a very short time."

By persistent effort Catherine produced a long, successful concert at her school. Every child took part, much to the pleasure of parents. Father Macieszek played Santa Claus, for under the Christmas tree decorated with donated ornaments was a gift for each child. Sister Guest, who had more students and was particularly skilled in singing and teaching choirs, put on an even more "splendid and inspiring concert to a keenly appreciative audience." Catherine was very moved, "knowing the condition of the school and the lack of aid given a teacher. The tone has been raised already, a very great deal. Only teachers could understand the difficulty of doing this."[18]

By Christmas Eve, a few of the local men had managed to line the interior of the church with brown paper, install a camp stove and place around it benches of planks supported on boxes. The sisters worked at cleaning and decorating it until after midnight. The music for the Christmas Day High Mass was sung by the new choir; the sermon was delivered by Father Macieszek in English, German and Polish. When they finally ate their dinner in the little cabin at 8 p.m., Catherine was so tired she could hardly eat. But they all enjoyed their priest's expert violin playing after the feast.

Fatigue had to be ignored next day, when they moved into their new convent. Catherine carefully noted that their helpers were young Paul Biys, and Pat the horse, who hauled the sleigh. The frame story and a half building was about 26' by 34' feet. It had no plumbing or running water, but to the sisters a furnace, kitchen, sitting room, bedrooms and a separate chapel were a great improvement on the cabin.

A few days later they attended a public reception held in their honour at the cathedral rectory in Winnipeg, arranged by Archbishop Sinnott and the Diocesan Laymen's Retreat group. Many laity and representatives of the religious orders in the diocese were present to acknowledge their success in the demanding field of the rural apostolate. In his report to Father Daly, Archbishop Sinnott declared:

The First Mission at Camp Morton

They have gone about their work quietly and unostentatiously and as a consequence they have gained the confidence and esteem of every parent and ratepayer of the district ... More and more does my conviction grow that the Sisters are an invaluable contribution to the solution of the problem presented by the New Canadian ...

To instil the principles upon which our social order is established, we must have some one who will bridge for the New Canadian the chasm between present environment and old-world conditions — some one who will reconcile and bind together all that is best and worth while in national and religious inheritance with what this country offers in prosperity, liberty and established self-government. The Sisters of Service ... are admirably adapted for this work. Each member is particularly trained for it.[19]

After the public reception, Catherine collapsed from fatigue and a nagging cold. She had worked without a break for five months. She rested for three days in Winnipeg at the convent of the Holy Name Sisters, and was well enough to come home to Morton for the great day on 4 January 1925, when Archbishop Sinnott officially opened the new convent in the presence of Mother Lidwina, Sister Schenck, the Superior of their Toronto hostel, and Superiors from two Winnipeg orders. The occasion was made more festive by good news from Toronto. Mrs. Ambrose Small had given $3,500 to pay for their building and another benefactor, who had already sent clothing and bedding, was donating $500 to furnish their chapel. Mother Lidwina remained at Camp Morton a few more days, inspecting every aspect of their work. She played the new organ at the parish church service; with such an expert musician leading them, the congregational singing showed marked improvement. She enjoyed visiting the schools; the children were friendly and respectful and put on a little recital for her.

After the busy holiday season, their Camp Morton schedule of teaching school, Sunday catechism classes and running the health clinic was resumed, with the addition of a new Sunday class at Berlo. Mass was now said every day in their chapel, and every second week at St. Anthony's where the congregation was steadily increasing. One Sunday in January their horse, King, ran away with Paul Biys in the cutter, and the animal suffered a serious gash in his foot. Catherine concluded that the accident was due to the boy's fear of King, which had made the sensitive horse nervous. A few weeks later he bolted when Catherine was driving him, but her unusual strength and skill enabled her to bring him under control. Again, she did not fault the horse; she decided that he had been hitched too short. The only other events of note in the scanty Annals of that winter were that "Rastus was badly injured by the train," and Father Daly visited the mission and was pleased with all he saw.[20]

The never-ending work at Camp Morton completely absorbed Catherine's attention and we find no comment in the Annals on Father Daly's extensive plans for new missions. She might not have been aware of them, or of his intensified efforts to recruit candidates and benefactors to staff and finance them. He wanted more urban womens' hostels, similar to their Toronto mission which in its first four months of operation had helped 966 young women in a variety of ways — meals, inexpensive lodging, counselling and employment placements. Archbishop O'Leary of Edmonton had been one of the first of the western bishops to support the formation of the new order and invite them into his diocese, so the two men agreed that the first step should be to found a Religious Correspondence School in Edmonton, with the expectation that when a suitable building could be purchased, a hostel would be added. Catherine had noted in her early reports to Archbishop McNeil in 1920 that the Protestant denominations were using a similar method of reaching farm families in remote areas. Her advice was not sought by Father Daly on this or any other occasion on the nature and location of the new missions. Perhaps he avoided the subject because she had not approved of the Toronto hostel. In late January 1925 he chose three newly professed sisters to open the Edmonton mission. One of them was Catherine McNally, Catherine's friend from novitiate days, whom he appointed Sister Superior.

Father Daly felt confident about founding the new mission because word had finally been received from Rome that the Sacred Congregation of Religious had approved "the Title, Habit and characteristic of our Order ... By this appointment the Archbishop [McNeil] has the required permission for our Canonical Erection ... This letter implies the validation of the Novitiate and the Profession of Vows."[21] As well, the application to the Canadian government for the legal incorporation of the Sisters of Service had been approved, which meant that the order could now possess property in its own name. The governance of the order was still the direct responsibility of the archbishop, through his delegate, Father Daly.

In early February serious diseases hit the community. Many

The First Mission at Camp Morton

families had influenza and two families were quarantined for scarlet fever. Fortunately Sister Mary Bridget Burke had been added to the Morton staff in January. She attended to the cooking and housekeeping, while the other three sisters did their best to help the community through the crisis. Sister Wymbs eventually found time to send a report to Toronto:

> One family had six children ill [with scarlet fever]. I was there for three nights they were very sick. I came home during the day. The conditions the poor souls live in is most pathetic. There were three children in each of the only two beds in the home, the father and mother sleeping on the floor, no extra mattresses or bedding. The same conditions exist in many of the homes. They do not undress to go to bed. I have not found one patient (with the exception of the Canadians) who has a night gown.
>
> We are all well. Father Maciesek [*sic*] had a bad cold and cough. We are to have Holy Week services ... the singing is improving. The snow is going very quickly, the roads are in terrible condition ... the sisters send fondest love and Sr. Burke wishes to tell you her bread is a great success.[22]

Easter had always been celebrated with special pomp in the Catholic Church in the old world, but many people in the area had not attended such services in many years. The church walls were still covered in brown paper and very little money was available for decorations. Yet when the services started on Holy Thursday there were white curtains made by the two teachers hanging on the wall at the side of the church to provide a bright backdrop to the candles and white carnations on the Altar of Repose. The community responded with marked devotion; in ever-increasing numbers they visited the church. On Holy Saturday they followed the old-country custom of bringing baskets of food from their homes to be blessed, and on Easter Sunday the church was filled with worshippers for the first time.

A spring teachers' convention in Winnipeg gave the teaching sisters a much-needed respite from their routine, and Catherine came home brimming with ideas. In her enthusiastic report to Father Daly she outlined a plan to help children, particularly "backward" boys who had difficulty mastering academic subjects. She felt that they would benefit from more instruction in practical subjects like manual training.

> I hope we can get a real good chest of tools and some lumber. The

tools could be used by both schools. I understand the tools myself — took the manual training course at Normal School and through our Inspector we could secure the services of a specialist in this subject to direct us now and then. The boys love this kind of thing. Before Easter, they made about two dozen bird houses to be put up in the trees and on the fence posts near the school, to help our little bird friends and keep them near us.

Hygiene lessons, actually put in practice are the only ones of use here. Miss Wells [the public health nurse] called to see us in Winnipeg and told us how to secure free tooth-paste and tooth brushes at reduced prices. We will have to use these at school. Miss Wells is coming up to this part of the country soon to make an examination of the school children and secure dental services free for the children. The case of eye trouble which you noticed when you visited our school will be attended to also. I fear it is a very serious one.

We appreciate greatly the opportunity of attending the Convention ... We went to the Parliament Buildings and got the necessary information about circulating libraries, also a supply of literature helpful in teaching Agriculture, Geography, and Civics.[23]

The final school term passed quickly. The school inspector gave the sisters a good report and recommended that Catherine's teaching certificate be made permanent for Manitoba, with a waiver of an academic course requirement. In mid-May, Sister Guest, who was not physically strong, succumbed to exhaustion and bronchitis and was put in the hospital in Winnipeg for two weeks. Even when she was released, she was unable to finish the teaching year. Catherine took over her school while Father Macieszek became a substitute teacher for a time. There were no arrangements for payment when a teacher was on sick-leave at that time, thus Sister Guest was not paid during her illness. Her total salary for May and June was only $49.50, and the loss seriously reduced the mission's available funds for food and other necessities.

Spring brought increased activity in the religion classes, as thirty-nine children were being prepared to receive their first communion. To the sisters, this was the most satisfying climax to their first year's work at Morton. They managed to provide the customary white veils for the girls and arm bands for the boys, and organized two days of services and receptions at the church to celebrate the event. As the school year drew to a close the inspector made his final call. He was very complimentary, and expressed the hope that both teachers would return in September.

Soon after the schools were closed, the Camp Morton staff returned to Toronto for a much-needed rest. On 15 August the four of them made their first renewal of their vows at the motherhouse; Sister Agnes Brunning RN, took her first vows and prepared to join Sisters Donnelly, Guest and Burke at Camp Morton. Father Daly appointed Catherine as Sister Superior of Camp Morton, as Sister Wymbs was being transferred to Vilna, Alberta, to supervise the opening of the order's first small hospital.

Early in September, Sisters Catherine and Mary Burke returned to Camp Morton and took up the now familiar routine. When Catherine retrieved King from the local farm where he had summered, she found that he was still lame from the winter mishap with the cutter. A search began for a new, heavier horse to relieve Pat. As Sister Guest was not arriving until mid-September, only one school was opened; but, as in the previous year, most of the students remained at home for another week, occupied with farm work. The good news was that improvements were being planned for the mission: electric light was to be installed in the convent and in the new stable and barn. The distressing news was that Father Macieszek would not be returning, and no priest was going to be appointed in his stead. Again it would be the sisters who would be responsible for leading the small congregation on Sundays.

Sister Guest returned and resumed school teaching, but Sister Brunning took over her Sunday catechism class. The latter was soon at home in the community, since she spoke fluent German and proved to be competent with horses. This was fortunate, for their new horse, Dolly Grey (Doll), turned out to be a strong, wilful animal who showed her displeasure by kicking the local farmer when he put her in her new stable and did not give her water or food. A few days later when Catherine hitched Doll to fetch Sister Guest from school, Doll objected, bucked, and with powerful kicks freed herself from the buggy and took off. The box, crossbar and harness were broken, and as the buggy flew apart, Catherine received a severe blow on her knee. She limped down to the lake to search for the horse. She found her, "standing motionless with her back to the lake and head up — a beautiful looking creature. I took the harness off and tied her to a fence till she'd be less nervous."[24]

To Do and to Endure

The next day Catherine's swollen leg kept her in bed and Sister Brunning took her class. Nevertheless, a few days later Catherine took the horse out for a drive.

The second winter, with its severe cold and worsened living conditions, again left the community open to infection. Five new students from two families who had enrolled in Catherine's school in February came down with measles. In a few weeks the cases of the disease increased to become an epidemic which closed the school from 18 March until after Easter. In May one of Catherine's students died of meningitis.

The greatest advance for the order that spring was the opening in April of the Winnipeg hostel for transient women and immigrants. Archbishop Sinnott and Father Daly had made an agreement with the Winnipeg Catholic Women's League that they would purchase and furnish a very large, handsome house, centrally located in the city, and the Sisters of Service would run it. Winnipeg was the strategic location for such a mission, for it was the gateway to the prairies, the route followed by all trains going west. The new hostel was intended also to be a useful temporary home to Sisters of Service when they needed a rest from their work in the rural districts, or had to come to Winnipeg for medical examinations, dental appointments, or for academic study during the summer.

Catherine made no comment on this important event in the Morton Annals, perhaps because she was preoccupied with a difficult problem which had arisen during the year with the four trustees who comprised the school board. The trustees allowed the schools to be used by the community for dances, but they did not arrange for them to be cleaned up before the students arrived at their schools for class on Monday morning. They expected the teachers to do the cleaning.[25] Catherine, as principal, warned them that this was against provincial regulations. The situation did not improve, and as they continued to ignore her protests, she reported the situation to the Department of Education.

When the time came in June to renew the sisters' teaching contracts, they were told that the trustees did not want to engage them any more. After Catherine informed Archbishop Sinnott, he went to see the secretary-treasurer of the board, who confirmed that "they appreciate and want the sisters, but they do not want the two sisters who are now teaching." As Archbishop Sinnott probed further, the

The First Mission at Camp Morton

whole story came out:

> The Sisters ... reported dances and other things to the Department, and the Trustees were in trouble over it. Everybody resented the action of the Sisters and they did not want them back. In fact, they would hire other teachers rather than the two Sisters.
>
> It was useless to argue with them. They blamed Sister Donnelly particularly and would have none of her under any circumstances. I showed them how Sister Guest had nothing to do with it ... They had nothing against Sister Guest, in fact they loved her. It did not take much persuasion to make them relent in the case of Sister Guest, but I could do nothing in the case of Sister Donnelly.
>
> Yesterday morning, Martin Keller brought me to the Camp the contract of Sister Guest signed by the Trustees in Triplicate, and another contract signed by the Trustees in blank. At my assurance, Mr. Keller inserted the name of Sister Donnelly, but I promised him that she would not come back ... You must send me another Sister in place of Sister Donnelly. No one realizes more than I do how hard Sister Donnelly has worked and what she has put into the work of zeal and devotion, and I am sorry to make such a demand. But you will realize that it does not mean any lack of appreciation on my part. The contracts are signed, but another Sister must be substituted for Sister Donnelly. Sister Guest must come back.
>
> Next winter I'll have a priest at Camp Morton and it will be more agreeable.[26]

Catherine left Camp Morton for Edmonton on 1 July 1926 after closing the schools and mission for the summer. Whether she knew that her signed contract was a fictitious one is uncertain; there were no entries in the records or her memoirs to indicate that her new posting to Vilna, Alberta, was for any other reason than to pioneer again in opening a new school. She carried with her commendatory reports on her teaching, gratifying recollections of the excellent rapport she had enjoyed with her school inspector, and fond memories of the children's eagerness to learn both their school and religious lessons.

The worth of all the difficult times endured in those first two years at Camp Morton was impressed on her by a letter of thanks that she received from Metro, one of her students, four months after she had left. Metro was a very bright boy, older than most of his class, quite shy and sensitive, and one of the most willing to help the sisters with any

139

heavy tasks. He was completing elementary school, and Catherine expected that he and one other boy would sit the stiff departmental examination required for entry into high school. As she was making out his application form he informed her that he had no intention of writing the examination. She was very puzzled and disappointed, for he had worked hard at his studies and she was sure that he had great potential. The more she thought of it, the more she suspected that loyalty to his parents might be causing him to hide the fact that they could not afford the $2 fee. To solve the problem, she hatched a scheme. She filled out the two application forms and sent in the $4 registration. The next day she spoke casually to Metro about writing the examination, as if she had forgotten what he had said.[27] When he still declared he would not be writing it, she said, "You must write, your application and fee have gone, and of course you don't need to return the fee to me. I want oats for the horses and I wish you would kindly bring me some." Metro smiled a little, and the next Saturday, looking much happier, he delivered three bags of oats. He wrote his exams; but Catherine had returned to Toronto before the results were announced, and after her move to Vilna she became preoccupied with another set of problems.

That autumn she received a letter of thanks from him. "I am a scholar again, something I never expected ... but for you I would not be where I am today ... I guess you remember. I always will."[28] Catherine learned that when word had been received that Metro had passed, Father Morton had offered him free room and board while he attended high school in Winnipeg. In half a year he had completed one grade and was on his way to a promising future.[29]

Progress like that made at Camp Morton in only two years was proof to Catherine that the new approach to the rural apostolate envisioned by her and Father Coughlan could produce results. The urgently needed medical services and education given by the sisters to people of any religious faith had gained them acceptance into the community. Money had been scarce but the continuing donations of produce from their farms and kitchens had been constant reminders that they were welcome. Lowering the barrier between the secular world and that of the religious order had helped persuade those who had been indifferent or hostile to the church to accept its ministrations. If only more teachers and nurses would join the Sisters of Service, what great opportunities awaited them!

CHAPTER 7
RETURN TO ALBERTA: PIONEERING IN VILNA

AT THE END OF THE SCHOOL YEAR, FATHER DALY decided that Sister Josephine Fallon was the teacher who would replace Sister Catherine at Camp Morton. In August 1926, Catherine, who had spent the summer in Edmonton attending summer school at the university, was told that she was being transferred to Vilna to be the Superior of the Vilna Hospital Mission as well as principal of the Vilna public school.

Vilna was a little town ninety miles northeast of Edmonton, mainly populated by Ukrainian, Polish and German settlers. The town was growing but its facilities were few. There was no Catholic church, and the lack of medical facilities limited the local doctor when he had to treat seriously ill or injured patients. The road to the hospital in Edmonton was long and winding and a hazardous drive in winter. The train came from Edmonton only every second day, after a trip taking many hours because of the lengthy and frequent stops along the route.

Archbishop O'Leary felt that the area's most urgent need was a small hospital, and suggested to Father Daly that this would be a splendid opportunity to introduce the Sisters of Service to the opportunities awaiting the order throughout the rural districts in his diocese. A nursing sister would be in charge of the small hospital and a teaching sister would be hired by the public school board to teach in the Vilna public school. The two male authorities decided that the hospital could be housed in an empty wooden building on the town's main street which had formerly been the local branch of the Canadian Bank of Commerce. They thought that part of the second floor of the building could also be sectioned off as a convent to house the sisters. When the archbishop presented the plan to the townspeople, they agreed to help pay for remodelling the old building into a hospital. In September 1925

To Do and to Endure

Father Daly purchased it for $1,500, with occupancy to be on 1 November.

Sister Catherine Wymbs had been assigned the task of designing and overseeing the building's conversion. Her final instructions from Father Daly were received shortly before she arrived in Vilna, and his note was typical of many letters of caution and support he would send to sisters undertaking difficult assignments.

> I come to you with a word of encouragement for I know you will find many difficulties in your undertaking. At times you may perhaps feel that the obstacles are unsurmountable, but I know that you are ready to give the best you have in you for the cause of the souls of the poor people with whom you will come into contact.
>
> Go quietly. Do not hurry. Take your bearings cautiously. Try, as I said, to collect the money from the people as they promised to give it when I met them with Father Hughes [archbishop's representative] in September. If you see that the money is not coming in fast enough, write to me and I will get in touch with His Grace the Archbishop and ask him to advance you what is necessary to start. Get acquainted with the Department of Health in Edmonton and take advice from them. Visit other small hospitals and get all the information you can before launching out. I repeat, you may at times be prone to get discouraged, but always seek refuge in prayer, and look ahead ten years from this when your humble beginning will become a factor for good in the community around you.[1]

When Sister Wymbs and Sister Geraghty, the young novice who accompanied her, inspected the building on 11 November 1925 their spirits had "dropped to zero" at the sight of the dirt and decay in the derelict building.[2] The basement was in very poor condition; it leaked badly, the water which had come in during the autumn rains was already frozen on the floor. There was a coal bin, but it contained more logs and scrap wood than coal. Sister Wymbs was more optimistic when she wrote to Father Daly a few days later, and described it as "a very nice building and should make at least a ten-bed institution."[3] The hot-air furnace was now working; she noted the water in the cellar had been drained. The sisters were cooking on a borrowed camp stove, and had already decided that the long bank counters could be remodelled to make a desk, a storage facility for kitchen supplies, and an altar. The last would be put in a room at the end of the hall upstairs, in the small

Return to Alberta: Pioneering in Vilna

section which, Sister Wymbs considered, would serve as the convent section and contain the sisters' bedrooms and chapel.

Contact had been made with some local residents and on Sunday Sisters Wymbs and Geraghty were driven to a farm eight miles from town. Here a priest stationed at a nearby Indian reservation came once a month to celebrate Mass for the owners, who were Romanian, and two visiting families from Vilna. Afterwards, everyone remained for dinner — "such a meal ... perfectly cooked and served. The mother and daughter-in-law do not speak English, but the men in the family understand very well. They are sending [us] potatoes and other vegetables next week."[4]

In two months the shabby building had been transformed into a small hospital. The main floor was divided into five rooms separated by a wide central hall. One side contained the doctor's office in the smallest room; a second room held two beds for women patients and a third room had three beds for men. The other side of the hall was divided into two rooms: an operating room which also contained the autoclave for sterilizing instruments and dressings, and a kitchen. The latter also served as a combined dining room, laundry and sisters' recreation room. The smaller area upstairs was sectioned into a maternity ward and a nursery, while the space under the eaves became the sisters' sleeping quarters. Their "rooms" here were small cubicles, separated only by heavy curtains. Each contained a cot and a wooden crate for clothes, and "you needed to stand with care or you really banged your head on the ceiling."[5]

There was no running water in the building. The well in the backyard had to supply water for cooking and drinking, bathing patients, and cleaning. To do laundry, the sisters used big wash tubs and wash boards in the kitchen. As one of them would record, "All water carried in, also had to be carried out!" The sisters' toilet facilities were an outhouse, located at the back of the yard over a ditch; and whenever the well in the yard dried up, they carried water in pails from either the railway station across the street, or the public well on the main street. There was no electricity in the town; the power to run the autoclave and light the hospital came from gasoline.

The first patient, a Ukrainian boy, had arrived on 12 December 1925; ten days later Sister Geraghty caught the measles. Clearly, Vilna was not going to be an easy posting. Yet the report of the government

To Do and to Endure

deputy minister who inspected the hospital six months later noted that:

> The nursing sister seemed to be a very competent woman and the wards, building, etc. were in excellent condition.
>
> I recommended the building of a chute from the maternity ward on the second floor as there was no adequate fire escape. This they agree to do.
>
> Dr. Eddy, a recent graduate of the University of Alberta is practicing in the place.
>
> Case records are well kept, order books signed.
>
> I was favorably impressed with the Hospital.[6]

In February 1926 another novice, Sister Fallon, arrived to teach in the two-room school. The government inspection report noted that Vilna General Hospital had "nine beds operated by the Sisters of Service, four of whom are in residence. One Graduate Nurse who is also a Registered Nurse, and three others doing the housekeeping. 3 Wards. 1 nursery." He had included Sister Fallon as one of the housekeeping staff! And true, she did help in the general duties when she was not teaching or preparing lessons.

Sister Catherine's position as Superior included the responsibility for administering the hospital as well as being principal of the school. She was also to oversee the financial affairs of the mission and, last but not least, she was the spiritual leader of the sisters on the mission. Her salary would be used to help defray the expenses of the hospital, for it had become apparent soon after the opening that the hospital venture would not likely be self-supporting.

As the year progressed, Catherine found that she had little time to rest. Five days a week she was at school all day, teaching the senior group, which included students from grades 5 to 11. She reported to Archbishop McNeil, "Our lives are quite crowded with duties. Crops have been a failure this year and money is not in the country, but we are holding our own so far. All the Sisters are well. God is good to us!"[7]

The real situation was more arduous than Catherine had reported.

> When she [Catherine] was free from school she would help with the cooking and other chores. Sister Pickup was night nurse. Sister Geraghty was officially the cook, but like myself, when finished with special chores we did dishes, cleaning and washing and ironing and anything else that needed doing.
>
> We had four or five men and women on the Main floor, also

The Clergy Co-Founders of the Sisters of Service

Archbishop Neil McNeil of Toronto.

Father Arthur Coughlan, CSsR.

Father George Daly, CSsR.

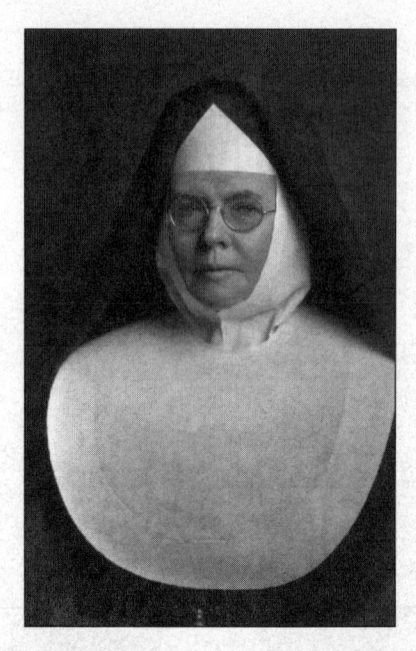

Sister Lidwina CSJ, Superior-General of the Sisters of Service, 1922-1926.

Sister Othelia CSJ, Superior-General of the Sisters of Service July 1926-1928.

2 Wellesley Place, Toronto, the Motherhouse of the Sisters of Service from 1922-1969.

The Motherhouse Chapel at 2 Wellesley Place where the novices made their first vows.

The novices with Mother Lidwina: L-R Srs. J. Stokes, C. Donnelly, K. Schenck, M.A. Burke.

Leaving for their first mission at Camp Morton: Srs. Catherine Wymbs, Margaret Guest and Catherine Donnelly.

The first SOS mission, 1924 – The house at the Camp Morton Mission.

Setting out for school 1924-1926.

King Edward School, Camp Morton, 5 miles from the house.

Recess at St. Brides, Alta. 1932.

Celtic school, St. Brides, Alta., 1932.

The medical-dental clinic arrives at St. Brides
The school was closed for three days while teeth
and tonsils were removed.

The house built for the Sisters at St. Brides in 1931.

The dental van at St. Brides.

The horse stable and students at St. Brides School.

Return to Alberta: Pioneering in Vilna

many minor accidents. Any children we had were on cots in any available space or in the hall. We enjoyed ourselves and though we had plenty of hard work, there were many things that were funny which helped us through our long days and nights.[8]

Their work was appreciated in the community. A writer for the local paper commented: "This useful institution was opened last December by the Sisters of Service — veritable guardian angels, I call them ... Altogether, Vilna [hospital] is a jewel on the plain."[9] But this local appreciation did not produce much revenue to fund the hospital, and the constant shortage of money was a nagging worry to Catherine. Soon the mission owed $1,134 to the bank, and their bills with local merchants were overdue. In response to her plea for money to placate her creditors, Father Daly sent $100 and promised a little more would be forthcoming. He cautioned her "not to worry too much about the financial side of your institution. Do what you can and God will do the rest."[10] He also expressed concern that she was working too hard at school by undertaking to teach so many grades, and advised that she cut down her teaching load next year to "allow you more leisure." He did not seem to realize that it was the Vilna Public School Board which decided on the number of staff they would hire. Catherine does not appear to have been consulted about her salary or conditions of work when the contract employing the order was negotiated by the archbishop. Yet, as principal, she was duty bound to answer the educational needs of all of the children enrolled by their parents in the school.

The hospital report which Catherine, in her capacity as Superior, submitted in May 1927 to Father Daly, stated that the hospital's receipts had totalled $4,136. This was made up of a $180 government grant, $346 from donations, $880 from Catherine's own salary, and $1,984 from dispensary and patients' fees. Under expenditures, only $1,236 was listed for "provisions" for both the patients and the sisters: a sure indication that they had lived very frugally and had been very dependent on the produce received from the farmers, many of whom gave donations of food in lieu of fees. They had no money to spare, for the final entry, "cash on hand," was only $1.20.[11]

The statistics on patients indicate that both patients and the sisters lived in very crowded conditions and that a larger hospital was desperately needed. The small building had received a steadily increasing stream of patients. During 1927 eighty-two patients were admitted; twenty-six had operations, six babies were born, and nine patients had died. They had also served 727 outpatients requiring examinations, prescriptions, dressings and treatments.[12] Hampered by cramped quarters and a small staff, the sisters had all worked to the limit of their strength to keep ahead of the work.

Father Daly wrote to Catherine that if they could be assured of a municipal grant of $1,500, he would consider building an extension on the hospital. "If this is not possible I would like to make some addition to your present premises, so as to give a little more privacy and comfort to the sisters."[13] He also requested her to write a short article for the order's little magazine, *The Field at Home*.

This letter also included other news. Their new Mother Superior, Mother Othelia CSJ, would soon arrive on an inspection trip. She had replaced Mother Lidwina who had to retire from her post due to ill health. Two sisters were being sent to Quebec to meet the immigrants on the boats arriving during the shipping season, and the sisters who had the double task of running the hostel in Halifax and meeting the transatlantic liners were still very busy. Father Daly was sorry to report that a young novice, one of the few trained teachers who had applied, had to leave the order because of a lung hemorrhage. Lastly, he advised that Father Coughlan had been transferred to a parish in Quebec, and Father Gerald Murray was now Provincial of the Redemptorists in Canada. This last bit of news would make it difficult for Catherine, as Father Coughlan was the priest on whom she still relied for spiritual direction as well as practical advice on her work. His transfer took him out of her orbit, and never again would she have special access to him through the personal meetings that she had enjoyed whenever she was in Toronto.

Catherine responded to Father Daly's request for a brief article with "Out Where a Teacher Is More than a Teacher," a short item which was published in their magazine's July issue. In it she noted that a Sister of Service teacher had a variety of worthwhile tasks, for as well as teaching, she could branch into social service work as well as giving religious training to the little ones.

> Each of these western schools is capable of such a marked individuality. That is a very interesting thing about them. They are filled with children who are very frank and trusting, many under no religious direction whatever from parents. Others have

attended non-Catholic services, prayer-meetings, revival meetings and the like, till they have become distrustful of all.

Mother Othelia's report of her visit to the western missions provided Father Daly with a realistic perspective on the working conditions of the pioneering sisters. She was shocked by their crowded and substandard living conditions at the Vilna hospital and warned Father Daly that improvements should be made soon or the sisters' health would fail and the order's work would not flourish. Indeed, Catherine had already had one serious bout of illness. She came home from school one day and asked what was "St. Anthony's Fire," as one of her pupils had come to school and announced that he had it. Sister DeMarsh told her he should not be at school or in contact with other children as he had erysipelas, a very infectious, painful, skin disease. Catherine caught it, and had to stay away from school while the disease had run its course.

Catherine made her third renewal of her vows on 15 August 1927 in Edmonton, and because she was preparing for her second year of teaching at Vilna, she was not in Toronto for the special celebrations which marked the fifth anniversary of the founding of her order. Father Daly used the occasion to issue press notices to the Catholic newspapers publicizing the latest evidence of the order's progress. To accommodate an increasing number of applicants, the Sisters of Service had acquired an imposing house on Glen Road in the heart of the beautiful district of Rosedale, Toronto, to be their official novitiate. The purchase of this property, which had been owned by Sir Casimir Gzowski, had been made possible by a generous donation from Mrs. Ambrose Small, in celebration of the order's fifth anniversary.[14]

In a stream of articles and public addresses, Father Daly joyfully reported the amazing progress made by the order in five short years. In Toronto, the Sisters of Service were in charge of a large hostel for immigrant women. At Camp Morton, Manitoba, two sisters were teaching in two public schools and another was operating their small medical clinic; a catechetical centre had been opened in Edmonton; in Halifax, another benefactor had given his house to the order to use as a hostel and headquarters for their port and social service work. The sisters were also in charge of a hostel in Winnipeg; in Alberta, small hospitals had been founded in Edson and Vilna, and another sister was teaching in the Vilna public school. The order also now owned a house in Montreal which was both a hostel for girls and a residence for the sisters meeting the transatlantic liners. Similar work had been started recently in Quebec City. Father Daly's reports and advertisements always included a plea for both more applicants and donations. The names of the donors and the amounts given, no matter how small, were always acknowledged in *The Field at Home*.

The down side of all of this successful expansion was that with each property purchase, the order was acquiring a large debt load of mortgages. There was little money to spare for easing the living conditions, and life on the isolated rural missions was particularly spartan. The sad fact was that from its founding, few qualified teachers had joined the order. This had been noted by Archbishop McNeil in his sermon at the ceremony admitting a new candidate:

> The many friends of the Sisters of Service will be glad to know that another has been added to the number of the Professed Sisters of Service. On the other hand we, who are more intimately connected with the progress of the Institute are somewhat disappointed at the small number of *teachers* that have come forward to dedicate their lives to this great work. It is not that teachers are lacking in faith or piety or seriousness of purpose. Last year twelve teachers gave their lives in a certain diocese in one religious order — not a large diocese — a diocese in Nova Scotia.
>
> Evidently the call is there and the response to a certain extent is there, but equally evident is it that it is a special call.[15]

This shortage of teaching sisters had resulted in fewer guaranteed salaries, which Catherine and Father Coughlan had anticipated would provide the order with the secure income to finance its social and medical apostolates.

There were several reasons why Father Daly and Archbishop McNeil always stressed that the city hostels for single young women should be an important part of their social outreach strategy. First, they met urgent and immediate needs, and provided a setting in which the sisters could make an early contact with recently arrived immigrants. Second, the skills involved in running a hostel made good use of the domestic talents of novices who did not have educational qualifications for entering teaching or nursing courses. During the 1920s the Catholic hierarchy became increasingly alarmed at the vigorous religious proselytizing being directed to the European immigrants by the large, prosperous Protestant denominations. An important adjunct to their religious message was their extensive network of social and educational services. Father Daly reported to Archbishop McNeil that the United Church of Canada was supporting 268 missionaries and assistants at eight-five missions, forty social centres, fourteen hospitals, and twenty-one schools, as well as funding several Ukrainian and Hungarian newspapers.[16]

Thus this dilemma of a shortage of Catholic teachers and little income to support those who were working with Catholic immigrants surfaced early in the order's history. Father Daly's policy of assigning more money and personnel into hostels to meet the urban female immigrant's immediate need for shelter and wholesome companionship would, as time went on, be a source of disappointment and depression for Catherine. She felt this policy was a short-sighted solution which sacrificed her order's commitment to an apostolate of meeting the long-term educational, social and spiritual needs of the families of the rural western immigrants. After school and in the summer the teaching sisters could teach the faith to the children and their families. In her view, organizing and managing city hostels for unmarried, transient women was a worthy undertaking for Catholic laywomen in the Catholic Women's League. But not only immigrants, but whole rural communities would be exposed to the Catholic faith in action through the caring, personal example of the sisters living among them. Until more teaching and nursing sisters were recruited or trained, the tension between two needed and worthy kinds of work would not be resolved.

The beginning of September 1927 also saw changes in the staff at the Vilna hospital. Father Daly appointed a new nursing sister who would take charge of the hospital and also replace Catherine as the Superior. From the founding of the mission, Vilna Hospital, not the little public school, had been the most important part of the order's work in Vilna, and the greater of the Superior's responsibilities. With the number of hospital patients increasing, it was obvious that a professional nurse should be the Superior of the mission. Catherine had been a conscientious administrator, but her professional expertise was in teaching and running a school, not nursing. When crises and tensions occurred among the overworked sisters, her lack of nursing experience and overload of responsibility were handicaps which hampered her when she had to solve hospital problems. What was most urgently needed, however, was a larger hospital and better living conditions for the sisters. In May 1928 word was received that improvements were pending as plans had been approved for a new and larger building. The Vilna Annals noted that that same month workers started drilling for their well, and on 1 June they struck water at 115 feet!

It was fortunate that these changes had been made before the school year began, for Catherine's teaching load would prove to be even heavier than the previous year. When school resumed in September 1927, she reported that pupil enrolment had increased and a third teacher was urgently needed. But the school board said they did not have any more money for staff. Catherine and one lay teacher would have to be responsible for all of the children. Within a few weeks, her colleague Isabel Davidson, who had been assigned the junior grades, had discipline problems with her Grade 4 pupils. As principal, Catherine made the decision to relieve her of teaching the troublesome grade and put those students in with her own group. All that year she taught grades 4 to 8 elementary, and 9 to 11 secondary, in one school room. Many years later this teacher recalled the situation and wrote to Catherine, "I shall never forget your help and support the year we taught together in Vilna (1927-28). You were a tower of strength."[17]

A milestone in the order's history had been reached in May 1928 when Father Daly and Archbishop McNeil decided that the Sisters of Service were now securely established, with personnel capable of accepting "full responsibility for their future development." The task undertaken by the Sisters of St. Joseph was completed; they would no longer be responsible for the religious formation of the postulants entering the Sisters of Service, and Mother Othelia would now retire from her duties as their Novice Mistress and Superior. Usually when a new order reached this level of maturity, it was granted the authority to elect its own Superior, Novice Mistress and councillors. This did not take place. The archbishop's decree stated that this was because "the Sisters of Service cannot now be assembled for the election of general Superiors."[18] Therefore for a period of three years he appointed Sister Florence Regan as Sister General, Sisters Kathleen Schenck and Carmel Egan as councillors, and Sister Margaret Guest as Mistress of Novices. At the end of that time, on 15 August 1931, members of the order would meet in Toronto to elect their general Superiors "according to regulations drawn up for that purpose." All of these women had entered the order after Catherine, and only one, Margaret Guest, now Superior at Camp Morton, was a teacher. The other three had been Superiors of hostels and had taught the catechetical correspondence courses.

No written records have been found which explain why Catherine, whose inspired insight and persistence had persuaded Archbishop McNeil and Father Coughlin to support her vision of a new kind of Canadian religious order, was its first member, and the founder of its first mission was thus passed over. The sisters who were selected to lead the Sisters of Service were her juniors in the order by at least a year. Perhaps Catherine's early outspoken misgivings about undertaking hostel work were remembered by Father Daly and Archbishop McNeil. Moreover, her feelings on that issue had not abated. As well, a shadow had been cast over her splendid work at Camp Morton by the unfortunate run-in with the chairman of the school board. Her forthright protests about the board's lax supervision of school property and unreasonable demands on the teaching staff, even though justified, were not conducive to a peaceful settlement of the problem.

But although the clergy ignored both her original contribution to the order and her considerable knowledge of the nature of immigrant society, Catherine never commented on what must have been a publicly hurtful decision. Perhaps the other sisters did not even think about the slight, because her contribution had never been told to the postulants when they were learning the history of their order. After Archbishop McNeil had announced that the names of Fathers Coughlan and Daly were to be entered in the Annals as the founders, Catherine had not pressed for any official recognition. Humility was one of the virtues the sisters were always enjoined to exemplify.

When Vilna school was closed in June 1928, a tired Catherine went to the order's Winnipeg hostel for a rest. Sister Church, on staff at the hostel, was scheduled to do a catechetical tour of southwestern Manitoba that summer, but at the last moment she was unable to go. Catherine forgot her fatigue when she was asked to take her place, for she was scheduled to visit areas where there were no resident priests, and prepare the children for first communion and confirmation. An

151

added enticement was that she had the use of a car which would enable her to visit centres scattered over a large territory.

Her first assignment was to spend a week in Minnedosa, a town 150 miles west of Winnipeg, whose Catholic population was English, Ukrainian and Polish. After calling on all the Catholic families in the town, she had garnered twenty-five children whose parents had given permission for them attend her classes, and one family offered to board her for the week. Another woman offered to teach the smaller children while Catherine took the older ones, for it would take marathon teaching sessions morning, afternoon and evening to cover the lessons in that short period. The weather was fine, and so instead of confining the children to a building, Catherine held classes outdoors. Once a day she took them out in the car, away from town to scenic locations nearby and taught them as she drove along. Her method was based on the philosophy that "Catechism classes are not so unappetizing when they are given among flowers and trees and there are recesses for picking flowers and berries."[19] "The boys were won that way. It didn't require two outings to make them feel at their ease and interested in seeing the course of study through till after Confirmation." On 20 July she had to move on, but the parents were assured that the archbishop would come to the town and confirm the class on 19 August.

Her next stop was Neepawa, a town eighteen miles east, where the local Catholic church was small, but very beautiful. There were several English-speaking Catholic families in the parish. At first only a few children attended, and it took several visits to the homes of the Polish and Ukrainian families to persuade them to allow their children to enrol in the class. The woman at whose home she boarded was a recent convert who

> threw herself into the work, helped me with the children's choir and came with me to the homes ... In the same town there's a very remarkable Catholic family, delightfully refined and most strongly Catholic. They worked wonders in the short time I was with them. They welcomed the Polish and Ukrainian children with such a beautiful well-bred spirit, it was inspiring to me. Once we got the little timid ones started they loved to come. They loved the singing, especially singing themselves. They began to love the religious instruction and prayers too, which were difficult at first.[20]

While at Neepawa Catherine encountered her first anti-Catholic

Return to Alberta: Pioneering in Vilna

opposition. Some local "bible students" took two of the children into their house to keep them away from the confirmation class. When the district priest was passing through the town he heard about it and went to the house demanding the children. "She harangued him about not teaching the Bible and about the wickedness of the Popes," and with the consent of the mother, the children were kept from the class. Catherine heard later that all the other children had been approached to abandon her classes but none did. On another occasion, she drove fourteen miles east to the village of Arden and called on several Polish families. When she told them the archbishop would be coming, they promised to instruct their children and bring them to the confirmation service and the celebration breakfast on 19 August.

Catherine then took an eight-day break from teaching, and went as prearranged to the convent of the Sisters of Our Lady of the Missions in Brandon to make her annual retreat. The obligation for an annual retreat was (and is) an important part of the Holy Rule of all Catholic religious orders. The Sisters of Service always arranged for this retreat to be taken away from their own small, busy missions, for this was intended to be a time for personal meditation and prayer, as well as a much-needed physical rest.

As she reflected on her summer missionary experiences, Catherine was moved by the memory of the eagerness of the children who were receiving their first formal religious instruction. The Catholic community too had accepted her, a sister who travelled and worked alone, away from the formal restrictions imposed by convent life. With freedom to accept their hospitality, she had used the opportunity to forge personal bonds with the children and their families. This was how she had envisioned the order would establish contact with the immigrant communities. In the towns, a start had been made on bridging the cultural and linguistic gulf between the Central European immigrants and the Catholic English-speaking citizens when the latter became involved in coaching the choir for the confirmation service, and organizing the celebration breakfasts for the newly confirmed children.

A refreshed Catherine returned to the catechetical trail and taught for a week in Russell, a small settlement eighty miles northwest of Minnedosa on a branch line of the Canadian Pacific near the western boundary of Manitoba. The tiny church was new and the congregation was very poor. Racially her class was mixed: "Polish, Ukrainians, 'half-

To Do and to Endure

breeds' Scotch, Belgians, and a Negro. Seven or eight adult Indians were [to be] confirmed. The Negro is a boxer." There was also a large class of young immigrant children who had never received any Catholic religious instruction. "The sign of the Cross, the Lord's Prayer and the Ten Commandments were quite new to them."[21] She also noticed that the houses of the Catholic settlers had no religious symbols on the walls nor books of any kind.

She taught the children from nine to twelve in the morning and again after lunch. It was a test of concentration both for herself and her pupils, as the weather had turned very hot. The adult class met in the evening. When the district priest and the archbishop arrived by train on 12 August, awaiting them were one young man for baptism, twelve for first confession and communion, and twenty-one for confirmation. In the afternoon her negro pupil was married to an Indian girl.

Catherine renewed her vows in the town of Oakburn three days later, in a little Polish church which had been founded by Father Macieszek, her former priest at Camp Morton. Only a mile away was a large Ukrainian Catholic church, and to her it was indicative of the fact that in Canada, neither at that time, nor in the foreseeable future, would this generation of disparate Catholic national groups worship together or integrate socially in their communities. She also saw that when the children were put all together in one class, taking religious instruction from her in English, they began to understand that they all shared a common bond of religion and Canadian citizenship. Her six weeks of teaching catechism had made her buoyant with hope:

> What possibilities there are in children, no matter of what nationality! They respond to sympathetic encouragement in such a marvellous way. There must be hundreds of Catholic children in every Western province who get little or no religious training.
>
> Surrounded by the rank growth of weeds I saw some exquisite cultivated flowers. It was the most glorious thing I saw; unselfishness, intelligence, culture, true piety.
>
> Among the Catholic children of the East, whom I have known well, I can truly say I have never seen any with a greater share of these charming qualities than had some children I taught this summer in Manitoba. The West is full of such flowers.
>
> Altogether, it was a delightful vacation for me, a holiday of thrilling adventure, full of inspiration — something worth remembering always.[22]

Return to Alberta: Pioneering in Vilna

She returned to Vilna for her third year as teaching principal of the school. It was a posting where she felt there were not the opportunities to work as effectively with the children and their families as she had at Camp Morton. She confided to Archbishop McNeil that although she had enjoyed

> two wonderfully successful years of school-work ... its not so satisfying as it might be. There is no organization so one can go ahead instructing the children. The church is only a shell and so far not heated. There is no place where one can welcome the children in and make them comfortable. The summer has given me a vision of what might be, and so I serve because I stand and wait.[23]

Catherine's letter pinpointed the difficulty of operating a mission in a location which lacked a local priest and a church building. The sisters missed the spiritual and moral support which was given by attending celebrations of the liturgy regularly, and the comradeship of working together with the priest in the common cause of the parish community. At Camp Morton, Father Macieszek had given them strong and sympathetic assistance, and he had appreciated their efforts to make meaningful for the parish the special holy days of the Christian year. The sisters' enthusiasm in arranging Christmas concerts, decorating the shell of their half-finished church at Easter and training the choir had all helped the people feel they were a community which had common values and traditions. That priest had used his religious authority to urge the men parishioners to complete the church building. After their initial resistance was overcome, it was finally completed, and became a community gathering place for times of celebration and sorrow.

At Vilna the sisters had to depend on the occasional visits from an itinerant priest for the sacraments, and Catherine could see that apart from the hospital, the sisters had no involvement with town life. She felt that the sisters and the Catholic laity, especially the children, were being short-changed by the lack of a priest. Father Daly recognized the problem, but he had no authority to remedy the situation as it was the archbishop who decided which communities could have a full-time priest. But Father Daly did draw the archbishop's attention to the problem:

> I hope, Most Reverend and dear Archbishop, that by now you

To Do and to Endure

> have given our Sisters in Vilna a priest who will be in their rather arduous undertaking an advisor and a Father. These poor Sisters, I can assure you from intimate knowledge, need all the spiritual help they can obtain. The mission is a hard one, and as far as religious influence is concerned, Mother Church has yet before her an arduous task.[24]

That year Catherine's teaching load did not diminish; the patient load at the little hospital continued to increase, and the sisters' cramped living conditions were still a trial. They were buoyed by the knowledge that relief was in sight as construction of the new hospital was proceeding well. During the winter Catherine caught a severe case of the flu and struggled with it for several weeks while she continued to teach. But she was heartened when Archbishop Sinnott asked her to embark on another catechetical mission for two months during the summer of 1929. She sent him a joyous letter of acceptance:

> School closes here June 28 and I could leave here next morning. Two months is a pretty short time to get over much ground isn't it? I am feeling fine, and the change is as good as a rest — much better. Last summer was so satisfactory because I could get around to the houses. I should hope, though, the next time to have more literature on hand and make the time count for more. I'm hoping to be ready for anything, and get over a lot of ground. Don't you think that what the children need is a welcome — they need us to believe in them! God willing, we can do something worth while at least, and I do hope our plans will materialize.[25]

Catherine returned to Winnipeg to pick up a car and her itinerary and set off for Roblin, Manitoba, a town on the provincial border. As she drove the 250 miles north and west of Winnipeg, the flat prairie farmland changed to hill country populated by people of French and Indian descent. She made her headquarters for a week at Duck Mountain, a hamlet twenty-five miles farther north. There had been a resident priest in the parish but he had left a few years before. His house, where Catherine was to stay, was still in fairly good condition, but little St. Clare church was only a shell and unfit for use in winter. She called on as many families as she could, and sent messages throughout the area that classes would be held in three different locations each day — in the church and two of the schools.

Catherine's efforts were well received by the parents, yet although she located fifty Catholic children, attendance at the catechism class was small and very sporadic. She was sure these children did not attend school regularly, many of them were behind in reading ability. They enjoyed the singing, but the catechism course would require further work, so she enrolled them in the course being given by the order's Correspondence School in Edmonton, hoping that when the lessons arrived in September, their parents would help them. She was told that the three public schools in the parish were taught by non-Catholic teachers. One little nine-year-old French-Canadian boy responded to her question of whether he was Catholic with, "Well, no, not much — just a little bit."[26]

On her return south to Roblin, Catherine drove about searching for Catholic families. The few she located had no way to get to a Catholic church, as only one or two had cars. The only religious training in Roblin was being given by the Salvation Army. She continued on to Russell, where she visited the families of the children she had instructed the year before. She was heartened to find that the majority had attended church regularly during the year. The Polish and Ukrainian children at Minnedosa, Neepawa and the surrounding hamlets were also doing well and fitting in with the other Catholic children in Neepawa.

The Sisters of Service were not the only Christian group to use the mails for instruction or send out religious teachers to travel the dusty prairie roads in the summer. In 1907 a western Anglican bishop had started a "Sunday School by Post" and by 1929, 20,000 people were on its mailing list. In 1920 an Englishwoman, Eva Hasell, originated the idea of sending caravans staffed by two young women, a driver and a teacher, to travel throughout the prairie provinces, especially searching out the immigrant communities. She had a private income, and each winter returned to England to raise funds for caravans and recruit crews of adventurous young women. By 1929 there were nine caravans which were receiving financial support from the Anglican Women's Missionary Societies in eastern Canada.[27] Catherine's papers never mention meeting any of these itinerant church workers, but she probably knew about them, and their presence would reinforce her certainty in the rightness and urgency of the cause to which she was dedicating her life.

Catherine returned to Winnipeg in August only to set out again, this time for the fertile farm lands around Boissevain in the southwest corner of Manitoba. It was an old settlement into which twenty Catholic Belgian families had immigrated in the early 1920s. They were good farmers and their new life in Canada held promise of prosperity. The men and a few of the women spoke some English, and were grateful for Catherine's interest in their children, about twelve of whom attended the town public school. They admitted that their only contact with the Church was through the priest from Deloraine, twenty-five miles west, who came occasionally and said Mass in a small farmhouse in which only some of them could be accommodated. They seemed to want a church in Boissevain, but when Catherine asked them why they did not build a little one, they replied that they had no capital for such a colossal undertaking. Their only ready capital was their hands and they were still trying to build secure houses for their families. The rest of the town population was nominally Protestant and she thought the Belgians might be concerned about anti-Catholic prejudice.

Catherine's last mission stop was Killarney, a hamlet ten miles east of Boissevain, where she found only three Catholic families and five little girls who were eager for lessons. At the end of the week she felt these bright, willing children were ready for their first communion the very next Sunday in Deloraine.

On her return to Vilna, Catherine prepared to move to Edmonton. She had been reassigned to work in the order's Correspondence School in Edmonton. The order had sent three sisters, led by Catherine McNally, to Edmonton in January 1925, fulfilling Archbishop O'Leary's early request to Father Daly that he send Sisters of Service into his diocese as soon as they were available. Their first task had been to conduct a religious survey of the five Catholic parishes in the city. Within three months they had located five hundred children, mostly of Polish and Ukrainian descent, who were attending the city public schools. For them, they organized religion classes at the city churches. They had then visited the immigrant families in the little settlements surrounding the city where there was no Catholic church. To their children, they offered to send weekly religious lessons by mail. Reverend James McGuigan, the Vicar General of the diocese, was delighted with the results achieved by Sister McNally in ten months, and informed Father Daly that "she and her companions will do more among these poor people than we priests can do."[28] In January 1926 the Edmonton Catholic Women's League helped the order purchase a large house on 85th Street to accommodate the Religious Correspondence School. The sisters were hard-pressed to keep up with the demands in Edmonton for their local Saturday classes in religion and also attend to the requests of increasing numbers of rural children who were enrolling in the correspondence courses.

Giving religious instruction by correspondence, mailing out and marking the children's answers was not Catherine's favourite method of teaching. But she worked at it conscientiously for she realized that it was, of necessity, becoming an increasingly important part of the order's apostolate. The isolated farm families were pleased to have a regular contact with the Church, and the children were delighted when the mail arrived with packages of papers and magazines addressed especially to them. Sister Regan, the Superior at Edmonton in 1926, had reported that 3,043 catechism lessons had been sent out, and 1,781 corrected; 10,900 papers and magazines had been mailed to the scattered rural Catholic population in Alberta.[29] Far more families were being reached this way than through teaching in the public school system. Moreover, this project attracted financial support from the Catholic community in the East. Those who could give only a few coins were assured that in so doing they were partners in an important missionary effort, for their contributions paid for the stamps for several children's lessons. Father Daly had been successful in persuading Frank O'Connor, the wealthy founder of the Laura Secord Candy Company, to donate $100 a month to the Correspondence School so that it now had a firm financial foundation.[30]

Catherine was exhausted from three continuous years of teaching so many grades in Vilna, and two summers of work in the summer mission field. Relieved of Vilna's hard physical labour and heavy teaching load, she benefited from a change of pace and tasks done in the quiet setting of the order's community spiritual life in the Edmonton convent. By spring she was revitalized and in April 1930, she requested permission to attend summer school where she could continue to upgrade her qualifications in preparation for returning to teaching as soon as possible. Sister General Florence Regan agreed and made the necessary staff arrangements with Catherine's Superior, notifying her that the course would start on 7 July, and authorizing payment of the fee of $15. "You will be teaching Catechism in the country and Sr. D. will live at the hostel."[31]

Summer school was all that Catherine had hoped. She enrolled in the first class teachers' professional course, and studied psychology, educational problems and school administration as well as an extra course in music methods I. At the conclusion, she wrote a twelve-page letter to Sister General Florence Regan recounting the experience. "I was steadily on the go from 9 to 4 ... but I enjoyed every bit of it and certainly needed it greatly." She had been particularly pleased to have as classmates sisters from seven other teaching orders, for together they had examined the enlarged roles now being planned for teachers. Their instructors stressed that the new methodology required teachers to become more involved with the social problems of their students and to communicate more with parents. She had also learned that the Edmonton School Board was now engaging only teachers with first-class certificates. Catherine reported also that the Depression was now affecting teaching opportunities. Several teachers taking the course did not have a position for the coming year. "Times are not any better ... there is no money in the country ... Domestics are asking only their board. I feel sure the distress this winter will be worse that ever and it was very serious indeed last winter."[32]

She was delighted when she received a telegram from the Sister General three weeks later, informing her that, starting in September, she and Sister Fallon would be teaching at St. Bride's School in the Edmonton diocese.[33] As usual, the employment arrangements had been made by Father Daly and Archbishop O'Leary, and the Sister General had only been involved as the conveyer to the sisters of the news of their appointments. At a meeting with the archbishop, Catherine was told that she was to start school on 2 September and that everything needed would be provided. Catherine's telegram to the Sister General confirmed that "We start school September the second near St. Paul Archbishop Gave us information everything needed has been provided we will report on conditions immediately on arrival at st birdes [sic] both ready for work will do our bit God helping.[34] The next day a telegram from the Sister General told her she would be in charge of the new mission at St. Brides, and that further particulars from her were anxiously awaited.

CHAPTER 8
SERVING IN A DEPRESSION-WRACKED COMMUNITY

THE HAMLET OF ST. BRIDES, 115 MILES NORTHEAST of Edmonton, had been established in 1927 by the Canadian government through the purchase of an eight-thousand-acre block of uncultivated land from the Saddle Lake Indian Reservation. It was then divided into fifty-one quarter sections (160-acre lots). The settlement was managed by the Soldiers' Settlement Board, who offered the lots to fifty families, who emigrated in the spring of that year with a priest, Father W.M. McPhee. Most of them were Irish, from the counties of Tyrone, Derry, Fermanagh and Antrim, with a few from England and Scotland.

The federal authorities had prepared for their arrival by first digging a well on each farm and breaking the soil on forty of their 160-acre lots. After the settlers had arrived, some of the land was fenced, and small houses were to be built for them. Each family was also given a grant of $1,500 with which to purchase livestock, a team of horses to plough the land, and some equipment. This was not free land. The terms were that all families were on probation for a year, and if they succeeded in settling in, they would be asked by the Soldiers' Settlement Board to sign an agreement to purchase their farm for $4,000. The board then held the mortgage with interest at 5 per cent, to be repaid in twenty-five years.

When the settlers arrived they saw a vast rolling plain where the climate and living conditions would be unlike anything they had experienced in the old country. They had to live in tents until the frame cottages were completed. There was no church or any other public buildings, and religious services were held in the open air. After the spring thaw the mosquitoes which infested the area hampered their work. They were unused to working large tracts of land; it was exhausting work getting the soil ready for spring seeding and building

To Do and to Endure

barns to shelter and store the expected crops and livestock.

No provision had been made for the education of the settlers' children. The nearest school was ten miles to the west, in the town of St. Paul, which was a French-Canadian community, and at an impossible distance for daily travel by horse. Thus while their parents worked, the settlement children were left to roam the prairie and amuse themselves as best they could. A small Catholic church was the first public building started by the newcomers; but it was only an unheated shell. Rooms which could be heated were built behind the church for Father McPhee. One of the settlers who was a qualified teacher started classes for children in the church basement, but attendance was spasmodic. The next common building project, however, was Celtic School, the small two-room building to which Sisters Catherine Donnelly and Josephine Fallon had been assigned.

The sisters arrived in St. Paul by train in late August 1930, and were driven by the Settlement Board agent to a small cottage on a deserted farm, two miles over a rough country road from the hamlet of St. Brides. No car, or even a horse, was among the necessities covered by the archbishop's declaration that everything needed had been provided. Their salaries of $1,000 each, negotiated by the archbishop, were barely sufficient for a minimum of supplies and equipment to furnish their living quarters. It was obvious that this cottage adrift in the middle of the prairie and far from the school, was an impossible location for the sisters. The land agent thought that another house, also on a deserted farm and "about" a mile from the school, would be available in a week or so. The rent was $5 per month, provided they signed a caretakers' agreement. No lease was possible, as both farms were for sale, but they would be given five days' notice to vacate in the unlikely event that the farms were sold. Optimistically, Catherine said that she and Sister Fallon could sleep temporarily at the school on the little folding cots if their dwelling was sold.

In her first report to the Sister General, Catherine commented on the poverty and isolation of the settlement. Although their land was fertile, and they were expecting an abundant harvest, the immigrants had few possessions, for they had left Ireland with very little money or goods. Few had cars, and distance and language separated the community from St. Paul, where two religious orders of French-Canadian nuns ran a school and a hospital. There was no telephone in

St. Brides, mail only came twice a week, and telegrams were very expensive as they had to be hand-delivered from St. Paul.

The school arrangements made by Archbishop O'Leary were equally as confused as the sisters' housing. The school inspector, Mr. Gibault, was also the official in charge of the administration and organization of the school. He told Catherine that there was a male teaching principal at present, and that three teachers might not be needed if more settlers moved out or some were deported. They would have to wait and see. Nevertheless, Catherine's first letter closed with the assurance that "We are really just fine and everything will be alright."[1]

Once school had started, Catherine wrote to Archbishop O'Leary reporting the delay in obtaining suitable housing. However, she was pleased with the little school; the rooms were bright and airy and filled with children. But she noted that:

> They have had many disadvantages and are backward, so there is a great deal of work to be done in the class-room alone. It's a pity the church isn't warmly fixed up for the winter, for the children's sake, isn't it? Some of them come four and a half miles to school, and several three miles.
>
> The landscape is pleasing and I don't think I have ever seen grander sunsets ... The people have been kind and willing to help us when they could. The children all show a real good spirit.

The archbishop responded promptly, noting "it is surprising how backward are some of those coming from the old land." He feared that nothing could be done about finishing the church as "the debt is too great."[2]

By mid-October it was clear that three teachers were required. Mr. O'Dwyer, the principal, was teaching in the church basement and Catherine had forty-seven children in her school room. She was happy planning new and interesting additions to their curriculum at minimum cost. Eaton's catalogue supplied the words for calling dance steps she had decided to teach the little children to perform at their first school concert. At her request, the Sister General sent the scripts of several of the plays, skits and poems that Catherine and her classmates had performed in the novitiate. She planned to introduce the older children to the fun and skills of producing a play. The concert was a great success and a first for the community.

To Do and to Endure

Fortunately the local farmers had moved the sisters into the cottage a mile from the school, just before the first winter storm struck with sudden fierceness on 16 October. The cold wind spurred Catherine to prepare their dwelling for winter. Manure and earth were banked on the north-end wall, and earth around the other three sides. Storm windows and a storm door were put on and coal ordered for the stove. In her reports, Catherine had not complained about the muddled housing arrangements which had necessitated scrubbing the dirt out of two deserted houses and settling in twice in the first six weeks. But she did admit that she and Sister Fallon had found the long walks to school and back very tiring. After school, the housekeeping chores awaited them; hauling and heating their water, chopping wood, cooking and cleaning had to be done before preparing their lessons for next day. They were pleased when Sister General assigned Sister Mary Bridget Burke to St. Brides as their housekeeper.

The arrival of cold weather made the poverty of the community more obvious; some of the children were coming to school in scanty summer clothing. Catherine requested her Sister Superior in Toronto to appeal to the Catholic Women's League for donations of warm clothing, shoes, stockings and underwear as well as outer garments, so that the children would not have to miss school. Catherine also asked for toys and candy treats to give the children at their first Christmas tree party at the school in December. The London and Chatham CWL branches and the motherhouse responded with large boxes, and every child received a Christmas gift.

One of the other benefactors who responded generously was a Miss Eleanor McMahon from the town of Dundas, Ontario, whose name appeared several times during the 1930s in Catherine's reports. She was born in 1865, and was a faithful attender of St. Augustine's Church. She was not a wealthy person, but she did her best to answer the appeals of the Sisters of Service for donations to the poor in western Canada. She did not send money, but she gathered up clothing, toys, house furnishings, religious and secular books, newspapers and magazines, and sent them by freight regularly for several years at considerable personal cost.[3] It was generosity such as this from people of modest means that supported the order's missions during the Depression. For the sisters' first Christmas at St. Brides, Catherine was delighted to receive a big box from Miss McMahon, whom she called their "fairy godmother," filled with clothing and hand-knitted woollens for the children, new blankets, quilts and curtains for the sisters, as well as preserved fruit and pickles and fresh pears. Shortly after, Eleanor McMahon sent altar linens for the church, and large quantities of Catholic literature and childrens' books. The latter became the nucleus of Catherine's classroom library.

The first glimpse of serious dissension within the community was revealed when Catherine reported in November that their splendid church choir had resumed practising. The choir and the altar society had been on strike for some time. No specific reason was apparent but Catherine felt that

> there is so much poverty and such large families, the people get quite excited over anything ... No one is satisfied to have anyone in charge among the people around here ... [The church] is not fit for winter use. The people certainly have a good excuse for not coming to Mass on Sundays in winter ... The people and Priest here are quite hopeless about raising funds to finish the church. Miss MacMahon [*sic*] of Dundas is making a drive now for a new altar for here, instead of these old boards. She'll get it too, I expect. She sent us a gramophone which she obtained from a friend and it has already given entertainment to quite a number. Sr. Burke enjoys it very much. It's company in the house ... It's wonderful to come in and find the house warm and supper ready.[4]

Transportation had become a priority for the sisters as Father McPhee and his car, on whom they had relied for transportation to St. Paul, were to be away from the parish for some time. Buying a car was financially impossible. Rather than buy a horse, Catherine arranged with Father Claude, the priest who replaced Father McPhee, to feed and take care of his team and cutter in exchange for their use. Her low opinion of his horse skills was obvious when she reported to Sister General:

> The new priest took the team out the other day and left them standing while he shut a gate. They ran away of course, and smashed the cutter. It has to be mended, but I think there will soon be snow and I'll have a way of getting to town — not enough snow for sleighing yet.

Catherine's first financial report to the Sister General revealed the precarious financial position of the whole community of which the mission was now a vital part. Prices for the settlers' crops had been declining steadily, and by the autumn of 1930 they were receiving only five cents a bushel for their oats. As the grain elevators were full of wheat, many farmers were unable to sell even at that price. Very few could pay their taxes, so that only $140 of the $600 due the two sisters for three months of teaching had been received. The bank had refused to advance money on the credit of the district, and even the teachers' partial salaries had only been received because the Soldier's Settlement Board had paid some of the taxes. The Settlement Board had then added these amounts to the mortgages which they held on their farms. The board had also been forced to build a stable at the school for the horses, as the parents had no money to buy lumber for its construction, and they would not send their children to a school where their animals would be unsheltered. Catherine reported that as a result of the community's financial crisis their mission was also $454 in debt, of which $254 was for unpaid bills for food and supplies bought from local merchants, and $200 for a bank loan.[5]

Part of the problem, in Catherine's opinion, was that many of the Irish settlers were not good money managers. They were not even able to manage the school properly and the inspector had to attend to it. "They got a good chance on these farms but they are a very easy-going, ne'er do well kind of Irish people."[6] Catherine did not take into account the fact that these Irish, like many of the immigrants, were unused to the Alberta school system of having elected school trustees in charge of a community's school. Most of them were not familiar with the details of the Education Act; thus in some areas, including St. Brides, the local school inspector was authorized by the Ministry of Education to attend to school business.

The sisters' isolation and confinement to the small cottage was one of the most trying of the conditions during that first year. The sisters at nearby Vilna urged them to visit their new, spacious convent whenever they needed a change, but there was no direct or easy means of getting there. Catherine longed to accept their invitation to spend Christmas at Vilna, but she felt they could not leave at a time when the priest obviously required their help to prepare for the Christmas services. The people showed their appreciation by giving the sisters several chickens and some vegetables for their Christmas dinner, as well as a live goose and two roosters. The latter were soon strutting

Serving in a Depression-Wracked Community

around their stable yard as Catherine didn't want to kill them. After Christmas, Catherine arranged for Sister Fallon to have a few days at Vilna, for she had been suffering for some time from fallen arches exacerbated by the long walks to and from school. Catherine drove her the ten miles to St. Paul in the cutter, where she caught the train. She also gave her permission to miss two days from school during the first week of January so that she could go to Edmonton for dental work and a medical consultation about her feet. Catherine taught Sister Fallon's classes as well as her own while she was away.

In January the community embarked on a sudden spurt of fund-raising, and formed work teams to finish the church. An interesting glimpse behind the scenes in the hamlet was revealed by Catherine's remark about Father Claude whom she had begun to admire after his misadventure with the horses. "The little French priest [from France] is doing splendidly ... speaks typically when attempting to speak English and is very firm but winning ... Father Claude is stopping the public dances — they are terrible affairs. He said today he'll go to the next one — and he will! He says little but acts promptly."[7]

For six weeks winter colds and flu afflicted all three sisters and by April Sister Fallon was showing signs of stress. Catherine reported: "I think it would be better for her to live in a place where there is less walking, a larger number of Sisters and not so much isolation. Sr. Burke is as lively as a cricket and interested in everything. She has been a real treasure here ... She loves the West — has become a real Westerner."[8] She concluded her letter with some cheering news: Father McPhee had returned; the parishioners, both men and women, had worked so diligently that the church interior was almost completed; and the Alberta government school grant had enabled the trustees to give the sisters "quite a bit" of unpaid salary.

In April the Sister General announced the summer assignments for the St. Bride's staff. Sister Fallon was to go to the Edmonton house for a short rest, and then to Vancouver to teach catechism. Sisters Burke and Donnelly were to return to the motherhouse in Toronto as soon as possible after school closed and they had closed down the convent for the summer. There they would prepare to make their final religious vows on 15 August. Their eight-day retreat before the ceremony was to be directed by Father Coughlan.[9] Catherine was overjoyed at the prospect of a reunion with her old adviser.

To Do and to Endure

Catherine then wrote a long, very frank letter to Father Daly outlining the options for the sisters' accommodation at St. Brides for the next year. The farm land around their cottage was leased; their rights to the building next year were uncertain, unless they paid rent for July and August to hold it. In the event it became unavailable, they could move back to the original cottage two miles from the school. In either case

> a car of some sort would be a necessity if we stayed here ... It is impossible to get out anywhere without a car, and there are no cars near here except the priest's. We just go to school and back, and to the church and back and that is all we have time for. We don't meet the people at all, nor see their homes. It's not exactly a satisfactory way to work. It's better to know the people don't you think?

Catherine had heard that Father Daly was trying to persuade the Church Extension Society and Archbishop O'Leary to build a proper house for the sisters at St. Brides. She boldly cautioned him that it "would be well to think twice about it." The priest needed a house for himself, which the men of the parish could build for him quite cheaply. If they built one for the sisters, it should be on a piece of land bought by the order, and not too near the church.[10]

Then she revealed the most urgent of her problems as Superior of St. Brides Mission. The first was her relationship with Sister Fallon, which was so serious that she didn't feel she could continue to work with her. Catherine had taken the primary class because Sister Fallon did not want to teach it. She had found it a good experience and had enjoyed the work. But this concession had not alleviated Sister Fallon's discontent. "She has been moody — extremely so — since the first day we came here ... I feel quite hopeless about being able to 'carry on' while associated with her." Catherine named another teaching sister, Madge Barton, whom she thought would be an excellent replacement for "she is bright and cheerful and ready to try anything which might be helpful."

The next problem was that "the idea of having a lay teacher for principal over sisters doesn't work so very well in a country place like this." In her experience in the city, she had seen men teachers taking some of the senior classes in the Catholic schools, but a sister was the principal. "The Sisters, then, have control of the school and get the proper respect. With a lay principal, the scope of the Sisters' work is

Serving in a Depression-Wracked Community

narrowed down till it becomes monotonous." Moreover, she had found that a man teaching in a little place like St. Bride's usually boarded with a local family and "is tempted to cater." She had been given to understand by Archbishop O'Leary last year that he expected the Sisters of Service would be teaching under a lay principal for only one year. It had not been easy, as "I have found this Principal so touchy that teaching is very trying. He has made grave trouble for me too with Sr. F." But she thought now that the situation might continue, for

> perhaps Father [McPhee] is in favor of a male principal because he can help him in many ways. He wants Sisters too for different reasons — to keep the altar linens clean and in order — and help sometimes in other ways around the church. To take the responsibility of the children knowing their catechism. To help out with meals for the priest. Sr. Burke cooks Father's dinner in our oven sometimes and he calls for it. She has him and Mr. Walsh [the carpenter who was living with Father McPhee] for dinner nearly every evening. He would like us to give his rooms a general cleaning-up when he happens to be away from them, but that is really a lot of work for Sr. Burke and we have no time. I think Fr. would like Sisters living near enough to him to take charge of his house-work entirely and provide all his meals. He detests cooking for himself and he can't afford a housekeeper.

She also felt that three teachers, whose salaries totalled $3,400, was a large burden for a poor community to support. "I think the whole school could be managed by two teachers without either having as much work as I had in Vilna."

Her final observation about the St. Brides assignment was a candid observation about the usefulness and suitability of the presence of the Sisters of Service in an Irish community with a priest and people still strongly attached to the culture and mystique of the religious orders they had been used to in the old country.

> I do not see why a community like the St. Joseph Sisters might not come here. I'm sure the men would build them a house. A community which has a good supply of teachers — music teachers also — would just suit this place. It doesn't seem exactly the place for our Sisters does it — as we can go where others would not be accepted, and here, its the old type of Sisters that would feel quite at home. I am ready for anything though except difficulties which one is sure cannot be overcome. The inconveniences of living

conditions don't worry me at all. Sr. Burke has been a wonderful little home-keeper.

Now that I have told you the way things are, any arrangement you may advise, would suit me.[11]

Thus, in spite of her conviction that the Sisters of Service needed to be freed from the restrictions that prevented them from having close contact with people, Catherine was beginning to see that the traditional religious habit, the strict Holy Rule, and the financial stability of the older religious orders did have important advantages. For although these were barriers which separated them from the world they sought to serve, the old familiar ways had also established, and then reinforced, the respect which they automatically received from priests and laity as easily identifiable religious. The Superiors of these other orders chose the tasks they would undertake within the mandates of their own apostolate, and specified the living and working conditions which enabled them to carry out their work effectively. If their sisters required further training to keep them up to date in their professions, there still remained others in the order who could take over at their place of work.[12] Their experience and expertise had become so respected, that these orders attracted many applicants with qualifications in the same professions as those which Catherine had hoped would be attracted to the Sisters of Service — that is, teaching and nursing. Because of this strong foundation, the Sisters of St. Joseph had been able to spare two of their most qualified sisters for six years, to complete the task of training the novices of the Sisters of Service.

It would take time for the majority of the Canadian Catholic clergy and laity to catch the vision of the opportunities which awaited the Church if only they would give recognition and financial support to a truly revolutionary order like the Sisters of Service. Catherine's view that the Church needed such an order in a rapidly changing Canadian society had certainly been recognized and supported by Father Coughlan, Father Daly and Archbishop McNeil. But Father Daly had had to struggle to raise the funds they all knew would be required to establish the order's financial security; in the 1920s the Catholic Church did not have proportionately as many members who possessed great wealth as did the Protestant denominations. Just when the Sisters of Service needed infusions of capital, the Depression had struck the Canadian working class with particular harshness, and it was this element which formed the majority of Catholic church membership.

In view of these circumstances, Father Daly's fund-raising efforts had produced amazing results. Yet he had stretched the order's financial and physical resources to the limit in order to open the new missions requested by those bishops who really needed the sisters' presence in their dioceses. Money was not available for anything but the bare essentials, and too often the Sisters of Service had to forgo even these. It was so at St. Brides, where, for example, the lack of a car was a serious impediment to their work among the poor and abandoned immigrants. Six weeks after the sisters had arrived there, the mother of one of Catherine's little Ukrainian pupils died suddenly. Father McPhee was away in Edmonton for three days, and Catherine felt badly that they had no way of getting to the farm to offer both spiritual and practical help. Sadly, she had written to her Sister General, "I suppose the poor woman was buried somewhere yesterday."

Catherine's mood seemed to have lifted shortly after she had exposed her resentment over Father McPhee's domestic demands. Perhaps this improvement came because Father Daly, on a brief visit to St. Brides, succeeded in calming her outrage that her sisters were being regarded primarily as housekeepers for Father McPhee, and in persuading the priest to be more tactful about his domestic needs. In her next letter to Sister General Catherine seemed more resigned to the situation, "Sister Burke often gives meals to Fr. McPhee and his friend the carpenter. They are badly off in that line. Father asked for a little help that way and Sister Burke certainly is kind to them. There seemed no other solution so I thought you would wish it."[13]

The school year 1930-31 ended with attendance much improved, and a large number of children were expected to enroll the next September. Catherine was very pleased with her pupils' academic progress, along with the community's success in completing its own church. There was now a confessional at the back; a new altar and railing were coming; names had been put on pews; and High Mass was again being sung by the choir. When they had closed the school, both sisters had signed contracts to return for the 1931-32 year. Their salaries would remain the same in spite of the fact that the boards of all of the other adjacent communities, including Vilna, had reduced their teachers' salaries. Catherine then sent another request to Father Daly about Sister Fallon:

To Do and to Endure

> I find it extremely uncomfortable teaching in the same school with Sister. Some improvement would be for her to take the primary room next year. They are more easily controlled. She is not able for a large class of lively children.
>
> Could you possibly make a change and have Sr. F. take one of the schools at Camp Morton again. I'm sure it could be arranged with Mr. Gibault to make the exchange. Sister would be happier in a little school with only one teacher. Her system of conducting school is so very different from anything I am accustomed to in Alberta, that I can't understand it. I really feel so depressed when I think of being in the same school with her again that I am almost ill and hopeless ... I am trusting that you will find some way of taking sister back to a Camp Morton school. She was bitterly disappointed on leaving there.[14]

In spite of her own difficulties with Sister Fallon, Catherine did tell Father Daly that the people of St. Brides had said they wanted the sisters to return to Celtic School.

On her return trip to Toronto that summer, Catherine stopped in Winnipeg for a few days, as she had been given permission to have a visit with Sister Justina, her "little sister," who was now teaching in a Winnipeg separate school. Then she and Sister Burke were given the great treat of returning home by boat from Fort William. They were welcomed back into the motherhouse family with great joy. Along with Sister General Florence Regan and Sisters Ann Geraghty, Catherine Wymbs, Margaret Guest, Carmel Egan, and Kathleen Schenck, they began an eight-day retreat in preparation for taking their final vows. These eight women, of whom Catherine was the oldest at forty-seven, were the first Sisters of Service who had stayed the course of yearly renewal six or seven times, and were now permitted to pledge lifelong commitment to the service of God and their order. The simple private ceremony took place after Mass in the chapel of the motherhouse on 15 August 1931. A few days were allowed for visiting friends and family, and then it was time for all of them to return to their respective mission posts. The Sister General and Sister Guest remained in Toronto at the order's headquarters, the latter as Novice Mistress. Sister Schenck returned to her work with German immigrants in Toronto, and Sister Egan to the Toronto hostel. Sisters Geraghty and Wymbs went back to the Edson Hospital Mission, accompanied by Sister Burke, who was transferred from St. Brides. Catherine herself returned to St.

Brides in time to prepare for the fall school opening. She had considerable preparation to do because her teaching assignment had been changed. Her pleas had been heard; Sister Fallon had been informed by the Sister General that in September she was to teach the junior class in the school.[15]

Father Daly had long been concerned about the lack of adequate housing for the St. Brides mission. Archbishop O'Leary declared that the diocese could not donate any money for a house, but the parishioners of St. Brides would supply the labour if Father Daly would buy the materials. After Father Daly had persuaded the Church Extension Society to give $500 for the project, Father McPhee stated that this would not buy all the building materials required. To complete a "respectable shelter" would require between $1,500 and $2,000, as the plan was to build a plain two-storey building 24' by 30'. He suggested, that as both sisters were receiving "a very fair salary," this money should be offered as security on a credit note for the building supplies purchased from the lumber company.[16] Father Daly rejected that solution. However, a site was obtained near the school, and during the summer of 1931 the basement was dug. When the time came in July to start building the house, the archbishop told Father Daly that an additional amount of at least $1,000 was required to build the house. Father Daly replied that he had understood that the house could be built for $500 and free labour, and that he was not in a position at that time to put more money into St. Brides. He regretted that the delay would inconvenience the sisters, but work on the house must be deferred until he could discuss the problem with them in September.[17] Some sort of arrangement was evidently made, for when Catherine reopened the school she reported to Father Daly that Father McPhee was trying to get the farmers to finish the basement. She was pleased that the house was on a good, well-drained site on a knoll just west of the church. "Mr. Walsh, the carpenter who stays with Father, is a real good carpenter — an artist at his work."[18]

However, Catherine's report on the local economic situation was gloomy. She painted a realistic picture of the effects of bad weather on a prairie community. The harvest was still lying in the fields, as it had rained day after day for three weeks. The wheat would therefore be a very poor grade and fetch low prices, if it could be sold at all. No financial contributions towards the church could possibly be expected

To Do and to Endure

from the people; she knew several families who were destitute. Among these were some whose men had been making illegal liquor with the little money they had received. Moreover, the Red Cross, which had been helping these destitute families, was out of supplies. School attendance, too, was unexpectedly low, because the children had no clothes. Catherine asked Father Daly to appeal for clothing for children of all ages, for they were in desperate need.

School was cancelled for the first three days in September 1931, as the sisters were occupied with helping to run a medical clinic given by a team of government health workers. This team had arrived in St. Brides driving vans outfitted with medical as well as cooking facilities, and with a cook and driver. In three days the four nurses, two doctors and two dentists had extracted over two hundred teeth, and given fifty-one anesthetics for removal of teeth, tonsils and adenoids.

Catherine's next big project was to organize the Celtic School entries for the annual St. Paul's school fair in mid-September. This was only possible because the mission now had a car of its own. When Catherine had returned to Edmonton after the great celebrations at the motherhouse, she was delighted to take delivery of a secondhand car which Father Daly had managed to procure. The rains were still making the roads nearly impassable, but Catherine put chains on the tires, loaded the car with the school's own contest entries and some children, and drove through the mud into town. She was followed by the parents with their wagons, loaded with more children, and their vegetables, animals and poultry. Catherine gleefully recounted that "We took so many prizes I haven't counted them yet ... firsts for the calf, pigs, turkey, writing ... the whole four turnip prizes — and many 2nds, 3rd & 4ths on other vegetables, sewing etc. Best of all the children got a real impetus to do better work."[19]

In spite of the bad weather, Catherine was optimistic about the coming school year. She expected to be able to keep up the payments on the car as long as their salaries were being paid. "Our car gets real good care, *I see to that.*" They were comfortable in the little cottage, although they had only the bare necessities

> We always get plenty to eat and its delightful to get into this warm little shack, after the day of mud and rain and cold ... The people all seem quite pleased to see us with a car. I hope Fr. doesn't take a notion to borrow it for he is not good with a car. His own is

174

usually out of order ...

Father is badly off for meals too. He and Mr. Walsh get their "one meal a day" at our house. I think we can arrange to get meat and some other staples wholesale. We are planning and hoping for some improvements on last year's prices for food — I'm sure we can manage it. Sr. O'Reilly [the housekeeper who replaced Sister Burke] is very kind and willing and Sr. F. seems more cheerful.[20]

The new teaching arrangement worked well, and Catherine felt that the general spirit of the school was greatly improved. She was now the principal; both she and Sister Fallon had large classes of about fifty children, and the new young male teacher, whom Catherine liked very much, was teaching a class of forty in the church basement. The children were all at varying stages of knowledge, since their school attendance had been so spasmodic. Each pupil had to be individually assessed and lessons prepared to raise all of them to their proper grade level. Catherine thought this process would take three or four years, but she felt optimistic that it could be done. Sixty years later, one of the St. Brides' students recorded her own memory of Catherine's work at Celtic School:

> The Sisters of Service came to St. Brides in 1930. They lived in a farm house 3/4 of a mile east of the school. Sister Burke the housekeeper worked hard to make living comfortable for the Sisters.
>
> The Sisters taught grades one to nine. Sister Donnelly was the principal and Sister Falon [sic] one of the teachers. Another teacher was Mr. MacDonald.
>
> Sister Donnelly was very strict but fair. She believed in getting things done today, not putting off till tomorrow. Her goal was to help each student achieve to the best of his or her ability. She believed they were capable of doing well. Sister was a born leader. She stressed the importance of school, church and home all being equally important in the upbringing of children.[21]

Work on the house was continued throughout the autumn, as Father Daly had managed to raise the extra $1,000 to buy the building materials. He and the diocese, however, signed an agreement which stated that this sum was a loan, and the terms were that "should the Sisters of Service at some future date be removed from this place it is understood that the parish of St. Brides refund to you or to the motherhouse of the Sisters of Service this sum of one thousand

To Do and to Endure

dollars."[22] Father Daly then explained the agreement to Catherine:

> I have been meaning to write to you for some time past to explain to you our position in St. Brides concerning the house Father proposes building for the Sisters. Seeing the difficulty of his position and the rather restricted quarters of our Sisters I agreed to get him from Extension $500.00 and I advanced for the building $1,000.00. Now this money was given to Father with the present restriction: — The Convent will belong to the Parish, and were we to leave St. Brides Mission one day the Parish would refund to us the sum loaned when they would be able to do so, and without interest. So you see in reality, my dear Sister, I have done this for the benefit of the Sisters. You have no financial responsibility as far as the house is concerned, and the building I left entirely in the hands of Father, only I asked him, which is only natural, to consult you in the matter as to the disposal of the rooms. Keep this for yourself, and if Father does not bring up the subject, let it lie quiet.[23]

With these arrangements in place, the house construction continued, but very slowly as it was too cold to build during the winter.

The rest of the year passed without incident. The school Christmas concert and party was a great success. Thanks to a large donation of gifts and clothing from the Church Extension Society in Toronto, all of the children at the Celtic School received toys and clothing. Catherine often said that she found it worth while to teach the St. Brides children because they were eager, bright and fun-loving. In spite of her criticism of some of the Irish settlers, she did feel sorry for them, as they had had a different vision of Canada before they left the old country. The realities of the severe extremes in the Canadian prairie climate, the loneliness of living on a vast plain with no immediate neighbours, and the mixed racial and cultural groups they encountered within the area had made their adjustment to the new land an unexpected ordeal.

Catherine spent the summer of 1932 in Edmonton attending summer school at the university with Sister Fallon. As they had finally moved into their new house in St. Brides, there was now room for Sister Agnes Dwyer, whom the school board had hired to replace young Mr. MacDonald as teacher. Catherine was very grateful when Sister Burke was reassigned to St. Brides to be their housekeeper. They would

Serving in a Depression-Wracked Community

now be a convent of four sisters, with Catherine as the Superior. The school year ahead looked promising, but Catherine herself had worries about Father McPhee and finances, and she sought her Sister General's advice. Father McPhee had hinted to her that he expected to do no more cooking. Catherine avoided discussing this by asking him for the present to just continue coming to the convent for dinner in the evenings. Mr. Walsh was still living with him, for the convent was not completed and much more work was required on Father McPhee's house — "enough to keep a carpenter going for a year yet. Then there will be other men too for meals, no doubt. How are we going to finance such an expense for boarding men?" The school board still owed the sisters $600 from the previous year, and she doubted if their salaries would be paid in the coming year. Teachers' salaries were an important source of income for the order; it distressed Catherine that her original plan to use this income to train sisters as teachers and nurses for the western missions was not working as well as she had planned.

> They seem to think the Sisters will do everything and wait indefinitely for their salary. I have been quite firm about it and have been careful to give the Trustees no excuse for thinking that we can wait.
> On the other hand, everyone expects us to pay promptly for wood, groceries etc. It is impossible to get loans from the banks. When they pay us what they owe us now, we will have to stretch it very far, and depend on very little in the future ...
> There will be very large grocery and meat bills if we undertake all the cooking Father MacPhee wishes us to do for him and his men. We will hold off a decision till we hear from you. The sisters will look after the sanctuary, Father's rooms and the altar linens.
> Unfortunately our water supply is not satisfactory. It would take an engine to pump it. When we do get it, it is yellow with iron and really unfit for washing white things. It will be necessary for us to get eave troughs on the house and a soft-water tank in the basement. Also, the pump will have to be fixed in some way to make it easier.[24]

The reply from Toronto instructed Catherine to agree to Father McPhee's requests and do the best they could for him; but by November the financial situation was getting serious. The Sister General's only suggestion was for Catherine to ask Father McPhee for some donations of vegetables and fowl, try to get a bank loan on the security of the salary owed to her by the school board, and use some money which Catherine had hoped to give her sister.[25] Catherine also decided as an economy measure not to use the car during the winter months. She felt this would not be too inconvenient as the roads were blocked with snow, and the horses and cutter were still available.

In spite of their poverty, the community's Christmas celebrations included toys and clothing for the children thanks to appeals to donors in eastern Canada. In gratitude, the people gave the sisters some of their farm produce. But in January there was no cash in the community to pay school taxes, as there was no market for their products. "One young man told me he killed a young beef and took it to town and couldn't get money at all — had to take store goods at 4 cts. a pound for the beef ... Wheat went down to about 14 cts. a bushel."[26] Only when a Ministry of Education grant was awarded in March, did the sisters receive the balance of their salaries owed them since June 1932.

At this time a local feud which had been brewing within the St. Brides community heated up. At first it was focused on the financial accounting of the former school board treasurer, but the real issue were disagreements between the community's ethnic factions. The Irish were a cohesive cultural group among other settlers of Ukrainian, Scottish and English origin. The whole community was beset with financial problems and the taxes needed to pay the teachers' salaries were, as Catherine had noted, a heavy burden. Their salaries, negotiated by the archbishop, had been authorized by the inspector and the three Irish board members who had hired the sisters. These issues and personal quarrels bitterly divided the community in the election for school trustees in April 1933. Catherine wrote to Father Daly, explaining that this situation pitted "three Irishmen on one side and opposing them were a triumvirate, an Englishman (Mr. Hornby), a Scot (Mr. McIntyre), and a Ukrainian (Mr. Sheput)." The opposition team got in by six votes, on a platform of lower taxes to be achieved through the lowering of the teachers' salaries. Catherine felt it was the Ukrainian vote, which the "Irish candidates never cater for of course," which had really carried the election. "The Board that got in canvassed and organized for weeks ahead, and allowed the communists to use the most disrespectful language against the Church."[27] This faction wanted a male principal, and the favoured person was Mr. Hornby's son, who

Serving in a Depression-Wracked Community

had not had a teaching job in the previous year. Catherine observed that in the past, "Mr. M. used to board the teacher ... about the only way anyone around here could get a little money."

Catherine was particularly distressed that the board planned to do away with the senior school rooms. This would, in effect, cancel the high school grades and limit the number of teachers to two, one of whom would be the principal. The salary to be offered was rumoured to be $600 or even lower. The board might, she thought, offer to keep one sister on staff at the lower salary. Catherine reported that she had been asked in February by the board secretary about the sisters taking an immediate decrease in salary. The inspector had been consulted, and he had advised that "we take $840, $840, and $900 from March 1st. I agreed to that, but nothing official has been done yet."[28] Another tactic being used to dislodge the sisters was the claim of the new trustees that Sister Dwyer was not qualified because she did not yet have her first-class teaching certificate. (She was only short two subjects, one of which she was due to write when the school year was completed.) Catherine felt this was unjust, as Sister Dwyer was a good teacher, was well liked by the students, "handles the people pleasantly, and at the same time in a dignified manner," and was conducting the choir with splendid results. Catherine wondered if she should resign if the board replaced her as principal, even though the Irish were very pleased with having a sister for principal and the inspector had spoken highly of all her work at the school. The whole situation was uncertain, but she told Father Daly, "We are all real well and thankful to be so."

Catherine's next report to Father Daly described the school trustees' open declarations that they could hire teachers at much lower salaries, and asked, "What is the lowest you would advise us to take? or would you advise me to take just whatever they would offer — even if only a couple of hundred each?" The vote had shown that the trustees did not have the support of the whole local community, but no opposition could be organized as "not an Irishman has a bit of influence at present ... The inspector can do little. They will not heed him." Catherine was ready to do battle, or at least consult the Alberta Teachers' Association about the whole situation. She mused, "I'd like to win in the game against these 'Reds'. Father McPhee doesn't enjoy a combat very much. He gets discouraged."[29] Catherine does not seem to have appreciated Father McPhee's dilemma in the squabble over which

179

group should control the school. He was caught between factions which included some of his own parishioners. Indeed, only the year before Catherine had written that "The organist is a splendid player and very religious and loves to play and help the choir. She is Mrs. Hornby who used to teach here." In his reply, Father Daly tried to rein in the feisty Catherine and advised her to

> ... ask Archbishop O'Leary's advice and follow it to the letter. I would not take the matter up with the Teachers' Association as this would lead to undue publicity and would eventually do us harm. Any how, if the people do not want us the field is big enough to go elsewhere ...
>
> Keep Father McPhee posted on your doings. Remember, he is your parish priest and everything must go through him. This is the way things are done in the Church of God ... Close no deal with them without communicating with here even by wire, if necessary.[30]

As advised, Catherine consulted the archbishop in Edmonton. He did not think the trustees were capable of managing the school, and said he would send a priest to the community to organize the people if the sisters were dismissed. But then Catherine pointed out that the board had the right to dismiss the teachers without stating a cause. At that, Archbishop O'Leary said he felt their only hope was for a change of trustees after the election in April 1934. He was truly worried about deepening the divisions within the community, and in the meantime they would just have to await developments.

With only a month of school remaining, Catherine worked ceaselessly to prepare her students for the important final examinations only a few weeks away. By the end of last teaching day she was very tired, but optimistic that her pupils would do well. They had worked right along with her, as they struggled to complete all the work in their respective grade levels. On the last day of school, Catherine was told that her contract was terminated by the board. On 1 July she wired the Sister General, "Each Teaching Sister here received legal official notice from trustees of the termination of her contract ... No reason Dismissal is signed by Hornby, MacIntyre, Sheput, Archbishop is being informed we expect to reach Vilna Sunday Edmonton Monday."[31]

Shortly after, the archbishop sent one of the diocesan officials, Monsignor M.J. O'Gorman, to meet the trustees in St. Brides. As

Serving in a Depression-Wracked Community

Sheput refused to attend, only Hornby and MacIntyre were there to face his wrath:

> He threatened them by telling them the Priest would be taken away and the Church and Sisters' House closed. The two of them were so frightened about what the Irishmen would do to them that they signed an apology to the Archbishop. Msgr. O'Gorman says they didn't do it because they were sorry at all, but because they were so scared of the people up there. Msgr. O'G advised His Grace not to have Sisters go back under the present Board of Trustees. He says that Father MacDonnell wired his Grace strongly urging that the Sisters stay away for the present.
>
> Rev. Father MacPhee [*sic*] ... reports that the Ukrainian Trustee has quarreled with the others and resigned. It seems that young Hornby was engaged at a salary of $900 and Mr. Sheput had a friend who would teach for $750.
>
> That leaves it that there must be another election for a third trustee. No doubt an Irishman will go in now. His Grace says, however, that it would still be one against two ... The apology for dismissing the Sisters is to be read in the Church on Sunday to the Congregation ...
>
> His Grace says the Inspector was interviewed and also the Department of Education and both spoke highly of the Sisters ... His Grace told me today that its all nonsense this thing of wanting a man for a principal ... Everybody dealing with the matter here seems to think the Sisters had better wait and not go back with John Hornby as Principal ... and his father as Chairman.[32]

During this uncertain state of affairs, Sisters Catherine and Dwyer attended summer school together at the university in Edmonton and lived at the order's hostel there. Catherine studied music and Sister Dwyer took her last course, which qualified her for her first-class teaching certificate in both Alberta and Manitoba. Some good news came from St. Brides, however, in the form of letters to Catherine from two of her students, Kathleen Maguire and Peter Boychuk. Kathleen Maguire said that she had passed five units of Grade 11. Catherine praised her for succeeding in the most difficult of the courses and told her she could review the other subjects and write them off when she took Grade 12. Peter had passed with high marks every one of the eight units he had written. Catherine was pleased to report Peter's success and that of the other students to Sister General.

> He was in grade X and I made him take Agri.2 extra. He is deeply grateful and wrote me a lovely letter and asked me what he should study next year. He says Francis McVea passed on everything too (8 units). 6 units is considered a very full years work so they have had wonderful success. Jack Maguire had all the exams to write for the three years of High School. He passed on fourteen units I think. No doubt Laura Hornby passed well. I haven't heard. The results of the examinations are excellent. I used to be in despair of ever getting the work taught for the attendance was so irregular. It was really a steady year's desperate struggle and I thank God it turned out so well.[33]

The results of the senior room departmental examinations were printed in the local paper with the student's name, subjects passed and grades recorded. Under the headline "No Better in Alberta," the paper noted that eighteen-year-old Jack Maguire, who had only been able to attend for seven months of the school year, had passed nine out of eleven subjects taken in Grade 11, and was awarded credit in seven subjects in Grade 10. He had arrived from Belfast, Ireland, three years before with his parents, who were now farming in St. Brides. The article concluded, "We think that the teacher, Sister Catherine Donnelly, is deserving of part of the credit for this boy's success."[34]

The salaries still owing the three sisters were paid by the Department of Education in late September, and Catherine used some of the money to meet the mission's levy for the support of the motherhouse. Another portion was spent on Catherine's own dental work which was long overdue, and the third portion paid for the fees and books for several summer school courses taken by herself, Sister Dwyer and three other sisters. Catherine had urged the Sister General to allow them to pursue summer courses that would upgrade their education, so that they would be eligible for teacher training. She was pleased to report to Father Daly that one of the three involved, Sister Domatilla Morrison, was now attending the Normal School.

Sister Catherine forwarded Sister Fallon's cheque to Father Daly with no comment, in spite of the shocking news that Sister Fallon had not been permitted to take her permanent vows, and had been "dismissed" from the order on 14 August 1933. As was customary, no explanation was recorded in the order's personnel records. When Father Daly acknowledged receipt of the cheque he made no comment about Sister Fallon's exit, except to say, "I am forwarding it to her and naturally leaving her the use of it, as it is the only honourable thing to do under the circumstances."[35] In this letter Father Daly wrote finis to the St. Brides mission. "As to the St. Brides issue, it is a dead one for the present as far as we are concerned. I met the Archbishop of Edmonton here and I told him that we will only go back when the Board will be changed."

The Sisters of Service never returned to St. Brides, but in the 1940s and 1950s they did establish teaching missions in other locations in northern Alberta. However, the matter of the financial obligation of St. Brides parish to the order was not settled for some years. Father Daly did not forget that the diocese still owed the order the money he had advanced to build the convent at St. Brides. The contract had stated that this was a loan, that the building belonged to the parish and if the order left St. Brides, the money would be repaid without interest. In August 1948 Father Daly acknowledged receipt of a cheque forwarded as "part payment from the parish of St. Brides. I presume that this obligation will continue from the new Diocese. The change of diocesan lines will not, I am sure, make any difference in the obligation of St. Brides Parish to the Sisters of Service."[36]

Father Daly did not find a teaching position for Catherine for the next year. He was becoming less energetic in locating public schools for the sisters, partly because so many of the rural school boards were defaulting on the teachers' wages, but mainly because he felt the hostels and catechetical schools offered more promising missionary opportunities. Catherine was assigned to the Catechetical School in Edmonton. She continued with her university studies as well, working towards her degree at the University of Alberta. Father Daly knew that she would find mailing out lessons and marking papers less to her liking than teaching in a school room, and ministering to the families of her students; but he tried to console her:

> I am glad that you are busy in the great catechetical work. It is quiet work, but the thought that you are reaching out to hundreds and hundreds of souls of children should encourage you. I look upon that piece of the S.O.S. work as one of the most beautiful and most consoling. His Grace, the Archbishop of Regina, wants me to start a similar centre for Saskatchewan; the matter is under consideration.[37]

Catherine could do nothing about his schemes to enlarge this aspect of the order's work. She only hoped that opening another urban centre would not drain away too much of the order's meagre funds and personnel.

CHAPTER 9
CREATING A NEW RULE FOR A NEW ORDER

ONE OF THE MOST IMPORTANT TASKS WHICH Archbishop McNeil had assigned to Father Daly was to draw up the Holy Rule and Constitutions of the Sisters of Service. It was a heavy responsibility, for according to canon law, each order's Rule was to provide the spiritual and constitutional foundation which would enable it to carry out the approved work or apostolate for which it had been founded.

The Rules of the religious orders of the Catholic Church were based on those written by either St. Augustine in 423 A.D. or St. Benedict in 540, and had certain principles in common: members were to live in a community and apart from the secular world; they were to take part in the community's regular, disciplined prayer life; they were to take perpetual vows of personal poverty, chastity and obedience to their Rule and to the Superiors of their order. As the number of religious orders increased, each one was obliged to compose its own Rule which, while including the ancient principles, would reflect in its particulars the vision of its founder. 'Approbation' of their Rule by the Sacred Congregation for Religious was the final Vatican declaration recognizing the new order's official status within the Church. The Rule of an order whose founding had been previously approved could only be presented to the Sacred Congregation for approbation "when the congregation should have sufficiently expanded, brought forth good results, given a good trial to its constitutions and are possessed of sufficient means."[1] The normal time considered necessary to achieve this was ten to fifteen years after an order's foundation.

The canon law pertaining to the religious formation of applicants to approved new religious orders which did not yet have their own Rule was very precise. They were to spend at least six months as postulants,

185

To Do and to Endure

followed by a two-year uninterrupted novitiate supervised by a Novice Mistress who would be on loan from an established order. Wearing the religious habit of her own order, she would live with the novices of the new order and they would all follow the senior order's daily routine and Rule. She trained them in the obligations and lifestyle they would undertake when they took the traditional vows to live according to a Holy Rule. The sisters in the new order could design and wear their own order's dress, and once out on their own missions they would live under an interim Rule, which included the distinctive principles proposed for their own order. It had to be composed by a clergy adviser and approved by the bishop (in the case of the Sisters of Service, the relevant two were Father Daly and Archbishop McNeil). During this interim period, the Rule could be amended until presentation to the Vatican authority for approval, rejection or modification.

Thus Father Daly would have to draft a formal version of the Rule of the Sisters of Service which would reflect Catherine Donnelly's vision of service as accepted by Father Coughlan and Archbishop McNeil during their discussions between 1920 and 1922. They had both agreed that hers was the most feasible and effective way for the Catholic Church to serve Catholic immigrants in remote rural areas. Sisters would provide secular and religious education for their children, health care to all people in their small communities, and through social work aid them to adapt to Canadian ways and undertake the responsibilities of Canadian citizenship. To achieve these goals, the Sisters of Service would have to break free of some of the most revered traditions and regulations of the womens' religious orders established in Canada at that time.

From 1922 to 1928 the applicants to the Sisters of Service were trained by two sisters of the Community of St. Joseph, who acted in the dual capacity of interim Mother Superior and Novice Mistress, and lived according to a slightly modified Rule of the Community of St. Joseph. Thus when Catherine began her religious formation as a novice of the Sisters of Service under Sister Lidwina, she obeyed a Rule with which she had some familiarity from her previous five-month postulancy in the St. Joseph's Community. According to her memoirs of this period (written after she had retired), she still felt that living according to the sections of the St. Joseph's Rule which restricted the sisters' free movement in the world outside the convent community

Creating a New Rule for a New Order

was not adequate training for sisters who were destined to have more personal involvement with the world of the laity. Essential to the success of their mission would be the freedom to travel many miles alone when necessary, to teach and to minister to people in their homes in remote western communities. Catherine's defiant refusal to undertake as their first mission the supervision of an Indian school in Manitoba was based on her interpretation of the order's purpose to avoid the impersonality of large institutions like boarding schools. Unquestioning obedience to her Superiors when she felt the original purposes of the order were being constrained or thwarted would always, for Catherine, be the hardest of the vows to keep.[2] But she did persevere, and at the end of her novitiate there had emerged a sister who freely accepted the sacrifices involved in the vows of poverty, chastity and obedience. She had undertaken conscientiously the cultivation of the virtues of humility and zeal, and a disciplined prayer life, which Father Daly had informed them would be the heart of their own Rule.

Father Daly had begun to draft the Rule for the Sisters of Service in 1929 when he had written to each mission telling them of the impending visit of the Sister General Florence Regan and Councillor Sister Kathleen Schenck: "As I am now re-writing the Rule, I am relying on the information they will gather from the visits to you, for the practical changes or new suggestions which would work out for the greater good of our humble but dear Institute."[3]

He worked on the text for some years before presenting it to Archbishop McNeil in late May 1934. Signing the document authorizing its presentation to Rome was one of McNeil's last official acts before he died a few days later. In composing the text, Father Daly had to keep in mind that canon law stipulated a certain style of presentation, "short, clear and well arranged," and in the acceptable language of presentation to Rome, which could be either Latin, French or Italian, but not English. Canon law also stipulated that the order's general objectives, principles, and daily schedules for prayer and study were to be outlined, as well as the particular disciplines which would indicate their obedience to separation from the world, even though they would be participating very actively in it.

The Rule of the Sisters of Service as formulated by Father Daly was unique among the Rules of Catholic religious orders working in

To Do and to Endure

Canada at that time, in that it introduced several novel provisions and omitted some traditional prohibitions. It was these changes which enabled its members to be in the vanguard of a movement to allow the Sisters of Service more freedom in their work and personal relationships with the secular world. The Rule justified these changes because they would work "for the salvation of the most abandoned souls ... especially in the outlying districts of our New Provinces, where the Church with the Country is still in the making [and where] the activities of the various non-Catholic bodies among our Catholic Immigrants have prompted its policy and particular methods."[4]

In the section detailing the religious work of the Sisters of Service, Father Daly wrote that they were "To be always and everywhere the hand-maidens of the Lord, the devoted auxiliaries of God's priests."[5] Such a clause was not in the Rule of the Community of St. Joseph or any other English-speaking order with apostolates in teaching, nursing and social work. One reason for this inclusion was that the sisters were assigned other duties along with the traditional tasks of preparing children for first communion and confirmation, and caring for "altar, ornaments, and linens of the chapels or churches in their district." They were "to gather together the Catholic people on Sundays, in the absence of the priest, say the Rosary, sing hymns, and read to them the Gospel or other spiritual book — all with the approval of the local priest."[6] The latter admonition was an official brake on the sisters' decision-making powers. Yet in practice, frequently and for extended periods, they would act on their own initiative and organize services for the laity, and also instruct male and female adult converts. Even when the mission was on a priest's regular circuit of rural parishes, bad weather, impassable roads, illness, or car breakdown could prevent his arrival. In this case, too, the priests expected the sisters would take charge and conduct a parish worship service, although it could not be a Mass.

Father Daly also took account of the fact that if there was no priest in residence at the mission station, the sisters would not be able to attend Mass and receive communion every day as they had during their novitiate in Toronto, and as was requisite for the sisters of all orders in the urban centres. In some locations a month or more might go by before a priest could visit the Sisters of Service at their little mission. This had occurred at Camp Morton during Catherine's last year there, when there had been no resident priest for a year. This irregular situation was taken into account in their Rule, where Father Daly had written that, after rising in the morning, following private meditation: "Mass and Communion will follow. Where there is no Mass, they shall spend ten minutes in making a Spiritual Communion. As this may often be the case in the missions, the Sisters should give great attention to this spiritual exercise."[7]

It was expected that their work of teaching and nursing would bring the sisters into regular contact with non-Catholics where proselytizing would not be accepted. Therefore the Rule defining the order's educational work simply stated that they were to "take charge of schools as qualified teachers in the Province in which they live."[8] Their Rule did not confine them to teaching in separate schools or demand that their pupils be Roman Catholic. Nor in their teaching and welfare work were they confined to Catholic agencies; the Rule stated simply that they were to "co-operate in as much as possible with official agencies that have in view the betterment of the people," and "co-operate with social agencies in their community."[9]

Both Catherine and Father Daly were worried that thousands of recent immigrants were receiving no government help to learn English, no instruction in the Canadian system of government or in their duties as future citizens of their adopted country. Hence, as well as finding suitable places of employment for newcomer women in hostels, the sisters were also to "help the immigrants to understand their new environment, teach them the elements of true citizenship, and assist them in every possible way during this crucial and trying period."[10] All this was added to their traditional role "to combat all proselytizing influences in order to safeguard the faith of these New Canadians and other Catholics."[11]

Catherine had insisted that even if they did some immigrant work in the cities, the order's principal efforts must be directed to their rural apostolate. To ensure that their work would be centred on the rural folk in small settlements, the Rule stated, "So that the Sisters may always maintain their missionary character, they shall not accept the direction of large boarding-schools, academies or orphanages."[12] Catherine's two clerical colleagues had agreed such work would detract from the intimate, individualistic character of their educational and social service, and also with her view that other Catholic women's orders

To Do and to Endure

were already doing this work.

The archbishop and Father Daly did disregard Catherine's contention that lay women could found and run hostels for single immigrant women in the large urban centres. Shortly after the order was founded, Father Daly had established a hostel in Toronto, followed as soon as possible by others in Montreal, Winnipeg, Edmonton and Vancouver. Many young women lived for short terms in hostels such as these, but they were never large institutions on the scale of the residences founded by the YWCA. That would have required more capital and personnel than the order ever had available, and such hostels would have been contrary to the mission of the Sisters of Service to provide personal guidance in a home-like atmosphere to young women needing temporary shelter and employment.

One of the most conspicuous of Catherine's breaks with tradition had been her insistence that the Sisters of Service discard the long, cumbersome religious habit, which up to 1923 identified the members of all female religious orders as women who lived strictly separated from the secular world. The Rule of the Community of St. Joseph and those of other orders as well, declared that their distinctive clothing was a "holy habit" to which it was "strictly forbidden to make any changes without the permission of the Holy See."[13] Catherine and Archbishop McNeil had agreed that the dress of a Sister of Service was to be much less conspicuous and confining, and easily maintained, as befitted women who would not be living in large convents supplied with all the conveniences and space of city houses. As she had once pointed out to Sister Lidwina, Catherine wanted clothing which enabled her to travel on horseback if necessary.

The Rule confirmed the clergy founders' support of this radical concept when it stated that:

> The uniform of the Sisters of Service shall be of a grey woollen material, and made in every detail according to the design adopted by the Community. In view of the nature of their work, it shall always be a uniform rather than a strictly religious habit.
>
> The head-dress shall be grey, with a white band, somewhat like that of a nurse. Sister General and her Council will decide if, in certain cases, the head-dress and the wearing of the cross are to be dispensed with, as, for instance, for our teachers in public schools, where wearing them could give rise to objection.
>
> The Professed Sisters shall receive at their profession a plain

silver cross with S.O.S. engraved on one side, and "I HAVE COME TO SERVE" on the other. A plain silver ring shall be worn after final profession.[14]

The wearing of the simple hat meant that the Sisters of Service did not cut their hair at the time of their investiture, as had always been done in the women's orders up to that time. As one sister recalled,

> In 1922 mature women generally wore their hair long, so the first sisters would have entered with long hair. Later when short hair was fashionable, cutting and styling could have been a problem to those not in the city. Long hair seemed to complement our uniform when worn in a bun or a braid. When the habit was modified, this called for other changes including hair styling.[15]

Their simple practical dresses and a small plain silver cross on a blue cord rather than the large, conspicuous crucifix worn by many traditional orders, identified the Sisters of Service as a Christian religious group with a charitable and educational purpose, and one that fitted in comfortably and unobtrusively with the laity. The Rule's final word on dress instructed that "If in the future, the present design of their costume should become conspicuous by its oddity, the General Chapter shall, with the permission of the Holy See, have the right to change it as they see fit."[16]

The remarkable personal freedom permitted Sisters of Service by their Rule was instituted by the omission of the usual clauses on enclosure in the Rules of the other orders, designed to ensure separation from the lay world. Sisters traditionally remained in the convent unless they were given permission by their Superior to leave. Permission had to be sought even for short errands or medical appointments, and they were always to be accompanied by another sister, or an approved lay female escort.[17] Nor were they allowed to stay overnight "even in the father's house, without special permission from the Mother General, who shall not grant it except for serious reasons."[18] In contrast, the Sisters of Service were allowed to visit their parents, and were even granted permission to stay a considerable time if a serious family situation justified their absence from the convent. They regularly went out alone by horse (later by car) to their schools in the country, and into the community to do their works of charity, even nursing the sick in their own homes if necessary. If they could not get back to their convent at night, they gratefully accepted the hospitality

191

of the local folk, whether they were Catholic or not. As a professional teacher, Catherine went to out-of-town teachers' conventions, and attended their social occasions with her lay, non-Catholic colleagues. When alone on such occasions, a Sister of Service observed the spiritual directives of her Rule privately, as it noted only that, in their public demeanour, "their zeal shall be always directed by obedience, governed by prudence, and accompanied by meekness and humility."[19]

The established orders reinforced their sisters' separation from family connections by changing the Christian name and dropping the family name of the novice when she took her first vows. The new name, that of a saint, was chosen for her by the order. Thus Catherine's young sister Mamie had become Sister Justina in 1918. In contrast, the Rule of this new order stated that, "The Sisters keep their family name."[20] Nor did they change their Christian names, because it was anticipated that their work would bring them in contact frequently with the secular and non-Catholic world, "and they were careful to avoid anything which might be a barrier. Requesting strangers to address them by a Saint's name might prove to be such ... to those not of the Catholic faith."[21] In their professional certificates and contracts for their work as teachers and nurses, they were always addressed by their own Christian and family names.

The vow of obedience for the established religious orders stated only that a sister owed obedience to her local Mother Superior, and the Mother General. The Rule of the Sisters of Service stated that in addition to "obeying the command of their legitimate Superiors in all that regards directly or indirectly the life of the Institute ... the duty of reverence and obedience to the bishop of the diocese and to the pastor of the district in which they are called to work shall be considered most sacred, and as a condition of success in their missionary life. They are indeed the handmaidens of God's anointed."[22] This clause confirmed the subsidiary status of women religious in the Catholic Church, as opposed to that of the priest and the male hierarchy. In spite of the considerable freedom which the established womens' orders had achieved concerning their internal governance and institutions — such as deciding who was to be admitted to the order, the extent and location of their vocational activities, and the control of raising and spending their financial resources — in practice their authority was limited when they

The First Final Profession; August 15, 1931, at the Motherhouse, 2 Wellesley Place. Standing: Sr. A. Geraghty, Sr. C. Wymbs, Sr. M.A. Burke, Sr. M. Guest, Sr. C. Donnelly
Seated: Sr. K. Schenck, Sr. F. Regan, Sr. C. Egan.

A trapper's cabin in the Cariboo.

The road to Big Bar Mountain Creek.

Driving through the 40,000 acre Koster Ranch.

Setting off to ride over the mountain to see Violet Grinder and arrange for her baby's baptism at a forthcoming Mass.

Big Bar Mountain Creek in congregation after Mass.

The Kostering family on the Koster Ranch at Big Bar Mountain. The Sisters parked on the open ranchland and ate at the ranch house. Archbishop Duke standing beside Mrs. Koster, second from right.

Sr. Catherine Donnelly with the Denardy Family and Fr. A.L. McIntyre.

Catherine's "dressing room" on the Koster Ranch.

Crossing the Quesnel River on the Cantin's ferry.

Sister Faye chopping wood for the dinner fire on the Quesnel River Camp site.

The Sisters lived in this rented house at Marquis, Saskatchewan 1938-1939.

The Chapel in the house at Marquis. Morrison Sillery made the furniture and altar for the Sisters.

Marquis High School Grade 12 Class. Teacher Morrison Sillery, front right. Sr. I. Faye, back left, Sr. L. Trautman, back right. 1938-1939.

After Catherine's troubles at Sinnett in 1940, she worked for three years at the Order's hospital at Edson, Alta.

Father George Daly with the 1937 General Chapter of the Sisters of Service.

Creating a New Rule for a New Order

worked outside in parishes.[23]

Catherine's own conviction that the nature of her new order's service would require freedom from the traditional monastic ascetic practices, such as frequent fasts and early rising hours, was written into the Rule in their "Order of the Day." Their rising hour of 6 a.m. was later than was usual in religious orders, and their food was to be "simple, yet wholesome and sufficient,"[24] and silence at meals was not obligatory. The old monastic practices that were retained included "the Great Silence" (no conversation in the convent from the hour of the night prayers, which were said in common, until after Mass the next day); "Before dinner Particular Examen [of conscience] and prayers of the Community Prayer Book"; and the short noon and evening recreation periods, that were "always to be taken in common." Each sister, moreover, was to spend one day a month in silent retreat, relieved of her duties, and annually, "five entire days on Retreat in strict silence."

In addition to its particular Rule, each order had a set of "Customs" which governed everyday behaviour and routines in the convent, and obedience to these was strictly enforced. Sister Lidwina had introduced the Customs of the Community of St. Joseph into the convents and novitiate of the Sisters of Service. These were retained even after 1928, when Sister Othelia CSJ, Father Daly and Archbishop McNeil had decided that sufficient numbers of Sisters of Service were now competent to act as Superiors and as the Novice Mistresses of their own community. Most of these Customs were retained for many years, even after the Rule had been approved. They were intended to reinforce the obligations of constant humility and obedience, whilst enabling the convent's Superiors to organize its domestic routine, and to supervise the allocation of duties. The most elaborate and strictly enforced of these was the necessity of seeking "Permission" for any contemplated action which was outside obligatory group activities or assigned duties. A sister had to make a formal request to her Superior for a myriad of activities: using the telephone for a private purpose, or writing a personal letter; taking even prescribed medicines; requesting an appointment with a doctor; discarding worn clothing and acquiring replacements; even taking a rest during the day, or retiring early. In a large convent this detailed control enabled the Superior to keep track of the occupants and of the many activities which were needed to keep the organization running smoothly, but they could prove petty and irksome when there were only three or four sisters living in a tiny house on a rural mission.

Customs also prescribed the penances for such breaches of convent etiquette and discipline as breaking a silence through banging doors or dropping things, being late for communal meals or spiritual exercises, or accidentally breaking convent property. To the novices, the long list of infractions seemed endless and trying, especially since a reason was never given for them. Customs could be changed by the members of the order at their annual general chapters. When the reform of the religious orders began in the 1950s, it was the obsequious, obsolete, and impractical ones which were first deleted. In the case of the Sisters of Service, who would often be sent out in twos and threes to a location where they cooked, ate, slept, worshipped and received visitors in the crowded space of a small cottage, many of the order's Customs which they had obeyed in the novitiate were not enforced. But to the best of their ability, they were conscientious about keeping the all-essential Rule, whose obligations could not be waived.

When, as a result of Vatican II, the Sacred Congregation of Religious instructed the Catholic orders to re-examine their purposes and lifestyle in the light of the new pronouncements on religious life, it was the revisions made in the Holy Rules of these orders which proclaimed the new approaches which were being taken. The most drastic changes took place in the traditional orders, but the Sisters of Service introduced changes too, including discarding their distinctive dress. But they had already achieved in their 1934 Rules and Constitutions the practical freedom which Catherine Donnelly, sponsored by Archbishop McNeil, Father Coughlan and Father Daly, had deemed necessary for an active apostolate in the twentieth century.

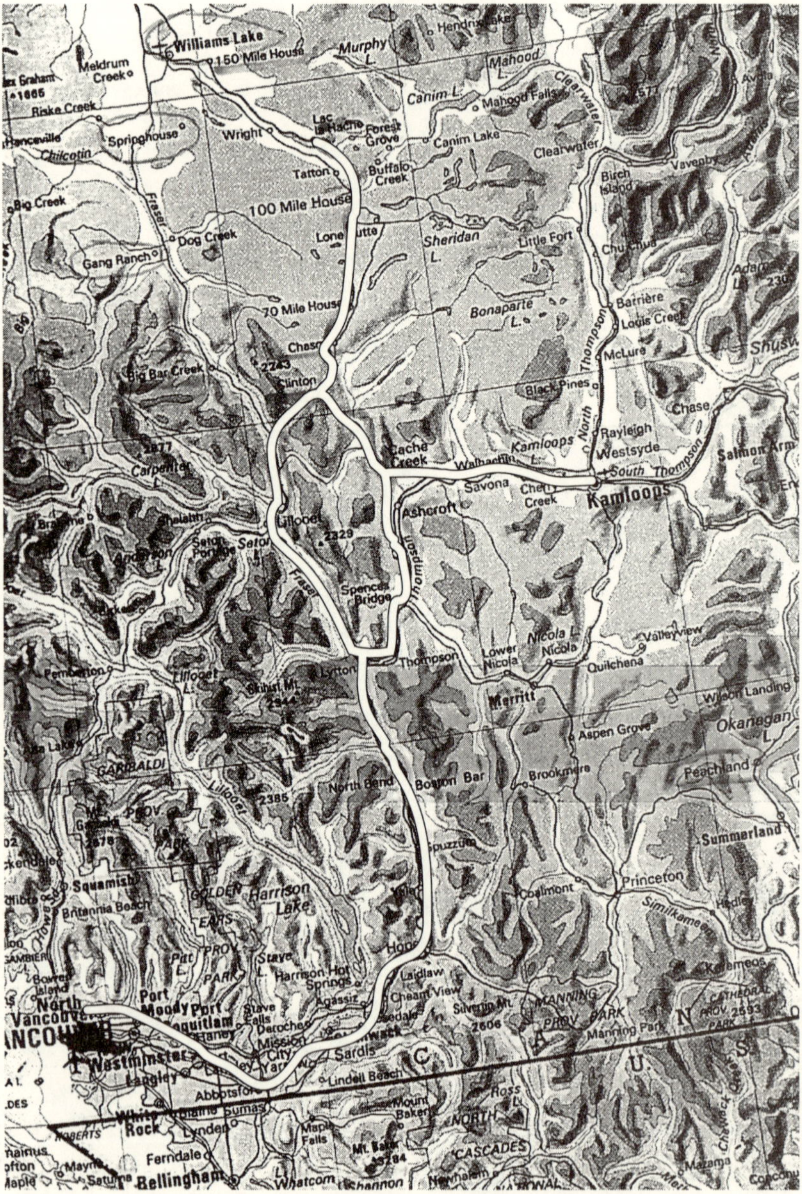

Williams Lake
150 Mile House
Murphy L.
Mahood
Meldrum Creek
Riske Creek
Canim L.
Mahood Falls
Clearwater
Springhouse
Chilcotin
Wright
Lac la Hache
Forest Grove
Canim Lake
Tatton
Buffalo Creek
Birch Island
Vavenby
Big Creek
Fraser
100 Mile House
Dog Creek
Lone Butte
Sheridan L.
Little Fort
Gang Ranch
Chu Chua
70 Mile House
Bonaparte L.
Barrière
Louis Creek
Thompson
McLure
Big Bar Creek
2743
Clinton
Black Pines
North
Chase
2877
Carpenter L.
Cache Creek
Walhachin
Kamloops L.
Rayleigh
Westsyde
South Thompson
Salmon Arm
Savona
Cherry Creek
Kamloops
Ashcroft
Lillooet
2329
Seton Portage
Seton
Anderson
Fraser
Spences Bridge
Thompson
Nicola L.
Nicola
Lower Nicola
Valleyview
Quilchena
Pemberton
Lillooet L.
Lytton
Skihist Mt. 2944
Merritt
Wilson Landing
Okanagan L.
GARIBALDI
Aspen Grove
Peachland
Lillooet
2385
North Bend
Boston Bar
Brookmere
PROV.
PARK
Summerland
Spuzzum
Squamish
GOLDEN
Harrison Lake
EARS
Coalmont
Princeton
Britannia Beach
Similkameen
Hope
Pitt L.
PROV.
Stave L.
PARK
Harrison Hot Springs
Laidlaw
Cheam View
Keremeos
Bowen Island
North Vancouver
Port Moody
Port Coquitlam
Stave Falls
Agassiz
Silverhope
MANNING
PROV. PARK
CATHEDRAL PROV. PARK
2606
Dewdney
Deroche
Mission City
Yarrow
Sardis
Manning Park
Westminster
Langley
Abbotsford
Lindell Beach
Sumas
Mount Baker
Ross L.
White Rock
Lynden
Maple Falls
NORTH
Ferndale
Mt. Baker 3284
CASCADES
Bellingham
Whatcom
Shannon
Newhalem
Mazama

CHAPTER 10
PIONEERING IN THE CARIBOO

FROM SEPTEMBER 1933 TO MAY 1934 CATHERINE LIVED and worked in Edmonton at the order's Catechetical School. She also took more courses towards her bachelor of arts degree, since there were no teaching positions available in the few Alberta separate schools. Father Daly did not actively search out positions with the provincial public school authorities, and it would have been a serious breach of discipline if Catherine had used her good contacts to search out openings on her own. Even if she had done so, the sisters might not have found employment in the public system. Rural teaching positions were becoming increasingly scarce as drought and falling wheat prices caused many settlers to abandon their farms and move to the cities in search of work and unemployment relief. Many other school boards besides St. Brides were unable to pay their teachers, because the farmers who continued to live on the land could not pay their taxes.

Thus the religious instruction given by the Sisters of Service through their correspondence schools became the most effective way of teaching the faith to the thousands of rural people who requested help for their children. Proof was in the large increase of students enrolled in the catechetical courses. The school's annual report in 1933-34 noted 3,274 lessons were corrected and 22,409 papers and magazines mailed. The next year the sisters corrected 5,140 lessons, wrote 967 personal letters and mailed out 32,468 papers and magazines to Catholics who could not have afforded literary subscriptions of any kind. The magazines were supplied by Catholic Women's League groups from Edmonton and Eastern Canada, as well as by individuals like Miss McMahon of Dundas, Ontario, who continued to send books and reading materials to Catherine wherever she was posted. Not untypical

To Do and to Endure

was a letter addressed to the Edmonton House from Chard, Mile 210, on the Northern Alberta Railway:

Jan 26th. 1934

Dear Sisters.

We were wondering if your Society is sending out Catholic literature.

We have been making our living up here since 1923. We have two children, one boy 13 years old, which we managed to send to school, at the convent of Lac la Biche for 4 years when our funds would permit no more, and another baby boy born a year ago.

We get the visit of our good missionary from [Fort] McMurray two or three times a year. Our nearest neighbors are 15 miles away, which we seldom see. We have no radio or gramophone, so you may well imagine that we are too much alone. It is to bad especialy [*sic*] for the boy.

If your service includes sending out literature it sure would be appreciated by us all. Either French or English would be very much welcome. French for the boy would be more appreciated, but English would do for all if you are sending only English. I am from French Canadian parents, but born in the States, and had only English schooling. My husband is a French Swiss, and can read both languages just as well also. We subscribe to "Our Sunday Visitor" from the States which I like so very much and read over and over ...

Some reading for the boy would help such a lot, especially Religious, as he is apt to feel or think about all the religious teachings he had at the convent as if they were more like Fairy tales for children. Though we sincerely try to teach him and pray all together every night and on Sundays. He is a nice boy though and not rough, is big and tall and works like a man. It is just from being alone and not seeing other children and people and not going to church often.

Thanking you and hoping to hear from you soon.

Sincerely yours,

(Mrs. Js. B. Currat)

Catherine responded immediately and received the following reply from Mrs. Currat:

February 2, 1934

Dear Sister:

Thank you ever so much for your nice letter, books, literature and Catechism Lessons. I never expected an answer so soon, and with such a lot of interesting things ... I was all excited about it and so was my boy, after he had read your letter, he said it was too bad we did not know and wrote before. My husband is away working at tie cutting, and will not be home for over a week yet. We will wait for him to see those lessons before sending answers in. The boy would like to send them back right away but I want my husband to go over them to. They are interesting and so instructive.

I wonder if you can imagine what it will mean to us all, to the boy, and to me. The boy will go out with his dad working outside and I'm always alone with my thoughts all day, nearly the year around, I haven't seen a woman since last summer. I remember one summer I saw only one Indian throughout the whole summer. I need some reading so that I will have something to think about while working, as I am quite busy with all kinds of housework. I like Religious reading we are so ignorant about our Religion, and can learn so much ...

I shall write next week to Miss McMahon. Thank you ever so much for giving me her address, and for all your kindness. Will write again when I return books, etc. We will pray God to bless you all dear Sisters for all the good you are doing.[1]

Letters such as these spurred Catherine to work steadily at her marking tasks. Her own academic studies, however, kept her ever-mindful of the changes in teachers' qualifications being instituted by the provincial departments of education. As she looked ahead to the time when more teaching positions would be available, she became increasingly concerned that there would not be enough Sisters of Service qualified to seize the opportunities to serve in rural schools. She pressed the Sister General to arrange for more sisters to undertake part-time study to qualify for their high school certificates and subsequent professional teacher training. Since the four western provinces each had their own teacher licensing system, she wrote to their respective departments of education to verify the grades and courses required for entry into their teachers' colleges. The Sister General approved of Catherine's suggestions, but funds were scarce, and sometimes the young novices who had only an elementary education were not interested in teaching, or were reluctant to undertake the strenuous high school program with its dreaded provincial examinations.

Catherine persistently encouraged the novices, particularly those who were assigned to the hostels and catechetic schools in the cities, to further their education to become teachers, nurses or social workers. When they did enroll in courses, she kept track of their progress as they worked at accumulating their academic credits. In this vein, in March 1934, she wrote to Sister General Regan outlining with approval the success and further potential of five sisters, who had been working hard at their studies, and suggested that another young novice on the staff in Edmonton would make a good student:

> I think it would be nice if she could go to High School next year. She could start in grade 9 anyway and see how she'd get along. She would make a bright and pleasant teacher.
>
> This is just my opinion. It would be better for them all to have several attending school at the same time. The majority of our Sisters have no inclination for High School work or teaching. Opportunities may yet be plentiful for schools — will be, if we keep on trying.[2]

Undergirding these ambitions for the order's future was her own joy in teaching, and her longing to be in the classroom again, where she could transmit personally her passionate love of academic and religious knowledge. She was excited when she was told a few weeks later that she was to leave in early May for the order's hostel in Vancouver, where she would join forces with Sister Irene Faye. They were to spend three months travelling into the remote valleys of the Cariboo district, in the interior of British Columbia, giving religious instruction to children in the little settlements which dotted the area. This new venture was part of Father Daly's strategy that summer to respond to as many as possible of the bishops' requests for help with religious instruction of the young, by sending into the hinterland mission fields every Sister of Service who could be spared.

Irene Faye was a twenty-four-year-old novice, originally from Toronto, who after taking her first vows in August 1933, had been sent immediately to join the staff at the Vancouver Girl's Hostel. A sheltered city girl, and not very robust, she had not acquired the skills or physique required for roughing it in the isolated, sparsely settled expanses through which the dangerous upper Fraser River flowed. But she was game to try, and eager to work directly with children and their parents.

The Cariboo is a two-hundred-mile series of mountain plateaus and valleys, bounded by the Coast range on the west and the Cariboo range on the east. Until 1857 it was inhabited mainly by various Indian tribes. The discovery of gold in 1857 had brought the first non-aboriginal settlers into the valleys whose creeks flowed into the Fraser and Thompson rivers. Soon, over thirty thousand prospectors were pouring into the area, in whose little creeks fortunes in gold were found. But unfortunately for the majority, the profits would be retained by only a lucky few.

In 1862 the Roman Catholic missionary order, the Oblates of Mary Immaculate (OMI), had built St. Joseph's Mission as well as an Indian school at Williams Lake in the heart of the mining district. When the easily accessible gold was depleted and most of the prospectors left, the ones who stayed became ranchers, lumbermen and subsistence farmers. Most of the homesteaders were very poor; they could earn money only by working on the big ranches of the few wealthy settlers, by lumbering and taking short-term occasional work when they could get it. The cattle ranchers owned huge tracts of land, and employed cowboys to look after their cattle. They would drive them to the summer pastures on the high mountain plateaus, guide them back down in the autumn, and drive those which were ready for market to the cattle auctions. Cattle ranching was a physically and economically risky business, for it depended on the owner's good health and business acumen, the cowboys' skills and reliability, and on good weather and good beef prices.

Father A.L. McIntyre, the priest whose mission territory covered the large area between Williams Lake and Clinton, heard of the work and lifestyle of the Sisters of Service, and felt they would be the ideal women's order to help him minister to the settlers. He appealed to Father Daly, who agreed to send two sisters to teach catechism for at least three months during the summer of 1934. It was Catherine Donnelly whom Daly selected to lead the way into this new, exciting locale. She was an ideal choice, for the task required a person of great physical endurance, who was also resourceful and unafraid of primitive living conditions, and at ease in meeting the varied social and racial groups she would encounter on the western frontier. She undertook the assignment with great enthusiasm, since the Cariboo could provide the ultimate testing ground for her conviction that a religious order of

To Do and to Endure

adaptable women with professional skills and an unencumbered lifestyle could be effective missionaries to many Catholics for whom the Church was not providing adequate services.

Father McIntyre's instructions were that the sisters were to drive to various hamlets in the Cariboo district and, keeping to his prearranged timetable, organize classes in religion for the children of his parishioners at the local school houses. The sisters had to be prepared to camp out or board with the local inhabitants he had selected for each of the two-week sessions. Father McIntyre was hopeful that they would attract the children of the practising and lapsed Roman Catholic families in each area. He said he would notify people who could give assistance to the women as they passed through. To reach these areas Catherine was to drive an Essex Super-Six car, which he decided would be better than a van for navigating the winding, steep mountain roads, most of which had no guard rails.

With Catherine at the wheel, the two sisters left Vancouver on Monday, 7 May, in a heavy rain which followed them as they drove east through the rich farm land of the Fraser River delta to Chilliwack, where the river swerved northeast to Hope and the beginning of the Cariboo Road. Their destination was Lytton, 180 miles northeast of Vancouver where the Thompson River joined the Fraser. They had expected to reach the town before darkness fell, but the muddy, narrow, twisting road, and poor visibility slowed their progress. They could not see the river, yet could hear it rushing along beside them in the dark. It was a wild, cold, weird sound that almost made Catherine shiver, but she shook off her fears by concluding that they were merely signs of fatigue from driving all day.[3] The final frightening drive up and then down Jackass mountain into Lytton was a chastening introduction to the motoring conditions of interior British Columbia.

They stopped overnight at a tourist home, and early next day drove to Clinton which was considered the gateway to the Cariboo, and the southern limit of Father McIntyre's "parish." All along their route they had met friendly, helpful people. At a gas station Catherine spent $6 of their scanty funds on chains, after being warned by the garage man that even steeper, muddy, slippery roads without guard rails lay ahead. On reaching Clinton, they lodged with the Smith family who always gave free overnight accommodation to the missionary priests when they came by. In the morning, a parting gift from their hostess

Pioneering in the Cariboo

was a packed lunch "to keep them going" until they reached their destination, Charlie Kostering's house on the Big Bar Ranch.

In the afternoon the food and the winding bumpy road made Irene Faye car-sick. Catherine noted in her diary, "cheese sandwiches and banana ... didn't affect me so. Nothing does. I can enjoy every kind of lunch and every kind of road without a fear of that kind of thing, thank the Lord. I have enough of other things to attend to." Sister Faye sang hymns to keep her mind off her misery. It was to no avail, and Catherine stopped the car and spread their blankets on the sloping rock of the mountainside so that Irene could rest until her heaving stomach calmed down. They stopped again a few miles farther on at Jesmond, where they collected their mail and bought gas for the car. A letter of instructions from Father McIntyre included the request that at Jesmond they call in at a Gus Haller's house, and notify him that Father would say Mass in his home on 23 May. He also included some directions on how to proceed with their work in this, their first camp-site.

It was after dark on 9 May when they arrived at the Big Bar Ranch and saw a house built up against a hill, where Father McIntyre had arranged for them to camp on the property for the week. Mrs. Kostering and her children came out to welcome them and she gave them supper. There was no level land for a camp-site, but they made do by parking the car in the best location, which was near the far end of the hen-house. This would be their base while they taught religion to the children in the area. The seats of their Essex Super-Six made into a car-bed, into which the two found they could fit, provided Catherine slept with her head at the back of the car on the driver's side, and Sister Faye put her head at the front and stretched out on the passenger side. Within a few days they had mastered fitting into the space which, although crowded, would at least be dry during the rainy months to come.

The next day they met Mr. Burtt, the teacher at the local public school, where they would conduct their classes, starting after school on 11 May. He gave them helpful information and advice about local conditions and offered them a four-gallon gas can for an emergency supply of fuel, and the loan of a coal-oil stove for cooking. He also advised them to always carry their chains, a good tow-rope (which he gave them), a search light, and an axe.

Eleven children were enrolled in their first class, including two

To Do and to Endure

Kostering girls and the Haller children. Sister Faye was very successful in capturing the interest of this group after she discovered that they liked to sing. She was particularly gifted in teaching choral music, and she began to rehearse them in hymns to sing at the forthcoming Mass in Jesmond. During the week Catherine also found time to call on other settlers in the area, including several non-Catholic families, who welcomed her warmly. One day she helped her hosts with the milking, the first she admitted that she had done in twenty years. By 16 May they had to move on as, according to Father McIntyre's schedule, they were expected on the other side of the mountain at Big Bar Creek. The sisters gave small parting gifts to the Kosterings, and were touched by their "teary" goodbyes.

They left the main Cariboo Road and drove west on a narrow precipitous trail, up around and down the mountain to the Grinder farm. It was only a few miles as the crow flies, but it was such a harrowing drive that for the first time Sister Faye was frightened and gasped, "We don't have to go down there, do we?"[4] They made it safely down to the farm on Big Bar Creek, and parked under a cottonwood tree. Mrs. Grinder, their hostess, supplied them with splendid meals for the week that they taught seven Grinder grandchildren at the local school after classes were over for the day.

The sisters found great gaps in their pupils' religious knowledge. When Sister Faye asked one of the children if she knew any hymns she replied, "I don't know what you mean by hymns." Neither the children nor their parents had ever heard a hymn, but they were so glad to learn some.[5] Thus with stories, pictures and music, of which they too were particularly fond, a second class and their parents were prepared for the forthcoming Mass which Father McIntyre hoped would attract a large congregation from the district.

He had also asked Catherine to visit Mrs. Grinder's cousin, Violet Grinder, to arrange for her baby's baptism at the church service. She lived several miles away on an abandoned sheep ranch which was accessible only by a narrow stony trail. Saddles were found for five horses, and Catherine and Irene, accompanied by Mrs. Grinder and her two married daughters, set off after lunch on Sunday, 20 May. Irene wore blue trousers underneath her SOS uniform, while Catherine used a wide black scarf which was draped across the saddle and hung down her legs on either side, with the ends folded loosely and pinned at the ankles. Catherine thought the scarf made fine chaps.

Sister Faye was given a quiet horse, Sailor, a pretty, plump bay which she was assured would stop if the rider pulled the reins. She found the journey a real test of her nerve and endurance, for as she later confessed:

> I never rode a horse in my life, but I made up my mind to do my best. A nice gentle horse was picked for me. We got along beautifully until he started to trot, and then I seemed to be going up when he was going down. When I got off the horse my knees were knocking enough to play a tune ... Coming back I was more used to the horse and didn't bounce so much, but I'll stick to the Essex whenever possible.[6]

They met Violet Grinder at the old ranch house, and she promised she would come to her cousin's farm on Wednesday to be there on time for the Mass at 10 a.m. the next day. Father McIntyre arrived at the Hallers' house on the 23rd, where he celebrated Mass. For the sisters, it was their first church service since they had left Vancouver. The service for the whole district was held next morning in Big Bar Creek Hall at 10 a.m. The children of the two classes which Sister Faye had taught sang splendidly, and when Father McIntyre questioned them on their lessons they answered well. The Koster and Grinder families attended, as well as many other local folk whom the sisters had visited. Only Violet was absent. At the end of the service she arrived on horseback carrying her two-month-old baby, and explained she had been unable to come the night before. She had ridden seven miles that morning, hoping to be there on time. Catherine was pleased to record that "the baby was baptized with all ceremony." Breakfast was an informal 'pot luck' arrangement in a beautiful picnic area overlooking the mountains. After photographs were taken, it was time to say goodbye, as the sisters and Father McIntyre had to drive on to Springhouse, their next stop eighty miles north.

> We shook hands with all the people before leaving. It is a nice custom with Father McIntyre. He is very careful to make a thorough success of this ceremony. The children we had taught, especially the Hallers, were very solemn about it, and seemed thoroughly to regret our departure and anxious to be in touch with us again soon through the Correspondence Course.

With Father McIntyre leading the way, the two cars loaded with the sisters' supplies and camp gear took off on the winding mountain road to Canoe Creek. Although it was hazardous, Catherine was struck by its beauty:

> A rare drive — one of those I shall perhaps never be privileged to see again. Once Father McIntyre stopped, got out of his car and came back to draw our attention to the vast outlook across the Fraser Canyon to the left — the great mountain piles reaching away and away, part of the Gang Ranch.[7]

They drove through the Canoe Creek Indian Reservation, met some Indian women, and inspected their little church, one of the two Catholic churches in Father McIntyre's Cariboo parish. At Canoe Creek their hosts were the Kosters, who owned a large ranch. Mrs. Koster had a delicious and generous lunch ready for them. Catherine noted with pleasure the attractive ranch house with its comfortable armchairs, large pictures of cattle on the walls, and pretty dishes. The Kosters ran a prosperous enterprise of forty thousand acres, which employed many cowboys to care for up to four thousand cattle and three hundred horses. Before they departed, Mrs. Koster donated $4 to the sisters' work, took out a subscription to *The Field at Home,* and gave them canned goods from her larder.

As they continued driving north, Father McIntyre introduced them to his parishioners at the farms along the way and also explained what he described as the "trigonometry" of some of the parish families they would be meeting. That some of the local marital arrangements shocked the sheltered Sister Faye was evident in her report to Father Daly: "Some of the parishioners are unable to receive the Sacraments as they have no regard for the moral law whatever. It is so common here that people think nothing of it. Father McIntyre says he does not think God will hold them responsible as they have had little opportunity to know what is right."[8]

She was nevertheless impressed by the warmth of the welcome wherever they called; Catholics and non-Catholics always offered them food and a place to camp if they wished to stop. At Springhouse, Father McIntyre introduced them to the families whose children he hoped would be enrolled in their catechism classes for the next two weeks. Six miles north of Springhouse they pulled into Williams Lake, the site of the first church built by the Oblate Order in the Cariboo. Catherine thought the design "artistic" and noted that everything was very neat

Pioneering in the Cariboo

and in good order in the two rooms attached to the back of the church for the use of the priest. Father McIntyre paid for an overhaul of their car, filled the gas tank and, as a parting gift, sent them back to Springhouse with a can of mosquito repellent. Their task was to prepare the area children and some adults for their first communion. They set up camp on the farm of Mr. and Mrs. James Isnardy, and with their help made a fireplace, backed by a piece of sheet-iron.

It took them a few days to round up their class, as many lived miles out on the back trails. Many times their way to a cabin in the woods was blocked by fallen timbers which they had to clear away with their axe, a skill at which Irene Faye was becoming expert. On one particularly difficult trip into Williams Lake on a cold, rainy day, the car skidded over a ditch and the front wheel jammed on a gnarled pine root. They chopped the root away but one of the car wheels was still suspended in mid-air. An elderly man came out from a little cabin and helped Catherine cut brush to put under the wheel to form a base for some gunny sacks he offered to place on top to give the wheels some traction. Sister Faye decided that this might not be successful and set out to walk five miles to Williams Lake for a tow truck. Just as the garageman was preparing to go for them, Catherine arrived, having won the battle with the ditch thanks to the help of old Mr. Millar. They had become better acquainted while they worked in the rain. She reported to Irene that he did not charge for his hard labour, but she had given him a dollar to buy himself "some comfort," as he had been ill and did not look well.

Both women were soaked, cold, and miserably tired. Sister Faye asked hopefully if they were going to stay in town for the night, as their camp-site at the Isnardy farm would be wet and they would have great difficulty lighting a fire. Catherine decided they should not stay in town as they would have to search for a place to sleep. She did admit that she too felt depressed about the wet camp awaiting them. When they arrived, their belongings had disappeared. Mrs. Isnardy ran over to tell them to go over to a little cabin nearby. It was formerly their milkhouse, and in it she and her husband had placed an old stove they had repaired, along with their camp supplies. Catherine stood in the doorway of an eight-foot square cabin, and stared at the stove through whose cracks and holes a fire was glowing:

> It smiled and beckoned to us to come in out of the teeming rain. It

was a never-to-be-forgotten sensation ... It was a royal welcome we received and [in] that little log cabin with its mud floor and its crevices stuffed with moss ... I felt like a queen in a palace and said so. The three-legged stove, though it was old and broken, rusty red, and its thin pipe edges all curled, was surely the most beautiful stove I ever saw ... Mr. Isnardy brought a sheep skin and spread it on the floor in front of the stove for our feet ... We got our supper and said our prayers and it was 1 a.m. before we left that fire.[9]

The next day Mrs. Isnardy asked the sisters if they would keep six of their children (aged two to eleven) while she and her husband fixed the sod roof of their farm house. The constant rain had so saturated the sods that water was dripping down the walls inside the house. They were going to cover the sods with some boards from their barn roof. The children crowded into the little cabin; the baby howled. An exhausted Irene Faye fled to the car which Catherine drove into a quiet field where she could sleep in peace. Catherine amused the children by taking them outside to gather kindling and pile up the wood which she began to split for their stove. "We had a real pleasant time in the rain ... The B.C. fir blocks split easily and are beautiful wood. To me there is poetry in a wood pile, and there is no more pleasing way of heating than a plain wood stove or fireplace."[10] The children returned home in the afternoon when the repairs were completed.

For two weeks classes were given nearly every day, for in spite of the incessant rain, the children would walk long distances out to the main road from where Sister Catherine could drive them to the school house. About seventeen were in the class, only four of whom attended school. The others ranged in age from six to sixteen and could neither read or write. Where the population in the Cariboo was so sparse and scattered, the schools were few and far between, which accounted for the high rate of illiteracy. School attendance was not compulsory if the child lived more than three miles from the school, and some families lived in isolated cabins away from a drivable road.

It was Irene Faye's first experience of a community in which the people had to do without schools and churches. "I never knew that a place could be so entirely ignorant of God and His Church."[11] Catherine commented, however, that although some were unschooled, their students were bright, and some were very witty. They liked the music that accompanied their lessons, although they were completely untrained. One day Andrew Westwick, who did attend school, told Catherine that next day their school teacher was expecting a visit from Mr. Lord, their school inspector. He remarked, "When Mr. Lord comes tomorrow wouldn't it be funny if we all sang 'O Lord I am not Worthy.'" (This was the latest hymn taught to them by Sister Faye.)

By 7 June Catherine felt she was making good progress, especially with the big boys who were listening attentively. They did grow restless when the sessions were lengthy, but she observed:

> They would make good students in religious doctrine if a teacher who would be firm and very active could stay with them. Evidently they have never been under control and have learned almost nothing. But at least the soil is Virgin soil. If there have not been Catholic instructors there have been no others, until lately the Anglicans have come. Communism seems to have kept away too.
>
> The children are good natured, warm-hearted towards religion, eager to learn when convinced they should. I'd like a class of fifty children like these. Only the gay spirit of the times which seems to find its way into the farthest recesses of the mountains holds them back a bit from attention to things of value.
>
> Adults are busy with horses and cattle. The cowboy rides the range, picturesque and self-sufficient, often as unrestrained as if he were living here a hundred years ago. Luxuries don't exist here and the arts don't flourish. And born amidst all this, the child is surprisingly free and easy, if not crude.[12]

At the Mass on 10 June, their last day at Springhouse, a class of eleven came before Father McIntyre for their first communion. Sister Faye's report noted that they had expected seventeen children would be presented, but one five-year-old was considered too young, and the parents of six children "would not let them come." She also noted that although many people attended, "the majority are unable to go to the Sacraments on account of the way they live."[13] Father McIntyre made it a special event for all who were there, regardless of their circumstances. Both sisters hoped that they had laid a foundation for growth in the years to come, but in her report Catherine, because of her wider experience, stressed that most of the community, which rarely met together, had made the effort to be present, and were participating in a religious celebration:

To Do and to Endure

> No Sunday Mass Service I've attended in city church or Cathedral has ever had the effect on me, that this worship has in the tiny log school with the teacher's desk for an altar. Here at Mass are the people of simple faith, no matter what the conditions of their lives may have been or are. Their sins are not the sins of the rich and sophisticated. They still believe in God. Their homes have no luxuries. They have no church. The children have never seen one. There is none to teach them except the lone Missionary Shepherd who travels constantly and smiles ever ... There could be no closer imitation of the Great Master, human and divine, who travelled over the hills and stayed in the homes of sinners, than a man who labors alone in this vast parish of ninety thousand square miles, without church-buildings or funds or a place to call his home.[14]

Again, photographs were taken, goodbyes said, and Father McIntyre guided the two Sisters of Service to the Oblate mission and the school a few miles south of Williams Lake where the five Sisters of the Child Jesus, who looked after the Indian school, had a convent. Catherine and Irene were very tired, and they were grateful for a comfortable room and the sisters' warm welcome. Catherine confessed in her diary that in spite of their good cooking and pleasant talk, she didn't sleep well in her comfortable bed. She felt depressed, because she felt the Cariboo people's poverty and lack of opportunity was giving some of them an inferiority complex which would blight their futures.

She felt better the next day after they arrived at Meldrum Creek when Father McIntyre joined them by their campfire for a few hours and talked about his work. Catherine found that he had faced situations similar to hers in his career, and had tried similar solutions. She realized that it was his ecumenical spirit, demonstrated by his affection for all of the people, regardless of whether they had a different religious affiliation or expressed complete unbelief, which earned him their respect and affection.

A typical incident happened the very next evening when a pleasant woman accompanied by three children visited the sisters' camp, and introduced herself as Mrs. McKay. Her children presented Catherine with a wild-flower bouquet and settled in for a chat. They told her about Father McIntrye's visit the night before to their beloved and very sick grandmother who lived with them. "He gave Grandma a prayer, would you please call at our house again tomorrow?" Catherine promised they would all come. As they left, they addressed her as Miss McIntyre, and it dawned on Catherine and Sister Faye that the family were not Roman Catholic, and they had become confused by Father McIntyre's talk about two sisters who would visit.

When they arrived at the house the next day, Mrs. Soules was dressed and sitting on the edge of her bed eagerly awaiting Father McIntyre. Although she was only sixty-three, Catherine noted that she looked much older. The priest sat in a chair they had placed for him. They chatted pleasantly for a short while, and Mrs. Soules told him that after his visit she had slept better than usual, and had been up early lest she would miss him. As he rose to leave, Father McIntyre told her he would bless her again:

> Eagerly and reverently her head was bowed under his hands as he said in English, the words of benediction. It was a great privilege for me to witness this. The family are all non-Catholics and this woman, at first, when Father came to the district was stiffly opposed to him and all priests. He has won!

To Sister General Regan, she confided: "Of course it was not her fault, and she and the rest of the family (all non-Catholics) have the courage of their convictions ... Such are the results everywhere of the patient efforts of this Apostle to the mountain people."[15]

The classes for the children at Meldrum Creek, which was their next stop, were cancelled after the first evening's lessons, as it was Stampede Week in Williams Lake and the whole community, including Father McIntyre, were caught up in the event.

The two women returned to the convent at the mission for a three-day rest, happy to return to a regular convent routine. They joined the sisters in their prayers and recreation, and enjoyed eating hot meals at regular hours, away from smoky campfires and damp firewood. Father McIntyre gave permission for the sisters at the mission to go out with Catherine for car rides, as they rarely left the convent. On their first jaunt, the Mother Superior came and directed them to a local store to see the beautiful Indian handwork on the buckskin garments and bags made by the mothers of the children who attended the mission school. She surprised her guests by buying each a present; Catherine was given a pair of white gloves with wide long cuffs, fringed and embroidered with violets; for Irene, she chose a sturdy camera bag and strap. On their final day Sisters Gonzalus, Trinity and Raphaelia of the mission

To Do and to Endure

came with them to Williams Lake to see their first stampede. Catherine's diary captured the hazards and excitement of the bucking contests:

> There were splendid outlaw horses and good riders. It is a cruel sport. The horse is to be spurred on the shoulders as soon as he leaves the corral. To win, the rider must stay on for eight seconds. Some riders went off immediately almost. The broncos escaped and were pursued by the cowboys. One little horse with lots of outlaw spirit jumped the fence and escaped to the mountains. It took six riders to round her up. We saw a horse bucking steadily and his rider remain till he must have been jerked to jelly. Then we saw the rider slip off behind. The horse fell also and one of the follow-up riders was so near that his mount tripped and fell over the other horse. The rider fell on his face. Next morning we knew who it was, Mr. J. Isnardy, our kind host at Springhouse. He came to Father's place to bid us farewell. His bruised lips and face told the tale. The cow-boy prize rider had been knocked out and Father McIntyre who was on the grounds had given him conditional absolution. These riders drink before they mount. One of the winners had taken so much that he couldn't talk but he certainly could ride. We left before the most dangerous and exciting performance — the mountain race.[16]

They left the convent next day laden with the sisters' parting gift of a big box of "goodies." At the gas station they met Mrs. Pinchbeck, Mrs. Isnardy's sister, who insisted they accept a dollar towards their gas bill. Their destination was the large town of Quesnel, fifty miles north of Williams Lake and more than four hundred miles from Vancouver. It was out of Father McIntyre's diocese, but it was more accessible from the south. Again he led the way, stopping at hamlets along the route and introducing them to parishioners. Quesnel had a church. A local member, Mrs. Lamb, called by and issued an invitation to Catherine and Irene to live in her house whenever they were working in the town; they accepted gratefully.

Two nights later they were camped beside the Quesnel River, at Gravelle Ferry, where Joseph Cantin operated the government ferry which took cars across the river. The Cantins were a French-Canadian family, and their farm was on the opposite side of the river near the ferry landing. When anyone wished to cross, they pulled a rope on a big bell which, Catherine noted, resembled an Ontario farm dinner bell.

Pioneering in the Cariboo

Across the river the Cantins' collie dog barked, and soon the customer would hear the sound of the cable as the ferry started up.

The sisters' task was to instruct the eight Cantin children for their first communion. They lived too far from the school, but their parents had tried to teach them as best they could until they obtained the services of a seventeen-year-old girl, May Probert, who lived with her aunt across the river and a few miles away. May crossed on the ferry two afternoons a week to teach them the elementary curriculum, but as she was not a Catholic, religious studies were not being included. Nevertheless, Catherine was very impressed with her, for it was obvious the children were making good progress and they loved their teacher. She observed that May dressed like a boy, as did all the young women in the area, and rode a "beauty of a saddle horse" with great assurance. She was amazed to be told that May shod him herself, for he had the most neatly trimmed horse feet Catherine had ever seen. "When she got off the ferry this evening, it dashed off home like a flying vision before she was rightly in the saddle, and I know how proud she was of the lovely creature. I've felt the same thrill."

Catherine came to admire the Cantin family. The parents were interested in the children's catechism lessons and enjoyed this rare chance to learn more about their religion. They taught their children to be kind and helpful, and were excellent examples themselves. They even took the trouble to set up a good camp stove and erect a canvas shelter to keep the sisters' wood and supplies out of the ever-present rain. In spite of the fact that isolation and distance kept the family's education and religious knowledge at the bare minimum, Catherine reflected that "they are better living away out here than in the wicked little towns."[17] Catherine wrote this rare judgmental remark about Cariboo townlife in a mood similar to that which had overcome her years before, during the Spanish flu epidemic. This time, however, she had no doubts about what her role should be in righting what she had discerned was absence of opportunity to learn spiritual values, and acquire even a basic education. She rejoiced that now she and Irene Faye, along with other Sisters of Service, were being recognized as capable of working in places like the Cariboo, combatting ignorance and materialism in partnership with priests like Father McIntyre.

When the rain ceased a few days later, camping at Gravelle Ferry became very pleasant. Catherine and Irene crossed the river in morning

To Do and to Endure

sunshine, taught the children and returned to camp in the evening to eat venison, vegetables and strawberry pie supplied by the Cantin family. On 26 June, Father McIntyre conducted Mass at the Cantin house in which their five daughters and one son participated for the first time. Catherine could not help but notice that the little girls did not wear the dresses usually donned for first communion, and realized that they did not own any. After having experienced some of the privations that were part of everyday life in the Cariboo, she concluded that such customs were unimportant details.

That same day they returned to Quesnel, and enjoyed the luxury of living in a house for four days with the hospitable Lamb family. They visited several other Catholic families in the town, toured the small cottage hospital, and met Dr. Barker, the town doctor, whose medical exploits were a legend in the area. One day was devoted to a visit to the once famous but now deserted mining town of Barkerville, sixty miles east. Catherine was fascinated by its colourful history, its derelict buildings and the relics of gold mining on exhibit in the hotel, which appeared to be the only business still functioning in the town. On their return visit south they stayed again with the Sisters of the Child Jesus at the OMI Mission and met the famous Father F.M. Thomas, the pioneer priest in the Cariboo, whose sole responsibility, since Father McIntyre's arrival, was working exclusively among the various Indian tribes in the area.

On 2 July Catherine and Irene set out again with Father McIntyre, this time for the settlements fifty miles to the southeast which were on the list of seventy-five mission locations which he tried to visit at least once a year. The rains had started again and driving continued to be difficult. In two weeks they managed to visit Catholic families scattered around the communities of Forest Grove, Bradley Creek and Bridge Lake and give shortened courses of a few days to the children. Both sisters agreed that more instruction was needed in this area, but as their time was growing short, it would have to be a project for another year. Irene Faye used some of this time to begin driving lessons with Catherine. She made good progress, for in ten weeks she had come a long way in conquering her fears (but not her car-sickness) on the narrow, steeply graded roads.

At Roe Lake, their last planned stop, all of the Faessler children had the chicken-pox and were very disappointed when their classes had to be cancelled. Father McIntyre and Catherine decided they should start their return journey to Vancouver, and by 13 July they were all back in Clinton being welcomed again by the Smith family. As Catherine and Irene said their goodbyes to Father McIntyre, he gave them a cheque for $15, a large sum for a priest who was continually short of money. Even more valuable was his letter which accompanied it:

> With genuine regret do I say goodbye and God bless you. I am very glad indeed to have met you and known you long enough to be able to say in all truth and sincerity that the Lord most likely is pleased with your zealous intelligent efforts to save souls for Him. I am sure I am, and even now, would ask you to put yourselves on order in my district next year ... Later on I will write good Fr. Daly to whose kindness and missionary zeal I am largely indebted for your efficient and willing service this season.
>
> I very much regret one thing and that is my inability to do much for you in a financial way for reasons as well known to you as to me ... The enclosed small cheque is to help you on your way home ... it goes with a good heart in which there is deep appreciation of your kindness and assistance in the work assigned me by the Archbishop.[18]

Such praise from a priest they had come to admire meant much to Catherine and Irene. They were indeed willing to return, for as Catherine reflected, "the second trip over the same territory could accomplish ten times as much. We could have our day's program planned, prayers in their place, retiring usually at nine so as to be able better to face strenuous days. The people are not timid of us now, respect and admire our work and all of them ask for us to come next year."[19]

They arrived back at the hostel in Vancouver ten weeks after they had set out for the Cariboo. In that time they had driven 2,200 miles. On instructions from Father Daly, Catherine remained at the hostel for a short rest, and along with Irene made her annual retreat. Then it was time for the sisters to part. For the next two years Irene Faye remained on staff at the hostel in Vancouver, and Catherine continued her work at the Edmonton Catechetical School coupled with part-time studies at the university. The Catechetical School continued to flourish. By May of 1936, the sisters were marking over 8,500 papers a year and mailing out over 32,400 papers and other literature.

Father McIntyre's request that Catherine Donnelly and Irene Faye

To Do and to Endure

return to the Cariboo mission work was answered in 1936 when they were told to leave Vancouver on 2 May and spend another three months working throughout the territory. Both sisters were now experienced drivers, and although the roads were just as rough and precipitous as before, the prospect of driving them, even alone when necessary, did not frighten Irene Faye. As Catherine had anticipated, for this session they were better organized in their lesson preparation, and more expert in setting up camp. Father McIntyre was pleased to welcome them since he had more children and adults spread over a larger area, for whom he hoped they would be able to organize classes. The children they had taught two years before were now to be instructed for confirmation by Archbishop Duke, and there was a new, younger group, as well as some adults to be prepared for first communion. As before, Father McIntyre prepared their itinerary and notified the Catholic families of the dates on which they would be camping on their property.

As they drove into Clinton, the two women were welcomed as old friends by Miss Mary Smith and her mother, who had given them overnight lodging two years before. This time they boarded at their house for nine days, preparing the local senior and junior children for the Mass Father McIntyre was to celebrate at the Smiths' house. One day they drove fifty-nine miles north into the mountains to Big Bar Creek to make a special parish call on behalf of Father McIntyre concerning the forthcoming wedding of a young woman to a non-Catholic.

On 10 May they were back at the Convent of the Sisters of the Child Jesus near Williams Lake for eleven days of classes at a new location, the village of 150 Mile House. Every morning they drove ten miles into the country collecting children from two ranches and conveying them to a third ranch, the La Bontys. Here they again organized a senior class of six girls and boys of high school age, and a junior group of seven small children. Class hours for the senior children had to be flexible as they were helping with the farm work. Classes over, they drove those children home and returned to the village where four seniors and thirteen juniors awaited them. Some classes were continued in the evening after they had supper at the convent. It was a strenuous day with no rest for either of them, but Catherine was pleased with the response, particularly of the village senior class which included high school boys and girls, up to the age of seventeen. She found them to be "a very live class and learn through questioning and discussion. They have the makings of enthusiastic Catholics ... They are 'good soil' and will live constructive lives."[20]

They left the mission on 22 May and drove to Quesnel for a teaching session for six seniors and seven juniors. As well they called on Catholic families both in and outside the town as directed by Father McIntyre. They had no spare moments to struggle with campfires, and appreciated the hospitality at the house of Mr. and Mrs. John Lazzarin. They moved thirty miles southeast on 30 May to stay at Gravelle Ferry for six days to prepare seven of the Cantin children for confirmation. They used their old camp-site, and found that nothing had changed: the district by the ferry landing was as isolated as before, and there was still no school nearby for the children who, unfortunately, had lost their tutor. May Probert now had a full-time job.

The most noticeable change was in the river flow, which due to the spring rains, was so high that it had carved ten feet into the banks. One hundred and fifty foot trees were felled by a current that was so swift that Catherine lost their water pail when the rope broke in the rough water. The Cantins erected a tent for them and again set up the stove, so they could cook their breakfast and dinner. The sisters taught the little children during the day and returned on the ferry in the evening to teach the boys who were working during the day to keep the ferry pier clear of the driftwood surging down the river. The weather was very hot, and the mosquitoes at their pretty camp-site were the worst they had ever encountered, particularly at night when they were sleeping in the car. The first night was the worst, "at 4 a.m. both of us were desperate. Evidently the car door had not been perfectly tight. I had a bite on the sole of my foot, on my fingers & face, and one wretch bit me on the end of the nose."[21] Relief only came when a change in the weather brought a strong breeze. The six days went by all too quickly. The sisters regretted having to bid goodbye to the family they admired so much, but their itinerary still listed several other places where children awaited them. Some days later, Archbishop Duke came to the Cantins cabin and confirmed the children.

Forest Grove and Bradley Creek, where they had spent only a few days two years before with the children of two Catholic families, was their next stop. These were very isolated settlements enclosed by high mountains. All the farms were small, as flat land was scarce. To make a camp they backed the car into a clearing at the side of the trail, and built a barricade of dead trees in hopes of keeping the inquisitive cattle at bay. Catherine was amused by a little mongrel dog who came when they whistled and chased the cattle away from their tent. There was a small log school nearby, and across a creek a tiny log cabin housed a young teacher who told them that this was his first job in a few years. They admired his sincerity and devotion, for he was up every day at five a.m. to prepare his lessons before breakfast. As he was not Catholic, he did not give religious instruction to the children of two Catholic families who attended the school. The children's mothers were Swiss, and did not speak English well enough to help them with their lessons. Until Father McIntyre had called in at their little settlement, they had not seen a priest for many years. Nevertheless the fathers made certain that they all celebrated Sundays together. They dressed as if they were attending church, and the fathers read and explained the lesson to the children. They were so happy to have the sisters give formal lessons, that one of the mothers offered to cook meals for the two women during their stay. Knowing how poor they all were, Catherine used this as an opportunity to give them some of their food supplies.

It rained incessantly during their six-day stay, and they were grateful for the teacher's offer of the use of his cabin while he was teaching at the school. Irene Faye taught her class there and Sister Catherine used their car. It was a strenuous week; but they both found satisfaction in the close relationships they were able to forge when they called on the people, listened to their accounts of trials and difficulties, and extended to them the comfort of their support and friendly advice. "This seems almost as important and effective as teaching the children."[22] In this they were consciously following the example set by Father McIntyre, who visited everyone and accepted them regardless of the circumstances in which he found them.

They were reminded of this a few days later on their way to Meldrum Creek in the Chilcotin District across the Fraser River. They dropped in on Mrs. McKay, whose home they had visited with Father McIntyre two years before when her mother, Mrs. Soules, was ill. The old lady had died two weeks before, and Mrs. McKay was grateful that to the end, Father McIntyre had continued to call on her to give her his blessing.

During six days of splendid weather they camped at Meldrum Creek to give classes to a large Indian family of seven adults and four children. Generous amounts of milk, butter, eggs and fresh vegetables from their farm were a welcome supplement to own their supplies. Again, they had to leave before the bishop arrived on 4 July for the confirmation service at the school house.

Springhouse, thirty-five miles south, was an opportunity for a reunion with the Isnardy family. This time Mrs. Isnardy had their camp already set up on a hill with a spacious tent complete with a table and a sheltered stove outside which Catherine felt was, "the best camp we have had as yet." It was a happy prelude to a very busy week in which their car was continually on the road with one of the sisters driving children to and from their classes at two local schools, which were about five miles apart. Irene recorded, "They were exceedingly busy days. We drove fast and worked hard ... managed to call at a dozen houses ... were invited out for some meals."[23] The community had recently built a small church and its dedication as well as the first communion and confirmation ceremonies were to be all held on 5 July.

It was a complicated task for the two women to organize the cleaning and decorating of the church and the yard, as well as arrange for the Sunday picnic, as there were no phones, and the people's farms were so scattered that they were not used to taking part in such a co-operative effort. But the local folk answered the sisters' requests as best they could. They scrubbed the church and brought boughs of evergreens to decorate the yard and exterior of the church, as well as huge bouquets of wild tiger lilies, asters and white mignonette for the interior. The archbishop was delighted to see the Williams Lake choir there to sing at the service. The church was filled with the overflow of the congregation standing outside, and three adults and nineteen children ready for confirmation. Everyone had brought lunches, and good hot coffee was made by an Irishman who happened to be an expert cook, and enjoyed his task. After this first great community celebration it was again time for the sisters to move on.

The narrow trail from the north via Dog Creek, which led to Kosters' ranch was just as harrowing as when they had first driven it, but Catherine and Irene were too weary and happy even to worry. They were welcomed with a good dinner, a good bed and breakfast, and were

To Do and to Endure

sent on their way for the long drive south to the Kostering ranch at Big Bar Creek. They camped in their old location, and organized their classes for the service on 12 July. There was still no church building, but after the service in the Community Hall, the large crowd, which included the non-Catholic population, met to discuss building a church. Then came the community breakfast outside with vegetables from local gardens and fresh salmon, some of which had been caught by the archbishop in the Fraser River. Catherine thought it was a glorious way to celebrate the Twelfth of July, 1936.

During the final two weeks, they returned to some people whom they had bypassed or only visited briefly two years before. Six days were devoted to the Faessler children, before Catherine and Irene departed for Vancouver on 23 July. Their second trip had been even more successful than their first. The people now knew and welcomed them as friends as well as teachers. Statistically, they had travelled nearly three thousand miles to prepare almost three hundred children and adults for first communion and confirmation. Father McIntyre summed it all up in his final letter to them which was waiting for them at Clinton when they passed through:

> My Dear Sisters:
> Before the toll gates of Clinton clang behind you and you turn your backs once more to the Cariboo, I wish to express my appreciation for the very wonderful service you have rendered us during the past three months ...
>
> The circumstances must have been most trying at times, but you never once showed any signs of weakness, discouragement or gloom. It was a severe test over a prolonged period, for the Cariboo shows no quarter to those who come to labor within his boundaries; but you have won his heart and you go away with a great load of love and the hearts of the poor little children who can never forget the Sisters of Service. God bless them![24]

The two summers during which Catherine and Irene worked together had two fortuitous results. The experience contributed immeasurably to the maturing of Irene Faye and confirmed that she was a capable teacher, able to withstand hardship and physical danger as a Sister of Service. For Catherine, the memories of their successful work, the kindness of the people of the Cariboo, and the experience of working with a priest who respected her ability and trusted her judgment, would sustain her in the difficult, frustrating situations she would meet in the future. She would always recall with gratitude the Cariboo mission where they accomplished so much in spite of the hardships they endured.

CHAPTER 11
KEEPING THE ORDER ON COURSE

IN JANUARY 1936 CATHERINE HAD BEEN TRANSFERRED from Edmonton to the order's new Catechetical School in Regina. It had been established by Father Daly in September 1934 to be the catechetical teaching centre for Saskatchewan and Manitoba, and as a base for the Sisters of Service who would go out on teaching missions on weekends and in the summer. It was a busy mission, and Catherine was happy enough to return to marking catechism lessons and writing to the students and parents. She was a good letter-writer and by praise and encouragement established a good rapport with these isolated farm families.

This job also allowed her more leisure time to write to the large circle of friends and relatives with whom she kept in regular contact. At the top of that list were her two sisters and her nieces and nephews, her old friends Achsah and Ruth MacDonnell, several clergy and sisters in other religious orders, as well as faithful benefactors such as Ellen (Eleanor) McMahon in Dundas, Ontario. Her closest confidant continued to be Father Coughlan, with whom she had planned the adaptation of the concepts which defined the traditional religious orders for women into a new Rule which would reflect the spirit and particular mission of the Sisters of Service. He had also acted as her spiritual adviser even before he undertook that position for the whole order after it was officially founded.

Father Coughlan had been transferred out of Toronto, and in 1935 he was the Rector of St. Alphonsus, the Redemptorist seminary at Woodstock, Ontario. The time required for this new responsibility and Catherine's own heavy assignments on the western missions meant that their correspondence was limited. But in December 1935 Catherine was able to return to Toronto for Christmas; and there they met privately because he wished to discuss with her, at length, the details of the sequence of events leading up to the foundation of the Sisters of Service. He asked her to write down all she could remember of those events as he wished to incorporate them into a history of their founding. When he acknowledged receipt of her memoir, he thanked her for

> the pains you took to make it correct and complete. It was just what I desired ... In due time, I shall write my own account of them and I presume you will grant me permission to use them for the purpose. The Sisters at Toronto have asked me repeatedly to write such an account. I shall propose to them that along with mine, your memoirs be preserved in the archives of the Sisters of Service. Thus when you and I pass away, there will remain sufficient data for future history ... You may certainly be proud of your share in the beginnings of the Institute.[1]

He added that he was pleased that she had been doing summer catechetical work "in abandoned places" but added that he was "very much disappointed that teaching opportunities had ceased, and that their original idea of working among the Ruthenians appeared to be an almost impossible mission until some young Ruthenian women joined the Order."

Father Coughlan was probably responsible for Catherine's second summer mission assignment to the Cariboo, for during his Easter visit to Toronto in 1936 he had recommended her to the Sister General as "the ideal sister for summer catechizing."[2] Thus it was bad news for Catherine when he told her in September, just after her return from her successful Cariboo summer, that he was being transferred back to his native country, to St. Mary's College in Erie, Pennsylvania. He was to be the confessor to two big convents, and at his own request had been relieved of the superiorship. This meant that his official role with the Sisters of Service was ended. Catherine should still, however, feel free to consult him. This generous offer was indeed fortunate, as Catherine was becoming perturbed about Father Daly's policies in his role as the clerical director of the Sisters of Service. She wrote to Father Coughlan in October and early November 1936, and his reply showed the issues that were bothering her.

Her main complaint was Father Daly's partiality for founding hostels rather than seeking out teaching positions for the sisters.

Hostels were absorbing the order's funds and personnel to the detriment of their rural teaching missions. If the trend continued, she feared that their teaching and nursing apostolate would eventually become negligible. In his reply Father Coughlan shared her concern, and said he had spoken with Father Daly about it. The situation was caused partly by the scarcity of teaching positions, but mainly by the fact that very few qualified teachers and nurses were joining the order. Father Coughlan emphasized, however, that he believed the order's other projects which Father Daly had initiated, such as operating the catechetical schools and sending sisters on summer missions, were worthwhile endeavours and true to their apostolate. Father Coughlan suggested that the obvious way to overcome this shortage of professionally trained sisters was for the order itself to educate some of its most promising and capable members to qualify them for further training in nursing and normal schools. This was not a radical idea, for it was being done in other Catholic womens' orders. He also advised that this matter should be discussed at her order's official meetings.

Regarding the history of the order which he had undertaken to write, he confessed that he had not written a line of it; he was being held back by an awkward situation:

> Father Daly is acknowledged everywhere as the founder of the Institute, and deservedly so from the standpoint of the most valuable services he has rendered to it, services which I could never have given. Indeed I cannot see how the Institute could have contined its existence without him. But from a historical standpoint he is not the original founder. As far as I am concerned, I would be glad to be forgotten entirely, to be left completely out of the picture. But if I am to write the history of the foundation of the S.O.S. I must tell the whole truth, and coming at this late date I am afraid my account would annoy Father Daly and would give the impression that I wish to deprive him of the prestige of being the founder. The truth is, if you had not come to me with your story of Western conditions and your offer of yourself to make a beginning, there would be no S.O.S. today. And so I am waiting and will continue waiting until I can see my way clear to write the true story ...
>
> God had his own designs in bring us together years ago, and I am consoled to feel that we both have tried as best we could every since to carry out His designs for the salvation of abandoned souls.[3]

To Do and to Endure

In January 1937 Father Daly and Sister General Florence Regan began preparations for the order's first general chapter, which was to be held at the motherhouse the following May for the purpose of electing a new Sister General and two councillors. All Mission Superiors would attend, along with five delegates elected by each of the five geographic groups into which the order was being divided for voting purposes. The choice of delegates eligible to be elected to the chapter was limited to the professed sisters with perpetual vows, but all sisters who had taken vows, temporary or perpetual, had a right to vote for their group's representative.[4] Catherine Donnelly was elected as a delegate by the Winnipeg, Camp Morton and Regina group of fifteen sisters, and arrived in Toronto for the chapter meeting on 9 May.

Father Daly opened the chapter with a frank and detailed summary of the order's achievements in the fifteen years since its founding. Its membership had now reached ninety women: thirty-nine were fully professed sisters, thirty-one were under temporary vows, fourteen were novices; and there were six postulants. They were working and training at the motherhouse and the novitiate in Toronto, and in twelve missions scattered between Halifax and Vancouver. Residences for girls were located in Halifax, Montreal, Ottawa, Toronto, Winnipeg, Edmonton and Vancouver; the cottage hospitals were in Vilna and Edson, Alberta; religious correspondence schools were in Edmonton and Regina; and two Sisters of Service were teaching in two public schools in Camp Morton.

In Father Daly's financial report, the order's total assets had been credited at over $602,000. They consisted mainly of the properties he had purchased on its behalf for hostels. It was an amazing accumulation of capital considering the depressed state of the Canadian economy since 1930. However, $100,000 of these assets were a recently credited but not yet received legacy from the estate of the late Theresa Korman Small.

The order's liabilities were $283,000 in bank loans owing on their properties. He admitted that the buildings were a heavy burden on their mission staff because interest payments of $11,000 a year had to be found from the order's current revenues. Since this was a troublesome responsibility for the order's administrators to oversee, he intended to continue managing their finances, but would gradually withdraw from the internal administration of the order. For this reason the forthcoming elections were very important, as a new Sister General must be chosen. Sister General Florence Regan could not be re-elected because, by canon law, the term of office for a Sister General was six years with a twelve-year maximum. Sister General Sister Regan had already served for nine years. Because it was essential that the new Sister General and the councillors leave their missions (and their salaries) and live in Toronto, they should choose their councillors very carefully.

He also reported that fourteen Canadian bishops had sent splendid letters praising the order's work in their dioceses and supporting their request for approbation of their Rule by the Sacred Congregation of Religious in Rome. Typical was that sent by Archbishop P.J. Monahan of Regina, who had declared that "the task they undertook was daring and new in our land. The results have been surprising." He noted that the small Catholic hospitals they had built "where the older communities would not venture" had been highly successful. Since coming to Regina they had done work no other community would have attempted. "To illustrate this statement may I point to the fact that these Sisters are in direct contact with no less than *Seven Thousand* children of the Archdiocese through their Correspondence Course."[5]

Several western bishops had appealed for Sisters of Service to establish more missions in their dioceses, and Father Daly said he was making plans to respond to these requests. Teachers might be required in Marquis, which was northeast of Moose Jaw, Saskatchewan; the Bishop of Peace River had requested that sisters come and work in his diocese; and Father Daly would like to accept a similar invitation from the Bishop of Fargo, North Dakota. The latter could be the vanguard project by which they could establish an American Province.

In his summary, Father Daly did admit that by extending the work of the order so rapidly, he had strained both its financial resources and the stamina of the sisters. "Some have criticized me very bitterly for the rapid development of the Institute ... but the principle I went on was that ... I had contacts which you had not, and I tried while I was still in my vigor to get you to the centres which could be looked upon later as a nucleus for future development."[6] He concluded with the optimistic prophecy that when the doors to immigration opened again "we will be ready to go back to the first idea that dominated the institute in its foundation." Father Daly then withdrew from the chapter meeting and the elections proceeded.

To Do and to Endure

The delegates elected a teacher, Margaret Guest, as their new Sister General. She had been sent to Camp Morton to work with Catherine in 1924. The two councillors selected were Sisters Carolyn Albury and Florence Regan, who had both worked in hostels. During the discussions which followed at the general sessions, questions were submitted to Father Daly on a variety of topics, ranging from delegation of authority within the order, minor changes to their style of dress, their group devotional practices, and the proper deportment to observe when dealing with the general public, particularly with regard to "familiarity with the people with whom we are working."

Father Daly's answers to the first three topics were clear, definitive and practical. For example, regarding their hats and collars, they should suit themselves, the only restriction to be that their habit "must always be a uniform." His answer to the question on familiarity revealed the attitudes which the sisters had encountered when they mingled with the world outside their convents. His advice was similar to that given at that time to all respectable secular women who dealt professionally with the public. They were to guard against discarding a "certain reserve," for it was like steel armour, and a better protection than a habit. "To say how far you can go, depends so much on the individual. There are some individuals who are naturally cold, others more expressive. Now we cannot judge everybody with the same yardstick ... I would not condemn this one or that one. Local custom comes into it." He then praised them all for their devotion and zeal, and said he was happy to be able to refute the sceptical archbishop who had decried their freedom to live and mingle with the people they served, "because before you know it they will all be married."[7]

There was no official recorded discussion held at the chapter sessions in 1937 on the topic of raising the level of the members' educational qualifications, but it was discussed at the council meetings which took place shortly after, in June and August. Two sisters who had been working in the hostels were selected to undertake further academic study. Sister Irene Faye, stationed at Vancouver, and Sister Leona Trautman, at Winnipeg were "to be sent to Regina Mission as students. There they will be taught by Sister Catherine Donnelly for one year, after which they will probably continue their studies at the Academy."[8]

Leona Trautman, the eldest of eight children of a devout rural

Ontario Catholic family, had entered the order in 1933 at the age of nineteen. Her father was a miller, who after working in the United States for a time, had returned to Canada with his family to take over his father's farm at Mildmay, near Wingham. Leona was educated in one-room schools, and was successful in passing her entrance exams after completing Grade 8. Like many of the children in large farming families, she was unable to attend high school the next year, as she was needed at home. Some time later she found work as a mother's helper. She had been working for five years for local and Toronto families when, on a visit to relatives in Kitchener, she read a pamphlet about nuns who did not wear the traditional long-skirted habits or veils, and who worked with immigrants in the west. This appealed to her and she applied immediately to enter the Sisters of Service in February 1933. Leona was one of five postulants who began the arduous two-year novitiate. She found the many rules for which no explanation was given, and the corrections by the alert Novice Mistress stressful. Would she be accepted as a Sister of Service? She need not have feared. Six months after taking her first vows in 1935, Sister Leona Trautman was assigned to the hostel in Winnipeg.

There were at that time twenty-eight girls boarding at the hostel. Many were daughters of recent Polish and Ukrainian immigrants. As well as teaching catechism, Sister Leona was one of a staff of five who taught housekeeping and cooking skills to the girls so that they could find employment as domestics. As soon as they found positions, which was usually about six months, a new girl would enter the program. When the graduates of the hostel had their days off, they often returned to have dinner and meet the new boarders. Out of these gatherings a club was formed, and the sisters were able to continue in the role as friendly advisers and teachers of religion and life skills. The club became very popular, its membership eventually reaching over a hundred. Moreover, when they married, many of these young women had their showers and wedding dinners in the big SOS house in Winnipeg. Altogether, Sister Leona found her work at the hostel very fulfilling, and was therefore surprised and somewhat apprehensive when she was told in August 1937 to report to the Catechetical House in Regina, where she, along with Sister Faye, would begin studying with Sister Donnelly for their high school diplomas.

She barely knew Sister Donnelly, for she had not been told during

To Do and to Endure

her novitiate of Catherine's pivotal role in founding the order; nor had she ever worked with her, as had Irene Faye. This would also put her at some disadvantage, since Irene's talents were already known to Catherine. Their classes were held in the Regina convent in a small room on the second floor converted into a school room. Catherine soon made it apparent that she expected them to complete three years of high school in one year! Unfortunately, she also indicated that Irene Faye was being prepared to take teacher training. The council had stated this in its directive, but as it had not mentioned any specific professional goal for Leona Trautman, Catherine did not either. As the two young women sat side by side at a long table facing a blackboard, Leona naturally felt some concern as she worked through what she would remember "as the most exhausting year of my life."

Catherine drove her students with an energy whose source lay in her realization that this was the opportunity she had craved so long. Even if fewer teachers than she had expected had joined the order, teachers could and would be made from some of their own members, by setting them to the task of upgrading their education; and their vows of obedience would oblige them to put all of their effort into their studies. Catherine's methods with these first two sisters were, unfortunately, not those that she had used in her schools in years past, nor with the adult students to whom she had taught religion so successfully in the Cariboo. She did not take time to make learning an exciting and fun-filled adventure. Rather she concentrated on drills based on the textbooks and "wrote scads of paper slips with questions for us to work on."[9]

Today such methods are not acceptable in any classroom, for they are based on learning by rote for the purpose of passing an examination. And in truth, that was Catherine's immediate objective, as the diploma certifying the successful completion of high school would be the sisters' ticket of admission to Normal School or a School of Nursing. Time was too short, and the task too urgent for her to worry about her methodology; it was the results which mattered. Unhappily for the two sisters, Catherine was so absorbed by this goal that she was oblivious to the stress that this abrupt change of career plan could produce, and also to the weariness which overcame Leona Trautman, as her teacher shouted and drilled their lessons into them hour after hour, and day after day. One of Catherine's mannerisms which Leona found

Keeping the Order On Course

very trying was the high volume of her voice when she was teaching them mathematics, science or history. If the window was open her shouts could be heard out on the street. "People ... stopped and would look up to see who was yelling what and to whom." Finally one day she spoke up and said that they could both hear well without the loudness. Catherine brushed aside her complaint with the reply, "When I teach I speak from my diaphragm."[10]

Irene Faye did not seem to feel the pressure as much as her classmate. After two summers spent keeping up with Catherine, she knew that she could master any new situation; and she had already received high praise for her teaching ability from Father McIntyre. Working with Catherine had also forged a bond between them; and she knew that when her teacher stopped to think of her pupils' immediate problems, instead of her own ultimate goals for them, she could be considerate and supportive. Catherine struggled just as diligently as her two pupils, as their progress proved. By the end of October they had completed Grade 9; Grade 10 was covered by the end of December. In January the sisters were enrolled in the Provincial Correspondence Course for Grade 11, but Catherine still supervised and supplemented their lessons.

Clearly, Catherine did not fit into the current stereotype of the gentle, mild-mannered, compliant sister which the clergy and the laity understood to be the proper mien for a woman religious. She was a person who pursued a goal persistently, vigorously and openly. As time passed, an adverse side of this single-mindedness emerged. Catherine became insensitive to the needs and abilities of the sisters who were working in the big inner-city hostels and the ocean ports far away from the settlers on the western plains. Her lack of appreciation for their work as "housekeeepers" (as she sometimes called them) could hurt, even though that was not her direct intention. Father Coughlan had recognized this trait some months before when he had written to the Sister General. "Sister Donnelly ... would never be at home in the East. I know her well, and she is really a woman of faith and high purpose, and her energy is unbounded. If she had more of the mother in her make-up, and a better grasp of spiritual values, what a flower she would be in your Institute!"[11]

The real test of the order's educational experiment came in June, when the two sister candidates went to the Sacred Heart Academy in

Regina to write the Grade 11 provincial finals. Leona Trautman triumphantly recorded that they both passed, "by our work and her managing skill." However, there was still the Grade 12 hurdle to pass before they could attend teachers college, which was Catherine's ultimate goal for them.

In the summer of 1938 Catherine was instructed to open a mission at Diamond Coulee, a tiny hamlet twenty miles south of Regina in the dry farming area of southern Saskatchewan. She was to teach Grades 1 to 8 in the one-room school and supervise Sisters Faye and Trautman in the Grade 12 correspondence course. When she inspected the school and the living quarters provided for the teacher, she realized the buildings were much too small to accommodate the three of them. She would have to find a teaching position which included suitable accommodation for three or four. She knew that the priest at Marquis, a larger centre twenty miles northwest of Moose Jaw, had been asking for some time for Sisters of Service to take charge of the local St. Mark's separate school. Moreover, the lay teacher at the school had resigned. Although she had misgivings about working for a Separate School Board, she persuaded the Sister General to allow her to apply to Marquis, and to send another sister in her place to Diamond Coulee.

Her interview with the board secretary was not encouraging. The community wanted a teacher, but no accommodation was provided, and the board might not be able to pay even the $60 per month teacher's salary. Catherine consulted Archbishop Monahan of Regina. He urged her to accept the job, rent a house in Marquis and hope for the best. She found an unfurnished house for $10 a month which would accommodate four sisters, and signed the board's contract. The motherhouse could not spare any money for start-up expenses, as the order was already beset with financial obligations. Catherine asked the bank manager in Regina for a loan. He refused, and pointed out that she had no security to offer. Her salary was no guarantee of repayment, as not all Saskatchewan boards were able to pay their teachers, even those with small salaries such as hers. After much "persuading and promising" she managed to get a loan of "ninety-some dollars" if she promised to pay back $100 dollars in three months. "Joyfully, anything to get going — I took the nine ten dollar bills."[12]

In late August Catherine bought a wood stove and an old armchair for $15 at a secondhand store in Regina, borrowed a double bed and a

Keeping the Order On Course

cot as well as a few bits of furniture and household items from the convent, and shipped them to Marquis. She followed, driving an old car loaded with her personal belongings and books, as well as those of the other three sisters who would be with her at Marquis. Two were her students, Irene Faye and Leona Trautman, and the fourth was a sister who would keep house for them. The car was then turned over to a young novice, Sister Mary Jackson, who was assigned to her position at Diamond Coulee.

As in Catherine's previous locations, moving into the neglected old house meant that they first had to haul some water from the cistern to scrub the floors and the walls as the house had no running water. Catherine noted that not one of the Catholic community came to assist them and it was one of their non-Catholic neighbours who came over and helped them connect up the stove which would be their sole means of heating and cooking.[13] The electricity rates were so high they would not be able to afford an electric heater in any room. Three orange crates had to suffice as chairs at the table where they would eat their meals. They discovered that their drinking water would also have to be brought in by the bucketful from the town water tank located at the CPR station some distance away.

They placed the blackboard brought from their school room in Regina in an upstairs room with the intent that Catherine would coach the two sisters in the evenings. She immediately realized that this would be inadequate instruction for anyone preparing to write the provincial Grade 12 examinations in June. What to do? There was a public high school in town and Catherine hastened over to introduce herself to the principal, Mr. Morrison Sillery. He had a few Grade 12 students studying at his school, whom he taught during the recess period. Catherine persuaded him to let Sisters Faye and Trautman join this class, and also to teach his now enlarged Grade 12 during the regular school hours. In return, Catherine arranged to teach the twelve Grade 9 Catholic students who would otherwise have transferred to the public school. In taking on this extra teaching load to secure proper classroom instruction for the sisters, she was also saving her Separate School Board the fee of $35 a year per pupil which it had to pay the Public School Board to educate Catholic high school students. But when she asked her board to provide the Catholic school with proper seating for six big boys in the Grade 9 class who had outgrown their

To Do and to Endure

elementary school desks, they refused to provide any funds. It was not a good omen for the future.

The situation was saved by Mr. Sillery, who made a large, solid table to serve as a common desk for the six tall Catholic boys. It was the beginning of a splendid friendship between Catherine and her Protestant colleague. Mr. Sillery proved to be one of the most helpful persons Catherine ever encountered in her professional life. He was "clever, kind, generous, [and] proved to be our best friend in Marquis."[14] A month later, when she received permission from the archbishop to have a small chapel in their house, it was Mr. Sillery, who was also an excellent carpenter, who volunteered to make the liturgical altar, credence table, and four prie-Dieu to furnish it. He and his wife went out of their way to be helpful, and unusually good cooperation was soon established between the two schools. When St. Mark's had a Hallowe'en party, the public school students were invited. When Catherine's Grade 9 science class needed equipment for experiments, they used the science room at the public school.

It took the town's Catholic community a few weeks to realize that these Sisters of Service were living on the same poverty level as the rest of the community. Then a few of them responded with great generosity, sharing their garden produce, eggs, their home-baking and even their meat and fish with them. One of the first to recognize their need was Mrs. Contini, whose husband was the section man for the railway. He was one of the few breadwinners in town who could count on a regular salary. The writer of the convent's Annals listed a steady flow of gifts of food from her and from several other women, as well as Father Lukas, their priest, who appreciated the work the sisters were doing in the community. The donations of food were truly life-saving, for Catherine's salary of $60 a month was the only money available to pay the rent, heat and light for the house, to feed the four sisters, and give some donations to some local families who they discovered were in desperate need. They would assuredly have been very hungry had it not been for the generosity of a few friends.

It was soon obvious to Catherine that there was tension between their parish priest and the Catholic population in Marquis. She never mentioned the cause, but the feud was evident in the attitude of the Separate School Board, who from the beginning maintained a chilly distance from the teacher they had hired to run their school. Catherine

Keeping the Order On Course

thought part of the trouble was the general discouragement caused by the increasing poverty of the whole community, for which no relief was in sight. Marquis was in an area which had suffered successive years of drought and severe dust storms, as well as falling grain prices. Taxes were unpaid, and the Separate School Board was several years in arrears for the fees due the Public School Board for the education of their previous Grade 9 students. They did not wish to meet with her to discuss providing any facilities for St. Mark's School. Catherine, however, also observed that the Catholic population of Marquis was sufficiently large to be entitled to control the public school, which was better equipped. But the reason they did not do so was lack of lay leadership.

In the spring of 1939 Father Lukas was to celebrate twenty-five years in the priesthood and the diocese made elaborate plans to celebrate the event. A large public dinner, to be put on by the Catholic Womens' League, was to be held in the Marquis community hall. Several notables, including the mayor of Moose Jaw, the Redemptorist priests stationed in that city, and the famous Catholic educator, Father Athol Murray, were coming. Also on the guest list from Moose Jaw was Father Lukas's sister, Gertrude, who belonged to another Catholic women's order. On the great day Sister Gertrude arrived at the convent in Marquis with a companion nun, and requested that they be given their dinner there, as their Rule forbade them to eat in public. As Sister Trautman later recalled:

> It was out of the question as we had no food in the house nor time to cook up stuff with all the preparations for the program, the High Mass etc. So they had to go to the head table. We S.O.S. had no place at the head table. We asked CD [Sister Catherine] what we were to do, go home, eat, and come back? She said, "We will mix in with the farm people at any place. We must not expect any place special. Our place is with the ordinary people.[15]

In spite of the heavy teaching load and the spartan living conditions, Catherine felt that first year in Marquis was a "fine experience" for her and the sisters. Mr. Sillery was delighted to have two hardworking Sisters of Service in his class to provide an example for his students. They led the class in the final examinations; both of them received over 70 per cent. Catherine's Grade 9 students were also succcessful, and indicated they were looking forward to staying with

To Do and to Endure

her in St. Mark's for Grade 10.

In August, Sister Faye took her final vows, and in September entered the Normal School in Regina. Sister Trautman took her place at the Vancouver hostel for a year. After taking her final vows in August 1940, she entered Normal School in Winnipeg. Catherine was particularly proud of these two pioneers, and many years later she still remembered the "valiant sisters" who had worked so hard and had proved that lack of education when entering the order need be no barrier to becoming successful teachers.

When school began again in September, Sister Mary Roberts, who had just taken her first vows, was assigned to Marquis and enrolled in the Public High School under Mr. Sillery. Catherine again taught Grade 9 as well as the elementary grades, and life in the convent followed much the same pattern as the year before. Catherine's low salary was again fortunately supplemented by the generous donations of their friends in the town. Mr. Sillery again made it clear that his extra pupil was an asset, not a burden. At Christmas he wrote:

> Dear Ladies — allow me on behalf of myself and family to thank you very heartily for your gifts. I may assure you that the Sisters of Service is an organization worthy of whatever support I or others can give.
>
> I daily do favors for people who do not give me the moral or spiritual support that I receive at your hands, not to mention practical aids that I receive. Speaking as a teacher to a teacher, do we not welcome a "peace-maker" in a grade, do we not welcome a student who adds to the moral stability of a class.
>
> Hence accept our little bit of Christmas Cheer and know that we are giving it because we *want* to not merely because it is the proper thing to do. Further I would like Sister General to know we appreciate your friendship and co-operation.[16]

In another letter to Sister Catherine he revealed an educational philosophy identical to her own:

> A teacher's duty is to make citizens when and where opportunity presents itself, and if I have been able to help my neighbours and future students then it is a duty to continue to do this. Let us keep the war in Europe, while we work together both teachers and students, for the total betterment of the community.
>
> May I humbly thank you for your kind wishes and generosity and be assured that, in the future as always, I will be only too

willing to assist you in any way that I can.[17]

In spite of the kindness of some individual Catholics towards the sisters, the situation between the priest and the parish members did not seem to be improving and this put the sisters in an awkward position. Archbishop Monahan was very concerned, because when the numbers warranted it, he wished to have the Catholic secondary school students in the rural parts of his diocese educated under the auspices of a Separate School Board. There was little chance of that happening in Marquis with the priest and the congregation at loggerheads. But he saw an opportunity to put such a scheme in place in Sinnett, another town in the archdiocese with a substantial Catholic population which had no Catholic school available for secondary students. He decided to start a Continuation School there under a Catholic School Board. After discussing the situation with Sister General Guest, the decision was made to send Catherine to Sinnett in September 1940 to start the new venture. Sister Roberts was to continue with her studies at the Marquis Public High School for another year, and Sister Barton, who was a qualified teacher, would replace Catherine as Superior and teacher at St. Mark's School. This, too, worked out successfully, and a few years later Sister Roberts graduated from the Misericordia Edmonton Hospital as a nurse. In 1944 she had begun a new career at her order's hospital at Edson, Alberta.

By 1940 Catherine was middle-aged; and she had witnessed significant developments in the order. It was not as she would have wished it to be in its primary focus or in numbers, but in her optimistic moments she was heartened that after eighteen years they were accomplishing many of the goals in immigrant rural communities which she had hoped and prayed that such an order could prove were attainable.

CHAPTER 12
THE HARDEST YEARS

IN AUGUST 1940 CATHERINE MADE HER ANNUAL RETREAT at Regina along with Sister Faye and Sister Anne. Irene Faye had graduated from Normal School in June, and followed this with a summer school course in Regina, in preparation for her first teaching assignment at Bergfield, in southern Saskatchewan. Sister Anne, age twenty-five, had taken her first vows (for three years) in 1938, and since then had been stationed at the Regina Mission. She had been chosen to keep house for Catherine while she established the order's new project, the Loyola Continuation School at Sinnett.

The hamlet of Sinnett was an isolated settlement just over one hundred miles northwest of Regina. Its railway connection to Saskatoon, the nearest large city sixty miles west, was at the hamlet of Lanigan eight miles south. The settlement had been founded in 1905, and was named after its founder, Father John C. Sinnett SJ. During the Boer War he had served as a chaplain to the volunteer Canadian contingent and was mentioned several times in despatches. On his return he had worked in Catholic missions in the Prince Albert area, and also as an immigration and land agent for the federal government. As land agent, he had observed the successful German settlement at Muenster, thirty-eight miles north, and the arrival of a French-Canadian group who took up homesteads in 1904 at St. Brieux, in the same area. Father Sinnett wanted to found an Irish settlement, and in 1905 investigated some unclaimed land twenty miles south of Muenster for seven Irish immigrant families in Prince Albert. He reported that it was fine, level prairie, with plenty of wood and water, and good soil for grass and hay. On his advice, the seven families registered their titles to the quarter-section homesteads which the Canadian government was offering to immigrant settlers, and moved to the area. Father Sinnett also obtained some land, gave up his position as land agent, and joined the group as their priest. In 1906 a little log church, named St. Ignatius,

To Do and to Endure

was built, soon to be replaced by a larger frame building. The first one-room elementary school was built in 1909 on a site purchased from the Hudson's Bay Company. Father Sinnett encouraged parents to give their children some secondary education, but the farmers could not afford to send them to the city schools. The students who were ambitious had to make do with correspondence courses. For years, Father Sinnett hoped that the settlement would have its own continuation school, but when he retired to Guelph in 1922 his dream had not been realized.

A larger church was built in 1926 and the old frame church became a parish hall. In their planning for the Loyola Continuation School in the spring of 1940, Archbishop Monahan and the local priest, Father Dunphy, agreed that the hall could be partitioned to provide a one-room school for the students, and small quarters for two Sisters of Service. Since this would be the first secondary school in the hamlet, it would qualify for a government grant.

Catherine, very enthusiastic about her new assignment, bought food supplies, some second-hand furniture, including a piano, in Regina, and had them trucked to Sinnett. On 23 August she and Sister Anne were met at the train by Father Dunphy and driven to their new home, a mile north of Sinnett hamlet. The rectory and garage were near the hall; a small barn and cemetery were close by, and dominating all was the big parish church.

On entering the hall, Catherine's first impression was of a long building whose dark brown walls were lit by its country-gothic church windows of clear glass. The only progress visible in the conversion was one partition, which did not reach the high ceiling, but did divide the building into two sections. In the front section which was to be the school, no furniture, school desks, cupboards or bookcases were to be seen. The priest's housekeeper was busy painting the classroom walls. There were no partitions in the living area where their furniture was scattered about, but the kitchen stove had been connected, so the two sisters unpacked some supplies, cooked their supper, made up their beds and wondered what lay ahead. All they knew was that school was scheduled to open on the fourth day of September.

That week Father Dunphy, the carpenter and the two sisters ran the marathon race of building, scrubbing, cleaning and painting which was now routine whenever the Sisters of Service arrived at a new

The Teacherage at Diamond Coulee School, Bergfield, in the Dry Belt of Southern Saskatchewan in 1938.

Post office, Bergfield, Saskatchewan.

Rycroft Mission, Peace River Country, Alberta, in 1952.

The staff at Rycroft, Catherine's last school where she taught from 1952-1956. Sr. O'Kane is back row farleft, Sr. Marie McDougall on far right, C. Donnelly is front right.

Camp Morton in 1956 to which Sr. Catherine Donnelly retired from public school teaching at 72 years of age.

Catherine was still teaching the Sisters when this was taken in 1966.

Sr. Lena Renaud with Betsy, the Camp Morton dog.

Cardinal Flahiff celebrated the Order's Golden Jubilee Mass at Camp Morton August, 1972. The Sisters who have served at Camp Morton are lined up behind and beside Catherine Donnelly and Margaret Guest.

Sister Lena Renaud with Ms. Sadie MacKinnon, a co-member of the Order, Betsy, and Duchess have just been given tidbits by Sr. Catherine.

Cardinal Flahiff presents the Papal medal Pro Ecclesia to Sister Catherine Donnelly, August, 1974.

Srs. Catherine Donnelly and Margaret Guest at their Golden Jubilee, August, 1974.

The Residences and Catechetical Houses where Catherine Lived and Worked

Toronto — Headquarters

Vilna

Edmonton

Edmonton

Toronto-Novitiate

Vancouver

Camp Morton

Regina

Edson

Winnipeg

Catherine Donnelly celebrated the Order's Jubilee at the Motherhouse in Toronto, August 1972.

The present Motherhouse of the Sisters of Service, Toronto, built in 1969.

The Hardest Years

assignment. Partitions were erected to make two tiny bedrooms, a chapel, small dining-room, kitchen and narrow living-room; windows were cut out and doors installed. The water for washing was obtained by opening a trap-door cut into the kitchen floor, climbing down dangerously steep steps to the basement, and crawling behind the steps to an uncovered rainwater cistern sunk in the muddy clay floor. The heavy pail of water was then carried back up the stairs to the kitchen. This was such a hazardous operation that Catherine decided she should fetch the water herself in case of injury to the young, inexperienced Sister Anne. The drinking water for the convent and the school had to be brought in daily from the rectory property in a cream can, carried by Father Dunphy or the students. Of course there was no electricity, as the lines had not yet been extended to Sinnett. It would be 1953 before the hamlet was electrified.

Although nothing was ready on opening day, thirteen "quiet, courteous, eager" students arrived. The temperature was 104 in the shade, but they were ready to start. As the classroom was still empty, and the construction of the sisters' living quarters incomplete, Catherine sat with her students outside on the grass and chatted with them about their goals and their general educational background. Using this information she organized them into grades in which, from their varied responses, she concluded she would be teaching all subjects from Grades 9 to 11, and eventually 12. To her surprise, several girls were determined to take chemistry as they wanted to enter nursing. Catherine was surprised and pleased when the board secretary, "good, kindly, gentlemanly" Mr. Cunningham, called by and helped her choose from a catalogue her own and the students' desks, blackboards and other equipment, including those for a chemistry class.[1]

When Catherine discovered that no latrines had been built for the school, she enlisted her students to dig two pits west of the building, and helped them build the outhouse. She discovered that "it was quite a simple thing to erect a small building, if one had 2 by 4's, a little lumber, a few shingles, hammer and nails — and TIME!" Later in the week the school inspector, Mr. Murphy, arrived from Humboldt and asked some pointed questions about her plans and her qualifications. Catherine sensed that he was fearful lest this new teaching sister might break the provincial education act by introducing crucifixes and religious pictures into the classroom. Once she had reassured him that

To Do and to Endure

she was familiar with and would, of course, abide by the regulations, they got along very well, and he said he was pleased with her plans and their progress to date.

Father Dunphy was anxious to have the students perform in concerts and "entertainments"; he thought "once a month or so" would be very nice. Catherine did not think that with her teaching load it would be possible to achieve that goal, but agreed to prepare a concert for Hallowe'en. Her students were an exceptional group, and they cooperated willingly:

> I prepared a little play or skit, some lively French songs and others and some instrumental selections. Teddy Dodd and Eddie Kowalski provided the latter. From the very first day it was a custom accepted by all that every child called upon to play a part or even to sing alone was to respond without hesitation. This became a tradition. The sportsmanship was superb. The little concert had a most appreciative audience. The pupils gained in self-confidence, poise and ambition.
>
> There were not many of them, so that each had to work at full capacity to make any little social event a success. In fact, with the heavy program of studies, the numerous grades, and the desire of every pupil to accomplish a full grade in a year, there was really no time for any extras whatever.

Catherine's thirteen students were thus a delight to teach, and faithful in their attendance, but an average attendance of fifteen students was the requirement necessary to secure the full government grant for secondary schools. Without it Catherine knew that her salary of $700 a year would be a heavy burden for the community. She grasped at every idea which would help. Father Dunphy's housekeeper, Florence Blanchard, decided to enroll in the school to increase her knowledge of French and music. When Sister Anne was registered to take some Grade 11 subjects, all fifteen school desks were occupied; the grant was assured. But Catherine's teaching responsibilities had increased considerably. Music was also supposed to be on their curriculum and a sister qualified to teach music was supposed to join the staff as several children wanted piano lessons; but the teacher's arrival was delayed because of sudden surgery. Catherine had no training in teaching piano; all she could teach was elementary theory. To keep the children's interest alive she encouraged them to practise a little, but she felt her teaching time in school hours had to be devoted to the academic high school courses.

Sister General Margaret Guest arrived on 12 September for a four-day visit, and experienced the chaos being caused by the building renovations. While she was there, Father Dunphy was helping the carpenter nail on the eavestroughs. She was cheerful and encouraging, and praised Catherine for her organization of the school, and the students for their diligence. As well, she had some private discussions with Father Dunphy. When he returned from driving Sister Guest to the train on 16 September, he headed for the basement to do some some work on the cistern.[2] Catherine reported to Father Daly on the Sister General's visit and also made some pointed comments about their difficulties at Sinnett when she wrote to congratulate him on the jubilee celebration of his ordination:

> You will be out to see us here this autumn, I hope. You may expect to see quite a rough place and quite a bit of disorder. All our most strenuous and constant efforts since coming here have failed to conquer the millions of flies and the chaos in general.
>
> It is the usual thing in the West, for everyone to "pass the buck" and perhaps it is the case everywhere so we should learn the lesson to provide everything possible for emergencies when we go to new places. Why not? It's all for God's work and we should be practical.
>
> Sister Anne is well and quite interested in her work here ... The first year of school is keenly watched. I'm trying to play the game well, I hope the Lord will step in quickly and help me. We want to win in this endeavor.

Catherine probably could have coped with better humour with the dirt, flies and mess caused by the prolonged construction if any explanation had been given for the lack of workers on the project. What really bothered her was "why the men of the district had not been organized or the trustees informed about these necessary provisions is a mystery."[3] When the schoolroom became noticeably dirty, Catherine asked Father Dunphy if any caretaking arrangements had been made. He replied that "it was left to her for the present and the floor was supposed to be scrubbed once a month."

As winter approached, the lack of heating equipment or chimneys in either section of the building became a matter of real urgency. Only the cook stove in the kitchen was operating. The mason built the chimney for the classroom stove while Catherine and the students tried concentrate on their school work. Then, "a small stove was brought in which smoked and continued to smoke. The pipes came apart and fell down regularly, a constant wear on our patience and precious time." Abnormal cold and high winds in October revealed that the window-frames in the kitchen and classroom were not weatherproof, and the snow was blowing in because none of the window panes had been puttied. The porch fell away from the outside wall and snow blew in on the students' clothes and boots. Catherine rearranged the kitchen and hall so that they could at least keep them dry, but the extra traffic added to the dirt and disarray. Catherine had understood that wood was to be supplied by the school board. On a cold weekend the small supply gave out and Catherine had to round up some young men to bring in a load of wood on Sunday. More repairs and wall insulation were urgently required. Gradually the insulation was put in place by Father Dunphy, who had to work up on a ladder and stuff the insulation through a hole and into the space between the walls. Every so often his knock on the classroom door called Catherine out to hand up the basket of insulating material.

In November a shed for the children's horses had to be built. Most of the children came to school driving or riding a horse, especially in the cold weather. The boys had to spend hours of their precious school time erecting the shed among the trees west of the church. Catherine was proud of their work, for although it was rudely and hurriedly thrown together, it served as a very good shelter. The lack of heat in the school building was supposed to be solved when Father Dunphy installed an oil burner in his house, and put his old furnace in their basement. Catherine found that it, too, smoked.

Preparing lessons and teaching completely occupied the week days, and the housework had to be done on Saturdays. Catherine did the washing and hung it in the classroom to dry while Sister Anne, at Father Dunphy's request, accompanied him to Wynyard, a mission station nearby which was settled by French-Canadians. He said that she could be a great help as she spoke French and could sing French hymns, and visit with the people. As she worked about the house alone, Catherine found her cat, Gibbs, to be a good and helpful companion, for the animal made regular raids on the large mouse population which

The Hardest Years

infested the basement. When Gibbs had a large litter of kittens, Catherine persuaded some pupils to adopt them, pointing out that they would be wonderful mousers if they were at all like their mother, and also that instead of being destroyed after the summer, cats "ought to have a winter life too."

There were no mail, banking or shopping facilities in Sinnett and as Catherine had no car, she was dependent on Father Dunphy to do these tasks for her. She also relied on him to take her to the teachers' convention in Humboldt, and to the convent of the Sisters of Loretto in Sedley to pick up some boxes of chemistry equipment for her class. Catherine wished she could call on the families in the area, particularly the parents of her students, but she had no time to spare, nor a car to do so even if she had made the time. The open house that she arranged for the parents on 8 November was a disappointment. A snow storm blocked the roads and only the Dodds' team of horses got through to enjoy the lunch prepared by the sisters and Miss Blanchard. Not many visitors came to see the school, but those who did brought little gifts of food, and the neighbouring clergy offered some furnishings for the chapel.

Unknown to Catherine, Father Dunphy was becoming equally frustrated. He had been in Sinnett for some years, and when war was declared he wanted desperately to join the airforce as a chaplain. To date, he had not been able to do so. Undoubtedly he had not expected to have carpentry and house-building added to his other duties. Nor was it pleasant to have to face the complaints, no matter how justified, of Sister Catherine. There is no record that they quarrelled, but Catherine was not one to be silent if she thought that the confusion caused by lack of planning by the clergy was hindering her efforts. Father Dunphy wrote to Sister General Guest in mid-November, and from her reply it is obvious that he had demanded that Catherine be removed, and soon. Sister Guest asked him to bear with her while she thought of a way to change teachers. As she explained:

> Every one of our teachers is in school. Next year we could manage very well as we have two at normal school this year. I had hoped that everything would be fine for this year and that next year we would be in a position to make adjustments ...
>
> Please do not think, dear Father, that I blame you in the least. I understand perfectly how things are and will do my very best to

To Do and to Endure

> bring the matter to an end as peaceably and quietly as possible. You have been very kind to the Sisters and in every letter Sister has told me of your co-operation and kindness. That is what I cannot understand.
>
> In the meantime I shall be very grateful if you keep me informed as to any new developments. I am sure you realize what an awkward position we are in and how difficult it is for us at this time of the year to do all we would like in the interests of the Foundation. The Sister who I hope is going there soon has completed a full high school course and has several optional subjects also and besides is very talented in music. I hope this will be a great help right now.[4]

Four days later Sister General Guest wrote to Catherine in response to her pleas to her to "try and come at once to look things over." Her reply was that she regretted that it was impossible for her to do so at that time, and that Sister Mary Phillips, their new music teacher, was en route. Her presence would allow Catherine to get some rest and some help with her heavy teaching load. Then she concluded with the remark that it might be necessary to make changes:

> I must have time to think. For you, *do not worry* ... When you are over-tired get into bed ...
>
> I appreciate so much your ready willingness to go anywhere and do any work. You are very tired, I know and it was a big undertaking to start a Continuation school but everything will come right in the end.[5]

Sister Mary Phillips did arrive a few days later. Her first impressions of Sinnett confirmed the harsh conditions the sisters were expected to endure, and reported that Catherine was stressed and testy. "A kitchen stove which continually went out when a wind from a certain direction was blowing ... I do remember that I had decided to do nothing to upset C.D. because she would come down hard on a person who did!"[6] Catherine did not realize that something was seriously amiss, for in her letter to Father Daly a few days before she had praised Father Dunphy and described him as a

> splendid, enthusiastic, good young priest. He is always helping his people in a very practical way — digs and hammers — anything to make a success of his undertakings. His High School is started well and is a real going concern, with a marvellous spirit. The

children are very keenly in earnest, exceedingly anxious to make the best of this splendid opportunity. Many a young rural priest will follow Father Dunphy's example and organize a Continuation School some way for other boys and girls.

I'm glad I've had the great privilege of doing a little bit in the organizing of this one. Please pray for me ... I'm real well but — tired.

Sister Anne is doing great team-work — she says to tell you she still likes candy.[7]

On 4 December, Catherine was teaching when a message was delivered to Father Dunphy. He gave it to Sister Anne to deliver to Catherine in the classroom. It was a telegram from Sister General Guest which said, "Please leave today for Edson. Notify Sister Quinn [the sister in charge of Edson hospital]."[8]

Catherine went numb with shock. As soon as class was over she immediately prepared to do as she was directed. She packed a few clothes and prepared to leave, despite the heavy snow storm that was blowing and filling the ruts in the roads. As Catherine approached the rectory she could see Father Dunphy starting his car. She asked him to take her to Lanigan where she could catch the next train west. All she recalled of that ride was "I knew that something was exceedingly wrong — but that I must not delay! I have never seen that disturbed man since."[9]

As the train would not arrive until early next morning, Catherine took a room at the little Lanigan hotel. She never forgot that night and referred several times in her letters to close friends, to her feelings of despair, bewilderment and determination:

> I took it passively, utterly sick at heart, trampled in the dirt, completely friendless and despised apparently — but I sat quietly in the Lanigan hotel in a little chair in the corner of my bedroom and said to myself, "I will have *Faith*. This thing will pass away and time will make me able to laugh at it."[10]

In another letter, written on the thirtieth anniversary of the event, she recounted again her despair at what had happened, her resolve to keep her faith, and added that the kindly hotel owner had sensed her disturbed state and brought her some food. They chatted for a while and Catherine remembered that "We even had good laughs together that evening." Early the next morning, as she trudged along a

To Do and to Endure

Saskatoon street to the station from where she would catch the 8:50 a.m. train to Edmonton, she was hailed by her cousins, Betty Ogle and her mother, who greeted her with great affection and concern because she was obviously upset and unwell. She later reminded Betty Ogle of the time, "When I saw you in 'Stoon on my way to Edson. You were most kind to me Betty and I do not forget such kindness."[11]

Catherine arrived in Edson at 6:25 p.m. obviously distraught and very weary. This was not surprising considering the working and living conditions she had endured in Sinnett since August, and the humiliation of being summarily removed with no reason given. To this day the reason is still not clear; no evidence exists of any friction between Catherine and Sister Anne. What is known is that Sister Anne was removed from Sinnett and sent back to Regina in April 1940, and recalled to Toronto in June. On 15 August 1941, the day she was to renew her vows, she left the order.[12] Sister Catherine seems to have believed that Father Dunphy and the Sister General had been misled by Sister Anne. Conceivably, recognition of that fact led to Sister Anne's sudden departure from the order. Later that same year Father Dunphy was given permission to leave the parish and join the Royal Canadian Air Force.[13]

Catherine's abrupt departure with no explanation or letter of resignation alarmed the school board, particularly Mr. Cunningham, who was baffled by her sudden action. He was very concerned for both the students and the ultimate future of the new Loyola Continuation School. Sister General Guest's order to leave Sinnett immediately for Edson, which Catherine, under obedience had followed to the letter, placed her in peril of severe professional discipline. Legally Catherine was under contract, and should not have left her position without giving notice in a letter of resignation. The Sister General also realized that her order to Catherine, however justified, had blighted the good name of the order. She hastened to explain to Mr. Cunningham that Sister Donnelly had become suddenly and seriously ill, and had to be sent to the hospital. She assured him that Sister Phillips would take over Catherine's classes until Christmas, and that an additional qualified teacher would be assigned to Sinnett. He could count on the school reopening on schedule following the Christmas holidays. This explanation was accepted by the board, and the sick leave salary due to Catherine was forwarded to the order shortly after.

The Hardest Years

Irene Faye was hastily transferred from Bergfield to take Catherine's place. She had graduated from high school under Catherine's tutelage eighteen months previously, and had only just completed Normal School. The two teachers rearranged the schedule, divided Catherine's teaching load between them, and managed to complete the school year.[14]

Catherine's illness was reported and accepted throughout the order as the reason for her sudden hospitalization in Edson. Only her many references in personal letters and memoirs written some years later to the "trauma" of Sinnett offer some clues that, in addition to her breakdown from exhaustion, there had existed a different and more serious reason about which she did not hear for some time. Her mental stability may have been undermined by the suspicion that her removal had been brought about by more than her obvious fatigue. She later referred to the person who, "afterwards had to confess her treachery and deceit, her plotting with the Pastor and had to sign her confession and leave the SOS Community."[15] Many other similar references indicate that the physical breakdown, which most certainly overwhelmed her, was exacerbated by the revelation of underhanded plotting against her by her two Sinnett colleagues.[16]

For a few days after her arrival at Edson, Catherine's condition continued to deteriorate, which was not surprising considering the traumatic events which had turned her life upside down. Sister Mary Quinn, the Superior of the hospital, was very professional but gentle with her, and Catherine always attributed her recovery to her understanding and skilful nursing. Sister Quinn had her hands full, for St. John's Hospital was a busy institution. The hospital had been founded to served a town which was at that time primarily a divisional point for the Canadian National Railway. However, it provided medical sevices not only for the railway workers and their families who lived in the vicinity but also the general populace who were involved in the farming, mining and lumber industries in the area. The CNR, the mining company, the Compensation Board, and the provincial government all gave financial subsidies towards its operating costs. It was not, however, equipped to deal with a person who required any psychiatric therapy. At that time very few hospitals in Alberta had such specialists on staff.

The majority of the patients were not Roman Catholic, but the sisters' hospital was highly valued by the community.[17] It was also a source of revenue for the order, because the majority of the patients could pay for their hospital care. In 1941, of 713 patients admitted, only thirty-nine were listed as "non-paying." Father Daly counted on the hospital's assessment to the order to help towards paying off its very large bonded debt. "You are my unique resource in days of penury — and there are plenty of those."[18]

Sister Quinn reported Catherine's arrival to the Sister General:

> Sr. D looks fine, from appearances there is not much wrong. Her appetite is splendid. She has told me a few things but as far as the Community is concerned she is here for a rest as she has had it hard at school during the past term. She speaks highly of the people, etc. She has let off some *steam* to me though. Isn't it a pity she has these trials as she is so well intentioned and generous to a fault. If we were only as cunning for God's interests as Satan is for his eh! I know this is a difficult affair for you but God will surely reward Sr. D's efforts and all will be for His greater glory.[19]

Catherine found rest and compassion at Edson, and began slowly to regain her mental and physical strength. The first indication of recovery was her request to be assigned the most ordinary, unskilled work available, and for some time she worked in the kitchen where her main job was peeling vegetables. Sister Quinn gave very frank progress reports to the Sister General:

> We finished Murder in a Nunnery. It is a great book ... Sister D. read it to us at table. She surely can read. I told her the other day I thought she should see Dr. Tiffin. I think she is having her menopause. Really she is quite a character. I do not bother offering an[y] corrections as I do not think they would go over very well. I do intend to watch my chance and tell her of a few glaring things though. For instance bringing her mending to chapel and draping it over the organ. She has many odd ways eh! I have treated her up to now as a guest. I have always given her her mail withou[t] opening it. Had I better do otherwise do you think? I just could not do it before. I felt it made her feel more independent the other way and she was pretty well broken up over the Sinnett episode ...
>
> Sister D. feeds one of the patients who had one hand off and part of another. She rather enjoys it too I believe.[20]

The Hardest Years

Nevertheless, supporting Catherine in her struggle to recover did try the patience of Sister Quinn. Two weeks later, she reported that "Dr. Tiffin checked Sr. Donnelly last week. He says she has a chronic arthritis. Nothing else serious heart O.K. blood pressure O.K. She is a problem." The report a month later indicated that Sister Quinn had brought her through the worst of her depression when she was able to say, "I admire her more than ever before. She promised to say a special prayer for me each day. There is a lot of good in her. It is a pity she puts her foot in it so often eh?"[21] By May, the report stated that, "everybody is busy, Sister Donnelly is now making beds for up patients, washing bedside tables and the drinking glasses for Sister DeMarsh on the men's floor. It helps out nicely."[22]

Sister Quinn gained a new appreciation of the situation Catherine had endured at Sinnett when, in May, she visited the mission there on an inspection trip for the Sister General.

> If we could talk we might be able to come to a decision re a Sister going to Sinnett. They really need a house-keeper there. The place is a wreck ... The Sinnett affair is a mix-up but nothing that cannot be smoothed out ... I feel certain if you saw Sinnett you would not send a young inexperienced Sister there. There is considerable school work to be gone over yet so Sisters F and P. have enough to do in the school. Cannot write the circumstances about the house to you ... I'll tell you *all* about my visit when we meet.[23]

Catherine's physical recovery was set back in mid-May when she caught erysipelas for the second time, but this did not deter her from seeking and receiving permission to study chemistry at summer school in Edmonton. In September she returned to Edson and continued to work at the hospital at any assigned tasks, and also tutored a local girl in trigonometry.

Hours of doing mechanical tasks gave Catherine time to brood about the current progress of the order. Although the members now elected their Sister General and council, the order was still, in all essential matters, controlled by Father Daly. Because he had spent order's money (which she did admit he had worked very hard to raise) on the urban properties used as hostels, very little would be available for the professional education of the sisters. This meant that the order would be ill-prepared to take advantage of the growing shortage of teachers and nurses. Catherine had met many of the novices at the

To Do and to Endure

correspondence schools in Regina and Edmonton, and she realized that during their training in Toronto they had never been told about her vision of women religious who would teach in the difficult rural areas. How could they understand the need for more training, if they were not told of the order's original purpose? Omitted, too, was any mention of the crucial role she had played in the design of the order's Rule to ensure that Sisters of Service would have the freedom to live and work in close proximity to their students and to patients in their clinics. The novices were only told that she was the first person to join the order.[24]

The one person to whom Catherine felt she could confide her disillusionment was Father Coughlan. She saved his replies to her letters expressing these feelings, for in them he confirmed her conviction that the order was going further off course. In one letter for example, he declared:

> I cannot see any point in the Hostel work ... if these hostels are to be merely lodging homes for Catholic girls or women. There are other agencies that could attend to this praiseworthy endeavor. There might be some reason for a small house at a few ports of entry for immigrant young women ... but immigration is practically non-existent at present ... It seems to me that the S.O.S. would lose nothing, save money spent, by giving up the Hostels and concentrating their attention and efforts on the three early aims of the Institute, rural schools, rural hospitals, and rural social service ...
>
> As to your idea ... of setting up a separate Institute for teaching at the present time I think that would hardly be feasible ... What could be done is to choose the young postulants who seem to have the capacity ... and assign them to the necessary training for the work of teachers ... I am of the opinion that enough efforts were not [sic] made to procure schools ...
>
> I need not assure you I would be very much gratified to meet you and talk with you about Everything! I appreciate more than I can say the confidence you have always reposed in me ... What an ordeal you went through at Sinnett! It would have broken the heart (as well as the health) of any other than the brave soldier you are.[25]

Six months later Father Coughlan responded to two more of Catherine's unhappy letters and in them he repeated his assurances that their visions of the order's apostolate were in harmony:

> Surely the S.O.S. were not intended for these magnified boarding-

houses, which swallow up needed money and deprive the West of services of many Sisters. I favor the correspondence courses for neglected children, but they should be conducted intelligently and according to a strict time schedule ...

Your list of Sisters fitted for teaching and their qualifications was most interesting. These should make a fine foundation for a great effort for the Institute to inaugurate. If I were in authority in the S.O.S. I would designate you to head this endeavor ... superintend the work of the teachers ... and investigate likely prospective places for new schools ... and arrange for the progressive education of teachers in the schools and universities ... Unless something like that is done, there will be no coordination in the school work, but instead a planless business, disorder, everything left to chance, a fitful changing.

And now, to speak very confidentially to you, I think Father Daly has outlived his usefulness to your Institute. While no doubt he achieves much good, I think he has got into a rut and that he is too old [seventy years] and too fixed in his outlook to extricate himself back to the original plans of its foundation, and I am afraid Father Daly is unequal to that change. I realize fully that he cannot be pushed out of his office. I do not think he will easily resign, so what have you? God alone can save the day, and God can only be reached through prayer. You cannot realize how I hate to say the above, I have such esteem for my dear friend, Father Daly, but truth is truth even if it is disagreeable ... Of course I am a fallible man and I may be mistaken ... There is an old saying: "*Deus Providebit*": "God will provide." Let us pray that He may do so in our present crisis.[26]

In spite of Father Coughlan's comforting optimism, the situation would not change. His letter did, however, help Catherine to put her anxieties aside for she realized that her greatest efforts must now be directed to returning to teaching.

CHAPTER 13
BACK IN HARNESS: THE LAST YEARS OF TEACHING

THE FOLLOWING SUMMER (1942) CATHERINE WAS again allowed to attend summer school in Edmonton and continue working towards her university degree. She was anxious to return to teaching full time, and it was decided that in September, a classroom would be outfitted in the basement of Edson hospital where she would teach the Grade 11 high school curriculum to Sisters Leona Rose, aged thirty-one, and Josephine Dulaska, twenty-nine. It was a successful year for the two students. Indeed, Catherine's contribution was recognized by Sister Guest: "I know that this year you have laid a foundation (and I think that is the only way it could ever have been done) which will enable them to go into a classroom next September and work as the other students do."[1] Catherine's mental and physical recovery was accompanied by a revival of her desire to keep abreast of contemporary political, economic and religious developments by reading secular authors. Sister Guest found a donor willing to send copies of *Time* magazine to her, and in return, Catherine sent her Sister General a book on "business economics." The strong friendship between these two women was never damaged by Sister Guest's swift and drastic action during the mysterious Sinnett troubles, and Catherine never faulted her Sister General for ordering her sudden withdrawal.

In the spring of 1943 Catherine was elected as the delegate from Edson to the order's second general chapter, which was held at the motherhouse in Toronto from 5 to 15 July. The minutes of those meetings indicate that Catherine participated prominently in the discussions, for her name appears as a mover or seconder of several motions. Many of these eliminated archaic customs or introduced changes of a more substantive nature in the order's lifestyle. Among

255

the recommendations by the Committee on Schools (of which Catherine was a member) were: "That more subjects be trained to be qualified teachers in the rural Public Schools"; and "that it be written into our Customs that, 'Our Sisters shall not wear the cap or cross in any school in which they teach or study, or help with teaching. This includes Normal Schools, Universities, and the Summer Schools under the direction of the Universities or the Department of Education. The cap and cross are worn in the convent'."[2] After a lengthy discussion and secret ballot, the motion passed almost unanimously.

Two notable changes passed by the council were that the hostels were to be renamed "Residential Clubs," and the committee on hostels also recommended "that some Sisters with an aptitude for social service work be given professional training." The latter was not voted on, but the discussion did draw attention to the need for more professionally trained sisters within the order. The recommendation spurred Catherine to be increasingly critical of what she considered to be the order's simplistic methods of performing social service work through hostels. She also believed that Father Coughlan's letters vindicated her harsh judgment of Father Daly for assigning so much money and personnel to their furtherance. Unfortunately, she could not reveal the source of her opinion as Father Coughlan had marked his letters "confidential," and they were not made accessible in the archives until many years after his death in 1943.

At the conclusion of the general chapter, Catherine was ready to return to her professional vocation as a teacher in the small public schools in the outlying districts. Her attendance at the council meeting in Toronto during the summer, however, and the fact that the Sister General was still uncertain whether she had recovered her stamina sufficiently to undertake a one-room school, had precluded her applying for any positions.

In October 1943 a suitable teaching opportunity became available when Sister Agnes Dwyer, who was teaching all the elementary grades at the Diamond Coulee School, in the south-central region of Saskatchewan, requested that Catherine be assigned to Diamond Crossing, six miles away, where Agnes lived in the former Royal Canadian Mounted Police barracks. Here, Catherine was to help out by teaching a small group of Grade 9 pupils.

The main town in the district was Minton, which was nearly one hundred miles south of Regina, and not far from the American border. It was an isolated farming district, whose bare, bleak hills were witness to years of severe drought. Fanning out from Minton and only a few miles apart were the hamlets of Jutland, Bergfield and Diamond Crossing. Each had a one- or two-room school, but because of their poor facilities and small teacherages, the few lay teachers who had applied for these schools had not stayed long. In 1938 Sisters of Service had begun teaching in the district because Archbishop Monahan and the local priest, Father A. Beechey, had persuaded Father Daly that teaching sisters were urgently required in the area, which was one of the poorest in Saskatchewan. One sister recalled that in the beginning, "in temporal goods of this world, priest, people and sisters had the bare necessities of life. The sisters were on relief with the rest of the parish."[3] Their willingness to share their hardships impressed the people in the struggling communities, and they were highly regarded.

The present priest, Father J.F. Volk, supported the sisters as much as he could, for he admired their willingness to undertake a ceaseless round of missionary work in the district. They taught in the public school all day, offered religious instruction after classes were over, and also travelled through the district on Saturdays and Sundays, calling on the people and conducting catechism classes. Still further, the sisters organized and trained a teenage church choir, gave lessons in handicrafts, housekeeping, art and woodwork, and distributed children's clothing to needy families. They felt, in fact, that in spite of the bleak landscape, it was a satisfying place to work, as long as their isolated posting did not last too long.

This would be a good posting for Catherine, moreover, as Sister Dwyer had a companion-housekeeper with her at Diamond Crossing, Catherine would not have extra domestic responsibilities along with her teaching. A section of their quarters in the barracks was curtained off to make a school room, and Sister Dwyer arranged with the school board that Catherine would start on 25 October to teach Grade 9 for no salary. Catherine's skills were a great gift to the children of the local community, for there was no way their parents could have transported them to the high school some distance away. Gas was rationed and even the sisters did not receive any extra gas coupons for their old Ford car. They were limited to driving to Minton for Mass and supplies, and making a few neighbourly calls.

Catherine settled quickly into the community and teaching routine. Sister Dwyer reported to the Sister General:

> Sister Donnelly has been marvellous so far, and it adds a great deal to have her here. She certainly is not hard to tell things to, and is, as you say, very humble, one, who is I think, truly humble. She tries to be cheerful and I think is really excellent. She has definitely made up her mind not to interfere with Father or anyone ...
>
> Sister Donnelly has Sister help her in the French class, and finds her a great help. She says Sister [who did not have teacher training] just goes about it perfectly, and finds the pupils are quite interested ...
>
> Sr. C.D.(please excuse these abbreviations) thinks Sr. P. and I are ideal S.O.S. according to the ideal she had, anyway, so we are feeling quite puffed up. We find Sister good company and I think three is much better than two ... [At school] we had a Welcome Program for Sr. C.D. and she was quite touched.[4]

After the Diamond Crossing school closed in June, Catherine attended summer school in Saskatoon. In September 1944 she was back in Edmonton working at the correspondence school and taking more degree courses at the university. In September 1945 the staff at Diamond Crossing was changed: Sister Agnes Dwyer was sent to Fargo, North Dakota, to be the Superior of the order's Religious Correspondence School which Father Daly had founded in 1939; an experienced teacher, Sister Mary Jackson, was assigned to the Jutland school; and Catherine was also assigned to Jutland to keep house for Sister Jackson in the small teacherage.

It would not be an easy year for either of the women, as both the Jutland school and their living quarters were in very poor condition in spite of the school board's agreement to improve them. For Catherine, it was a revelation of the physical and psychological difficulties endured for years and in many other locations by the order's housekeepers, who coped alone day after day, through trying inconveniences and lack of equipment when doing hard domestic work. She never forgot the unceasing tasks which occupied her every day that year in their deteriorating little house:

> I slept in a corner upstairs, did the cooking and housework, carried drinking and cooking water from a farm, and laundry water from

the big muddy stream — had to carry it up a steep hill. And I carried pails of coal up the flight of stairs to the 2nd floor stove and one flight to the kitchen ... But I survived it all.[5]

She later recalled: "My break from slavery was when I studied a university math subject by correspondence from Saskatoon University."[6]

Life was just as difficult for Sister Jackson; she taught all day in a run-down school house that lacked both teaching and playground equipment, and with little interest or co-operation by parents to make any improvements. After inspecting the area, Father Daly declared, "No man could survive here."[7]

At the end of June, Catherine was sent to Camp Morton to be cook-housekeeper under Sister Faye, who was now Superior of that busy mission. But while Catherine was in Toronto the following summer, she applied to fill the vacancy at Diamond Coulee Public School. In his letter of acknowledgment the board secretary of the district school units noted that as she held a "Superior First Class Certificate," she was eligible for a salary of $1,650 per year; but he also noted that a provision in their schedule stated that the maximum salary for a school with an enrolment of less than ten students would be $1,200 per annum. As he expected that the enrolment would be small, he set her contract at the smaller sum, with the understanding that "in the event that the enrolment should be 10 or more a new contract will be drawn up."[8]

Catherine arrived at Diamond Coulee in July 1947 to prepare the school for opening. After inspecting her new post Catherine notified the local school board secretary that it needed a coal shed. His reply was a graphic revelation of local farm life:

Dear Madam.
Re the coal shed I cannot do anything about it for some time yet, as I have 120 acres of flax to harvest as soon as it is ready and as you probably know I am the local Inspector for the P.F.A.A. [the farmers association] and I have to turn in a detailed report on every farm in the nine townships that comprise this Municipality in the not too-distant future. This on top of the usual work of running a 969 acre farm with a a big livestock population will keep me busy for a while, so do not depend on me for school work of this kind right away.

259

To Do and to Endure

> You are doubtless aware that the officer who has the executive authority in a Saskatchewan School Board is the Chairman, in this case Mr. Hoffart. Why not give him a chance at some of these things? He has a number of boys who, while not expert carpenters could probably do the work well enough and they could get to it long before I could ...
>
> Your suggestion re using old toilet lumber for coal shed is, I am afraid not very good. The lumber you mentioned could be used for roof boards where it could be covered with shingles perhaps but not elsewhere. We have far too many buildings of that type already alas.
>
> I am sorry I cannot fulfill your wishes right away but we poor dubs out here make our own living the hard way and if school Teachers' salaries are to be paid I have to keep my nose to the grindstone.[9]

The school opened in August and for the first month Catherine had for a housekeeper Bernice Anstett, a young sister, who up to that time had worked in the hostels. Her most vivid memory was Catherine's exuberant enthusiasm for her work, in spite of their poor living conditions:

> Our tiny unpainted house didn't boast a pump for either rain or drinking water. We depended on our neighbors across the road to attend Mass or to shop in the nearby town, Minton. Catherine seemed to thrive on frugality as long as she could teach! Each afternoon, after the children had been dismissed, she would hurry to our "posh residence" and recount exciting things that happpened. All the little tasks I did to make our living together enjoyable (such as making toasted orange and onion sandwiches and putting up a wooden plank to catch rain water in a barrel) she really appreciated and told me so. (Something unusual in those days, in religious life one was rarely complimented.)
>
> During the following years she wrote to me many times, encouraging me to go back to school and become a teacher. When I finally did make the move to complete grade 13, and go to teachers' college she was enthusiastic ...
>
> I find it interesting that I never realized that this woman CD — as we all knew her — was the woman with the vision that brought the Sisters of Service into being![10]

When Sister Anstett returned to the hostel in September, Dorothy Daley joined Catherine at Diamond Coulee. Catherine tried to broaden

Back in Harness: The Last Years of Teaching

the school curriculum by assigning Sister Daley to teach classes in knitting, sewing and music, in addition to her household tasks. The latter's past teaching experience in the order had been solely in the summer catechetical schools or hostels where she worked with larger staffs in the urban missions. These had provided companionship, and the structured religious routine of a large convent community which she had found were strong spiritual supports. Dorothy Daley had joined the community in 1932 because she had read some of Father Daly's recruiting literature describing the missionary work being done in the West. She had responded to his descriptions of the need for teachers of religion for the immigrant children. Professional teaching in secular schools had not been emphasized. "Since I did not want to be a teacher, this Order greatly appealed to me. When I entered we never heard of Catherine Donnelly for years. Our first knowledge of her was that she was the first Sister of Service."

The great influence in Sister Daley's spiritual formation had been Father Daly, for he had "opened the doors [of the Order] to all who were ready to live a religious life of poverty, labor, sacrifice and mortification for the poorest of the poor. He had visited the novitiate in Toronto every Sunday that he was in the city, and when he lectured the Novices he emphasized the importance of intense prayer and faithfulness to monthly and yearly retreats." He proclaimed frequently that, "It is quality and not quantity that counts. I'd rather see a small band of spiritual souls than an army of half-hearted Sisters. No Sister is consecrated to God for her own comfort and convenience."[11]

In Diamond Coulee Sister Daley learned about Catherine's role in founding the order, not once but "every Saturday morning ... I listened to her story of the foundation." As Catherine recalled how her design for the order had been thwarted by Father Daly, her resentment poured out. She admitted that she had not openly crossed Father Daly as she did not want to hurt him. Nevertheless, to Dorothy Daley she uttered the tactless and unfair accusation that "he took in all the riff-raff where I wanted professionals and opened up these glorified boarding houses (hostels)."[12] Pronouncements such as these from her Superior made Dorothy feel very isolated indeed.

When winter arrived the housekeeping chores became heavier, as in addition to hauling drinking water and chopping wood, snow had to be melted for washing, and coal carried from the shed. By January

To Do and to Endure

Sister Daley was limping badly from a damaged hip and had trembling spells. Catherine was concerned, and arranged for her to see a doctor in Regina. He reported that she was over-tired and weak, and had a chronic hip condition. Although she could return to Diamond Coulee, she must have more rest and not do any strenuous work or heavy lifting. The Sister General informed Catherine that to preserve Sister Daley's health, she should be relieved from these tasks. As well, she should "not be given too much to do in regard to the teaching of music etc. I know it is difficult for one to look after a house and prepare work for school too. Sister Daley has not complained but the doctor does find her in a weak condition so that is warning for us to be careful and not put too much on her."[13] Catherine willingly accepted the directive and did a larger share of the housework.

Sister Daley also recalled that life with Catherine was not all hard work and grim recrimination. "She had a good sense of humor, and we had many a good laugh together." Catherine was very fond of their priest, Father Volk, and they had a good working relationship. She admired his friendliness, and his humble piety, and praised him for treating the Sisters of Service as partners with him in the mission work. Nevertheless Catherine used her own judgment when it came to fulfilling her religious obligations. Sister Daley recalled that on Easter Sunday, Father Volk was to celebrate Mass at a church seven miles away and they had no ride arranged. She suggested that she and Catherine hitch a ride in the wagon of a local passing farmer as he passed the school. Catherine did not think she would be able to go:

> Sister had other projects on her mind but I said I was going anyway. I said, "here we are, no Mass for weeks ... didn't get our throats blessed ... didn't get the ashes ... and now, no Easter Duty? I'll never forget the imp in her eye as she looked up into my face, and suppressing a giggle she said,: "Isn't it a good thing we were baptized before we got here." We laughed with great mirth. Presently I saw horses approaching, and I ran and jumped on.[14]

Sister Daley was able to complete her year with Catherine, but it was obvious to the Sister General that living conditions in the area were endangering the health of all of the sisters working there. She wrote to Father Volk that Sister Jackson had permission to resign from Jutland School and Sister Catherine Donnelly would be resigning from Diamond Coulee. She asked him "how the people and Inspector found

Back in Harness: The Last Years of Teaching

Sister Donnelly as a teacher. Father Volk replied that the living and working conditions at the schools in the area were unfit for the sisters and he did not think that they could ask them to continue living under the present conditions, although many people had asked that they remain in the area. He had been told recently by the school inspector that he has a desperate time getting teachers for the district of Minton. The district board planned to build a three-room school at Minton, but he felt he would just have to wait and see how it will all turn out. In the meantime the living conditions at Jutland had not, and would not improve and he felt that

> we have waited long enough ... without success ... The Diamond Coulee school board wanted me to wire you to have the Sisters remain — but conditions there are worse than at Jutland and I made it clear to them. They made little effort to get the Sisters to Mass. Sister Donnelly told me that she had a letter from the Unit Board offering her any school she likes in this unit.[15]

With the clergy's approval, the Sister General decided not to replace the sisters who had resigned from the schools in the Minton district.

Catherine returned to Saskatoon after school was closed to attend summer school at the university. She passed her astronomy course and, to her great joy, was given permission to attend full time at the university for the 1948-49 year. She could now fulfill her life-long dream of completing her bachelor of arts degree. She submitted her application and underwent the compulsory X-ray examination in late August. To her horror, the doctor who read the plate saw evidence of an old infection in the right lung. It appeared to have healed, but further tests were ordered, and the doctor confirmed that tuberculosis bacilli were present. Catherine was put immediately into the sanatorium for further observation. A second test proved negative, but just to be sure, the doctor ordered another laboratory test, which would take at least two months for results. It was November before Catherine was informed that the germs observed on the slide in the first test were not tuberculosis. The old minimal pulmonary tuberculosis in her right lung was "inactive and non-infectious," and she was free to leave the sanatorium.[16] But now the year was too far advanced for her to attend the university.

To have been so close to fulfilling her ambition to be a university graduate was a severe blow. The opportunity to attend for a full year would never come again. This experience only hardened Catherine's determination to see that the younger sisters completed their secondary school education before they became too old to take university, college or hospital training which would earn them professional qualifications. But for now, her assignment was to work again at the Regina Catechetical School.

During the time she was in Regina her concern about the direction which the order was taking burst into the open in the form of a barrage of letter-writing to some of her clergy friends and several of the teaching sisters of her own order. She suggested that they join her in founding another order, dedicated solely to teaching in the rural areas. Only then could they recover the original purpose of the Sisters of Service. The sisters who received her long, rambling missives were disturbed, refused even to consider such an idea. and destroyed her letters.[17]

Catherine also outlined a similar plan to Bishop Henri Routhier OMI, and he was more sympathetic to her feelings of disillusionment and said that he understood her disappointment at Father Daly's dominating influence on the order's apostolate. He asked her to "let me know in detail what you think the rules of such an institution should comprise. The rule itself must be flexible, but there must be some organization to assure a deep religious life, a profound instruction in religion, not to mention absolute competence in teaching."[18] She responded immediately in some detail, outlining a proposed Order of the Day, and other details. She admitted that "the finances at first might be a problem of some proportions, but later on, not likely to be a difficulty at all." She also mentioned that Sister Guest would help launch such an initiative. "If her health improves sufficiently, she will be able for a big task."[19] In his reply, the bishop tactfully did not comment on the fact that her description of the new order matched that in the present Rule of the Sisters of Service, except that hostels were not included in their apostolate. He did most emphatically point out that the difficulties of financing the new order would be insurmountable. He encouraged her to continue with her teaching, and not lose sight of her goal of increasing the number of teaching sisters in the existing order. In other words, to establish the new religious order she had in mind was just not feasible, and she must accept that fact.

Catherine used poor judgment in plotting to found a splinter group, for it dismayed the teaching sisters and alienated those who were working in the hostels. Perhaps one cause for this serious breach of discipline during this period might be found in her anguish over Sister General Margaret Guest's severe mental and physical breakdown. Never a physically strong woman, Catherine's friend and oldest teaching collegue had worked without respite since her election as Sister General in 1937. She was the head of an order which was chronically short of money, yet was continually taking on new obligations. She worried about the sisters, who looked to her as their leader. She had first become ill in May 1947, shortly after her confrontation with Father Daly over his arbitrary decisions over the spending of the order's funds. He insisted on maintaining complete control of the order's finances, as well as making the living arrangements for all the projects he initiated. Yet it was Sister Guest who was nominally responsible for seeing that the Sisters of Service were adequately clothed and housed and placed in work suitable to their talents and training. One of the ablest women in the order, Sister Guest had struggled to carry out her duties. But by May 1948 she was unable to continue as Sister General, and asked to be replaced. She never undertook any administrative responsibilities in the governance of the order again.[20]

Catherine came to Toronto in August 1949 to celebrate her silver jubilee as a Sister of Service. She then returned to catechetical work until October 1951, when she was sent to the town of Peace River to serve as the cook for the sisters who were teaching there in the separate school. She remained there until the summer of 1952, when she was transferred to the order's mission at the hamlet of Rycroft, seventy-five miles south of Peace River. At the age of sixty-eight, she was to take up once more her originally intended vocation — a teaching sister in a rural public school. This time, however, Catherine would not be pioneering in a district which had never had teaching sisters in their school. The Sisters of Service had been active in the Rycroft public school since 1944.

They had come to this hamlet in the Peace River District in response to the repeated requests of Bishop Henri Routhier OMI, and the parish priest, Father Joseph Paquin OMI, to Father Daly and to Sister General Margaret Guest. Both clergy were convinced that the Sisters of Service was the only womens' religious order which could teach in the public school, conduct classes in religion for the Catholic

To Do and to Endure

children, and visit the families living in the isolated farming district, known as the Peace River Block, three hundred miles northwest of Edmonton. Its main link with Edmonton was the railway, as the one road could be impassable in bad weather. The farmlands in the area had been recently settled, mainly by Croatian and Ukrainian immigrants, along with some French-Canadians and a few English. Most of the settlers were nominally Roman Catholic, but many had lapsed in practice. In addition to supplying teachers for their children, Father Paquin had insisted that dormitory accommodation from Monday to Friday be provided for the elementary and high school students who lived too far away from Rycroft to commute daily.

The Sisters of Service had purchased a large empty house in Rycroft which was renovated to serve as a residence, complete with kitchen and a small parlour. The second floor was divided into several tiny bedrooms for the sisters. Most of the remaining area became dormitories for about twenty children, with boys on one side of the hall and girls on the other. The house had no plumbing; water for the students' washbasins had to be carried up and down the stairs. There was electric light, but heating and cooking were by wood stoves. As there were no wells in the town, and no town piping system for water delivery, the mission's water for drinking, cooking and washing had to be bought at 65 cents a barrel. The order's meagre funds were supplemented by citizens who donated furniture and linens for the house dormitory as well as food and used clothing for the students. The sisters' school regulations stated that the boarding charge was $10 per month, and that boarders were to return home every weekend with their dirty laundry unless this was absolutely impossible. Boarders were also expected to help with the housework each day; they had to make their own beds, do dishes, sweep and dust, and bring in the wood for the stoves.

From the beginning, the Rycroft Mission had been a popular community project, as parents no longer had to send their children to the school in Spirit River, five miles away, where there were no facilities for them to stay overnight during bad weather. But running the dormitory was also an extra burden for the small teaching and housekeeping staff, who were never free from their duties of teaching and supervising a lively group of children and adolescents in a building which was not designed to be a boarding school. The dorm was too often a noisy place. The boarders ate their meals with the sisters and, like all children, frequently needed their table manners corrected. The property was never empty or quiet, for the children used the house grounds for a play yard. Weekends did not bring the staff much respite, since all too often several of the students could not return to their homes for one reason or another. Staff changes had been frequent because of fatigue, frayed nerves, and poor health from the waves of illnesses which would afflict everyone living in the crowded building. These difficult living conditions were taken in stride by the students, and one, Paul Stanich, wrote a poem about life as a "Dormite," from the students point of view in the 1948 high school year book.

St. Michael's Dormitory

The dorm has got a set of rules
That we must all obey
They range from "Richard, bring some wood
To "Ernest hit the hay."

The strictest order must be kept
By boys and girls alike,
Or else we get a reprimand
From the Sisters of St. Mike's.

There's Father Paquin, lives next door
(He helps keep up morale)
And if we ever break the rules
He really gives us — well!

One night the boys were rather rough
Superior gave us a warning
Then later Father came and said
"Come see me in the Morning."

Next morn we went to meet our fate
In the reception room
Where Father Paquin awaited us
To send us to our doom.

We got a good stiff penalty
(It filled us with regret)

Which each and every one of us
Has not forgotten yet.

Our rules we seldom have to break
(Sometimes we do, no doubt)
And if the case is serious
Sister says,"Move out."

Yet we all love good old St. Mike's
We dread the thought of leaving
And when we have to leave the dorm
For it we will be grieving.[21]

By 1952 the venture was recognized as an educational and religious success. During the eight years it had existed, many immigrant children who spoke no English when they enrolled had become good students. One boy had boarded in the dormitory for five years, then attended agricultural college; by 1952 he was a successful farmer. Another student, John Duby, fifteen, was in Grade 11 when he boarded in the dorm in 1946. He later attended the University of Alberta, and in 1952 won a Rhodes scholarship.[22]

Every summer the sisters had taught classes in religion at Rycroft and throughout the Peace River District. Only a few people had attended the Rycroft Catholic church in 1942, but in eight years its congregation had increased to ninety-eight families. Bishop Routhier was impressed by the versatility of the Sisters of Service and described their unique qualities to their ecclesiastical superior, Cardinal James McGuigan of Toronto:

> Whereas all the other communities in our Vicariate are devoted in their teaching profession and in their care of patients in hospitals, while being faithful to the Rule, the Sisters of Service have this added quality that they alone have willingly and habitually visited the family [sic] of Catholics and non-Catholics, and especially neglected Catholics, to strive by all means to bring them into or back to the Church. Their manner has always strongly appealed to our population and they are beloved by Catholics and non-Catholics. They are the ideal type of missionary Sisters for many parts of our Vicariate where in small settlements people are unable to have mass regularly, being too sparsely scattered over vast areas ...

Back in Harness: The Last Years of Teaching

My only regret is that they are too few for the abundant work that would await them ... if they were more numerous.[23]

The sisters also cleaned and prepared the church for services each week, but this too was considered a worthy work, and Sister Superior Mary Phillips was pleased to report to Bishop Routhier that there was a "packed church each Sunday."[24]

Catherine arrived in Rycroft during the summer of 1952 to settle in and to teach catechism classes. Sixteen boys were being boarded in the dormitory for a week while they were instructed for confirmation. Catherine achieved immediate fame in the town for the wonderful stories she told the boys at bedtime. "These stories were almost 100% from the Old Testament and one could not hear a sound but Sister's voice, so great was the boys' interest."[25]

In September she was assigned to teach the Grade 9 students in the junior high school section of Rycroft public school, at an annual salary of $3,420. She attacked her teaching duties with her customary gusto, but at sixty-eight her energy and patience were not at the level that they had been when she was forty. Her Superior was apprehensive about this, and noted that her control declined when she was over-tired. "She is better right now and, oh, I certainly hope she stays that way. Sister is very anxious to be a success and I certainly would like to see her complete the year successfully."[26]

Near the end of March 1953, as she was leaving the house to attend the early Mass, Catherine fell. She said nothing about it, and sat through the service, until her Superior noticed her discomfort. They drove to the hospital at Spirit River where the X-ray revealed a severely broken wrist. It was set under a general anaesthetic "of which she was a little afraid."[27] Two months later one of Catherine's students noted that her wrist was still painful. Nevertheless, she managed to complete the school year.

July and August were spent in Saskatoon, as Sister General Quinn had given permisssion for her to take a course being given there in alcohol education. One of her great joys that summer was the visit of her old Baptist friends, Ruth and Achsah MacDonnell, with whom she had been corresponding regularly for years. In September Catherine returned to her Grade 9 class at the Rycroft school, where Sister Magdalen Barton was teaching the senior high school grades. It was a hard year for both of them. Catherine was ill several times with colds

To Do and to Endure

and then with pneumonia. By the end of May she was "too tired for us to discuss anything with."[28] Sister Superior Phillips talked this situation over with the third teaching sister on staff, Mary MacDougall, and reported their conclusions to the Sister General:

> Sister C.D. ... can't stay another year under this setup but, you know we do think Sister could last possibly for longer than we think [sic] if she had a quiet place to go after school and a real convent where the lights have to go out at a certain time. That is her downfall — she will not go to bed on time here and she knows there is no bell to tell her to go to bed — we can't have it as it would waken the children! ... For the sake of the community I would like to see Sister teaching as she will not be happy doing anything else — and yet without a [regular] convent [life], she can't continue. Isn't it a riddle!
>
> You have my prayers in your many dilemmas although I'll have to warn you, the Lord is turning a deaf ear to most of my petitions lately.[29]

The problem was that Catherine liked to read current books and periodicals to keep knowledgeable on world affairs, and the only time available was late at night, when she could be alone and silent. As a result of this ceaseless work and lack of sleep Catherine was frequently ill, to the detriment of her students and the life of her sisters in the convent.

Sister Barton was tired too, for she was preparing the Grade 12 students for the important provincial examinations in June. It was the first time a class at Rycroft had attempted the full Grade 12 curriculum in one year. The principal of the school, whom the sisters all liked and respected, taught some Grade 12 subjects as well. When he became ill near the end of the term, Sister Barton was the only teacher available to help them. The students' results reflected the lack of qualified substitute teachers for the senior grades when illness felled the staff: "The bright ones did not do too badly, but the weak ones went under."[30] Catherine felt it proved the urgent need for more teachers in the order, and in a letter to the Sister General she named two sisters whom she felt would make good professionals if they were given training.[31]

Catherine did not attend the fourth general chapter in July 1954, as she was not elected as a delegate. Father Daly, now eighty-two, gave several talks to the sisters, reviewing the order's progress and urging them to be faithful to their vows and their apostolate. He calmly reminded them that his own life and work with the order would probably soon end, but he had reached his goal, for the order was now free of debt. Sisters of Service were now serving in twenty-two missions across Canada as nurses, school teachers, residence workers, and teachers of religion through correspondence schools and summer classes. Their work had benefited thousands of immigrants and their children. All this was being accomplished by an order of only 119 women; ninety-three had taken permanent vows; fifteen were under temporary vows; nine were novices and two postulants.[32] He regretted that the order had not grown faster, but he assured them again that their quality more than made up for the lack of quantity.

In the months following the chapter, Father Daly's strength waned noticeably. He did not retire; members of his order worked until illness forced them to stop. He continued to conduct retreats when he was able, and although he cut down the hours he spent at his desk in the Sisters of Service motherhouse, he still came every day to oversee the order's affairs. Most important was the faithfulness with which he corresponded with the sisters, particularly those in the remote areas. He remembered their anniversaries, sent them books which he thought they would like to read, and assured them that their spiritual needs were not forgotten. His warm and friendly letters and little jokes made him a much loved father to the order to which he had devoted all the time and energy he could muster.

In faraway Rycroft the staff were preparing for another school year when tragedy struck the community. On the day before school reopened the principal committed suicide. When the school did open a week later, the teaching staff felt that they were working on a rudderless ship. They sorely missed his leadership and his teaching skills, and the school board had difficulty finding a qualified replacement.

The sisters boarded only eleven students that year, all of them in high school. Supervising them was a nerve-wracking task, particularly for the housekeepers who washed and cooked and cleaned in an inconvenient house amid the boisterous teenagers. Because of these unsettling circumstances and her own failing strength, Catherine's tempestuous outbursts at school and in the house became more frequent. Yet when the final results of the seventeen Rycroft students who wrote the provincial examinations were released, only two of the seven who failed were Catherine's students — and this in spite of illnesses which had hospitalized her twice that school year.

When plans were being made for the 1955-56 school year Catherine was outspoken in her objections to the continuance of boarding the high school students in quarters which were utterly inadequate for senior boys and girls, and at fees which she felt were too low. She also pointed out that the need was now less urgent, as transportation was more available and new schools were being built in the outlying areas. Moreover, the house was certain to be in turmoil during the fall term since, at long last, the town was installing sewers and a water system, and was about to start on the Sisters of Service property. The installation of the extensive plumbing required throughout the house would be disruptive; and the extra people living there would make it even more trying. It was finally decided that only senior girls would be accepted as boarders.

The new principal rearranged the teaching schedules and insisted that Grades 8 and 9 be taught by two teachers, Sister Catherine and a lay teacher. Catherine was to teach Grade 8 students in the morning and Grade 9 in the afternoon, for a total of forty-eight students. It was a taxing schedule and Sister Mary O'Kane, the new Superior, was not optimistic. "Its going to be very hard on her. She comes home quite played out, but she has grit and one cannot help but admire her determination. No one seems to think she will last the year."[33] But she did last, although she had some particularly big, rowdy boys in her Grade 9 class who delighted in riling her. She persisted in teaching while recovering from a bad case of shingles. Although Sister O'Kane admired her determination, she confided to Sister General Quinn that this must be Catherine's last year in the Rycroft classroom. Sister General Quinn agreed, and said she would break the news to Catherine as gently and considerately as possible.

On 31 May 1956 Catherine was notified by the Sister General that she was now seventy-two and well past the official retirement age. Her health was not good, and the shingles were not yet cured. For these reasons she would not be teaching in the school next year. The rightness of this decision was confirmed by Sister O'Kane, who reported that the exams were on and Catherine was still working with her students; the shingles had broken out again and "the poor soul is

Back in Harness: The Last Years of Teaching

suffering much. Believe me she is pretty relieved to know she does not have to teach next year. She lets it drop now and then. One has to admire her grit."[34]

As Catherine's teaching career appeared to be ending, Father Daly's life was ebbing. He died in Toronto on 3 June 1956 at the age of eighty-four.

CHAPTER 14
I DON'T WANT TO GROW OLD GRACEFULLY — USEFULLY — YES

THIS ANONYMOUS QUOTATION IN AN ARTICLE Catherine was reading caught her eye, and she wrote it down in a notebook in which she summarized articles and preserved sayings which pleased or inspired her. Then she noted in the margin, "Me too." It summed up precisely the philosophy of living which was to guide her throughout the years of her official retirement from the public school classroom.

After Catherine had received a formal letter from Sister General announcing her retirement, her Superior, Sister Mary O'Kane, made an appointment in June 1956 to discuss with the school authorities whether Sister Agnes Dwyer could replace Catherine at Rycroft school in September. It was with some trepidation that she invited Catherine to accompany her; as she explained, "my sympathies were with the old lady in spite of everything ... She was delighted and behaved beautifully."[1] When they met with Dr. Thomson, the superintendent of the Spirit River School Division, Sister O'Kane stated that the order felt that teaching alternating Grades 8 and 9 every day was taking its toll on Sister Donnelly's health. Catherine agreed that "it was very hard, but I feel able for it." The superintendent then confirmed that if the report from the registrar in Manitoba indicated that Sister Dwyer had the qualifications to teach Grade 9, she would be accepted in place of Sister Donnelly, if that was what the order wished. He then graciously thanked Catherine, and said that it had been a pleasure for the division to have her services, and that they would miss her. A relieved Sister O'Kane said a silent prayer of thanks that after all her worries, Catherine's departure from the Rycroft system took place without any trouble or regrets.

To Do and to Endure

Catherine spent part of the summer in Toronto, where she was able to visit with her sisters Tess and Sister Justina. Camp Morton was selected by the council as a suitable place for her to begin her retirement, for that was where she had started the order's first mission, thirty-two years before. The sisters' residence was now much larger, with many more conveniences, but their work was essentially the same, except that there were now three Sisters of Service teaching in three local schools. Catherine declared that her energy had returned after a summer off, and that she was fit and eager to resume teaching. The council decided that she could still give valuable service to the order if she undertook to tutor more sisters who required their high school matriculation before they could advance to professional training. Catherine was delighted to be able to continue working as a teacher, and in a situation where her skills were unique and needed.

A pleasant room with windows facing a splendid view west and north was fitted out as a classroom. Sister Mary Halder, who had entered the order in 1953, was the first sister selected to study there under Catherine. She completed Grade 12 successfully, entered a school of nursing, and graduated in 1962. Every year until 1968 Catherine taught either full or part-time in the "Camp Morton Matriculation School," as it was soon dubbed. People working in other parts of the house could not help but notice that even when teaching only one or two students, Catherine's method had not changed. She used all of her faculties, particularly her voice, to make a point. One sister remarked later that she addressed each one of them as if they were a large class, but she had not lost her touch for transmitting the essentials of a subject clearly and quickly. Another sister whom she taught from 1962 to 1964 wrote to her:

> I should have written you in view of the intense efforts you made with my education. Nothing is forgotten Sister. All that you taught me is tucked away ready for use, even the mathematics. The two years we spent together were a success, maybe not so much academically as a personal relationship trial — I have happy memories of Camp Morton and I think something fine was added to my character.[2]

Once or twice she substituted for the teacher in the local elementary schools, and one incident in particular made her yearn again for the classroom. She spent the day with fifteen elementary students who "gave me a royal welcome and were very disappointed that I couldn't stay for the rest of the week ... They thanked me again and again and coaxed me to come back. It was surely very moving. But I guess it was my swan song. I am glad I had this delightful experience. It was just marvellous."[3]

She also enjoyed tutoring the secondary students who required individual help for longer periods. Several young people from local families were listed in her letters as students she was helping in mathematics, Latin or French. Her remark in May 1966 to Sister General Agnes Dwyer was typical: "I have Freddy Schnerch for coaching every day after 4 in grade XI maths. He is desperately trying to get through high school."[4]

Catherine was still keen to continue with her own studies. In 1964, at the age of eighty, with Sister General Agnes Dwyer's permission, she attended a six-week summer session in senior French at the University of Edmonton. She was pleased to report that the course was taught in French, that the final examination consisted of three long essays in French and one in English, and that she had passed with 57 per cent.

A few weeks later, on 1 October, Catherine's sister Tess, died at the age of seventy-four. Tess and her beloved Arthur, a man whom Catherine greatly admired, had three children, one of whom, Barbara, had died at twenty-four, shortly after she was married. Their other two children were also married; daughter Renée had five children, and son Robert had seven. Catherine was a proud aunt as she watched her nieces and nephew grow up, receive good educations, and make successful marriages. At each milestone in their lives she had written cheery, encouraging letters which accompanied the little gifts she always managed to send. She also corresponded with the twelve children who were her great-nieces and nephews, and encouraged them to visit her. Catherine's nephew Robert Gifford, a successful American lawyer, was so fond of his Aunt Catherine that if a business trip brought him near Manitoba, as happened twice, he went out of his way to call on her at Camp Morton.

Her semi-retirement also gave her the time to be more regular in her correspondence. One of her personal beliefs concerning the proper lifestyle for those in religious orders, which Catherine transmitted to her own order, was that becoming a sister should not preclude her

To Do and to Endure

from maintaining frequent, close and direct communication with family and friends in the secular world. All Sisters of Service were allowed extended visits to their homes in family emergencies, and the sisters in Toronto visited Catherine's elderly Baptist friends, Ruth and Achsah MacDonnell, on her behalf whenever they were in hospital. When Catherine visited the motherhouse in Toronto, the sisters drove her to see all her old Alliston schoolmates. Father Daly agreed with her on this, for he too had a wide circle of all religious denominations with whom he kept in touch. As well, on his frequent travels across Canada, he would bring greetings to the friends and relatives of the Sisters of Service.

Another group who received Catherine's letters during the 1960s were selected sisters who were working in the residences. Catherine urged them to consider completing their secondary education, and then to take professional training. Several sisters did apply to do so, and when the news was announced that they were now attending high school, or had enrolled in courses leading to designations in social work, nursing, dietetics or teaching, her letters of approval would arrive shortly after. As they struggled with unfamiliar subjects, homework and examinations, Catherine would send them chatty, encouraging notes congratulating them on their progress, and urging them to persevere. She herself taught or gave short-term coaching to a total of twelve Sisters of Service who achieved their matriculation, and influenced several others to upgrade their academic qualifications in schools near where they were stationed. She was heartened when more substantial sums in the order's annual budgets began to be allotted to tuition fees. In spite of these successes, she still complained that the order was not making the most effective use of its members to achieve its original purpose. She was relentless in lobbying the order's council and the Sister General to pursue every work opportunity available in provincial government service to qualified Sisters of Service, particularly in the under-serviced northern sections of the western provinces. "The more SOS who work ... the better those governments will be."[5]

But what of the many sisters who were still working happily and effectively in the Residential Clubs, as they were now called? Many of them had not been interested in teaching school or nursing when Father Daly had accepted them into the order. In spite of Catherine's misgivings, they had been assigned important work in the SOS

I Don't Want to Grow Old Gracefully — Usefully — *Yes*

residences or in the country missions as housekeepers for the teaching sisters. There was still some demand for residence accommodation, although their clientele now came less frequently from the immigrant community. Not many of these sisters received Catherine's letters of praise and encouragement. In this, she did not seem to recognize that the sisters' residence work had generated a large portion of the order's income during the Depression, the war years and the postwar immigration period.

These issues came to a head in an unhappy meeting in the order's Winnipeg residence in May 1965 held to discuss the present and future role of the residence apostolate. Catherine was present when several residence workers contested her assertion that Father's Daly's insistence on spending so much money and personnel on the residences had thwarted the true purpose for which the order had been founded. It was heatedly pointed out to her that she was giving the impression that "you do not feel that we Sisters in the Clubs are *real* Sisters of Service." Catherine replied that she did not intend to give that impression, but only wanted them to know the truth about her own vision and role in the founding of the community. But this response did not win any approval. For, as one sister astutely observed, "If you eliminate our work, you eliminate us Sisters ... What were rural districts are now urbanized. We cannot prevent urbanization, but we can serve the people where they are — in the cities."[6] Catherine's weak reply that "we must prevent urbanization" did not contribute to a resolution of the controversy. Neither side realized how soon the changing circumstances in the world outside the order would make their differences of opinion less significant.

Catherine's hurt surprise at the attack on her declarations about Father Daly's purposes for the order was an example of her insensitivity to the difficulties Father Daly had encountered in securing clergy support, funding and recruits. For years he promoted the Sisters of Service in the face of opposition from some clergy and laity, particularly in eastern Canada, who could not believe that these were really vowed sisters whose freedom from the insularity of the enclosed convent life and its traditional clothing made them more effective in their varied ministries among the "abandoned ones."

Catherine's confrontation with the residence sisters did not divert her from her objective of persuading successive administrations that the

To Do and to Endure

order's future existence would depend on those sisters who were trained to work as professionals. If she was correct, the future of Catholic women's religious orders would depend on adapting to a world which needed workers trained as professionals or technicians either for the Church or for government agencies. At the same time they would be exemplifying a sister's caring concern for all the people with whom they came in contact. Keeping the residences going, she had concluded, would only delay the inevitable retraining of the residence workers. These adjustments would take time, money, and administrative and personnel skills. But, because her life had been centred on teaching and ministering to the country folk, Catherine did not take this into account; administration had never been her strong point. She had been successful in her own work because her professional skill had made learning a joyous and exciting experience for the children she taught, and because she had demonstrated genuine concern for the poor and discouraged rural settlers by her willingness to live in similar poverty and share the uncertainties of their lives.

Her stridently expressed belief that the order must recapture its founding charisma was amazingly in harmony with directives contained in "The Decree on the Up-To-Date Renewal of Religious Life," which was issued during Vatican II by the Sacred Congregation for Religious. These were the marching orders given to all of the Church's religious orders to counter what the Congregation perceived was an approaching crisis of purpose and numbers in these old and venerable institutions. Their "up-to-date renewal" was to be achieved by returning "to the primitive inspiration of the institutes, and their adaptation to the changed conditions of our time." The decree advised that "the spirit and aims of each founder should be faithfully accepted and retained ... for these constitute the patrimony of the Institute." Using the vision of their founder as a guide, every aspect of each order's lifestyle and work was to be examined and reformed:

> The manner of life, of prayer and of work should be in harmony with the present-day physical and psychological condition of the members. It should also be in harmony with the needs of the apostolate ... with the requirements of culture and with social and economic circumstances. This should be the case everywhere, but especially in mission territories.
>
> The mode of government of the institutes should also be

examined according to the same criteria.

For this reason, constitutions, directories, books of customs, of prayers, of ceremonies and such should be properly revised, obsolete prescriptions being suppressed, and should be brought into line with conciliar documents ...

The religious habit, as a symbol of consecration must be simple and modest, at once poor and becoming. In addition, it must be in keeping with the requirements of health and it must be suited to the times and place and to the needs of the apostolate. The habits ... which are not in conformity with these norms ought to be changed.

The up-to-date renewal of institutes depends very much on the training of the members. For this reason, ... religious women, should not be assigned to apostolic tasks immediately after the novitiate. Their religious, apostolic, doctrinal and technical training should, rather be continued ... in suitable establishments. They should also acquire whatever degrees they need.[7]

The 1966 general chapter of the Sisters of Service was devoted primarily to these tasks specified by the Vatican decree. Several committees presented reports proposing reforms in the specific areas mentioned in the document. Sister Catherine was not elected as a delegate, but she had responded vigorously to the request for comments and suggestions, mainly by reiterating her founding vision for the order.

The 1966 report on personnel showed a substantial increase since 1956 in the number of sisters who had secured professional qualifications. Membership in the order was now 121 professed sisters, four novices and three postulants. Of these, seventeen were registered nurses, seven were registered technicians, thirty-two were certified teachers (nineteen of whom were working in schools) twelve were housekeepers, twenty-three worked in the residential clubs, nineteen worked in the catechetical schools, and six were social workers and home visitors. Administrative tasks absorbed the remainder. The Sister General announced that in response to the increased demand for hospital care, the order's two hospitals were being expanded by the government of Alberta; Edson would have a new building with fifty beds, and Vilna was slated for an addition. Both would require even more trained hospital workers.

The residential clubs were still attracting a sufficient number of women who needed safe, economical places to live, and the mission report included a strong recommendation that the residences be retained as a vital part of the Sisters of Service apostolate. The other reports indicated, however, that the continuing decrease in the number of novices could restrict the sisters' ability to provide these services in the near future. As many of the recommendations regarding adjustment to this probability, and to the other proposed changes in the order's government and regulations, required further study, the chapter was adjourned for two years.

During this two-year period the order conscientiously followed the Vatican directive to reflect on their founder's original vision and use it as the basis for evaluating their present state, and future goals and organization. In their discussions they could not ignore the long-standing disagreement on whose vision the original apostolate of the Sisters of Service had been founded. Many had already concluded that Archbishop McNeil's directive in 1924 naming Father Coughlan and Father Daly as the founders was the correct one, for that was what they had been taught during their novitiate. Some of the sisters did begin, however, to take into account Catherine's declarations that the order had been founded when Father Coughlan had recognized that her particular vision was the catalyst for establishing a new order. The organization was to be based on her radical proposals and exemplified in their Rule, which would grant greater freedom and flexibility to its members. She claimed that the essential features of the new Rule had been agreed to by Father Coughlan, Archbishop McNeil and herself, before Father Daly was summoned to direct it. Furthermore, Father Coughlan had confirmed this in his letters. Archbishop McNeil's main contribution had been to give useful suggestions, moral support and the Episcopal approval required by canon law. Not unnaturally, Catherine was hurt that the three priests had omitted any acknowledgment of her role in founding the order. But she was even more concerned that Father Daly's past deviations from the founding principles could cause the order to plan its future on a misunderstanding of its original purpose. Catherine gave her version of the order's origins in an eighty-seven-page autobiography, *Ecumenism Blossoms,* in which she described the experiences which had inspired her to offer her vision, herself, and her savings to found a new ground-breaking order of women religious, particularly suited to a Canadian apostolate.

I Don't Want to Grow Old Gracefully — Usefully — *Yes*

In August 1968 Father Edward Boyce CSsR used this and the Coughlan letters, as well as other documents, to identify the founders in the first chapter of a survey of the order, which was commissioned by Sister General Mary Reansbury and the council as part of compliance with the directives of Vatican II. He wrote:

> All agree that the original initiative for the Sisters of Service came from Catherine Donnelly ... If it had not been for her insights, her generosity, and her persistence, the Sisters of Service as we know them today would not have come into being ... and it strikes me that the original inspiration was moulded through the interaction of four key people: Sister Catherine Donnelly, Father Arthur Coughlan, Archbishop Neil McNeil, Father George Daly.[8]

When the chapter reconvened in December 1968, the Sister General's report stated that during the two-year interval between chapter sessions, the order's residences in Edmonton, Toronto and Ottawa had been closed. The prime reason was economic. The big old houses had deteriorated; they did not meet current fire or building codes, and renovating them would be an impossible financial drain, as there was no public money available. Unfortunately, the houses which served as residences in Vancouver and Halifax were in a similar condition, and the number of sisters who now wished to undertake residence work was diminishing. Twelve sisters had left the order in the last two years; no younger sisters had entered this field in recent years, so that the large majority of those working in the residences were now over fifty years of age. Six sisters who had worked in the residences were now in full-time studies, and others had indicated that they wished to leave this work.

The Sister General then announced that as a result of the implementation of the order's educational policy during the last two years to assist more sisters in furthering their education beyond high school to prepare for careers, the following sisters had graduated: three with B.Ed.'s, one with a B.A., three welfare workers, four from Divine Word [for teachers of religion] in London, one in public health, one from Coady International Institute, one medical record technician. Twelve sisters were studying for a variety of careers in teaching, social welfare, public health, libraries and practical nursing.

In her outspoken approval of the residence closures, Catherine again offended some by her remark that their demise was long overdue.

Her convictions had been reinforced by her extensive reading of secular and religious authors who were warning that the process of reassessing their past and current apostolates would reveal to all of the Church's religious orders that significant changes would have to be made to their lifestyles and the work that they undertook henceforth. Many Catholic religious would become impatient with their order's reluctance to change; others would find that the reconstruction of their order's *modus operandi* diminished their belief in their own vocation. The critics were right, for nearly every apostolic order was experiencing a marked decline in applicants as well as the loss of their vowed members to the secular world. It was a trend that would continue throughout the 1970s.

Nevertheless, because many of these adjustments had been made when the Sisters of Service had been founded, their order did not undergo as severe a loss of their members who had taken permanent vows as some of the more traditional orders.[9] Although Catherine was saddened and worried when she heard of capable sisters, some of whom had been educated by the order, who were leaving, she was not bitter. She had gone through this experience before when Catherine McNally had left in 1928. It was a serious emotional blow to Catherine and had precipitated a bout of depression. But despite her disappointment, she never denounced or ostracized her; they had remained good friends, and through letters had kept in contact. A similar leave-taking was now occurring on a larger scale. Catherine and other members of her order strove to accept such decisions graciously, as the best solutions for the individuals involved. During this period of change, Catherine wrote to those sisters who did adjust to the changes, and who were determined to qualify themselves for new areas of service by undertaking further study. She urged them to have faith in themselves as well as in God, and assured them that their willingness to undertake new occupations would result in a return to the order's original field of action, to which more applicants would be attracted.

In the final sessions of the 1968 chapter meetings a motion was passed recommending that Sister Catherine Donnelly's name be added to those of Archbishop Neil McNeil, Father Arthur Coughlan and Father George Daly who were already recognized as co-founders of the Sisters of Service. Thus Father Boyce's declaration on Catherine's status was officially accepted.

Catherine adapted well to retirement at Camp Morton. She was happy to be able to chat frequently with their priest, Father Theodore Hoeks, whom she described as "one of the kindest and most intelligent of priests,"[10] and she got along well with her Superiors at the mission. They appreciated her sense of humour, her optimism and cheerful acceptance of her advancing physical infirmities which sometimes forced her to limit her activities. Her mental capacity had not deteriorated, and she insisted on tackling her share of the house and garden work. She loved meeting the new young sisters when they visited for their retreat or a holiday. One sister who lived with her at Camp Morton for four years and taught in Catherine's old school, wrote in her memoir of the Catherine who insisted on aging "usefully":

> She seemed to surround herself with papers, books, letters ... "Paper" was her medium, geraniums her project — she seemed to be either bringing the plants in for the winter, watering them, distributing them to the schools ... Her whole-hearted way of diving into a project would always leave its toll on her appearance — her cheeks would get red with enthusiasm. If she swept the dust would fly ... described by her peers as a "countrywoman" ... she revelled in the fresh air, pure water and black earth ... She made time for playing with the dog.
>
> She wasn't young even in 1960 but she would rip down the steep stairs and slide into the chapel as fleet as a teen-ager, I got the impression she was sliding on to her base.
>
> Gradually Catherine Donnelly became more and more sure of her ground with me. She began leaving me a few paper clippings on my desk ... each day ... I picture her surrounded with books to the ceiling and every type of paper imaginable, newspapers, magazines ... I would be amazed at her walls, they were covered with maps of the solar system ... she never missed the daily news; politics were her meat and potatoes.
>
> I teased Sister Marilyn Gillespie, her student at that time, about starting the school day with her by saluting the flag and singing O Canada. It was the comic relief she needed. I've heard this same Sister say that Sister Catherine Donnelly was the best teacher she ever had, and she has had plenty enroute to obtaining her Masters Degree after her teacher's certificate.[11]

In 1964 Sister Lena Renaud became the Superior at Camp Morton. She was a Franco-Ontarian who was raised on the family farm in southwestern Ontario. She had entered the Sisters of Service in

To Do and to Endure

1949, attracted as she laughingly said in an interview, by some pictures of one of them driving a dog sled.[12] The order sent her to the Normal School in Winnipeg in 1952, and the next year she began teaching in the old No. 2 King Edward School in Camp Morton. She shared with Catherine her love of the outdoors, her satisfaction in tending vegetable and flower gardens, her fondness for their dogs, and her reverent gratitude for the beauty of the lake and the countryside around their house. Like Catherine, Sister Lena had exceptional skill and enthusiasm for teaching, and an empathy with the children and their parents in the Camp Morton farming community. Catherine admired her artistic skills in art and carpentry which included making bird houses and whimsical toys for the local children. She was as adept at fixing the machinery and coaxing stubborn motors to work at Camp Morton as Catherine had been in handling their horses forty years before. Catherine's occasional boisterous outbursts and outspoken opinions did not jar Sister Renaud, and she handled Catherine's sometimes eccentric ways with tolerance and sensitivity for the twenty-four years that they worked there together. It was a place of great fulfilment for Catherine, for the mission's success was proof that her vision for the order was a living reality. Their daily routines of prayer, work and leisure were melded into the seasonal rhythms of rural life which Catherine found constantly stimulating. Their many visitors enjoyed her stories, and her knowledgeable comments on current religious and political affairs, as well as the jams and preserves she made for their meals.

    A special event took place at Camp Morton on 15 August 1974 when the order celebrated Catherine's golden jubilee as a Sister of Service. There was a special Mass, gifts, and congratulatory messages from her wide circle of friends in other religious orders, and from the laity, both Catholic and non-Catholic. The highlight of the day was the presentation of the papal medal, *Pro Ecclesia at Pontifice,* by Cardinal Flahiff, in recognition of her fifty years of work for the Church. The event was given special meaning for Catherine because her old friend, and former Sister General, Margaret Guest was present to celebrate the great occasion with her.

    Perhaps it was the memories which resurfaced on reaching such a milestone that caused Catherine's increasing anger at what she still considered was Father Daly's malevolent influence on the order's development. It was a subject about which Catherine had become more outspoken as she aged. Sometimes she linked it with the disadvantages women experienced in their status in secular society and in the Catholic Church. She spoke admiringly about Joan of Arc and the suffragettes because they strove for their rights as women to be part of the decision-making structures in their respective societies. She accepted without question the theological doctrines of her faith, but she told Sister Renaud that she "could not see why women did not have more say in what went on in the Church and why bishops and priests would not take any advice from them." She never claimed, however, that ordination to the priesthood was the goal for which women should strive. Nor, she declared, was she "one of those militant feminists who are so against men."[13] It was Father Daly who was the principal target of her wrath, for she felt that he had patronized her and the other sisters. She believed that in the Church, the clergy and the sisters should work as partners, each drawing upon the skills, spiritual insights and experience of the other. In places where Catherine had experienced such a partnership, as the Cariboo, she was sure that the people they ministered to had benefited.

Catherine was therefore very moved and proud when Sister Lena Renaud was the first woman in Canada to be appointed an Extraordinary Minister of the Eucharist. That meant that she could give Holy Communion to the congregation at the Camp Morton church, and also take it to the shut-ins in the parish who were unable to attend Mass. This unusual participation by a sister in the Eucharistic service was instituted because their priest, Father Theodore Hoecks, developed a heart condition which prevented him from performing any duties requiring physical stress, such as standing for long periods.[14] In his work throughout the rural West, he had come to admire the flexibility and freedom permitted to the Sisters of Service which enabled them to adapt to a variety of jobs and circumstances. To him, they represented the future of womens' religious orders, and he was grateful for Sister Renaud's special help at Sunday services and every day throughout the parish.

However, Catherine never ceased to blame herself for agreeing to have Father Daly appointed to help organize and direct the order in its early stages. She remembered that Father Coughlan had intended his appointment to be of limited duration. It had been circumstances, and

To Do and to Endure

Father Daly's own "chauvinist" ambitions, that had swerved the order from its intended course, and had done it great harm. This was unfair, and it was too simplistic an explanation for the direction which the order had taken. But Catherine expressed this view with increasing virulence in a flood of letters.

She became so openly obsessed with this grievance that Sister General Helen Hayes resolved that for Catherine's own good and that of the order, her incessant writing about it must stop. She wrote to Catherine demanding that she cease her "constant harping" about Father Daly.

> If you have been hurt, we know you have been hurt as you have not let us forget it but that does not change a thing *now* ... You are wasting so much energy writing about Father Daly and chauvinism. Storing up grievances is more than a waste of time; it is a waste of life that could be lived to greater satisfaction. If you keep a record of oppressions and indignities (chauvinism), you are restoring them to painful reality ... Sister so do not pick up your pen again and write about 'what might have been if Father Daly' ... You are an intelligent woman so I know you will understand that I am writing this because I am *very* concerned about your health physical and mental if you continue to harp and harp and play the same old record."[15]

The reprimand, which was really an order to her under her vow of obedience, seemed to shock Catherine. She had always taken her vows seriously and had done her best to observe them faithfully. On this occasion, after fifty-seven years of obedience to many less reasonable requests, she complied without comment or complaint.

Nine months later she received the recognition she deserved, when Roy Bonisteel chose Sister Catherine Donnelly and the order she founded as the topic of his popular television program, "Man Alive." Staff from the Canadian Broadcasting Corporation had descended on Camp Morton for a week at the end of June 1980. Sister General Helen Hayes came from Toronto to play a minor part, and to see that Catherine would be able, at the age of ninety-six, to stand the stress and the excitement (and, she admitted, to watch her remarks during the interviews).[16] As Catherine described it, she was too interested in watching the three "gallant" young men who were the technical crew and "clever" Azza el Sissi, the producer, to feel tired.[17]

I Don't Want to Grow Old Gracefully — Usefully — *Yes*

In the program, Roy Bonisteel first gave a brief overview of the conditions which led to the founding of an order of sisters, "which is part of our history." They had succeeded, he noted, because of their willingness to adapt to the Canadian frontier. "They broke new ground in their own Church and they are still at it." The producer had contacted the family of Edward Schreyer, the governor general, whose grandfather had helped build the original, small church in the village. Schreyer's aunt, Margaret Gottfried, was interviewed and recalled that many years before their large family of eighteen had been helped in many ways by the Camp Morton Sisters of Service. Bonisteel then interviewed the parish priest, Father Theodore Hoecks, who affirmed that in an age when many people thought that religious orders were no longer relevant, this order was still fulfilling a great need in the Canadian West. In his interview with Sister Lena Renaud, Bonisteel noted that her mentor had been Catherine Donnelly. She was filmed visiting the homes of her "family," the parishioners, and at the weekly Mass in the little Camp Morton church. The camera focused on her as she gave the Eucharist to the congregation.

But it was on Sister Catherine that Bonisteel mainly focused his commentary and interviews during the filming. She answered his questions thoughtfully and candidly, particularly those on the traditional role of women in the Church, and the first reactions of the public to the new women's religious order which did not adhere to a rigid prayer routine or obey restrictions which limited their freedom to work in the community. Her most revealing answers were given to two very personal questions: what did God say to her about founding a new order, and which of the vows had she found most difficult to keep? To the first, she answered that she felt that He said, "Get on to the right track; endure; and keep the Ten Commandments." Before she answered the second question, she paused with her eyes closed, as if her life was passing before her, and then said softly, "Not poverty, I could handle that,— not chastity,— obedience, yes obedience, I found it a little bit hard."

Roy Bonisteel's conclusions were that this "tough, enduring woman" had founded a religious order whose members were "a breed apart." In breaking free of restrictive rules and bending others, they had become pioneers in the women's movement in the Church.

It was fortunate that the film had been made during the summer,

To Do and to Endure

for in the next six months Catherine's physical strength declined noticeably, and she required more care. The program was broadcast on 29 December 1980, under the provocative title, "You've Come a Long Way, Sister." Catherine was inundated with a flood of congratulatory letters from across Canada, which she immediately set about answering. One of the most unusual was from her French professor at the University of Alberta from whom she had taken a course in 1964. He wrote that after seeing her on "Man Alive" he was vividly reminded of her presence in French 350 that summer. "But you are very modest. I had no idea at the time that you were the founder of the SOS. It was indeed an honour to have you in my class! I remember clearly your oral report on Damis, a character in Molière's *Tartuffe*."[18]

In early January 1981 Catherine contracted a more severe case of shingles than she had suffered previously. She spent two weeks in the Gimli hospital, but when she returned to Camp Morton she was still weak and pain-wracked. It was obvious that Sister Renaud, who was now teaching full time at the Gimli school, would not be able to nurse her through such a lingering infection, in a house unsuited to an invalid. Clearly Catherine would have to leave her beloved Camp Morton. On 25 January, Sister General Helen Hayes and one of the councillors, Sister Domitilla Morrison, flew to Camp Morton and accompanied Catherine on the flight to Toronto. She stayed at the motherhouse for a few days and was able to visit her dear sister Mamie who was now very frail, and living at the St. Joseph motherhouse in North Toronto. On 30 January Catherine joined the community of twenty other elderly Sisters of Service who were living at the order's nursing home in St. Catharines, Ontario.

Catherine adjusted well to the change. She wrote a cheerful letter to her cousin Betty Ogle, in which she briefly outlined the reasons for her sudden change of address and described her new surroundings. She was pleased to report that the head nurse was Sister Bridget Knopic, who had been very helpful when Catherine was recovering from the Sinnett episode at the Edson Hospital.

> [She] is the cheerful expert type God provides ... The shingles is not quite cleared up yet. The nurses here are working on it.
>
> I have not sorted my baggage here yet ... It is a big task here trying to get everything straightened out and placed properly and I get exhausted. This is a great set-up, fine management, a very big

business — haven't found my own way around here yet. There is a staff of every type connected with it ... My wrists are too arthritic to write plainly ...

Letters have been plentiful praising the TV show. Letters of great praise have come from non-Catholics — former pupils of mine too.[19]

In June 1981 Sister Justina died after a long period of steady decline. Sister Knopic accompanied Catherine to the funeral in Toronto. It was also the occasion for a family reunion, for her nephew Robert Gifford, his wife, one of his seven children, and his niece, came from New Jersey. Catherine's old friend Mary O'Connor, now Sister Ferdinand IBVM, attended, as did two old friends from Penetanguishene days.

If Catherine's physical life was now circumscribed, her mind never ceased to roam across the miles and the years. She followed the careers of the younger sisters, many of whom now held responsible positions in hospitals and social agencies. As other sisters reached retirement, she was proud when they received handsome awards thanking them for their service to the community. She gained great satisfaction from the letters of sisters who were working as teachers and social workers in new missions in northern Alberta and Saskatchewan. She was less prone to brood about the past as she felt that the order was now very much on the right track.

As her strength declined she became more mellow, but she did not lose her good humour. She was a favourite with the nurses; they enjoyed her sense of fun which bubbled up frequently into hearty laughter. She told them interesting stories about her adventures, and in turn, she was very interested in their careers. When she required extra help, she was sweetly grateful for their attentive care. Catherine passed her days contentedly, but actively, reading, writing, visiting with her old friend Margaret Guest, who was also a patient, and praying. When Catherine had been working, she had sometimes remarked in letters to her friends that she did not find the time to pray as much as she should; she had not excused her lapses with the Benedictine aphorism, that "to work is to pray." Now she was making up for it. Her Superior in the home noted that her eyesight dimmed and she could not see well. As she observed wryly, Catherine "got more prayerful after she stopped reading."[20] She added also that "she was never out of sorts ... the nurses and girls all loved her." Catherine's only serious request was that she receive the daily newspaper so that she could keep up with what was going on in the world. That was important to her as she "had no time for old news."

Catherine even began to take more philosophically her troublesome memories of Father Daly. She concluded that the root cause of their different methods of carrying out the apostolate of the Sisters of Service was to be found in the great differences in their backgrounds. His was an urban upbringing in a financially secure, socially conservative, traditionally devout, Quebec Catholic family, where women like his mother had clearly defined social and domestic roles. "He was brought up in the school of thought ... that Women were to listen, to leave leadership to men."[21] Her early life had been one of struggle against rural poverty, made more difficult by the heavy family responsibilities which had fallen on her shoulders after the death of her mother. But adversity had also taught her to be independent and resourceful. In her youth, her social and religious experiences were really wider than Father Daly's. As a student in Adjala township, and as a teacher in the Ontario public school system, she had been broadened by exposure to a greater variety of religious faiths and social classes. To an outsider, it was obvious that each of them had benefited from their experiences, and had been very successful in achieving their own goals for the order. It was unfortunate that they had been unable to combine their personal strengths of character and experience into a mutual collaborative effort.

Catherine lived to celebrate with her sisters the diamond anniversary of the founding of the Sisters of Service on 14 August 1982, rejoicing with them that they were finding new ways to serve a world experiencing profound religious and social change. When her eyesight was nearly gone, Catherine went into a slow decline. She was lucid to the end, and died peacefully on 8 September 1983 at the age of ninety-nine, just five months and eighteen days before her hundredth birthday. She had outlived her three co-founders by many years.

The funeral Mass was held at Holy Name Church where Bishop Robert Clune of the Archdiocese of Toronto presided, assisted by the thirteen priests who concelebrated the funeral Mass. Many old friends attended, including Sister Ferdinand, and her nephew Robert Gifford, his wife and daughter and three grand-nieces. She was buried in the

I Don't Want to Grow Old Gracefully — Usefully — Yes

Sisters of Service plot at Mount Hope Cemetery, Toronto. In her will, Catherine left modest sums of money to be used for the education of her grand-nieces and nephews.

Catherine Donnelly was declared the Founder of the Sisters of Service by her order in 1990. Hers was the first English-speaking Roman Catholic missionary order founded by a Canadian, and the first order in Canada to anticipate in its Rules and customs the new approach adopted after Vatican II by the Church's female religious orders. She had envisioned an order which would minister to people of all religions or no religion in the remotest sections of the country whose children needed education, health care, and moral and religious education. Catherine gave up her personal independence and a successful career because she believed that only a life-long commitment could ensure that the people of Canada who needed these services would receive them. She believed that education, combined with spiritual awareness, was the key to producing good citizens, and expressed this in a few reflective sentences:

> The religious orders ought to be in the world, a witness to God's existence and to His love for mankind ...
>
> It is extremely important not to separate the spiritual life and the training of the mind. The spiritual life and the intellectual life have the same root deep in the unity of the intelligence.

NOTES

CHAPTER 1: The Land of Her Youth: The Adjala Community
1. R. Cole Harris, Pauline Roulston and Chris de Freitas, "The Settlement of Mono Township," *Canadian Geographer* 19, no. 1 (1975), 7.
2. Ibid., 9.
3. Frances Morehouse, "Canadian Migration in the Forties," *Canadian Historical Review* 9 (1928), 311. In 1843, for example, out of 24,285 immigrants, only 10,000 were Irish.
4. Cecil J. Houston and William J. Smyth, "Community Development and Institutional Supports: Life on the Agricultural Frontier of Adjala and Mono Townships," in M. McGowan and B. Clarke, eds., *Catholics at the Gathering Place* (Toronto 1993), 11.
5. Bruce S. Elliott, *Irish Migrants in the Canadas: A New Approach* (Belfast 1988), 198, 210.
6. Sister Catherine Donnelly SOS, "Donnelly Family Information and Memoirs," written at Camp Morton, Manitoba, 11 January 1975. Unpublished manuscript in Sisters of Service Archives, Toronto (henceforth CD and SOSA).
7. CD in a taped conversation with nephew Robert Gifford, at Camp Morton, Manitoba, 15 July 1979, SOSA.
8. CD to Robert Gifford, 15 October 1980, SOSA
9. Interviews with Mrs. Mary Munnoch of Alliston, Supt. of Personnel, Metropolitan Separate School Board, Toronto, 23 November 1992, and Mrs. Margaret Donnelly, formerly of Alliston, at Toronto, 15 February 1993.
10. Interview with Mrs. Mary Munnoch, Toronto, 23 November 1992.
11. Elizabeth Smyth, "The Lessons of Religion and Science: The Congregation of the Sisters of St. Joseph and St. Joseph's Academy, Toronto, 1854-1911" (Ph.D. dissertation, University of Toronto, Faculty of Education, 1989).
12. CD, untitled paper on the founding of the Sisters of Service, December 1966, SOSA, RG1-01, box 9, file 14.
13. CD to Robert Gifford, 11 December 1980, SOSA
14. W.F. Sparks, Principal, Bradford Model School. Letter of recommendation for Miss Katie Donnelly, 2 November 1901, RG1-1,

Notes

box 9, file 7.
15 Robert Stamp, *The Schools of Ontario, 1876-1976* (Toronto 1982), 14.
16 A. Orton, Principal, Bradford Model School, to P.S. Trustees, RG1-01, box 9, file 7.
17 Sister Lena Renaud SOS, "A Memoir of Sister Donnelly," 6 March 1987, SOSA.
18 CD to Sister Patricia Ronan CSJ, 3 February 1978, SOSA.
19 Ibid.

CHAPTER 2: Life as a Teacher in Ontario, 1904-1918
1   Sister Catherine Donnelly, taped interview with her nephew Robert Gifford, at Camp Morton, Manitoba, 15 July 1979, SOSA.
2   SOSA, RG1-01, box 8, file 6.
3   CD, taped interview with Robert Gifford, 15 July 1979.
4   Ontario Archives, Land Records Item #3486 for Lot 1, Concession 5, Tossorontio Township. A Bargain and Sale on property with a mortgage held by Canada Permanent Trust for $4,200 is recorded to James Quayle of Adjala on 13 March 1905.
5   Richard Reid, "The Rosamond Woollen Company of Almonte: Industrial Development in a Rural Setting," *Ontario History*, LXXV, no. 3 (1983), 266-89. This article gives an excellent outline of the difficulties and risks of being in the wool trade in Ontario in the late nineteenth and early twentieth century.
6   CD, taped interview with Robert Gifford, 15 July 1979.
7   CD to Sister Pat Burke SOS, 21 November 1979, RG1-01, box 10, file 13.
8   *Alliston Herald*, 9 December 1905.
9   RG1-01, box 9, file 7.
10 CD to Betty Ogle, 25 June 1980, SOSA.
11 CD, memoir dated May 1973, RG1-01, box 9, file 9, SOSA.
12 CD to Betty Ogle, 25 June 1980.
13 Archives of the Sisters of St. Joseph, Toronto (ACSJ), box 5, *Academy Register, 1906-1907*, p. 6.
14 CD to Betty Ogle, 25 June 1980, SOSA.
15 CD to Sister Patricia Ronan CSJ, 3 February 1978, SOSA.
16 St. Joseph's Academy School, *Register and Accounts Book, 1905-1907*, p. 3, ACSJ. Catherine has left no written record of this incident, although she did mention it to Sister Leona Trautman SOS, and her nephew Robert Gifford confirmed that he was told the story by his mother.
17 The annual *Schools and Teachers of the Province of Ontario* was first published by the government in 1911. It listed the teacher's name,

Notes

certification rank, salary, and employing board. The salary information which follows is taken from these official records. In the SOS records where Catherine sometimes referred to her own salary, the two sources agree. In the 1911 government listing, the salary for Apto School was recorded as $525 per annum. It was probably less when Catherine worked there from 1 January 1907 to 31 December 1908.

18   Robert G. Gifford to Jeanne Beck, 23 March 1994, SOSA.
19   Elizabeth M. Smyth, "The Lessons of Religion and Science: The Congregation of the Sisters of St. Joseph and St. Joseph's Academy, Toronto, 1854-1911" (Ph.D. dissertation: University of Toronto 1989), Appendix 6, p. 256.
20   CD, manuscript, 27 June 1966, SOSA.
21   CD to Sister Patricia Burke, 20 December 1977, RG1-01, box 10, file 9.
22   RG1-01, box 9, file 7.
23   Ibid.
24   Ibid.
25   CD to Sister Burke, 29 September 1977, RG1-01, box 10, file 9.
26   CD, "Brief," December 1966, RG1-01, box 9, file 14.
27   Ibid.
28   RG1-01, box 9, file 7.
29   Ibid.
30   *St. Joseph's Academy Register and Accounts 1911-1912*, ACSJ, box 5, book 5, p. 413.
31   RG1-01, box 9, file 7.
32   Interview with Sister Leona Trautman SOS, 31 August 1993. Sister Trautman reported to Jeanne Beck that Sister Catherine Donnelly had told her this many years ago.
33   CD to Sister Patricia Burke, 2 October 1979, RG1-01, box 10, file 13.
34   St. Joseph's Academy, Toronto, *Annals*, entry for 9 June 1918, 544.
35   RG1-01, box 8, file 14.
36   Letter of recommendation from Jo. L. Garvin, B.A. I.P.S. North Simcoe, 16 June 1914, RG1-01, box 9, file 7.
37   Mark G. McGowan, "Sharing the Burden of Empire: Toronto's Catholics and the Great War, 1914-1918," in Mark McGowan and Brain Clarke, eds., *Catholics at the Gathering Place* (Toronto 1993), 155-76.

CHAPTER 3: Adventures in Alberta: Am I Called to Be a Religious?

1   Catherine Donnelly, "Why I am a Sister of Service," manuscript, 1949-50, SOSA, RG1-01, box 9, file 34.
2   Personnel Register, ACSJ.
3   Jos. L. Garvin, I.P.S. North Simcoe to CD, 10 July 1918, RG1-01, box 8, file 14.

Notes

4   CD, "Birth of the S.O.S.," manuscript, 1 August 1955, RG1-01, oversized box 1, file 5.
5   CD, unpublished manuscript, 1939, RG1-01, oversized box 1, file 13.
6   RG1-01, box 9, file 27.
7   CD, "History of the S.O.S.," 1939, RG1-01, oversized box 10, file 13.
8   CD, manuscript, undated, RG1-01, box 9, file 27.
9   CD, "Why I am a Sister of Service."
10 CD, manuscript, 1939.
11 CD, "A Minority Report," probably written in the latter half of the 1960s, RG1-01, box 9, file 24.
12 CD, "Birth of the S.O.S."
13 *Constitutions of the Sisters of St. Joseph* (Toronto 1935). This edition of their Holy Rule was just as strict in some particulars as an earlier version in use when Mamie had taken her vows. The 1935 version still had an injunction against "particular friendships." See chapter 13, 114 (f) 53.
14 CD, "Why I am a Sister of Service."
15 CD to Archbishop Neil McNeil, 11 January 1916, Archives of the Roman Catholic Archdiocese of Toronto (henceforth ARCAT), MN AH05.03.
16 CD, manuscript, undated, RG1-01, box 9, file 27.
17 CD, "History of the S.O.S."
18 CD, manuscript, RG1-01, oversized box 1, file 8.
19 CD, "History of the S.O.S."
20 CD, "The Sisters of Service," manuscript, 15 May 1965, RG1-01, box 9, file 31.
21 CD, manuscript, 1939.
22 CD, manuscript, 14 November 1969, RG1-01, box 9, file 30.
23 CD, "The Sisters of Service."
24 CD, manuscript, 18 January 1959, RG 1-01, oversized box 1, file 13.
25 Wellington Mackenzie to Archbishop McNeil, 25 January 1918, ARCAT, FW GC01.39; 15 May 1918, MN AH07.40; 22 January 1919, MN AH08.11.
26 CD, "Birth of the S.O.S."
27 Ontario Archives, Death Records, vol. 23, MO 935, reel 258, no. 028574.
28 No will of Hugh Donnelly registered for probate has been located. Presumably the estate was not sufficient or of a nature to require it. Catherine never referred to receiving any inheritance. She did save some family items for her sister Tess, and stored them with a local friend. Thirty-seven years later they were retrieved on a return visit to Alliston with Tess. Biographical sketch of Catherine Donnelly, 1961,

Notes

RG1-01, box 9, file 6.
29 *Constitutions of the Sisters of St. Joseph of Toronto* (Toronto 1935).
30 CD, manuscript, RG1-01, box 9, file 27. There are several documents in which Catherine Donnelly recounted her interview with the Peterborough Mother General. In all of them she notes that the Peterborough sisters did go to Calgary, but that they were withdrawn by the Mother General after a few years because of Bishop McNally's attempt to control their order.
31 Ibid.
32 CD, RG1-01, box 9, files 27, 30. This vaguely worded remark was probably a veiled reference to the period in late 1917-18, when Wellington Mackenzie was taking religious instruction from Father Coughlan. In another document Catherine stated, "I had once or twice consulted Rev. Arthur Coughlan CSsR, Toronto, on other matters. I knew he was well-informed about communities in general," manuscript, 1939.
33 Paul Laverdure, *Redemption and Renewal: The Redemptorists of English Canada, 1834-1994* (Toronto 1996), 115.
34 CD to Sister Patricia Burke, 21 November 1979, RGI-01, box 10, file 13.
35 *Constitutions of the Sisters of St. Joseph*, Chapter 7, "Vow and Virtue of Obedience," par. 69, 33.
36 CD to Sister Patricia Burke SOS, 21 November 1979, RG1-01, box 10, file 13.
37 *Constitutions of the Sisters of St. Joseph*, chap. 11, "The Mistress and Assistant Mistress of Novices," par. 269, 119.
38 CD, manuscript, 18 January 1959, RG1-01, oversized box 1, file 13.
39 CD, manuscript, "Why I am a Sister of Service."
40 *Constitutions of the Sisters of St. Joseph*, chap. 4, "Religious Habit," 14.
41 CD to Sister Patricia Burke, 21 November 1979.
42 CD, "Birth of the S.O.S."
43 CD, "Why I am a Sister of Service."
44 CD to Sister Patricia Burke, 21 November 1979.
45 RG1-01, box 9, file 6.
46 CD, "Why I am a Sister of Service." In her manuscript, "Birth of the S.O.S.," 1 August 1955, Catherine described their meeting, "Finally he amazed me by saying that I ought to start a new community. I told him that I would not know how, but he said we would discuss it and plan ... when the Christmas rush was over, we would work in earnest." In the manuscript written at Camp Morton, 18 January 1959, Catherine reported Father Coughlan as saying, "I guess we'll have to start a new community."

Notes

CHAPTER 4: Catherine Pursues Her Vision: The Founding of the Sisters of Service

1. Catherine Donnelly, manuscript, December 1966, SOSA, RG1-01, box 9, file 14.
2. Lawrence K. Shook, *Catholic Post-Secondary Education in English-Speaking Canada* (Toronto 1971), 7.
3. CD, "The Sisters of Service," 15 May 1965, SOSA, RG1-01, box 9, file 31.
4. D.I. Lanslots OSB, *Handbook of Canon Law for Congregations of Women Under Simple Vows*, 4th ed. (New York 1910). "The approbation by the competent ecclesiastical authority is required for every institution with a religious purpose; without it, it could not share the privileges of the church. The constitution 'Conditae' confer on the bishop the right to approve the constitutions of diocesan congregations. His approval is also required for every new foundation" (pp. 12-13).
5. More detailed information on Archbishop McNeil's background and work can be found in George Boyle, *Pioneer in Purple: The Life and Work of Archbishop Neil McNeil* (Montreal 1951), and also in Jeanne Merifield Beck, "Henry Somerville and the Development of Catholic Social Thought in Canada: Somerville's Role in the Archdiocese of Toronto 1915-1943" (Ph.D. dissertation, McMaster University 1977), chap. 3, 67-100.
6. Boyle, *Pioneer in Purple*, 127.
7. CD, "The Sisters of Service."
8. CD, manuscript, 1939, RG1-01, oversized box 1, file 13.
9. How aware these two men were of the difficulties encountered by the founder of the Josephites, Mother Mary McKillop, after she founded the order in 1869, is not known. The startling details of her life had not been publicized in North America. Only recently has the full story been told by a member of the order, Sister Marie Therese Foale ISJ in *The Josephite Story*, published by the Institute of St. Joseph, North Sydney, 1989.
10. Father Arthur Coughlan CSsR to CD, 12 March 1921, RG1-01, file 11.
11. CD to Arthur Coughlan CSsR, 20 March 1921, Archives of the Ardiocese of Toronto (henceforth ARCAT), MN AH10.43.
12. Father William Cameron to CD, 9 May 1921, RG1-01, box 7, file 9.
13. CD, *Ecumenism Blossoms* (undated, probably Autumn 1968), RG1-01, box 9, file 22, 27.
14. Frank J. Muzik to CD, undated, RG1-01, box 7, file 20.
15. CD, *Ecumenism Blossoms*, 28.
16. Father Arthur Coughlan to CD, 24 August 1921, RG1-01, box 7, file 10.
17. Ibid.
18. The great migration to Canada of what are now known as Ukrainians

Notes

was a lengthy and very complex phenomenon. The old Slavic kingdom of the Ukraine was divided in the late nineteenth century between Poland, the Hapsburg Austro-Hungarian Empire and Russia. The Slavic people who emigrated from the Hapsburg-controlled province of Bukovina were called Ruthenians. Those who came from Halychyna were called Galicians. They were Roman Catholic, but they had their own religious rites and customs in their own language (Slavonic). They associated the use of Latin with political and cultural oppression which they had endured under Roman Catholic European states and were strongly resisting attempts to latinize their services and clergy.

19 Mark McGowan, "A Portion for the Vanquished: Ukrainian Catholics and German Catholics in Canada, 1891-1948," in Stella Hryniuk and Lubomyer Luciuk, eds., *The Ukrainians in Canada* (Toronto 1991), 218-37. This excellent article explains the sources of the disagreements between the Ukrainian and the Latin Rite Catholic hierarchy which went on for many years and are still a contentious issue.

20 CD, manuscript, written probably in 1922. Appended to it is a note signed by G. Daly CSsR, stating that "this is an article which was written by Sister Donnelly when the idea of the Sisters of Service was first launched," RG1-01, box 9, file 33.

21 Father Coughlan to Archbishop McNeil, 9 September 1921, RG1-01, box 1, file 2.

22 Theresa Kormann Small was the wife of the wealthy and notorious Toronto theatre impresario, Ambrose Small. Mrs. Small was a devout Roman Catholic and one of the principal benefactors of many Catholic charities and religious orders in the city. Ambrose Small had disappeared suddenly on 2 December 1919, and the long and extensive police investigations failed to find any trace of his whereabouts or the reason for his disappearance. See Fred McClement, *The Strange Case of Ambrose Small* (Toronto 1974).

23 Father Arthur Coughlan to CD, 12 September 1921, RG1-01, box 7, file 11. Catherine's letter of 3 September 1921 to Father Coughlan has been lost, so one can only surmise its contents by his comments in his reply.

24 Father Arthur Coughlan to Father George Daly, 29 September 1921, RG1-01, box 1, file 6.

25 Brother Rogation of the de la Salle Christian Brothers, was the Superintendent of the Toronto Separate Schools. He admired Catherine for her teaching ability and supported her plans for a new order.

26 Catherine's chronology is vague on the date that she moved into 97 St. Joseph Street. Father Lozano, in *The Charism of the Sisters of Service*, has stated (p.16) that she moved there in March 1922. However, in *Ecumenism Blossoms* Catherine mentioned (p. 45) that she was living

Notes

there when Adeline McConnell wrote to her in March 1922. She does not state the date of her friend's arrival at the house.

27 Father Arthur Coughlan to Father George Daly, 31 December 1921, RG1-01, box 1, file 6. Father DeLaer who is referred to in the letter was a Belgian Redemptorist who had worked among the Ukrainians in the West since 1898. In 1906 he was one of the Redemptorist priests who had transferred to the Ukrainian rite (also called the Greek Rite). See McGowan, "A Portion for the Vanquished," 222.
28 CD, *Ecumenism Blossoms*, 48.
29 Copied from the *Redemptorist Chronicles*, RG1-2, box 1, file 6.
30 CD, *Ecumenism Blossoms*, 45.
31 Ibid., 49.
32 Father George Daly to CD, 6 May 1922. Quoted in ibid., 56.
33 Father Arthur Coughlan to Father George Daly, 2 May 1922, RG1-01, box 1, file 6.
34 Sister Katherine Schenck SOS, memorandum, "Motherhouse," RG1-02, box 1, file 4b.
35 Sister Kathleen Schenck, interview with Sister Mary Burke, November 1960, RG1-02, box 1, file 4b.
36 CD, *Ecumenism Blossoms*, 61.

CHAPTER 5: The Novitiate Years

1 Sister Katherine Schenck SOS, memorandum, "Reverend Mother Lidwina," undated, SOSA, RG1-02, box 1, file 1.
2 Ibid.
3 Taking the first and final vows together was the custom of the order at that time.
4 Father E.M. Bunoz OMI to the Reverend Mother General, St. Joseph's Community, 12 January 1916, *Published Annals, Vol 2*, ACSJ.
5 *Constitutions of the Sisters of St. Joseph of Toronto* (Toronto 1935), chap. 11, p. 119, par. 268, 269, 270.
6 "Reverend Sister Lidwina Henry," no date, SOSA, RG1-02, box 1, file 1.
7 George Daly CSsR to "Our Dear Sisters of Service," 12 August 1922. Memoranda of Sister Katherine Schenck, RG1-01, box 1, file 4b.
8 George Daly CSsR to Reverend Mother Lidwina, 14 August 1922, RG1-01, box 1, file 4b.
9 Sister Leona Trautman SOS, in a personal memorandum, "The Order of the Day," written for Jeanne Beck in 1993. Sister Trautman was a novice from 1933 to 1935, but her daily routine was identical to that described in the memorandum, "Early Days," written by the late Sister Kathleen Schenck, who entered the order in January 1923.
10 Sister Katherine Schenck, memorandum, "Reverend Mother Lidwina."

Notes

11 At that time the Redemptorists did not have a novitiate for English-speaking candidates in Canada. With very rare exceptions, English-speaking Catholics who did not speak fluent French had to study in the United States under the authority of the American Redemptorists. Many of them remained in the United States. The English-speaking students who wished to be stationed in Canada had to delay their entrance to the Belgian novitiate for at least two years while they studied French at the minor Redemptorist Seminary at Ste. Anne de Beaupré. Even then, many found their Belgian studies too difficult and they either left, or joined other orders in Canada. See Paul Laverdure, *Redemption and Renewal: The Redemptorists of English Canada, 1834-1994* (Toronto 1996), chap. 4.
12 Laverdure, *Redemption and Renewal*, 117.
13 Ibid., 119.
14 Ibid. The quotation is from a letter Patrick Mulhall wrote to Father Fidelis Speidel, the American consultor general, 26 February 1918. Archives of the Redemptorist Province of Toronto.
15 When Archbishop McNeil had agreed to the founding of the new order and asked Father Coughlan to undertake supervision of the process himself or through an subordinate, he was following a centuries-old Church tradition. When the Canadian branch of the Sisters of Charity was established in Nova Scotia in 1849 under Mother Mary Basilia, their Superior-General, usually a priest, was appointed by the archbishop. The priest controlled the affairs of the order until 1908, when it became a papal institute and the sisters were in charge of their own destiny. Sister Mary Olga McKenna SC, "Paradigm Shifts in a Women's Religious Institute: The Sisters of Charity Halifax," Canadian Catholic Historical Association, *Historical Studies* (1995), 137, 139.
16 Father George Daly, handwritten notes of his address to the CWL second annual convention, 26-30 Sept 1922, SOSA, RG5-2, box 1, file 7.
17 Sister Katherine Schenck, memorandum, "Uniform, Sisters of Service," no date.
18 Sister Katherine Schenck, manuscript, "Uniform Hats," 1962.
19 CD, "Charisma of the SOS," manuscript, 1972, RG1-01, box 9, file 15.
20 One of the most successful in Toronto was Georgina House founded in 1908 by the Anglican Church at the urging of Mrs. Georgina Broughall, the wife of an Anglican rector, whose parish was near the factory district on Spadina Avenue.
21 "The Annals of the Mother House," 19 January 1923, RG1-02, box 1, file 5.
22 CD, manuscript, dating from late 1960s, RG1-01, box 9, file 24.
23 CD, manuscript, RG1-01, box 9, file 30.

Notes

24 Ibid.
25 Sister Avila to CD, 21 February 1924, RG1-01, box 8, file 1.
26 Archbishop Neil McNeil to Cardinal Larenti, 12 August 1923, ARCAT.
27 Archbishop Neil McNeil to Le Secrétaire de la S. Congrégation des Religieux, 31 July 1924, ARCAT.
28 Ibid.
29 Father Daly to Most Reverend H. O'Leary DD, 11 March 1924, Archives of the Archdiocese of Edmonton.
30 Provincial Arthur Coughlan to Fidelis Speidel, Consultor General, Rome, Italy, 23 April 1924. AGR Toronto Provincialia, uncatalogued.
31 Letter to Sister Quinn from Fr. A.M. McBriarty CSsR, 14 August 1951 quoting from the *Annals* of the CSsR, Toronto, 2 August 1924, RG1-02, box 1, file 6.
32 A financial statement dated 31 May 1935, compiled by Father Daly, listed under Capital Liabilities, a loan, payable to Miss C. Donnelly, for $2,000, RG1-03, box 1, file 17. Catherine once told Sister Dorothy Daly SOS, that when she entered the novitiate, she had entrusted all of her savings to Father Daly to use in founding the order.

CHAPTER 6: The First Mission at Camp Morton

1 Archbishop Alfred A. Sinnott to Father Daly, 12 May 1924, SOSA, RG 6-04, box 1, file 1.
2 Father Daly to Archbishop Sinnott, 28 June 1924, RG 6-04, box 1, file 1.
3 Ibid., 14 July 1924.
4 Archbishop Sinnott to Father Daly, 18 July 1924.
5 Father Arthur Coughlan CSsR to Father Daly, 9 August 1924, RG1-01, box 1, file 6.
6 Annals of Camp Morton, 18 August 1924, RG6-04, box 1, file 1.
7 Sister Wymbs SOS to Mother Lidwina, 19 October 1924, RG6-04, box 1, file 1.
8 Sister Catherine Wymbs, "Gleaning from the Sister's Diaries," *The Field at Home* (January 1925).
9 The first payment ($2.00) received from a patient was not recorded in the Camp Morton Financial Records until February 1924, and a total of $9.40 was listed as receipts between 7 August 1924 and 29 June 1925, RG6-04, box 1, files 2 and 6.
10 Annals of Camp Morton, 1 September 1924, RG6-04, oversized box 1, file 1.
11 Archbishop Sinnott sent $275 in December 1924. Lunch boxes with thermos bottles were sent to Sisters Donnelly and Guest, and a set of medical instruments to Sister Wymbs shortly after the visit of Father Reardan of St. Paul, Minnesota. Financial Records and Annals of Camp

Notes

Morton, December 1924 and 20 October 1924.
12   Annals of Camp Morton, 11 September 1924.
13   Annals of Camp Morton, Sunday, 14 September 1924.
14   Annals of Camp Morton, Sunday, 14 September 1924.
15   Ibid., 2 October 1924.
16   Annals of Camp Morton, 11 November 1924.
17   Ibid., 1 December 1924.
18   Ibid., 22 December 1924.
19   Archbishop Sinnott to Father Daly, 31 December 1924; reprinted in *The Field at Home* (January 1925).
20   Annals of Camp Morton, 26-30 January and 24 February 1925.
21   Father Daly to "Reverend and Dear Sisters," 6 March 1925, RG1-01, box 1, file 32.
22   Sister Catherine Wymbs to Mother Lidwina, 6 April 1925, RG6-04, box 1, file 5.
23   CD to Father Daly, 19 April 1925, RG1-01, box 3, file 16.
24   Annals of Camp Morton, 19 November 1925.
25   Interview with Sister Lena Renaud SOS, 30 November 1993.
26   Alfred A. Sinnott, Archbishop of Winnipeg, to Father Daly CSsR, 5 July 1926, RG6-04, box 1, file 9.
27   This incident is not recorded in the Annals, but in the financial records of Camp Morton she noted on 31 May 1926, a payment of $4 to the Department of Education and the receipt of $2 from the other student. The same day, she also paid her regular horse feed supplier, who was another local farmer, $5 for oats for the three mission horses. Financial statement of Camp Morton, May 1926.
28   CD, memoir, "Metro N. A Sensitive Pupil," RG1-01, oversized box 1, file 1.
29   Catherine found out several years later that Metro more than fulfilled her hopes. He graduated from university and served as an officer during the Second World War. He became a university professor, a research expert in mines, and then manager of a mining company in New York. She was particularly proud that he was a happily married family man, still a practising Catholic, "devout and joyous in his faith."

CHAPTER 7: Returning to Alberta: Pioneering in Vilna
1   Father Daly to Sister Catherine Wymbs, 5 November 1925, SOSA, RG6-49, box 1, file 1.
2   Annals of Vilna, 11 November 1925, SOSA.
3   Sister Wymbs to Father Daly, 13 November 1925, RG6-49, box 1, file 1.
4   Ibid., 19 November 1925.

305

Notes

5   Sister Beatrice DeMarsh SOS, undated memoir "Hospital Days — Vilna, Alta. 1925," RG6-49, box 4, file 8. Sister DeMarsh arrived at Vilna in July 1926. Her pithy, six-page memoir vividly describes the facilities and the sisters' hardships in the early years of the Vilna Mission Hospital.
6   Alberta Government Report, "Vilna General Hospital," 26 June 1926, RG6-49, box 1, file 1.
7   CD to Archbishop McNeil, 11 January 1927, McNeil Papers, ARCAT.
8   Sister Beatrice DeMarsh, "Hospital Days — Vilna."
9   "Report from Vilna," *The Field at Home* 3, no. 2 (January 1927).
10 Father Daly to CD, 29 March 1927, RG6-49, box 4, file 1.
11 Yearly Report — Vilna Mission, May 1927, signed "Sr. C. Donnelly," RG6-49, box 1, file 1.
12 *The Field at Home* 4, no. 3 (April 1928).
13 Father Daly to CD, 12 May 1927.
14 The house at 60 Glen Road had been built in the 1880s and purchased by Sir Casimir Gzowski in 1904. He made many improvements and had lived there until he died in 1922. The property was acquired from his executors, the Toronto General Trust, for $25,000 on 8 August 1927. On 27 October 1936, the Sisters of Service were able to purchase the house next door for $8,000. This house was demolished and the land was used to enlarge the gardens of the novitiate.
15 Archbishop Neil McNeil, address at the SOS motherhouse, 2 February 1925, Archives of the Community of St. Joseph, Morrow Park, Toronto.
16 Father Daly to Archbishop McNeil, 25 September 1928, McNeil Papers.
17 Ralph and Isabel [Davidson] Steinhaur to CD, 9 May 1974. Isabel eventually married Ralph Steinhaur, who later became the Lieutenant-Governor of Alberta. Isabel's letter was in reply to Catherine's note of congratulation on her husband's appointment. Catherine included it in a letter to Sister Patricia Burke in 1974, RG1-01, box 10, file 6.
18 Archbishop Neil McNeil, Decreee Appointing First Sister General, Councillors and Mistress of Novices, 19 May 1928, RG1-03, box 1, file 5.
19 CD, *The Field at Home* 5, no. 1 (January 1929).
20 CD to Archbishop McNeil, 8 September 1928, McNeil Papers.
21 Ibid.
22 CD, "Summer Days," *The Field at Home* 5, no. 1 (January 1929).
23 CD to Archbishop McNeil, 8 September 1928, McNeil Papers.
24 Father Daly to Most Reverend H.J. O'Leary, Archbishop of Edmonton, 14 July 1928. Letter obtained from the Archives of the Archdiocese of Edmonton, courtesy of Sister Mary Phillips SOS.
25 CD to Archbishop A.A. Sinnott, 21 April 1929, RG1-01, box 7, file 5.

Notes

26 CD, "North-Western Manitoba," *The Field at Home* (July 1929).
27 "Caravans Carry Gospel to Many," Toronto *Globe*, 26 March 1929.
28 James McGuigan, Vicar General, to Father Daly, 24 November 1925, RG6-09.1, box 1, file 2. The writer soon became Archbishop of Regina and later Cardinal McGuigan of Toronto.
29 Sister Florence Regan SOS to Father Daly, "Yearly Report of the Edmonton Mission," 1 May 1926 - 30 April 1927, RG6-09, box 1, file 6.
30 Father Daly to Archbishop O'Leary, 20 May 1927, Archives of the Archdiocese of Edmonton.
31 Sister General Florence Regan to Rev. Sister Chisholm, Superior, 12 May 1930, RG6-09.1, box 1, file 7. In May 1929 the order had purchased another Edmonton house on 105th Street to be used as a hostel for "Immigrant Girls and girls from local areas." It was operated by the Sisters of Service until 1967.
32 CD to Sister General Regan, 9 August 1930, RG6-09.1, box 1, file 2.
33 Sister General Florence Regan to CD, telegram, 27 August 1930, RG6-38, box 1, file 1.
34 CD to Sister General, 28 August 1930, RG6-38, box 1, file 1.

CHAPTER 8: Serving in a Depression-Wracked Community

1   CD to Sister General Hayes, 31 August 1930, SOSA, RG6-38, box 1, file 1. In the absence of any annals for St. Brides in the Sisters of Service Archive, or private papers of the Sister General, the principal source of information about St. Brides Mission is the correspondence of Catherine to the Sister General and to Father Daly, and the Archives of the Archdiocese of Edmonton.
2   CD to Archbishop Henry O'Leary, 11 September 1930; Archbishop Henry Joseph O'Leary to CD, 19 September 1930, Archives of Archdiocese of Edmonton, St. Brides file.
3   The baptismal records of St. Augustine's Roman Catholic Church, Dundas, note the baptism of Eleanor McMahon on 28 July 1865. She lived in Dundas in the modest family home until 22 March 1939 when she entered the House of Providence, a local home for the aged, founded by the Sisters of St. Joseph. A year later she fractured her hip and died on 21 May 1940. The obituary in the *Dundas Star* noted that "she was a member of the family long associated with the town," and that "she has many friends among the older members of her community who will keenly regret her passing." The author acknowledges with many thanks the help of Rev. Father Ronald Synnott, St. Augustine's Church, and Sister Rose Pautler CSJ, archivist, who located these statistics in their records. With the death

307

Notes

of Miss McMahon's brother at the House of Providence the following year, the family line ceased.
4 CD to Sister General, 2, 30 November, 14 December 1930, RG6-8, box 1, file 1.
5 CD to Sister General, 14 December 1930, RG6-8, box 1, file 1.
6 Ibid.
7 CD to Sister General, 6 January 1931, RG6-38, box 1, file 2.
8 Ibid., 7 April 1931.
9 Sister General Hayes to CD, 9 April 1931, RG6-38, box 1, file 2.
10 CD to Father Daly, 10 May 1931.
11 Ibid.
12 The Community of St. Joseph expended much effort and money to ensure that their teaching sisters were fully qualified and up-to-date in curriculum and methodology. See Elizabeth Smyth, "Teacher Education within the Congregation of the Sisters of St. Joseph of Toronto, Canada, 1851-1920," *History of Education Review* 23, no. 3 (1994), 97-113.
13 CD to Sister General, 16 October 1930, 17 May 1931, RG6-38, box 1, files 1, 2.
14 CD to Father Daly, 6 July 1931, RG6-38, box 1, file 2.
15 Sister General to Sister Fallon, 18 August 1931, RG6-38, box 1, file 2.
16 W.A. McPhee to Father Daly, 29 January 1931, RG6-38, box 1, file 2.
17 The exchange of letters outlining the clerics' views resembled a chess match. Archbishop O'Leary to Father Daly, 8 July 1931; Daly to O'Leary, 13 July 1931; O'Leary to Daly, 23 July 1931; Daly to O'Leary, 29 July 1931; Daly to McPhee, 5 August 1931, all in RG6-38, box 1, file 2.
18 CD to Father Daly, 20 September 1931, RG6-38, box 1, file 2.
19 Ibid.
20 Ibid.
21 Mary Ellen McGonigal, St. Brides, to Sister Mary Phillip SOS, January 1993, RG6-38, box 1, file 2.
22 Rev. W.A. McPhee to Father Daly, 18 November 1931, RG6-38, box 1, file 2.
23 Father Daly to CD, 27 December 1931, RG6-38, box 1, file 2.
24 CD to Sister General, 28 August 1932, RG6-38, box 1, file 3.
25 CD, Last Will and Testament, 12 August 1933, RG6-38. As was customary, Catherine made a will just before she took her permanent vows. In it she left her capital, which totalled $2,080.39, to the Sisters of Service. The annual interest from this sum, some of which was invested in government bonds, she was allowed to give, with permission, to whomever she chose. According to *the Rules and*

Notes

Constitutions of the Sisters of Service (p. 22, no. 65), drawn up by Father Daly, a sister was not allowed to add to the capital or use it herself, but could dispose of the interest annually to whomever she chose. It was this sum of approximately $80 to which the Sister General was referring. Her will also stated that, "Should any money or property be bequeathed to me, I wish to will it to the Sisters of Service of Canada except the amount of one thousand dollars each to the children of my Sister, Mrs. Arthur Gifford for the Catholic education of these children if they are not grown up."

26   CD to Sister General, 8 January 1933, RG6-38, box 1, file 4.
27   Ibid. Whether the Ukrainian farmers who supported the new board were really communists is uncertain. The Ukrainian Labour-Farmer Temple Association (which was closely associated with the Communist Party of Canada) was actively seeking members at this time, and this group was anti-religious. See O.W. Gerus and J.E. Rea, *The Ukrainians in Canada* (Canadian Historical Association Series, Canada's Ethnic Groups, 1985). The Ukrainians who were members of either the Orthodox or the Ukrainian Catholic Church were resentful of the proselytizing by the Latin branch of the Catholic Church, to which the Irish priest and settlers belonged.
28   CD to Father Daly, 23 April 1923, RG6-38, box 1, file 4.
29   CD to Father Daly, 2 May 1933, RG6-38, box 1, file 4.
30   CD to Sister General, 22 May 1932; Father George Daly to CD, 10 May 1933, RG6-38, box 1, file 4.
31   CD, telegram to Sister General, 1 July 1933, RG6-38, box 1, file 4.
32   CD to Sister General, 21 July 1933, RG6-38, box 1, file 4.
33   CD to Sister General, 16 August 1933, RG6-38, box 1, file 4.
34   Unidentified newspaper clipping of a news report, dated 1933, from "Celtic S.D. 4337 St. Brides PO, RG6-38, box 1, file 4.
35   Father Daly to CD, no date, but probably early October 1933, RG6-38, box 1, file 4.
36   Father Daly to Reverend W.E. Doyle, 20 August 1948, Archives of the Archdiocese of Edmonton, St. Brides file.
37   Father Daly to CD, 23 November 1933, RG6-38, box 1, file 6.

CHAPTER 9: Creating a New Rule for a New Order
1   D.I. Lanslots OSB, *Handbook of Canon Law for Congregations of Women Under Simple Vows,* 4th ed. (New York: F. Pustnet 1910), art. 23, pp. 23-24.
2   CD to interviewer Roy Bonisteel on the CBC program, "Man Alive," broadcast 29 December 1980.
3   Father Daly, circular letter, 10 October 1929, SOSA, RG6, box 1, file

Notes

        36. This confirms the fact that their current Rule was not their own, and it would be rewritten and published as the *Rule and Constitutions of the Sisters of Service.*

4   *Rules and Constitutions of the Sisters of Service* (Toronto 1934).
5   Ibid., 8.
6   Ibid., "Religious Work," 9, nos. 12, 13, 17.
7   Ibid., "Order of the Day," 34, no. 103.
8   Ibid., "Educational Work," 10, no. 18.
9   Ibid., "Welfare Work," 11, no. 27 and 12, no. 29.
10 Ibid., 12, no. 32.
11 Ibid., "Welfare Work," 12, no. 33. It was understood that when the sisters did welfare work with Catholics, they were free to urge them to retain their faith. Father Daly was referring here to the persistent efforts of the Protestant missionaries in western Canada who were vigorously seeking converts among those immigrants who appeared to be indifferent to the Roman Catholic Church in their community.
12 Ibid., "Educational Work," 10, no. 22.
13 *Constitutions of the Sisters of St. Joseph* (Toronto 1935), 15, no. 33. Archives of the Community of St. Joseph, Morrow Park, Toronto. Their headress of a white linen cornet or cap and white headband, and the large white linen guimpe or collar, required good laundry facilities, quantities of hot water, and much time and expertise to wash and iron. During her postulancy in their novitiate, Catherine had pointed out that this was impractical clothing for anyone living and working on the dusty, and sometimes muddy prairie, and where running water was not available.
14 *Rules and Constitutions*, "Religious Uniform," 15 and 16, nos. 44 and 45.
15 Sister Catherine Schmeltzer SOS to Jeanne Beck, 8 May 1996.
16 *Rules and Constitutions*, "Religious Uniform," 16, no. 48.
17 "On no occasion shall a Sister be permitted to go out without a suitable companion, whom the Local Superior is to nominate or approve. In case a Sister cannot accompany her, she may take a prudent girl of the school, or some other exemplary person, who must not leave her until her return." *Rules of the Daughters of Charity, Servants of the Poor* (1913 ed.), no. 117.
18 *Constitutions of the Sisters of St. Joseph*, "Enclosure," 43, no. 94.
19 *Rules and Constitutions*, "Characteristic Virtues of the Sisters of Service," 32, no. 95.
20 Ibid., "Postulancy — Novitiate — Profession," 15, no. 43.
21 Sister Catherine Schmeltzer to Jeanne Beck, 8 May 1996.
22 *Rules and Constitutions*, "Vow of Obedience," 29. nos. 83 and 88.

Notes

23 In cases where a difference of opinion could not be settled by mutual agreement, the Mother General's only recourse was to withdraw her order from the parish or the diocese. The subsidiary role and authority of women vis-à-vis men at that time was not confined to the Roman Catholic Church. It prevailed in other Christian denominations (with rare exceptions) and most certainly in law, academia, politics and government.
24 *Rules and Constitutions*, "Order of the Day," 33, nos. 100 and 103.

CHAPTER 10: Pioneering in the Cariboo
1   SOSA, RG6-09.1, box 1, file 11.
2   CD to Sister General Regan, 25 March 1934, Edmonton, RG6-09.1, box 1, file 11.
3   CD, "Through the Cariboo, May 1934," diary, 7 May 1934, RG1-01, oversized box 1, file 4.
4   Ibid., diary, 15 May 1934.
5   Sister Irene Faye, "The Cariboo Trail, Big Bear Creek, May 21, 1934," *The Field At Home* (September 1934).
6   Ibid.
7   CD, diary, Thursday, 24 May 1934.
8   Sister Irene Faye to Father Daly, 1 June 1934, RG1-01, box 1, file 16.
9   CD, diary, 30 May 1934.
10 Ibid.
11 Sister Irene Faye to Sister General, 1 June 1934, RG1-02, box 1, file 16.
12 CD, diary, 4 and 7 June 1934.
13 Sister Irene Faye to Sister General, 14 June 1934.
14 CD to Sister General Regan, 19 June 1934.
15 CD, diary, 12 June 1934; CD to Sister General, 19 June 1934.
16 CD to Sister General, 15 June 1934.
17 Ibid., 19 June 1934.
18 Father A.L.McIntyre to Sisters Catherine Donnelly and Irene Faye, 15 July 1934, RG1-01, box 7, file 1.
19 CD, diary, 16 July 1934.
20 CD, "The Return to the Cariboo," *The Field at Home* (1936).
21 CD, Cariboo Diary, 2 June 1936, RG1-01, oversized box 1, file 3.
22 CD, "The Return to the Cariboo."
23 Sister Irene Faye, text of a talk on "Our Catechetical Work in B.C., Summer 1936," RG8-01, box 1, file 8.
24 Father A.L.McIntyre to "My Dear Sisters," 20 July 1936, RG1-01, box 3, file 16.

311

Notes

CHAPTER 11: Keeping the Order On Course

1. Father Arthur Coughlan to CD, 18 March 1936, Coughlan Letter Collection, SOSA, RG1-01, oversized box, file 6. Catherine's memoir was never placed in the SOS Archive, as Father Coughlan never did write the history. It must be assumed that her version was lost from his papers during his many changes of location after 1936.
2. Father Coughlan to CD, 2 May 1936, Coughlan Letter Collection.
3. Father Coughlan to CD, 23 November 1936, RG1-01, box 7, file 16.
4. Sister General Florence Regan to Sister Superiors and Sisters, 1 March 1937, RG3-01, box 1, file 1.
5. Archbishop P.J. Monahan to Rev. G. Daly CSsR, 4 December 1935, RG3-01, box 1, file 6.
6. Father Daly, address to the chapter sisters, 9 May 1937, RG3-01, box 1, file 1.
7. Minutes of the First General Chapter, May 1937, RG3-01, box 1, file 1.
8. Minutes of the Council of the Sisters of Service, 15 August 1937.
9. Interview with Sister Leona Trautman, 5 May 1993, and a memoir written for Jeanne Beck, undated, in the same year.
10. Ibid.
11. Father Arthur Coughlan to Sister General Florence Regan, 4 February 1936, RG1-01, box 1, file 12.
12. CD, two memoirs, "Marquis 1938-1940," RG1-01, box 9, file 10.
13. Marquis Annals, "Mission Notes," October 1938.
14. Ibid.
15. Sister Leona Trautman, memoir written for Jeanne Beck in 1993.
16. Morrison Sillery to the Sisters of Service, Marquis, 22 December 1939, RG1-01, box 9, file 10.
17. Morrison Sillery to CD and pupils of St. Marks, 17 June 1940, RG1-01, oversized box 1, file 10.

CHAPTER 12: The Hardest Years

1. CD, memoir, "The First Days of Loyola Continuation School." A note on the document states that it was written some time after 1950. There are two handwritten copies of this document in the same file which differ slightly in text but contain the same information. The file also contains a third version, which was typed and has an edited text with some additional bits of information. They are the main source of information in this chapter on the troublesome early beginnings of the school. These three documents are all in SOSA, RG1-01, box 9, file 26.
2. Annals of Sinnett, 12-16 September 1940, RG6-43, oversized box 1.
3. CD to Father George Daly, 24 September 1940, RG6-43, box 1, file 1.

Notes

4   Sister General Margaret Guest to Father W.H. Dunphy, 19 November 1940, RG6-43, box 1, file 1.
5   Sister General Margaret Guest to CD, 23 November 1940, RG-6, box 1, file 1.
6   Sister Mary Phillips SOS, "Memories of Sister Catherine Donnelly," undated, but received with a collection of sisters' memoirs sent to Jeanne Beck in 1994.
7   CD to Father Daly, 20 November 1940, RG6-43, box 1, file 1.
8   Sister General Guest to CD, 4 December 1940, RG1-01, box 9, file 26.
9   CD, memoir, 25 February 1977, RG1-01, box 9, file 26.
10 CD to Sister General Agnes Dwyer, 18 May 1966, RG1-01, box 8, file 6.
11 CD to Betty Ogle, 31 December 1968. In an interview with Jeanne Beck in September 1996, Betty Ogle clearly recalled the incident because the memory of Catherine's drooping gait and sad face was still etched in her memory.
12 Personnel records of the Sisters of Service. On the document no reason is given, as she had not taken permanent vows. During the period of temporary vows, neither the candidate nor the order is obliged to state a reason for withdrawal.
13 CD, memoir, 25 February 1977.
14 The Sinnett Public School would continue to be one of the successes of the Sisters of Service, as a succession of its teaching sisters were in charge of the school until 1969.
15 CD, memoir, 25 February 1977, "Behaviour of a certain human being is still amazing!"
16 CD to Sister General Reansbury, 7 October 1966. Reflecting long after the event, Catherine wrote that the "enemy" trying to thwart SOS work was "*not Protestants* but religious Catholics — Our own Sister (left afterwards) and a priest. God prevented catastrophe in that case and ultimately all went well," RG1-01, box 8, file 6.
17 The Hospital Report listing the religious denomination of the 713 patients admitted to the hospital during 1942 declared 196 as Catholic, 433 Protestant, and 139 as no religion. The principle nationalities listed were "English 173, Canadian 21, Ukranian 51, German 71, French 26, Scotch 67, Irish 58, Swede 29, 'Breed' 30, Russian 20, Polish 22, Norwegian 35, American 5, Danish 18, Czechs 17, Welsh 15, Jugo-Slav 11." The rest were scattered among the remaining European countries, RG6-10, box 2, file 3.
18 Father Daly to Sister Quinn, 4 September 1940, RG6-10, box 2, file 1.
19 Sister Mary Quinn to Sister General Guest, 9 December 1940, RG6-10, box 2, file 1.
20 Ibid., 8 February 1941, RG6-10, box 2, file 6.

Notes

21 Ibid., 23 February 1941, 25 March 1941, RG6-10, box 2, file 2.
22 Sister Agnes Brunning to Sister General Guest, 7 May 1941, RG6-10, box 2, file 2.
23 Sister Mary Quinn to Sister General Guest, 9 May 1941.
24 Several members of the order who were novices during the late 1930s have confirmed in interviews with the author that Catherine's contribution was never mentioned to them by Father Daly or the Novice Mistress.
25 Father Arthur Coughlan to CD, 11 May 1942, RG1-01, oversized box 1, file 11.
26 Ibid.

CHAPTER 13: Back in Harness: The Last Years of Teaching
1 Sister General Margaret Guest to CD, 19 April 1943, SOSA, RG6-10, box 2, file 6.
2 Minutes of the Second General Chapter of the Sisters of Service, July 1943, "Report of the Select Committee on 'schools'," RG3-02, box 1, file 3.
3 Sister Margaret Morgan SOS, memoir of Bergfield, undated, RG6-01, oversized box 1, file 7. Sister Morgan served at Bergfield from August 1938 to July 1939.
4 Sister Agnes Dwyer to Sister General Guest, 1 November 1943, RG6-01, box 1, file 6.
5 CD to Sister General Reansbury, 6 November 1968, RG1-01, box 8, file 12.
6 CD, memoir, "My Third Experience in the Bergfield Area," RG6-01, oversized box 1, file 7.
7 Sister Edith Wayland, interview with Jeanne Beck, 25 February 1994. Sister Wayland was Superior at Regina in 1947.
8 J. Williamson, secretary, Radville School Unit No. 3, to CD, 3 July 1947, RG1-01, box 9, file 11.
9 Stanley Hibbard to CD, 22 September 1947, RG1-01, box 9, file 11.
10 Sister Bernice Anstett SOS to Jeanne Beck, 22 April 1996.
11 Sister Dorothy Daley, memoir, "My Association with Catherine Donnelly and Father Daly," 6 June 1989, RG1-01, box 8, file 12B.
12 Ibid.
13 Assistant Sister General Quinn to CD, 30 January 1948, RG1-01, box 8, file 9.
14 Sister Dorothy Daley, "memoir".
15 Sister General Quinn to Father J. Volk, 7 May 1948; Father J.F. Volk to Sister General Quinn, 21 May 1948, RG6-01, box 1, file 11.
16 Dr. I.C. Molony to CD, 9 November 1948, RG1-01, box 8, file 14.

314

Notes

17 There are no copies of these letters, nor any listing of to whom they were sent. Three sisters who were interviewed by the author recalled receiving them, and noted that others who did have died. All stated they destroyed the letters as they were very upset by what they considered was an unthinkable and irrational idea.
18 Bishop Henri Routhier to CD, 30 August 1948, RG1-01, box 19, file 1.
19 CD to Bishop Routhier, 1 September 1948, McLennan Archives, McLennan, Alberta.
20 Sister Guest had a long recuperation at St. John's Hospital, Edson. As she improved, she began courses leading to qualifications as a medical record librarian, which she attained in March 1958. She worked at Edson in that capacity until Sepember 1973. With Catherine, she celebrated her golden jubilee as a Sister of Service in August 1974. She died in 1987.
21 Paul Stanich, "St. Michael's Dormitory," *Wheatfields and Wildflowers: A History of Rycroft and Surrounding School Districts* (Rycroft History Book Committee: Rycroft Alberta 1984), 110.
22 Sister Superior Mary Phillips SOS to the sisters at the Halifax hostel, 22 January 1952; Sister Phillips to Bishop Henri Routhier, 18 April 1952, RG6-37, box 1, file 9. John Duby received a D.Phil. from Oxford, and returned to the University of Alberta where he was listed as an associate professor in *Canadian Rhodes Scholars,* published by the Canadian Association of Rhodes Scholars, 1962.
23 Bishop Henri Routhier to Cardinal James C. McGuigan, 15 December 1951, McGuigan Papers, ARCAT.
24 Sister Mary Phillips to the sisters at Halifax, 4 May 1952.
25 Annals of Rycroft, 2 August 1952, RG6-37, box 1, file 1.
26 Sister Superior Mary Phillips to Sister General Mary Quinn, 1952, RG6-37, box 1, file 9.
27 Sister Mary Phillips to Sister Florence Regan SOS, 27 March 1953, RG6-37, box 1, file 10.
28 Sister Magdalen Barton to Sister General, 24 May 1954, RG6-3, box 1, file 11.
29 Sister Mary Phillips to Sister General, 3 June 1954, RG6-37, box 1, file 11.
30 Sister Barton to Sister General, 8 August 1954, ibid.
31 CD to Sister General Mary Quinn, 9 August 1954, ibid.
32 Report on Personnel, Discipline and Works of the Institute, submitted at the General Chapter, July 1954, RG3-04, box 1, file 12.
33 Sister Mary O'Kane to Sister General Mary Quinn, 9 September 1955, RG6-37, box 1, file 12.
34 Sister O'Kane to Sister General Quinn, 21 June 1956, RG6-37, box 2, file 1.

Notes

CHAPTER 14: I Don't Want to Grow Old *Gracefully* — *Usefully* — Yes

1. Sister Mary O'Kane to Sister General Mary Quinn, 8 June 1956, SOSA, RG6-37, box 2, file 1.
2. CD to Sister General Agnes Dwyer, 18 May 1966, RG1-01, box 8, file 6. In this letter, Catherine is quoting from a letter she had received from Sister Isabel Ellis, who was transferred to Halifax and had completed her education there.
3. CD to Sister Margaret Guest, 12 October 1966, RG1-01, box 8, file 6.
4. Ibid.
5. CD to Sister General Agnes Dwyer, 10 September 1964, RG1-01, box 8, file 6.
6. "Questions and Answers at Discussion in Winnipeg," 15 May 1965, SOSA, not numbered. The two-page typed document appears to be a transcription of a tape made at the meeting.
7. "Decree on the Up-to-Date Renewal of Religious Life," *Vatican II, Perfectae Caritatis,* 28 October 1965. *The Conciliar and Post Conciliar Documents,* translated by Austin Flannery OP (Collegeville, Mn. 1965), 612, no. 2b; 613, no. 3; 621, nos. 17 and 18.
8. Father Edward Boyce CSsR, *Survey — Sisters of Service* (31 August 1968), pp. 2,4, RG3-06, box 2, file 5.
9. The Redemptorist Order whose priests had contributed so much to the founding of the Sisters of Service, was also undergoing similar difficulties. See Paul Laverdure, *Redemption and Renewal: The Redemptorists of English Canada, 1834-1994* (Toronto 1996), chaps. 9 and 10. There have been many attempts to explain the widespread dissatisfaction with religious life which had surfaced as early as the 1950s, and which seems to have been accelerated by the soul-searching mandated by Vatican II. I am indebted to Father James Mason CSsR, for drawing my attention to a thoughtful sociological study on this topic by Sister Patricia Wittberg SC, *The Rise and Fall of Catholic Religious Orders: A Social Movement Perspective* (Albany 1994).
10. CD to Betty Ogle, 27 February 1977.
11. Sister Lita Camozzi SOS, "Memoir, Sister Catherine Donnelly," RG1-01, box 9, file 3, 1988.
12. Sister Lena Renaud, interview with Roy Bonisteel on the CBC television program, "You've Come a Long Way Sister", on *Man Alive,* September 1980.
13. Sister Lena Renaud, "Memoirs of Sister Catherine Donnelly," 6 March 1989, SOSA, not catalogued.
14. In recent years this practice has become accepted in the Roman Catholic

Notes

Church, and both lay men and women are now taking this role at Mass.
15 Sister General Helen Hayes to CD, 11 April 1979, RG1-01, box 8, file 12.
16 Sister Helen Hayes, interview with Jeanne Beck at Toronto, 11 February 1997.
17 CD to Anna McNally SOS, and Patricia Burke SOS, 4 July 1980.
18 J. Alan Dainard to CD, 4 January 1981, RG1-01, box 9, file 3.
19 CD to Betty Ogle, 19 February 1981, RG1-01, box 8, file 12b.
20 Sister Alena Bryden SOS, undated memoir, uncatalogued.
21 CD, memoir, December 1966, RG1-01, box 9, file 14.

SISTERS OF SERVICE MISSIONS 1924-1997

(numbers correspond to those on the endpaper map)

ALBERTA

1. Bonnyville
2. Drayton Valley
3. Dunvegan
4. Edmonton
5. Edson
6. Faust
7. Fort McMurray
8. Frog Lake
9. Goodfish Lake
10. Hawk Hills
11. High Level
12. Joussard
13. Manning
14. Meander River
15. Onoway
16. Peace River
17. Rycroft
18. Smoky Lake
19. Spirit River
20. Stony Plain
21. St. Brides
22. Vilna

BRITISH COLUMBIA

1. Fort St. John
2. Kelowna
3. Nelson
4. Penticton
5. Vancouver

MANITOBA

1. Camp Morton
2. Churchill
3. The Pas
4. Shilo
5. Winnipeg

NEW BRUNSWICK

1. Dorchester
2. Moncton
3. Saint John

NEWFOUNDLAND-LABRADOR

1. Bishop's Falls
2. Clarenville
3. Corner Brook
4. Northwest River
5. Petty Harbour
6. Sheshatshit
7. St. John's
8. St. Julien's
9. The Goulds

NORTHWEST TERRITORIES

1. Rankin Inlet

319

Sisters of Service Missions, 1924-1997

NOVA SCOTIA

1. Dartmouth
2. Halifax
3. New Glasgow

ONTARIO

1. Christian Island
2. Joyceville
3. Kitchener
4. Moosonee
5. Ottawa
6. Sarnia
7. St. Catharines
8. Thunder Bay
9. Toronto
10. Waterloo
11. Wyoming

PRINCE EDWARD ISLAND

1. Charlottetown

QUEBEC

1. Montreal
2. Quebec City

SASKATCHEWAN

1. Bergfield
2. Buffalo Narrows
3. Creighton
4. Diamond Crossing
5. Green Lake
6. Jutland
7. La Loche
8. La Ronge
9. Mayfair
10. Marquis
11. Meadow Lake

SASKATCHEWAN (continued)

12. Milestone
13. Minton
14. North Battleford
15. Paynton
16. Regina
17. Saskatoon
18. Sinnett

YUKON

1. Teslin
2. Whitehorse

U.S.A. - NORTH DAKOTA

1. Fargo
2. Grand Forks

SOUTH AMERICA - BRAZIL

1. Casa Nova

INDEX

A

Adjala Township, Ontario, 19, 21, 22
Alberta, Mother, 56-57
Albury, Sister Carolyn, 228
Allard, Miss C, 89, 95, 99
Alliston, Ontario, 19, 20, 21, 24, 32, 33, 35, 53, 54
Anne, Sister, 239, 241, 242, 244, 248
Anstett, Sister Bernice, 260
Apto School, Ontario, 33-35, 36
Avila, Sister, 59, 61-62, 81

B

Barkerville, British Columbia, 214
Barton, Sister Magdalen (Madge), 168, 237, 269, 270
Biys, Paul, 127, 129, 132
Blanchard, Florence, 242
Boissevain, Manitoba, 158
Bonisteel, Roy, 288-290
Boyce, Father Edward, 283, 284
Bradley Creek, British Columbia, 217-218
Brunning, Sister Agnes, 137
Burke, Sister Mary Anne Bridget, 88-89, 95, 135, 137, 164, 167, 172, 176

C

Caledon East Village School, Ontario, 39
Calgary, 50, 52
Cameron, Father William, 50-52, 75
Camp Morton, Manitoba, chapter 6; CD's retirement at, 276-290
Canoe Creek Indian Reservation, British Columbia, 206
Canon law, 67, 75, 96, 185, 187
Cantin family, 212-214, 217
Cariboo district, British Columbia, chapter 10
Cars, 152, 174, 202-203ff., 257; Father Daly and, 103
Catechism schools, rural/itinerant, from Camp Morton, Manitoba, 126, 129, 136, 137; in Cariboo district, British Columbia, chapter10; in Manitoba, 151-154, 156-158; at Regina, 223, 264; *See also* Religious correspondence schools (SOS)
Catholic Women's League, 80, 83, 87, 95, 105-106, 109, 116, 125, 138, 159, 164, 197, 235
Celtic School, Edmonton, chapter 8
Christmas celebrations, 131-132, 166
Churches, 219; Church of the Immaculate Conception,

321

Index

Arlington, Ontario, 19, 20, 22; St. Anne's Catholic Church, Penetanguishene, Ontario, 40; St. Anthony's, Camp Morton, Manitoba, 129, 131, 135; Ukrainian Catholic Church, 76
Claude, Father, 165, 167
Clinton, British Columbia, 202, 215, 216
Coleman Public School, Alberta, 52, 57
Colgan, Ontario, 19, 26
Correspondence schools SEE Religious correspondence schools (SOS)
Coughlan, Father Arthur, 55-57, 62-63, 94, 96, 146; is consulted by CD about beginning new order, 65-67, 71, 72-74, 76-78, 80-81, 83-84, 282; selects Father Daly to head new order, 84-85, 104; defends Father Daly, 116-118; considers writing memoirs of founding of SOS, 223-225; concerns about Father Daly's handling of SOS, 252-253, 256
Culross Public School, Ontario, 38

D

Daley, Sister Dorothy, 260-262
Daly, Father George, 81-82, 94, 95-96, 292; takes over from Father Coughlan as official clerical supervisor of SOS, 84-85, 104; pursues financial support and vocations for SOS, 85-87, 104; background, 99-103; and SOS habit, 108-110; defended by Father Coughlan, 116-118; negotiations with Archbishop Sinnott, 122-124; visits Camp Morton, 127; opens religious correspondence school in Edmonton, 134; makes arrangements for hospital in Vilna, Alberta, 141-142; negotiates about housing for SOS at St. Bride's, 173, 175-176; writes Holy Rule for SOS, 186-190; CD's concerns about Father Daly's influence on SOS, 224, 251-253, 256, 261, 264, 286-288; chairs general chapter meetings, 226-228, 270-271; death, 273; contribution to development of SOS, 279
Davidson, Isabel, 150
Denzil Public School, Saskatchewan, 72, 73
Diamond Coulee Public School, Saskatchewan, 232, 233, 256, 259-263
Diamond Crossing Public School, Saskatchewan, 256-258
Donnelly, Catherine, parents, 19-21, 29-32; elementary and secondary education, 22, 23, 24; Model School (teacher training) education, 24-25; character and views, 25-26, 33, 37, 57, 66, 130, 170;

friends and capacity for friendship, 26, 32-33, 277-278; first teaching positions, 26-27, 35-36; attends Normal School, Toronto, 29-30; teaches in Galt, 32-33; breakdowns, 33, 133, 249; teaches at Apto School, Ontario, 33, 34, 35, 36; teaches at Forrester's Falls, Ontario, 36-37; teaches at various locations in Ontario, 37-42; moves to Stettler, Alberta, 44; cares for rural people ill from influenza, 45-46; recognizes call to become a religious, 47-50, 51; teaches at Sacred Heart Catholic School, Calgary, 50-52; father's death, 53-54; first interview with Mother General, Community of St. Joseph, 54-55; talks with Father Coughlan about action to take, 55-56; meets Mother General Alberta, 56-57; joins Community of St. Joseph, Toronto, as postulant, 57-59; rejected by Sisters of St. Joseph, 60-61; decides to start own community, 62-63; consults Father Coughlan about beginning new order, 65-67, 71, 72-74, 76-78, 80-81, 83-84, 282; consults Archbishop McNeil about beginning new order, 69-70, 77, 80; teaches in Denzil, Saskatchewan, 72, 73; teaches in Stornoway, Saskatchewan, 75-76, 78, 82; returns to Toronto, 82-89; enters SOS novitiate, 95, 109; views on SOS women's hostels, 109-110, 149, 183-184, 224-225; depression and frustration, 111, 113; vow of obedience, 111-112, 247-248, 288, 289; first vows, 119; arrives at Camp Morton, Manitoba, 125; life at Camp Morton, 128, 130; attends teachers' conventions, 129, 135; leaves Camp Morton, 139-140; superior of Vilna mission, Alberta, 141, 144; life at Vilna, 144; passed over for leadership in SOS, 151; goes on retreat, 153; assigned to correspondence school work, 158-159; teaches at Celtic School, St. Bride's Edmonton, 160, 162, 163, 174-175, 181-182; life at St. Bride's, 166; takes final vows, 172; problems with school board at St. Bride's, 178-181; influence on formulation of Holy Rule, 189, 190, 193; works at catechetical correspondence school in Edmonton, 197-199; concerned that SOS sisters further their education, 199-200, 230, 278; travels Cariboo district giving catechism classes, chapter 10; concerns

Index

about Father Daly's influence on SOS, 224, 251-253, 256, 261, 264, 286-288; teaches Sisters Irene Faye and Leona Trautman, 228-232; teaches at St. Mark's Separate School, Marquis, Saskatchewan, 232-237; teaches at Loyola Continuation School, Sinnett, Saskatchewan, 239-247; life at Sinnett, 243-244; leaves Sinnett, 247-248; recuperates at St. John's Hospital, Edson, Alberta, 249-251; teaches at Diamond Crossing Public School, Saskatchewan, 256-258; works as housekeeper in Jutland, Saskatchewan, 258-259; teaches at Diamond Coulee Public School, Saskatchewan, 259-263; comes close to completing university degree, 263; teaches at Rycroft Public School, Alberta, 265-273; breaks wrist, 269; retirement at Camp Morton, Manitoba, 276-290; confrontation with residence sisters, 279; role in founding SOS acknowledged, 283, 284; celebrates 50th year as SOS, 286; topic of Roy Bonisteel's television program "Man Alive", 288-290; moves to nursing home in St. Catharines, 290; death, 292

Donnelly, Catherine (Mother), 20, 23, 29-30, 31-32

Donnelly, Elizabeth Theresa (Tess), 20, 29, 33-35, 43, 48, 53, 276, 277

Donnelly, Hugh (Father), 19, 20, 23, 30-32, 39, 44, 48; death, 53-54

Donnelly, Hugh (Grandfather), 19

Donnelly, Hugh Jr. (Cousin), 21

Donnelly, Mary (Mamie) Loretto (Sister Justina CSJ), 20, 29, 34, 35, 38-39, 43, 53, 61-62, 172, 276, 290, 291

Donnelly, Matthew, 21

Duby, John, 268

Duck Mountain, Manitoba, 156

Dulaska, Sister Josephine, 255

Dunphy, Father, 240, 241, 243, 244, 245, 247, 248

Dwyer, Sister Agnes, 176, 179, 181, 256, 257, 258, 275

E

Ecumenism, 33, 66-67; *See also* Protestants, relationships with Catholics

Edgeleys company, 107

Edmonton, 159, 283; *See also* Religious correspondence schools (SOS), Edmonton; St. Bride's School, Edmonton

Edson, Alberta, 248-251

Egan, Sister Carmel, 150, 172

F

Fallon, Sister Josephine, 141, 144, 160, 162, 167, 168, 171-172, 173, 175, 176, 182

Faye, Sister Irene, 200, 236, 239,

Index

249, 259; studies under CD, 228, 230-233; travels in Cariboo district, British Columbia, 203-220
Ferdinand, Sister SEE O'Connor, Mary
Ferguson, Hugh, 19
Ferry, Lenore, 72
Forest Grove, British Columbia, 217-218
Forrester's Falls, Ontario, 36-37

G

Galt, Ontario, 32
Garvin, Joseph, 41, 43
Geraghty, Sister Ann, 142, 143, 172
Gifford, Robert, 277, 291, 292
Gottfried, Margaret, 289
Gravelle Ferry, British Columbia, 212-213, 217
Grinder family, 204-205
Guest, Sister Margaret, 112, 123-124, 129, 131, 136, 137, 150, 151, 172, 243, 246, 247, 255, 286, 291; elected Sister General, 228; resigns as Sister General, 265

H

Habit (Religious garb), 60, 107-108, 190-191, 228, 256, 281
Halder, Sister Mary, 276
Hasell, Eva, 157
Hayes, Sister Helen, 288, 290
Heidelberg Public School, Ontario, 38
Hoeks, Father Theodore, 285, 287, 289
Holt Renfrew, 108
Holy Rule, 49, 54, 58, 70-71, 75, 93, 185-194
Horses, 23, 37, 44-45, 75-76, 125, 127, 128, 130, 133, 137-138, 165, 204-205
Hospitals (SOS), Edson, Alberta, 248-251; Vilna, Alberta, 141, 143, 145-146, 149-150
Hostels, SOS women's (Residential Clubs), 109-110, 134, 138, 148, 190, 229, 256, 278-279, 281-282, 283; CD's views on, 109-110, 149, 183-184, 224-225
Hudson Consolidated School, Ontario, 39

I

Immigrants, 69, 122, 158; Canadianization, 78-79, 189; *See also* Irish immigrants; Ukrainian immigrants
Influenza epidemic, 45-46
Irish immigrants, 17-19, 21, 161, 166, 176
Isnardy family, 207-208, 212, 219

J

Jackson, Sister Mary, 233, 258, 259, 262
Josephites (Sisters of St. Joseph of the Sacred Heart), 71, 73
Justina, Sister SEE Donnelly, Mary (Mamie) Loretto
Jutland, Saskatchewan, 258-259

Index

K

Killarney, Manitoba, 158
Killarney Public School, Ontario, 37
Knopic, Sister Bridget, 290, 291
Koster family, 206, 219
Kostering family, 203, 205, 220

L

La Bonty family, 216
Lawler, Gertrude, 38, 95, 106
Lazzarin family, 217
Lidwina, Sister, 91-94, 98-99, 107, 110-111, 133, 146; relationship with CD, 94-95, 111-112; and SOS habit, 108-109
Loretto, Sisters of, 77, 83
Lukas, Father, 234-235
Lytton, British Columbia, 202

M

MacDonnell family (Robert, Irene, Achsah and Ruth), 32-33, 61, 62, 63, 223, 269
MacDougall, Sister Mary, 270
Macieszek, Father, 131, 132, 136, 137, 155
Mackenzie, Wellington, 49-50, 52-53
Manley Public School, Ontario, 38-39
Marquis, Saskatchewan, 232-237
McConnell, Adeline, 39, 53, 72, 85-86, 88, 120, 127-128
McIntrye, Father A.L., 201-220
McMahon, Miss Eleanor (Ellen), 164-165, 197, 223

McNally, Catherine, 112, 134, 158, 284
McNeil, Neil, Archbishop of Toronto, 49, 55, 72, 93, 190, 193, 282; background, 67-69; is consulted by CD and Father Coughlan about beginning new order, 69-70, 77, 80; celebrates first SOS mass, 95; pleads for Vatican approval for SOS, 113-116; omits to credit CD with role in founding SOS, 119-120
McPhee, Father W.M., 161, 162, 165, 167, 169, 171, 173, 177, 179-180
Meldrum Creek, British Columbia, 210, 211, 218-219
Merriton Separate School, Ontario, 39
Metro (Student), 139-140
Minnedosa, Manitoba, 152, 157
Minton district, Saskatchewan, 256-257, 260, 263
Monahan, P.J., Archbishop of Regina, 227, 232, 237, 240, 257
Mono Township, Ontario, 18
Morrin Public School, Alberta, 57
Morrison, Sister Domitilla, 290
Morton, Thomas W, 121-122
Mulhall, Father Patrick, 103, 104
Murray, Father Gerald, 146

N

Neepawa, Manitoba, 152, 157
Newman Hall, Toronto, 82-83, 87

Index

O

Oakburn, Manitoba, 154
Oblates of Mary Immaculate, 68, 201
O'Connor, Mary (Sister Ferdinand IBVM), 39, 44, 45-47, 50, 52, 83, 291, 292
Ogle, Betty, 248, 290
O'Kane, Sister Mary, 272, 275
O'Leary, Archbishop of Edmonton, 116, 134, 141, 158, 163, 173, 180
150 Mile House, British Columbia, 216
Othelia, Mother, 146, 147, 150, 193

P

Paquin, Father Joseph, 265, 266
Peace River district, Alberta, 265, 268
Penetanguishene Public School, Ontario, 39-41
Phillips, Sister Mary, 246, 248, 269, 270
Poverty of rural areas, 162, 165-166, 173-174, 178, 235
Probert, Mary, 213, 217
Protestants, relationships with Catholics, 17, 21, 22-23, 32-33, 78, 234; during World War I, 42

Q

Quayle, James, 32
Quesnel, British Columbia, 212, 214, 217
Quinn, Sister Mary, 249, 250, 251, 269, 272

R

Reansbury, Sister Mary, 283
Redemptorist Order, 55, 100-101; *See also* Daly, Father George
Regan, Sister Florence, 150, 159, 160, 172, 187, 200, 226, 227, 228
Religious correspondence schools (SOS), Edmonton, 134, 157, 158-159, 197-199, 215, 258; *See also* Catechism schools
Renaud, Sister Lena, 285-286, 287, 289, 290
Riversdale Public School, Ontario, 38
Roberts, Sister Mary, 236, 237
Roblin, Manitoba, 156, 157
Rogation, Brother, 82
Rose, Sister Leona, 255
Routhier, Bishop Henri, 264, 265, 268
Russell, Manitoba, 153, 157
Ruthenians *SEE* Ukrainian immigrants
Rycroft Public School, Alberta, 265-273

S

Sacred Heart Catholic School, Calgary, 50, 52
St. Bride's School, Edmonton, chapter 8
St. John's Hospital, Edson, Alberta, 249-251
St. Joseph, Community and Sisters of, 22, 37, 40-41, 43, 52, 66, 80, 96, 170, 186, 193;

327

Index

and Tess, 33, 34, 35; CD's interviews with Mother General, 54-55, 56-57; CD joins order as postulant, 57-59; CD rejected by order, 60-61; CD decides to request a sister of St. Joseph to head SOS novitiate, 83; Sister Lidwina, 91-93; relinquish responsibility for SOS, 150

St. Joseph Street residence, Toronto (Newman Hall), 82-83, 87

St. Mark's Separate School, Marquis, Saskatchewan, 232-237

St. Paul, Alberta, 162, 174

St. Peter's Separate School, Toronto, 39

Schenck, Sister Katherine, 107, 108, 109, 133, 150, 172, 187

Schreyer, Edward, 289

Separate schools, 22, 39, 50, 52, 69, 232, 233-234, 235, 237

Sillery, Morrison, 233-234, 236

Simcoe County, Ontario, 17, 18, 21, 24

Sinnett, Father John, 239-240

Sinnett, Saskatchewan, chapter 12

Sinnott, Archbishop of Winnipeg, 81, 111, 112, 122, 127, 132-133, 138, 156; requests SOS sisters to work in diocese, 118-119

Sisters of Service order, founding, chapter 4; first mass, 95; first novitiate, 96-99; habit, 107-108; ministry in prairie Indian schools rejected, 111-112; awaits Vatican approval, 113-116; Archbishop McNeil omits to credit CD with role in founding, 119-120, 151; receives approval from Rome and legal incorporation, 134; celebrates fifth anniversary, 147-148; end of role of Sisters of St. Joseph, 150; financial difficulties during Depression, 170; first sisters take final vows, 172; Holy Rule, 186-194; CD's concerns about Father Daly's influence, and direction of order, 224, 251-253, 256, 261, 264, 286-288; general chapter meetings, 226-228, 255-256, 270-271, 281, 283-284; CD's advice and encouragement to sisters, 278; CD's views on certain aspects of, 279-280; Vatican II and, 280-281, 283; CD's version of founding, 282; CD's role in founding acknowledged, 283, 284; CD's lifelong contribution to, 293

Small, Theresa Korman (Mrs Ambrose), 80, 133, 147, 226

Smith family, 202, 215, 216

Springhouse, British Columbia, 205, 206, 209, 219

Stanich, Paul, poem by, 267-268

Stettler, Alberta, 44

Stornoway Public School, Saskatchewan, 75-76, 78, 82

Sullivan, Esther, 125, 126, 129

T

Teulon, Manitoba, 129
Thomas, Father F.M., 214
Toronto, 68, 76, 77, 85, 283
Trautman, Sister Leona, 228-233, 236

U

Ukrainian immigrants, 71, 75, 78-79, 104, 154

V

Vancouver, 67-68, 283
Victoria, Mother, 58, 59, 60, 80
Vilna, Alberta, chapter 7
Volk, Father J.F., 257, 262-263

W

Wellesley Place residence, Toronto, 87, 89
Whittaker, Mary, 89, 95, 99
Williams Lake, British Columbia, 206, 207, 212, 216
Winnipeg, 138
World War I, 40, 42, 68-69, 102
Wright, Nettie, 23, 26, 29, 30, 89
Wymbs, Sister Catherine, 118-119, 124, 125, 126, 127, 130, 135, 137, 142, 143, 172